SO FINE A PROSPECT

❧

Historic New England Gardens

W9-AOG-868

SO FINE A

PROSPECT

Historic New England Gardens

Alan Emmet

University Press of New England

Hanover and London

University Press of New England

publishes books under its own imprint and is the publisher for

Brandeis University Press, Dartmouth College, Middlebury College Press,

University of New Hampshire, University of Rhode Island,

Tufts University, University of Vermont, Wesleyan University Press,

and Salzburg Seminar.

University Press of New England, Hanover, NH 03755

© 1996 by University Press of New England

All rights reserved

Printed in Singapore

5 4 3 2 1

Library of Congress Cataloging-in-Publication Data

Emmet, Alan.

So fine a prospect : historic New England gardens / Alan Emmet.

p.   cm.

Includes bibliographical references.

ISBN 0–87451–749–4 (alk. paper)

1. Historic gardens—New England. 2. Gardens—New England—
History. I. Title.

SB466.U65N4825   1996

712'.6'0974—dc20   95–36320

Title page spread: *Grandmother's Garden*, Lydia Field Emmet, oil on canvas, ca. 1912.

(National Academy of Design, New York, New York)

"The Kingdom of England don't afford

so Fine a Prospect as I have."

❧

THOMAS HANCOCK

(1702–1764)

Acknowledgments

I could not have completed this book without the support and encouragement of my whole family, and of Ellie Reichlin, Cass Canfield, Harlan Hanson, Sally Brady and the Wednesday group. I am indebted to the late Florence Wolfe who said, "write," and to the late Nicholas King, remembering especially one sunny afternoon on Edith Wharton's terrace.

My favorite people are the librarians and archivists, too many to name, who helped me. I am grateful particularly to Lorna Condon at the Society for the Preservation of New England Antiquities, and to Sally Pierce and indeed to the entire staff of the Boston Athenaeum, that most felicitous of libraries.

October 1995   A.E.

Contents

Introduction

So Fine a Prospect

THE RASPBERRIES were dusted with frost this morning, so silvered with it that I could hardly tell which ones were ripe, but the sweet, perfect, dark red berries dropped into my hand as easily as ever. The sun shone through the canes, and the leaves and berries were translucent. The rough, whitened grass beneath the sugar maple was dappled with sparkling yellow leaves. As I picked, I thought of those other gardeners, the ones whose private letters and diaries I have been nosing so earnestly through. We must have something in common, they and I. Surely, all of them must have had those moments of pure delight in their gardens, when some homely detail or grand effect makes it all worthwhile.

Every year, every season, every day, and even every hour gardens change. Subject to natural rhythms of growth and decay, responding to care or neglect, gardens of every sort are continually evolving. Depending on the quality of light or the angle of the sun, the same place looks altogether different at different times and in different seasons. If constant change is the very essence of a garden, then there is no finished product and no point at which the need for upkeep ceases. There is no moment of which we can say, "This is it" or—looking back—"That was it." Certainly there are periods in the life of any garden when maintenance reaches its apogee, when the initial plantings approach maturity, and when painters or photographers are most likely to attempt to capture a moment of perfection. But the inevitably transient quality of a garden—the very fact of its evanescence—is reason enough to investigate its origins. For me the most intriguing questions about a garden are who built it and why.

Before the first spade cleaves the earth, before the first stakes mark the course of a new path, before the first tree is cut or the first tree planted, the garden maker has decided to alter the landscape. The chief reason for the change is to make a place more beautiful, more productive, or in the usage of the eighteenth century, to "improve" it. Inspired by pictures in the mind, the gardener seeks to make a fantasy become real.

Garden makers have always had visions all their own. One may have followed a modest dream of beauty, while another imagined a grand reordering of the landscape. A third may have aimed at rivaling the accomplishments of others. Some gardeners have deliberately adapted the dictates of contemporary fashion to their own terrain. Others have been influenced by current styles but less consciously, as if by osmosis. And then there are the innovators, whose gardens have been inspired by fresh insights and new possibilities. These gardeners may have followed literary sources, history dimly guessed at, or wisps of memory and dreams. Those who introduced novelty in design may have ended up as setters of the next trend or else were relegated to posterity as solitary eccentrics in their unique and private garden cul-de-sacs.

Curiosity led me to investigate the conditions under which some of New England's most important gardens were created during the first century and a half of this nation's independent life. People express through their gardens the degree of their self-confidence as well as their attitudes toward the land. Some have sought to dominate the place they called their own, whereas others have tried to enhance the inherent qualities of the landscape. The names that people have given to their places often reveal their intentions as well as the sources of their inspiration: Roseland, Bellmont, The Vale.

The gardeners of New England have always had much in common with each other. They share traditions, patterns of settlement, and a rigorous climate. Over the years many have been linked by their earnest efforts to expand knowlege and better the human condition through scientific experimentation in agriculture or horticulture. Many, too, have shared a moral bent, a belief in the ennobling influence of beautiful surroundings. In the first period of national life after the Revolution, New Englanders did not abandon the ways of the Old World but were quick to adapt to the opportunities offered by the New. As a result, they contributed far more to the national culture than might be expected, considering their numbers and the limited size of the area. Although the region's influence gradually decreased as the country grew, idealized images of New England are important national models to this day. Indeed, the developer of a recent subdivision in the dry prairie of central Texas named it "Nantucket," bringing in old dock pilings and maritime flotsam to create a "theme" landscape of the New England coast.[1] A village on a hill, white houses facing on a green, tall elms arching overhead, and a white church spire pointing heavenward: for many Americans this picture represents stability, tradition, national roots, and a retreat from urban stress. Revival styles based on New England examples have been popular for domestic architecture and garden design for nearly a century, within and beyond the region. The popularity of herb gardens for instance—

not strictly a revival of anything—represents more than anything else nostalgia for an imagined past, as often as not a New England past.

. . .

Leo Marx has pointed out two different meanings of the word "garden," meanings that are in essence contradictory. Both interpretations have played significant roles in American history. Marx quotes as one example Robert Beverley's comment in his 1705 essay, *History and Present State of Virginia*, that the reason there were so few gardens in Virginia was that the entire region was a garden.[2] In this sense, the term "garden" stands for the "Edenic land of primitive splendor," where Nature provides both bounty and beauty. This was the ideal that had drawn voyagers and settlers to America and that, despite deprivation, climatic extremes, and dread of the wilderness, continued for decades to inspire expeditions and expansion further westward. The other meaning of the word "garden," according to Marx, is a piece of cultivated ground, from which those who work on it can produce beauty and abundance. While sounding more prosaic than the proverbial "land of milk and honey," this definition describes the "middle landscape," neither wild nor densely urban, that represents the pastoral ideal so prevalent in American thought.[3]

This book is concerned with gardens made for private use, beauty, and pleasure. These gardens are not necessarily enclosed, but they are separated or set off in some way from the surrounding landscape. Their appeal owes as much to what they exclude as to what they contain. The best gardens convey this sense of their separateness, a feeling of seclusion and sanctuary from the workaday world. Ann Leighton put it almost biblically: "A garden, to be a garden, must represent a different world, however small, from the real world, a source of comfort in turmoil, of excitement in dullness, security in wildness, companionship in loneliness."[4]

Every garden is unique, depending on the purpose for which it was designed, the lay of the land, and any number of other factors. Size is one variable that significantly affects the character of a garden. The smallest might be a flowery, fenced enclosure adjacent to a house. At the other end of the scale would be a rural estate extending over hundreds or even thousands of acres. Traditionally, large landed estates were intended to be agriculturally productive; with imagination and skill, the whole rural scene could become a garden, a harmonious unity where use and beauty flourished.

Christopher Tunnard once referred to a garden as "a luxury of the imagination."[5] F. R. Cowell observed that only in periods of high civilization has gardening been elevated above a necessary and useful craft to become a fine art.[6] Both writers pointed out that with the opportunity for self-expression in the landscape there was room for eccentricity. Luxury, eccentricity, and sufficient leisure: it should come as no surprise that most of the creators of the gardens described in these chapters had either inherited money or achieved worldly success on their own.

The selection of the gardens to be discussed had a certain inevitability. The gardens I chose are not necessarily superior to others of their periods, even were it possible to make such value judgments. There are many other gardens worthy of study, some of which I wished I might include as well as others unknown to me. More gardens remain to be uncovered or discovered. The treasure hunt has no end.

The gardens included here provide a chronological sequence from the early years of the republic to the period prior to World War I. I chose gardens that either typify a particular period or exemplify an innovation. A third criterion was the existence of a written record. Whether or not a particular garden still survives in any form, it was the diaries, the correspondence, and the visual records that made it possible to study each garden's history and to inquire into the motivation of its creator. All of the garden owners in these chapters had their own reasons for doing what they did, beyond the inevitable influence of the social and cultural milieu in which they lived. The history of the relationship between garden owners and the professional designers some of them hired interested me for what it revealed about both. In this relationship the owner became a client, dependent on the expertise of the professional. At the same time, the owner was also a patron, with the opportunity to provide support and scope to the designer, as well as the ultimate power to terminate their association.

The gardens in these chapters are scattered across New England. Surviving records allowed me to discover four gardens that are entirely lost. Although this is in no sense a guidebook, most of the extant gardens that I have written of can be visited by the public. On the other hand, gardens that continue in private ownership are just that: private.

. . .

Before the Revolutionary War, during the first century and a half of New England's European colonization, gardens were seldom characterized as works of art. To the first settlers, luxury and leisure were inconceivable; survival was at stake. Utility was the chief consideration during the seventeenth century, when families had to produce their own food, clothing materials, and remedies against illness. People put their gardens near their houses and fenced them against the depredations of wild and domestic animals. Beds of vegetables and useful herbs were arranged for convenience, divided by straight and narrow paths, after the late medieval European fashion familiar to the settlers. The sole concession to fancy might be a sweet rose, grown from a precious slip carried on the long sea voyage.

As life in the colonies became more settled and secure, people inclined toward expanding and adorning their homes. Before the end of the seventeenth century those who were comfortably settled and reasonably well off felt free to make gardens purely for their own enjoyment. Few detailed descriptions survive of pre-Revolutionary gardens. Maps, deeds, and probate records are the most likely sources of evidence. In many cases, trees, walls, terraces, pathways, and the layout of beds survived well into the nineteenth century. Archaeology is a potential source for more information. Memories kept the early gardens alive, too, although reminiscences were often colored by sentiment for one's lost youth.

The gardens of the rich and prominent left a greater mark than did those of ordinary people. In Boston in 1700, Andrew Faneuil, a successful businessman, built a mansion house on the side of Beacon Hill, above Tremont Street. Here he and, after him, his nephew and heir, Peter Faneuil, developed a seven-acre garden famous for choice fruits, hothouses, and flowers imported from France. Terraces marked the descent from the house to the street and also rose behind the house, supported by walls and steps of hewn granite. Railings along the edges of the terraces were surmounted by gilt balls. At the top of the garden was a summerhouse with a splendid view of Boston Harbor. This fanciful structure, said to have been patterned after an oriental

Thomas Hancock's stone house, built in 1737, and terraced front garden on Beacon Hill, Boston, in a photograph taken by G. H. Drew, ca. 1860. The dome of the Massachusetts State House is visible at the right. The once magnificent garden was near its end; the house was demolished in 1863. (Society for the Preservation of New England Antiquities)

pagoda, had a spire topped with a gilt grasshopper as a weathervane.[7]

On another slope of Boston's Beacon Hill, overlooking the Common, Thomas Hancock built himself a fine stone house in 1736. He commissioned a local gardener to "undertake to layout the upper garden allys. Trim the Beds & fill up all the allies with such Stuff as Sd. Hancock shall Order and Gravel the Walks & prepare and Sodd ye Terras."[8] Before the establishment of local nurseries, Hancock and other American gardeners ordered all their plants from Europe. Hancock wrote to a London nurseryman to purchase dwarf trees, espaliers, and other plants. He boasted of his view in a letter to this nurseryman: "My Gardens all Lye on the South Side of a hill with the most beautiful Assent to the top & its allowed on all hands the Kingdom of England don't afford so Fine a Prospect as I have both of land & water. Neither do I intend to Spare any Cost or pains on making my Gardens Beautiful or Profitable."[9]

In nearby Medford in the 1730s, Colonel Isaac Royall, with a fortune from trade with Antigua, built the handsome house that still stands. The central walk was on an axis with the doors of the mansion. The walk extended five hundred feet behind the house, between garden beds to a terraced mount crowned with an octagonal summerhouse and a carved wooden figure of

Mercury.[10] A few miles away, in Lincoln, the Codman house, a close contemporary of Colonel Royall's, still overlooks a "Front Yard" noted in a 1778 inventory and stepped terraces that may be as old as the house itself.[11]

Estates of the Cambridge Loyalists were noted for their gardens, which contained similar features. Henry Vassall's garden, laid out in the 1740s, had the typical enclosed front yard, or forecourt, and central axial path. His path was paved with beach stones. Beds edged with boxwood were planted with fruit trees imported from France and England.[12] The forecourt of Richard Lechmere's 1761 mansion was enclosed by a fence with carved pineapple finials and was planted with rows of linden trees that stood until the hurricane of 1938. A broad path led to a raised terrace and the entrance portico. The center hall of this house opened onto the garden at the rear, where the path continued down some steps, straight through the garden, to terminate at an arbor.[13] At John Vassall Jr.'s house (now the Vassall-Craigie-Longfellow House, administered by the National Park Service), built in 1759, the landscape was arranged in the same typical fashion. The house was built on a terraced platform to provide a broad view of the Charles River marshes. A brick-walled forecourt was planted with rows of American elms.[14] These grand mid-eighteenth-century estates in and around Boston were alike in their geometrical organization around a central axis, of which the house itself was the focus. The desire for "Prospect" meant that elevated sites were preferred and that terracing was almost universal. The one landscape feature that more modest houses would have had in common with the great mansions was an enclosed and planted forecourt, scaled down to become a simple dooryard garden with a path from the gate to the house.

This cursory look at a few pre-Revolutionary gardens neglects their horticulture—the flowers, fruits, and trees in which the owners took such pleasure and pride. Plants were the life of these gardens, but it is their design features that characterize them as belonging to a particular period. These gardens near Boston were representative of their era; similar gardens were being made in and around other cities at the time.

Eighteenth-century estate owners imported not only plants and trees but also the books they depended on for guidance in the management of both the useful and the ornamental aspects of their grounds. There were no helpful American books at the time. Henry Vassall, for example, owned and presumably consulted John Mortimer's *The Whole Art of Husbandry* (London, 1716) and Richard Bradley's *A General Treatise of Husbandry and Gardening* (1725). The builder of the original Codman house, Chambers Russell, turned to William Ellis's *The Modern Husbandman* (1742) and Edward Lisle's 1757 treatise on the same subject.[15]

In their gardens, Americans of the colonial period

Terraced gardens at the 1760 East Apthorp house, off Linden Street near Harvard Square in Cambridge, Massachusetts; photograph ca. 1880. (Society for the Preservation of New England Antiquities)

adhered to the styles of the lands of their origin. When, in 1685, Sir William Temple described an English garden, Moor Park in Herefordshire, as "the perfectest figure of a garden I ever saw," he could have been writing about an eighteenth-century American garden.[16] Moor Park may have been more ornate than most New England gardens, but its major design features were the same: a close relationship between the architecture of the house and the plan of the garden, the bilateral symmetry of the garden along the spine of a central path, the use of terracing, and the inclusion of arbors and summerhouses. As we will see, New Englanders continued to make and maintain this type of garden long after the establishment of the new nation.

Notes

1. Greg McPherson, "Shedding the Illusion of Abundance," *Landscape Architecture* 79 (April 1989): 128.

2. Leo Marx, *The Machine in the Garden: Technology and the Pastoral Idea in America* (Oxford: Oxford University Press, 1964), 84–85.

3. Ibid., 104–5.

4. Ann Leighton, *Early American Gardens* (Boston: Houghton Mifflin, 1970), 6.

5. Christopher Tunnard, *A World with a View: An Inquiry into the Nature of Scenic Values* (New Haven, Conn.: Yale University Press, 1978), 67.

6. F. R. Cowell, *The Garden as a Fine Art: From Antiquity to Modern Times* (Boston: Houghton Mifflin, 1978), 8.

7. Abram English Brown, *Faneuil Hall and Faneuil Hall Market* (Boston: Lee & Shepard, 1900), 28.

8. Alice G. B. Lockwood, ed., *Gardens of Colony and State* (New York: Charles Scribner's Sons, 1931), 1:32. Hancock uses the word "allys," or "allies," to mean beds of planting.

9. Ibid.

10. Ibid., 1:39.

11. Middlesex County Probate Records (East Cambridge, Mass.), docket no. 19593.

12. Rupert Ballou Lillie, "The Gardens and Homes of the Loyalists," Cambridge Historical Society *Proceedings for the Year 1940* (Cambridge, Mass., 1940), 26:54.

13. Ibid., 57.

14. Ibid., 52–53.

15. Vassall's inventory is described in Lillie, "Gardens and Homes," 53. Russell's books are listed in a 1767 inventory of his estate, Middlesex County Probate Records, docket no. 19591.

16. Sir William Temple, quoted in Ann Leighton, *American Gardens in the Eighteenth Century* (Boston: Houghton Mifflin, 1976), 328.

SO FINE A PROSPECT

❖

Historic New England Gardens

Portrait of Chief Justice Oliver Ellsworth and His Wife Abigail Wolcott Ellsworth, by Ralph
Earl, 1792. The view from the window depicts the Ellsworths' neatly arranged domestic
landscape, indicating their strong attachment to their country estate, Elmwood.
(Wadsworth Atheneum; gift of the Ellsworth heirs)

Chapter 1

A Race of Cultivators

Theodore Lyman, John Codman, and

Other Exemplars of the Pastoral Ideal

Maybe there was a collective American memory of white meetinghouses and village greens that you acquired at birth or naturalization. New England was the promised land, even for those who had left it behind or who had never seen it, except in the movies. His mother said that was because New England *looked* like the ideal America that you studied in civics; it looked republican, with a small *r*.

—Mary McCarthy, *Birds of America*

OLIVER AND ABIGAIL Ellsworth are sitting in the book-lined parlor at Elmwood, the house Oliver's father built near Windsor, Connecticut. Abigail, stiffly upright under her enormous frilled bonnet, stares solemnly at the viewer. Her husband—hand on hip, legs crossed—looks more at ease. He holds a copy of the new United States Constitution, held so as to reveal just that portion of it that Ellsworth had helped to draft. The draped window frames a serene domestic landscape. Beyond a neatly painted five-rail fence sits a white frame house, typically eighteenth-century New England in style but expanded by wings at either side. The house is surrounded by young elm trees, planted by Oliver Ellsworth, we are told, to commemorate the thirteen original American colonies.[1] In a fine paradox, the house in the view is the very house in which the Ellsworths (and the viewer) are seated.

This double portrait, with its double view, was painted in 1792 by Ralph Earl. Earl, a native of Worcester, Massachusetts, had fled to England as a Loyalist in 1778 but returned to New England in 1791. The paintings he made over the next decade are visual evidence of the strong bond between New England landowners and their own domestic landscapes during the early years of the new republic.

Even after the Revolution, Americans had ties to the country from which they had won their independence. At the same time, they were anxious to prove that their country was as good as—indeed, superior to—the Old World. This competitiveness added zest to the pursuit of all the arts, including ornamental gardening.

With independence came a time of building. In New England, after years of disruption, merchants and shipowners were ready to turn their attention to refurbishing, renewing, and enlarging their public buildings and their homes. Paralleling the attention that prosperous New Englanders were paying to the design and decoration of their houses was their zealous adornment of their gardens and grounds.

The coastal cities—Portsmouth, Newburyport, Salem, Boston, and Providence—had suffered most. The building boom that came to these cities with peace and prosperity was marked by distinguished architectural design. Charles Bulfinch and Samuel McIntire were fortuitously on hand at a time when people were receptive of their new ideas and were willing to support fine craftsmanship and design. The work of these two architects has had lasting significance.

Outside the cities, rural seats abandoned by the Tory gentry sat neglected and desolate. The huge farms of Rhode Island's South County—southern-style plantations dependent on slave labor—were reverting to the wild. Their Loyalist owners had left, and slavery was formally abolished throughout New England during the 1780s. The elegant Medford, Massachusetts, estate of Isaac Royall, West Indies sugar merchant, was left to decline, as was the seat of the last royal governor of New Hampshire, John Wentworth. The time of decay did not last long. New owners and new fortunes soon filled the vacuum, along the coast as well as inland. "Interior" towns such as Worcester, Massachusetts, and Hartford and Litchfield, Connecticut, grew in prosperity after the war.

As a portrait painter, Ralph Earl had no difficulty in finding clients, particularly when he offered to include a glimpse of the house or the landscape of which the owners were so proud. Earl had studied painting in England, where he learned the convention of incorporating a landscape view into a portrait. But he provided something new to New Englanders at a time when land ownership was a primary status symbol. By depicting his confident patrons in their own environs, Earl conveyed their attachment to the land and their pride in it.[2] For Colonel Denny of Leicester, Massachusetts, Earl varied his custom by painting a pure landscape. This glowing panorama depicted the view from the windows of Denny's house. Beyond the pastoral acres of the Denny farm, we glimpse a winding river, white church spires, and low hills, all framed by trees. This is an agrarian landscape, not a wilderness. Although the land has been shaped and settled by people, human domination is not the chief message conveyed by Colonel Denny's view. Instead, this painting expresses love for the land and an appreciation of its beauty. That message was new.

The cultivated landscapes depicted by Earl would have delighted the French-American writer, J. Hector St. John Crèvecoeur (1735–1813). In his widely read *Letters from an American Farmer* (1782), Crèvecoeur had hailed the opportunity for the new nation to make a

Looking East from Denny Hill, 1800, oil on canvas by Ralph Earl. A landowner's view near Worcester, Massachusetts. (Worcester Art Museum, Worcester, Massachusetts)

fresh start. Contrasting the new world with the old, he wrote, "Here we have in some measure regained the ancient dignity of our species; our laws are simple and just, we are a race of cultivators, our cultivation is unrestrained, and therefore everything is prosperous and flourishing."[3]

Yeoman farmers, subservient to no one, were idealized by many Americans as model citizens and true patriots. According to Thomas Jefferson, an outspoken promoter of agrarian aspirations, "Those who labor in the earth are the chosen people of God."[4] George Washington himself, after all, was a farmer. Cleared and tilled land proclaimed the national virtue. The plow, with its biblical connotation "swords into ploughshares," was the perfect symbol for the young nation.[5]

Americans had ample space to become a nation of farmers. Although critical English travelers continued to observe with distaste the dense woods and rough grazing ground they encountered, the frontiers of farming were steadily being pushed farther inland. Neat farmsteads were generally admired for their beauty as well as their bounty. Diarist William Bentley (1759–1819), the Salem clergyman who wandered widely throughout the region, often noted with favor the flourishing farms he saw. He was moved by "the innocence of rural life, the happy application of riches to facilitate agriculture." Governor Gore's "splendid seat" in Waltham, Massachusetts, brought home to Bentley "the advantages . . . derived from an agricultural society, which has induced Gentlemen of taste to attend to the extensive experiments made to facilitate the managements of the farm."[6]

Some of Boston's leading citizens, following the example of a group of Philadelphians, banded together in 1792 to form the Massachusetts Society for Promoting Agriculture. They met to present and then publish papers on the techniques of farming. By encouraging experimentation and instructing others, they hoped to improve the lot of New England farmers generally. Only five years earlier, a hundred or more western Massachusetts farmers, a rowdy company led by Daniel Shays, had staged an armed rebellion against the state government to protest high taxes and low farm prices. The farmers fired their muskets at a troop of militia in an encounter that left four men dead. But that was the low point; the farmers' lot gradually improved. According to William Strickland, an English farmer who toured the United States in 1794, the efforts of the Society for Promoting Agriculture paid off. After talking with founding member and president Judge John Lowell at his estate in Roxbury, Massachusetts, Strickland reported that "[f]armers used to be very poor, but now are as generally rich."[7] If the United States was to be a nation of farmers, the Society's efforts to increase farm productivity and profits were nobly patriotic.

Other New Englanders sought to increase useful knowledge by scientific study of their environment. William Bentley walked almost daily in the vicinity of Salem, observing trees, plants, and wildlife. Sometimes he took groups of children along for instruction. Another scientifically minded cleric, the Reverend Manasseh Cutler of Ipswich, Massachusetts, made several botanical expeditions to New Hampshire's White "Hills," as he called them, starting in 1784.[8] Cutler hoped to advance medical knowledge by writing the first book on native New England plants, a goal he failed to achieve. Ezra Stiles, a minister who was named president of Yale in 1778, was also a scientist. He studied the climate, geology, and when a farmer turned up old bones, archaeology. Patches of primal forest survived in the Connecticut hills, and Stiles tried to ascertain the age of ancient trees when they were felled. In 1789 he distributed thousands of mulberry seeds to encourage the development of groves for the silkworm.[9] To such people as these, knowledge of the land was a means of controlling it. Profitable use of the land seemed the way to strengthen the nation.

.   .   .

John Adams, touring English gardens with Thomas Jefferson in 1786, found that one of his favorite places was William Shenstone's The Leasowes. Adams sounds like a stereotypical Yankee, saying he liked it because it was "the simplest and plainest, but the most rural of all."[10] To him, there was virtue and beauty in a useful landscape. Adams condemned many of the more elaborate English country seats as "mere ostentations of vanity." He hoped "Ridings, Parks, Pleasure Grounds, Gardens and ornamented Farms" would not soon—if ever—become fashionable in America, where "Nature has done greater Things and furnished nobler Materials."

Some Americans shared Adams's fear of the corrupting influence of wealth. As Neil Harris has pointed out, popular government seemed to demand restraint of the natural passions and adherence to moral virtue.[11] Virtue would hold the nation together; without it, decay was inevitable. Indulgence in luxury would surely weaken the fibers of liberty. Little more than lip service was

View of the Seat of the Hon. Moses Gill, Esq. at Princeton, in the County of Worcester, Massa'tts, from an engraving in *Massachusetts Magazine* vol. 4, November 1792. Gill's 3000-acre estate, famous for its gardens, made him the largest landowner in Worcester County. (Boston Athenaeum)

paid to these qualms, however, and those who had the means surrounded themselves with refinements both indoors and out.

During the first decades of their independence, New Englanders, like other Americans, were content to follow European styles. The American Revolution was political, not cultural. National pride among citizens of the new republic was accompanied by nostalgia for their homelands. Americans were surprisingly conservative in their choice of models for gardens, as well as for other facets of their lives.[12] England itself had undergone a gradual revolution in garden fashion, but its former colonies were slow to follow suit.

The Honorable Moses Gill's front garden of 1792 typified the genteel ideal in New England after the Revolution. Judge Gill was a prosperous landowner in

Princeton, Massachusetts, and a member of the Society for Promoting Agriculture. His mansion overlooked the several hundred acres he had under cultivation on his three-thousand-acre estate. A 1792 engraving of Gill's estate shows farm workers gathering in the hay. Gill undoubtedly employed a large staff to maintain his farmland and the gardens famous for their beauty. An elaborate fence separated his front yard from his fields and outbuildings. A straight walkway to the front door was flanked by statues set on square plinths. To one side was an area of rectangular planting beds, divided by narrow paths.

Henry Marchant, a member of the Rhode Island legislature and a federal judge, had a similar front garden at his manor house in South Kingstown. A pencil sketch from about 1790 shows his fence and small cone-shaped topiary trees in the center of the garden squares. Cultivated fields surrounded Marchant's house and garden. Either his estate or Gill's would have been a fit subject for the brush of Ralph Earl.

From the years prior to the Revolution through the first decades of the nineteenth century, the finest houses were built on high ground to gain importance and a

S.W. View of the Seat of Henry Marchant in South Kingstown, Rhode Island, ca. 1785–1790; an ink drawing by an anonymous artist. (Courtesy of The Rhode Island Historical Society)

view. The slopes were then terraced, with neat steps descending from the principal doors of the house. The Reverend William Bentley described William Brattle's four-and-a-half-acre Cambridge garden in 1792:

> We first saw the fountain and canal opposite to his House, and the walk on the side of another canal in the road, flowing under an arch and in the direction of the outer fence. There is another canal which communicates with a beautiful pool in the park and place for his wild fowl. The garden is laid out upon a very considerable descent and formed with terrace walks, abounding with Trees, fruits, and the whole luxury of vegetation, and is unrivalled by anything I have seen of the kind. The poultry was excellent and numerous. The parterres in fine order in the Garden. The Rabbit house had above fifty in it.[13]

The canals and fountain, while ornamental, were doubtless a means of controlling water, since the garden gave onto the tidal Charles River.

Other gardens of the 1780s and 1790s were equally regular as to geometry and perhaps even more fantastically decorated. Joseph Barrell's Charlestown garden, for example (also visited by Bentley), had four miniature ships at anchor in a circular pond, marble figures decorating the garden squares, a Chinese-style summerhouse, an aviary in the form of a globe, and a hothouse.[14]

The grounds of Thomas Kidder's estate, the Lilacs,

in Medford, Massachusetts, were developed after 1805 around a new house purportedly designed by Asher Benjamin. The Lilacs featured a curved entrance drive; an ornamentally planted circle replaced the traditional fenced front yard. Although symmetrically planned and planted, Kidder's garden included a latticed summerhouse atop a knoll off to one side. The Lilacs represented a modest break with the strict right-angled regularity of most earlier gardens.[15]

· · ·

In England, meanwhile, scores of terraced, fenced, four-square gardens, often differing from newly made American ones only in their greater scale, had been and were being "swept away," as some described the changes. Troops of workers were put to clearing out topiary that had taken decades to shape, breaking up straight avenues of full-grown trees, and reshaping terraced banks into smooth slopes. Stonework edgings were removed from geometric pools, allowing the water to form irregularly shaped ponds. Old flower gardens were often grassed over. At the same time, sunk fences, or ha-has, were installed around many English manor houses, giving their owners an unobstructed view of the countryside and of their grazing livestock. These vast open lawns represented, in J. B. Jackson's memorable phrase, "the triumph of sheep over horticulture."[16] The higher ground was planted with irregular clumps of trees, some of them of species recently

The Lilacs, Medford, Massachusetts, the residence of Thomas Kidder. The circular front garden was laid out between 1808 and 1812. Beside the house was a weeping willow, a tree that came to have romantic associations in the nineteenth century. (Society for the Preservation of New England Antiquities)

imported from the American colonies. Many landowners devoted considerable acreage to silviculture; a grove of young trees was like money in the bank.

The reasons for the wholesale changes in the English landscape may have been economic as much as aesthetic.[17] As landowners sought to increase their profits by adopting new agricultural techniques, their land reflected the shift from small-scale farming to large-scale. In village after village during the latter half of the eighteenth century, common fields and pastures were appropriated and enclosed by the local squire, under a series of Parliamentary Acts. The stated purpose of these Enclosure Acts was to boost agricultural production; but without land to support themselves, thousands of cottagers were driven to factory work—or to emigrate to England's former colonies. The landowners, meanwhile, grew ever richer. The new landscape was much admired, particularly by those who reaped its benefits.

The appeal of the so-called natural landscape style in eighteenth-century England has sometimes been linked to the struggle for political freedom.[18] Rigid geometry and authoritarian formality were frowned on as symbols of autocracy. All the more puzzling, then, that this natural style took so long to reach the new land of liberty on the opposite shore of the Atlantic.

In the United States the history, perception, and actuality of the landscape were entirely different. The land seemed vast; surely there was enough for everyone. In a country mostly wooded and still largely wild in its interior, cultivated farmland seemed especially beautiful. The fact that such land yielded profit made it look even better. But near people's houses, neatly fenced enclosures kept the memory and the fear of wilderness at bay. Trim flower beds, clipped shrubs, and straight graveled walks represented order and civility. Fountains and marble statuary showed off the owner's worldly success and cultural refinement.

Some European travelers to New England noted as they passed stretches of neat and fruitful farmsteads that the landscape bore an unintentional resemblance to a deliberately planned English landscape garden of the latest style. By carefully husbanding their land, the farmers of some fertile New England river valleys had inadvertently shaped scenery that, in its combination of the wild and the bucolic, impressed sophisticated observers with its beauty. The marquis de Chastellux, riding near Hartford in 1780, found in the valley of the Connecticut River "a *jardin anglais*, which art would have trouble in equalling."[19]

At the end of the century a few New Englanders, most of whom had traveled to the mother country, began deliberately to seek the so-called natural effect in their home grounds. Samuel Elam laid out winding paths in 1789 on the grounds of his poetically inspired estate, Vaucluse, near Portsmouth, Rhode Island (see chapter 4). In 1795, Elias Hasket Derby, Salem's richest merchant when he died in 1799, had an unidentified designer sketch three landscape schemes for the grounds of his McIntire-designed town house. The designs differ intriguingly in the degree of their "naturalism."[20] The most traditional shows a four-square garden with a fountain at its center, but even this scheme includes curving walks about the house. Another drawing proposes an open lawn with island beds along a circular path. This plan looks like Jefferson's Monticello lawn in

miniature. The third layout abandons regularity entirely. It suggests a circumferential path winding among randomly placed trees. There is no way of knowing which plan Derby preferred, but he may have deemed the third too radical. Certainly the garden at Derby's farm in nearby Danvers, Massachusetts, was entirely traditional, according to William Bentley's 1790 account of it. Bentley described a fenced, three-tiered garden with white-painted wooden keystone arches over each set of steps.

The Vale, the country estate of the Yorkshire-born Boston merchant Theodore Lyman (1753–1836), was one of the first New England gardens to be laid out in the English landscape style. Begun in 1793 in Waltham, a few miles outside Boston, it is the earliest garden of its type to have been preserved almost intact. Lyman appears to have laid out his grounds himself, with the help of his English gardener, a man named Bell. Lyman had undoubtedly been inspired by gardens he had seen in England. With its many firsts in design and horticulture, The Vale marks the transition from the conservatism of the first years of the young nation to the long period of change and experimentation that came with the new century. Fortunately, Lyman's estate is open to the public.

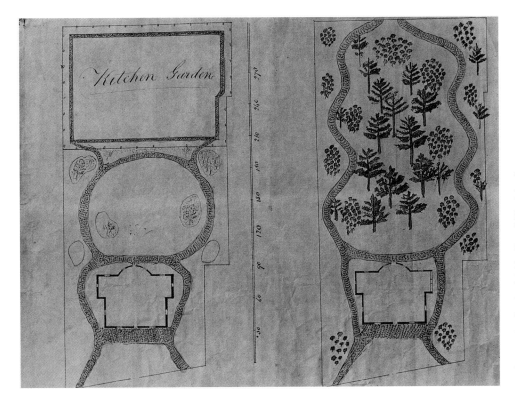

Two alternative schemes for Elias Hasket Derby's grounds in Salem, ca. 1800. The drawing at the left indicates island beds along curving walks, resembling the Monticello garden; the other drawing proposes a serpentine walk among trees and shrubs planted in a random pattern. (Courtesy Peabody Essex Museum, Salem, Massachusetts)

The Vale, Waltham, Massachusetts, painted sketch by an unidentified woman, ca. 1820–1830. A greenhouse can be seen to the left of the house; the summerhouse on the knoll at the right no longer survives. (Society for the Preservation of New England Antiquities)

The Vale, Alvan Fisher, pencil and watercolor, 1820–25. Theodore Lyman's mansion, designed by Samuel McIntire, overlooked a pond created by damming a brook. A carriage is coming up the original entrance drive at the right, having crossed a bridge that lay beyond this view. The layout of the grounds was inspired by English landscape gardens designed by Brown, Kent, and others. (Society for the Preservation of New England Antiquities)

Although The Vale has been diminished in extent over the years, the great change in scale that it represented is still apparent. Here the garden was the entire estate. The new appreciation for a sense of space allowed for wide pathways, broad expanses of grass and water, and unobstructed views of deer, cattle, and forest trees.

The very name of The Vale indicates the importance that Lyman attached to his choice of terrain for his rural seat. His use and accentuation of the natural contours of the land reflect the influence of William Kent, Lancelot "Capability" Brown, and the amateurs who had been designing and redesigning garden landscapes in England. Like Brown at Bowood or Henry Hoare at his own Stourhead, Lyman dammed a brook to form a lake that followed the contours of the ground and thus appeared natural. The original entrance drive at The Vale crossed the water, allowing a view in which the house appeared as one structural element in the garden landscape rather than its focal point. From the house a gentle slope of greensward ran toward the lake, which was enlivened by a few swans. The views from or toward the house are reminiscent of paintings by Constable. From such composed scenery we learn the meaning of the term "picturesque."

It may seem incongruous that one of the most prominent features of The Vale's landscape, notable for its novel breadth and openness, should be an eleven-foot-high wall. This long expanse of brick actually served two purposes. In part it screened such "useful and unpleasing objects" as the kitchen garden and the farmyard. The wall's chief function, however, was to support and protect the fruit trees espaliered against it and to hasten the ripening of peaches. The wall itself is indicative of an increasing interest in horticulture. Lyman and other New Englanders of the time were plunging with enthusiasm into the growing of exotic and ornamental plants. The hobby of a few rich people evolved over the next decades into a mania for many, as more and more foreign plants were imported into the country. Lyman raised lemons, grapes, and camellias under glass. One of his several greenhouses may be the oldest surviving structure of its kind in the United States.

At The Vale, trees were set out in random groupings on the higher ground, as English landscape gardeners had been doing for half a century. Native trees were combined with introduced species, and conifers were mixed with deciduous trees. The venerable purple beech on the lawn at The Vale may date from the 1820s and was certainly among the earliest imported to this country. The use of single trees, allowed to develop naturally to their fullest, reflected the horticultural concern typical of the nineteenth century.

Although Americans with modest demesnes clung to their traditional fenced foreyards and squared-off flower beds, affluent landowners throughout New England began to adopt the new, freer style that prevailed at Lyman's country seat. Elias Boudinot, a lawyer from New Jersey who kept a journal of his 1809 trip to Boston, was much impressed by the setting of merchant Stephen Higginson's elegant Brookline villa, where the varied scene "enchants the Eye": "The grounds around [the house] laid out much in the English style—The Shrubbery & Forest Trees extremely well arranged—The Walks beautifully romantic—The Kitchen garden at a distance, & thro' Which Walks wind so as to extend them about a quarter of a mile, all bordered with Grapes & Flowers."[21]

John Codman of Lincoln, Massachusetts, was another who undertook to transform an established landscape into a more modern form. In 1800, Codman traveled to England on business. Shortly before he went abroad, he had taken over the management of the rundown estate that had belonged to his wife's family. Although the place had been confiscated by Patriot rebels during the Revolution, family members had managed to reclaim it. John Codman's ambitious plans for refurbishing the property took a quantum leap forward as soon as he began touring English country seats. The letters he wrote to his wife convey his spontaneous delight in all he saw and reveal how his tastes changed in response. He was charmed by the seclusion of the estates he saw, where fine distant views were framed by trees. These belts of trees—products of the Enclosure Acts and of deliberate reforestation—seemed to Codman pleasantly unlike the more open landscape of his homeland. He was impressed by the deliberate use of planting to conceal every utilitarian structure. He marveled at the clean gravel walks "in serpentine and twisted forms" that circumnavigated the grounds he saw in England.[22] The grandest seat he visited was Wilton, where old geometric gardens and canals had been remade in the natural style.

Codman wanted to emulate the English estates in every respect. He sent messages through his wife to the manager of his Lincoln property, instructing him to start planting trees to hide the barns and the public road. His most cherished scheme he attributed to his

The Salem architect Samuel McIntire designed both the mansion and this summerhouse for Theodore Lyman at The Vale in Waltham, Massachusetts. The summerhouse is set against an eleven-foot-high brick wall that was built soon after 1800 to support espaliered apricot and peach trees and to hasten the ripening of the fruit. A door from the summerhouse opened into an ornamental woodland, where paths wound among the native American trees that Lyman had collected and planted. (Photo by Peter Margonelli)

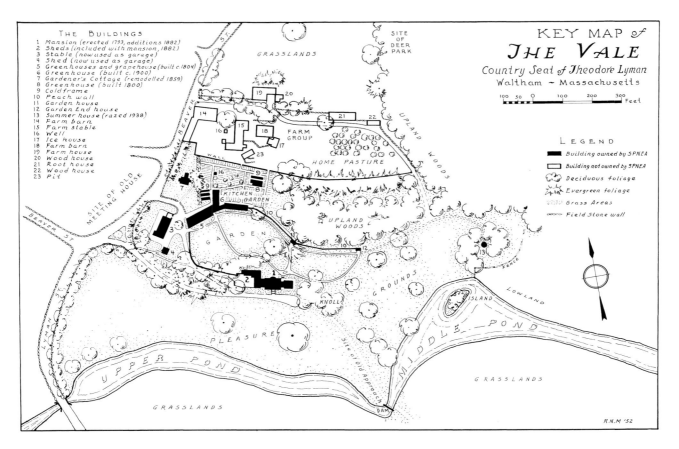

THE BUILDINGS
1 Mansion (erected 1793, additions 1882)
2 Sheds (included with mansion, 1882)
3 Stable (now used as garage)
4 Shed (now used as garage)
5 Greenhouses and grapehouse (built c 1804)
6 Greenhouse (built c.1900)
7 Gardener's Cottage (remodelled 1859)
8 Greenhouse (built 1800)
9 Coldframe
10 Peach wall
11 Garden house
12 Garden End house
13 Summer house (razed 1938)
14 Farm barn
15 Farm stable
16 Well
17 Ice house
18 Farm barn
19 Farm house
20 Wood house
21 Root house
22 Wood house
23 Pit

KEY MAP of
JHE VALE
Country Seat of Theodore Lyman
Waltham ~ Massachusetts

100 50 0   100   200   300
Feet

LEGEND
▬ Building owned by SPNEA
▭ Building not owned by SPNEA
🌳 Deciduous foliage
🌲 Evergreen foliage
Grass Areas
Field Stone wall

R.N.M '52

Plan of The Vale, R. Newton Mayall, 1952. (Society for the Preservation of New England Antiquities)

wife's cousin, Mrs. Christopher Gore, who had been living in England since 1796, during the term of her husband's diplomatic mission. As John Codman wrote his wife, "Mrs. Gore and myself have been planning improvements at Lincoln, she says it is the handsomest place in America and might be made a l'Anglaise with ease. I like her plan that the foreyard should be thrown down into a lawn that carriages may drive to the front door."[23] And six weeks later: "I do not know any place in America so much like Gentlemen's seats in this country as Lincoln (dear Lincoln) all it wants is the foreyard all knocked away and the house to stand in the midst of a lawn."[24]

Proud as Codman was of his estate, he now realized that the formality of its landscape was out of date and out of style. "I think I shall make some improvements when I return," he wrote. Within three years, sad to relate, John Codman was dead, at the age of forty-

The Codman house, Lincoln, Massachusetts, 1989. (Photograph by Peter Margonelli)

eight. He never completed the renovation of his old-fashioned foreyard.

Codman may, however, have been responsible for altering the wet meadow and pond overlooked by the Lincoln house, a part of his property still known as The Octagon. There is no sign now of the geometry implied by the name, but it seems likely that the pond may at one time have been a formal "bason." An English writer, John James, in his *Theory and Practice of Gardening*, a 1712 translation of a French treatise, included the octagon in his suggested forms for bodies of water. "Or if a bason be circular," he wrote, "the walk that surrounds it should be octangular."[25] Stowe, one of the most magnificent eighteenth-century English gardens, included a "large Octagon Piece of Water" with a seventy-foot obelisk fountain at its center. The garden at Stowe was laid out in the 1720s by Charles Bridgeman to include terraces and a canal descending from the house front to the octagonal lake. Stowe was well known from published plans and from poems written about it. It is entirely possible that, when laying out the estate in Lincoln in the 1750s, John Codman's predecessors had made there a modest imitation of Stowe's formal octagon. Even then, ironically, the prototype octagon at Stowe was being reshaped by landscape designer William Kent. Kent in the 1750s and Capability Brown after him continued to soften the edges of the octagon at Stowe until it resembled a natural pond.[26] John Codman would not have chosen to preserve at Lincoln a replica of a feature that had long been abolished at Stowe. He probably saw to it that nature was able to reclaim the pond on his property. Now, almost two centuries later, the inappropriate geometric term is still used at the Codman estate, as it is at Stowe.

. . .

Even as forward-looking New Englanders moved to incorporate the innovations of the English into their gardens, others expressed concern and fondness for those elements of the landscape marked with age. When Ezra Stiles counted the rings in the stumps of virgin timber in the 1780s, he touched base with presettlement America. The Reverend William Bentley felt a reverence for "antient sites," particularly those of historical significance. He was stirred by the pear tree that stood beside the ruins of Governor John Endicott's house in Danvers, Massachusetts, a tree that Bentley determined had been planted by Endicott in 1630. Every year Bentley made a pilgrimage to the old tree and collected pears from it. So fervently did he venerate this living link with the colonial governor that in 1809 he carried its fruit to President John Adams at Quincy, with a note attached saying, "To the Man worthy to eat with our forefathers."[27]

Adams's own patriotism was echoed by Bentley's. Both adhered firmly to their agrarian ideals for their country. Others, however, had different objectives. For New Englanders the sea, more than ever, was the surest avenue to riches. As American trading ships ventured all over the globe, the only caution was to avoid the conflicts between the English and the French. By the 1790s, certain New England entrepreneurs were developing still other sources of wealth. They built small factories along the river valleys of the northeast: lumber mills, textile mills, and ironworks. Alexander Hamilton, for one, thought manufacturing would help farmers by expanding the market for their produce and would prevent the United States from stagnating as a nation of "mere" cultivators. Others feared the changes manufacturing would bring.[28]

As to the arts, John Adams was not alone in thinking that Americans could do more than to follow slavishly after European fashion. Artistic endeavors, including garden design, should reflect the vigor, idealism, and self-confidence of the young democracy. But there was no final break. The tide of European influence upon American taste has continued to ebb and flow ever since.

Notes

1. Elizabeth Mankin Kornhauser, "Regional Landscapes in Connecticut River Valley Portraits, 1790–1810," *The Magazine Antiques* 128 (November 1985): 1015.

2. Ibid. See also Oliver W. Larkin, *Art and Life in America*, rev. ed. (New York: Holt Rinehart & Winston, 1960), 69.

3. J. Hector St. John Crèvecoeur, *Letters from an American Farmer* (1782; reprint, New York: Fox, Duffield & Co., 1904), 7–9.

4. Thomas Jefferson, *Notes on Virginia* (1784), in *Great Issues in American History*, ed. Richard Hofstadter (New York: Vintage Books, 1958), 1:170.

5. Michael Kammen, *A Season of Youth: The American Revo-*

lution and the Historical Imagination (New York: Alfred A. Knopf, 1978), 99.

6. William Bentley, *The Diary of William Bentley* (Gloucester, Mass.: Peter Smith, 1962), 1:374 (1792), 2:60 (1793).

7. William Strickland, *Journal of a Tour in the United States of America, 1794–1795*, ed. J. E. Strickland (New York: New-York Historical Society, 1971), 217.

8. Manasseh Cutler, *Life, Journals and Correspondence*, ed. William Parker Cutler and Julia Perkins Cutler (Cincinnati: Robert Clarke & Co., 1888), 1:96–108.

9. Ezra Stiles, *The Literary Diary*, ed. Franklin Bowditch Dexter (New York: Charles Scribner's Sons, 1901), 3:350 (9 April 1789).

10. John Adams, 7 April 1786. Quoted in Ann Leighton, *American Gardens in the Eighteenth Century* (Boston: Houghton Mifflin, 1976), 350, 359.

11. Neil Harris, *The Artist in American Society: The Formative Years, 1790–1860* (New York: George Braziller, 1966), 29.

12. Neil Harris, "The Making of an American Culture: 1750–1800," in *American Art: 1750–1800, Towards Independence*, ed. Charles F. Montgomery and Patricia E. Kane (New Haven, Conn.: Yale University Art Gallery, 1976), 29–30; Cushing Strout, *The American Image of the Old World* (New York: Harper & Row, 1963), 16.

13. Bentley, *Diary*, 1:398 (4 October 1792).

14. Ibid., 264 (1791).

15. Drawings of the Lilacs are in the Archives of the Society for the Preservation of New England Antiquities.

16. John Brinckerhoff Jackson, *The Necessity for Ruins* (Amherst: University of Massachusetts Press, 1980), 32.

17. For more on this subject, see Robin Williams, "Rural Economy and the Antique in the English Landscape Garden," *Journal of Garden History* 7 (January-March 1987): 73–96.

18. See David Watkin, *The English Vision* (New York: Harper & Row, 1982), 20–21. See also Christopher Hussey, *English Gardens and Landscapes, 1700–1750* (New York: Funk & Wagnalls, 1967), esp. p. 112, on Stowe, Buckinghamshire.

19. Francois Jean Chastellux, *Travels in North-America in the Years 1780, 1781, and 1782*, ed. Howard R. Rice Jr. (Chapel Hill: University of North Carolina Press, 1963), 1:76.

20. See Therese O'Malley, "Landscape Gardening in the Early National Period," *Views and Visions: American Landscape before 1830*, ed. Edward J. Nygren (Washington, D.C.: Corcoran Gallery of Art), 140–41.

21. Elias Boudinot, *Journey to Boston in 1809*, ed. Milton Halsey Thomas (Princeton, NJ: Princeton University Press, 1955), 42–43.

22. John Codman to Catherine Amory Codman, 20 July 1800, box 118, Codman Family Manuscripts Collection, Society for the Preservation of New England Antiquities.

23. Ibid., 18 July 1800. Upon their return to the United States in 1804, the Gores began transforming the landscape of their own estate in Waltham, Mass. The grounds and mansion are open to the public at Gore Place, as they are at the Codman estate.

24. Ibid., 24 Aug. 1800. The story of the Codman estate continues in chapter 8.

25. John James, trans., *The Theory and Practice of Gardening*, Antoine Joseph Dezallier D'Argenville (London: 1712), 20.

26. Hussey, *English Gardens*, 96; Michael McCarthy, "Eighteenth Century Amateur Architects and Their Gardens," in *The Picturesque Garden and its Influence outside the British Isles*, ed. Nikolaus Pevsner (Washington, D.C.: Dumbarton Oaks, 1974), 44. Stowe was commemorated by Rigaud's drawings (1733), Seeley's guides, and William Gilpin's "Dialogue upon the Gardens of the Right Honorable Lord Viscount Cobham at Stowe" (1748). In 1732, poems by Alexander Pope and Gilbert West sang the praises of Stowe. These works are reprinted in *The Genius of the Place*, ed. John Dixon Hunt and Peter Willis (London: Elek, 1975).

27. Bentley, *Diary*, 3:461 (30 September 1809).

28. Alexander Hamilton, "Report on the Subject of Manufactures," 5 December 1791, in *Great Issues in American History*, ed. Richard Hofstadter (New York: Vintage Books, 1958), 1:171–76.

Chapter 2

The Conservative Tradition

Gardens of Portsmouth, New Hampshire

LITTLE RIVERS, threadlike on a map, meander through southern Maine and New Hampshire, flowing south and colliding, finally, to form the Piscataqua River. At Portsmouth the Piscataqua meets the sea at one of New England's deepest and safest harbors. When all transportation was by water, prosperity flowed naturally along with shipping into Portsmouth. During the seventeenth and eighteenth centuries, quantities of huge logs from ancient pines, cut in the interior forests of Maine and New Hampshire, were floated downstream to Portsmouth. This timber, together with an unending harvest of fish, formed the basis for a lucrative trade with Britain, the West Indies, and the more southerly American colonies. Many and great were the fortunes amassed by Portsmouth ship owners and merchants. The Wentworth family, in particular, grew to preeminence; when New Hampshire was made a separate province in 1741, Benning Wentworth was appointed governor.[1]

Many fine houses were built in and around Portsmouth in the decades before the Revolution. The rich lived well. They surrounded themselves with fine furnishings, trim gardens, and servants to look after every need. Many households had slaves; in Portsmouth the infamous institution reached its peak in 1767, when 187 slaves were listed in town records.[2]

The War of Independence brought about a changing of the guard after the departure of the Tory Loyalists and occasioned a temporary setback to Portsmouth's economy. Shipping trade fell off, and "everything shows signs of being in a state of decline . . . many of the houses are dilapidated," according to a French traveler in 1788, who found people in rags.[3] The economy picked up again in the 1790s, and Portsmouth reached the peak of its vitality. The cosmopolitan port city remained the cultural, commercial, and political heart of New Hampshire. The inland valleys of the Connecticut and the Merrimack Rivers seemed remote and rustic. Ambitious young men from the hinterland—Daniel Webster, for one—were drawn to Portsmouth to seek their fortunes. They established banks and trading companies, built ships, churches, and fine houses, and laid out grand gardens. Many of these new rich encouraged local artisans with their support; talented craftsmen and carvers flourished under this patronage. Terrible fires destroyed whole sections of the city in 1802, 1806, and 1813; but after the ashes were cold, there was even more new construction.[4] Mansions and gardens were immaculately maintained to display

The South West Prospect of the Seat of Col. George Boyd, anonymous, oil on canvas, 1774. The garden at Colonel Boyd's estate in Portsmouth, New Hampshire, had an unusual plan of walkways radiating from a pool at the center. (Photo by Bill Finney; Phillips Exeter Academy, gift of Thomas W. Lamont, class of 1888)

the wealth and good taste of their owners. Some long-established householders continued to depend on their ex-slaves as servants, who in turn depended on their onetime owners. Mrs. Eleanor Shackleford, for example, lived for ninety-one years in her family home on State Street; three freed slaves—Adam, Bess, and Marcus—lived with her until the house burned in the fire of 1813.[5]

As was true in other coastal cities, many prosperous Portsmouth families owned farms outside the city to which they moved during the summer months. Even before the Revolution, members of the Wentworth clan had maintained rural establishments in addition to their city dwellings. The tradition continued into the nineteenth century. The March family's ornamental 275-acre farm, for instance, was handed on through seven generations, starting well before the Revolution.[6]

Visual images of post-Revolutionary gardens come usually from contemporary descriptions and the few surviving survey plans. Paintings of gardens of that era are rare. The anonymous 1774 oil painting of Colonel

George Boyd's Portsmouth estate is unique. Boyd, a shipbuilder, purchased property fronting on the tidal North Mill Pond in 1771. The mansion house, barn, and warehouses had been built by the previous owner. Boyd's neatly fenced garden is shown very clearly in the painting. Like many gardens laid out in New England during the years before and after the Revolution, this garden had a central walkway on an axis with the main door of the house. The Boyd garden varied from the usual four-square plan, however, in having subsidiary paths that radiated from a central point. In the middle of the garden was what appears to have been a raised water basin. From there one path led to a toolshed or

A View of the Mansion of the late LORD TIMOTHY DEXTER in High Street, Newbury port 1810

An 1810 engraving of the residence of Lord Timothy Dexter, Newburyport, Massachusetts. Forty brilliantly painted figures, erected in 1798, represented a range of people, from Venus to Louis XVI to Thomas Jefferson, as well as four lions and a lamb. (Society for the Preservation of New England Antiquities)

well house, and others fanned out like spokes in a wheel. The garden beds had an edging of greenery and a few randomly placed shrubs. A pair of tall pines flanked the garden gate. Along one side of the garden ran a formal canal. The well-organized pattern of the garden would have been clearly visible from the house.

The inspiration for the circular space at the center of the Boyd garden, with its pool and radiating walks, may have come from the early landscape gardens in England, where here and there a softening of strict regularity had lately begun. A 1722 survey of the grounds at Melbourne Hall in Derbyshire shows one of the first English examples of a *rond-point* similar to the later echo at Colonel Boyd's. As the term indicates, the English had adopted a French innovation, as seen, for example, at Marly, Louis XIV's last garden.[7]

Colonel Boyd's garden was intended to reflect well on its owner, whose mercantile trade had reportedly made him the richest man in Portsmouth before the Revolution. Boyd brought over a trained gardener from England to work for him. Charles Brewster, who chronicled the city's past as he viewed it during the 1850s, actually remembered Boyd's estate. He recalled that the place had been called the "white village," in reference to a paint color unusual when it was first applied to the house and its outbuildings. In his *Rambles about Portsmouth*, Brewster described Boyd's property as "a magnificent seat, such as a nabob might envy, enclosed within a white open fence, and at regular intervals of some forty or fifty feet, those handsomely carved towering Grenadiers' heads were placed on posts, and presented a very unique appearance."[8]

Unfortunately, the heads are not featured in the painting, but Boyd obviously had a sense of display. This row of busts must have been striking, perhaps surpassed only by self-styled "Lord" Timothy Dexter's flamboyant exhibit in Newburyport. There, in front of his mansion, Dexter in 1798 put up on his fence posts forty carved and painted statue figures, larger than life, of such notables as George Washington, King George III, Napoleon Bonaparte, and his own eccentric self.[9]

· · ·

Architectural historian Abbott Lowell Cummings pointed out another Portsmouth garden with paths radiating from a *rond-point*. This garden once adjoined the country house of the former royal governor, Benning Wentworth (1696–1770), at Little Harbor, just outside the city.[10] The Wentworth garden shows up as a tiny but clear detail on a 1774 map of Portsmouth Harbor. There may have been a summerhouse at the center. There are two plans of the Wentworth garden at Little Harbor. An 1812 survey plan documents a complete change in the layout of this garden since the earlier map was drawn. The flower garden now had straight paths intersecting at right angles, rather than the radial spokes of 1774. A larger garden behind the house had the long central walkway so common to urban Portsmouth gardens, with two cross-walks at regular intervals. This 112-acre estate was a working farm, with extensive orchards, pastures, and fields for row crops, as well as a wharf of its own.

Over the years the Wentworth farm was described in glowing terms in advertisements in the local newspapers as Benning Wentworth's heirs tried to sell it. In 1809 a notice announced that "a great quantity of box for large or small gardens" was to be sold from the garden at Little Harbor.[11] This boxwood—rare as far north as Portsmouth—probably edged the garden beds. According to an 1816 advertisement, the flower garden contained "a profusion of rose bushes making from 20 to 30 bottles of rose water."[12] The kitchen garden produced a variety of fruits and contained thirty large beds of asparagus. "The gardens and house would suit any gentleman of fortune or merchant for summer retirement." Another advertisement further proclaimed, "The situation is delightful and romantic, commanding a grand prospect of the seas and adjacent country."[13]

The words "prospect" and "romantic" were faintly alien to the Portsmouth of that era. "Convenient," "neat," even "elegant" were more typical encomiums. When this advertisement appeared, the Wentworth farm belonged to Martha Wentworth and her English-educated husband, "Sir" John Wentworth, a full-blown Anglophile who liked to be called by the title he thought he ought to have held. They were anxious to sell the family farm in order to move permanently to England, as they eventually did. Sir John's advertisement was a reflection of contemporary English land-

scape ideals in its emphasis on the emotional and sensory appeal that scenery could evoke. The natural landscape, once considered in America to be hostile territory waiting to be subdued, was now to be incorporated into the garden. Utilitarian elements could be arranged so as to enhance the view. Hinting at Italian villa prototypes, the Wentworths advanced their version of the design precepts of England's Humphry Repton and his predecessors to promote the sale of this Portsmouth country seat.

· · ·

Right in the heart of Portsmouth there was another Wentworth garden. This one belonged to another John Wentworth, the last royal appointee to serve as governor in New Hampshire and a nephew of Benning Wentworth, the prior governor. By all accounts, John Wentworth (1737–1820) was an excellent governor until forced by circumstances beyond his control to leave hastily and permanently in 1775. He lived in a fine Georgian house that still stands on Pleasant Street. The house was set close to the street on a narrow lot, far deeper than it was wide, the sort of lot that was typical of Portsmouth. The back garden of this property has only recently been obliterated by new construction. Charles Brewster, in his Portsmouth chronicle, described the garden as it survived in the 1850s, with "handsomely arranged walks and agreeable shade. At the bottom of the garden, beneath a summer house, a refreshing bathing-room is provided, which opens to the river."[14]

In a historical novel, *The Governor's Lady*, published in 1960, Thomas H. Raddall described this summerhouse as a Chinese-style pagoda enclosed in lattice-work. Raddall, accurate in many details, may have been right about the summerhouse. He may or may not have been right about the steamy interlude he described as having taken place there one summer night in 1769, when the buxom and beautiful Frances Atkinson submitted to the ardent importunings of the governor.[15] Ten days after the death of her first husband, Frances and the governor were wed, to live more or less happily ever after.

One of Governor John Wentworth's duties to the king had been to survey and manage New Hampshire's forests. He was conscientious in carrying out this responsibility. He traveled and explored throughout the province, concerning himself with the welfare of the

Governor John Wentworth, John Singleton Copley, pastel on paper, 1769. John Wentworth (1737–1820) was the last royal governor of New Hampshire. (Hood Museum of Art, Dartmouth College, Hanover, New Hampshire; gift of Mrs. Esther Lowell Abbott, in memory of her husband, Gordon Abbott)

inhabitants of the interior and striving to expand settlement and trade by building roads.[16] He founded Dartmouth College. His determination to enhance the prosperity of New Hampshire was aborted by the Revolution, which abruptly ended his tenure and the programs he had initiated.

In the course of his travels, Wentworth had found a site on Smith's Pond (now Lake Wentworth) in Wolfeboro, at the northern edge of Lake Winnipesaukee, where he decided to establish a "sylvan abode." In 1768 he began to acquire land at Wolfeboro, and eventually owned more than four thousand acres. James Garvin, architectural historian for New Hampshire, has summed up the scope of Wentworth's intentions: the Wolfeboro estate, "planned as an architectural show-

piece, a model farm, a junction for a highway network, and a magnet to attract inland development, . . . represents a monument to eighteenth-century planning and to the vision of one of New Hampshire's greatest minds."[17] A sojourn in England, where Wentworth had observed the style in which some of his kinfolk lived on their country estates in Yorkshire, had given him elevated standards for forming his own. The mansion house, now only a cellar hole, was apparently larger than any other dwelling in New England. Its appearance can only be guessed at. Wentworth designed it himself, consulting English architectural guidebooks and seeking advice from the leading architect in the American colonies, Peter Harrison.[18]

Wentworth's Wolfeboro estate, far surpassing in grandeur the rural seats of other Portsmouth gentlefolk, may have been New England's answer to the baronial plantations of Virginia and the Carolinas. The governor had as many as 150 laborers building roads and clearing land. He employed farmers, gardeners, and master craftsmen to work on the house, as well as household servants. He kept two slaves.[19] When it came to landscaping his grounds, Wentworth had ambitious plans. He hired a Scotsman as his head gardener. After the stumps were cleared away, Wentworth had a stone wall built to enclose a forty-acre garden on the lake front. He had hundreds of elm saplings shipped up from Portsmouth to line a straight, one-hundred-foot-wide "mall" leading to the house.[20] Large orchards were laid out with pear and apple trees, and six hundred acres were fenced in as a park for captive deer and moose. Forever experimenting, Wentworth attempted to introduce pheasants to his woods and ocean fish to the lake. The pheasants vanished, but the fish, unlikely as it seems, supposedly survived.[21]

The governor opted to spend six months of the year at the place he modestly called his "Farm."[22] His days were devoted to work. On occasion he would join his wife, Frances, and their houseguests for a picnic under a great pine that stood on the top of Mount Delight, overlooking the mansion. Another day, the party would sail out to an island in the lake to have tea on "Tea Rock." Lady Frances Wentworth, however, was usually lonely and disturbed by the ongoing construction. She called Wolfeboro a "solitary wilderness." Indeed, the place was surrounded by wilderness; it was situated fifty miles from Portsmouth, an arduous journey despite her husband's new road. Frances missed urban life and society. As she wrote to a friend, she—unlike the governor—was not "sunk in rural tranquillity half enough to prefer a Grove to a Ball-room."[23] Presumably, she had no pangs of regret for Wolfeboro when they were suddenly forced to flee the country in 1775. They had had no more than seven seasons there, not nearly enough time for Wentworth to carry out all his grand plans.

John Wentworth's plantation, like the estates of other Loyalists, was confiscated and later sold at auction. In 1820 the mansion was entirely destroyed by fire. The grounds reverted to forest once again. In 1933 the heart of the property belonged to Lawrence Shaw Mayo, a Harvard dean and John Wentworth's biographer. Mayo donated ninety-six acres to the state of New Hampshire as a historical park. From 1985 to 1988 a team of archaeologists investigated the site, adding to what was known about John Wentworth's bold experiment in agriculture, horticulture, and landscape design.[24] Were he around now, with his inquiring mind, Governor Wentworth might have enjoyed the archaeology. At least he would be happy that his pioneering efforts did not go for naught.

. . .

Inevitably, most eighteenth-century gardens have been lost or built on, but in Portsmouth there are survivors. One of the best known and best kept is that of the Moffatt-Ladd house on busy Market Street. This garden is open to the public in summer and early autumn.

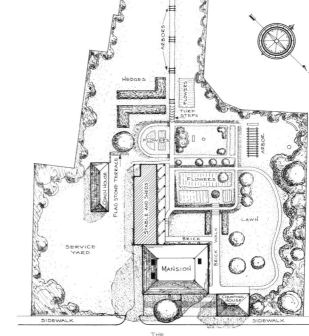

Plan of the terraced grounds of the Moffatt-Ladd house, Portsmouth, New Hampshire. (From John Mead Howells, *The Architectural Heritage of the Piscataqua*, Architectural Book Publishing Co., 1937)

The Moffatt-Ladd house, with the horse chestnut tree that still stands beside it. The gardens lie behind the house and its outbuildings. (National Society of The Colonial Dames of America in the State of New Hampshire)

Opposite: Terraced gardens rise behind Colonel John Moffatt's house in Portsmouth, New Hampshire. Grass steps, perfectly maintained, lead to the topmost level. (Photo by Peter Margonelli)

The Moffatt-Ladd garden is sheltered by the house and its attached outbuildings. A horse chestnut tree, visible to the right of the house, is said to have been planted to commemorate the signing of the Declaration of Independence. (Photo by Peter Margonelli)

Captain John Moffatt built the house—possibly the first three-story house in Portsmouth—in 1763. It remained in the care of his descendants until the National Society of the Colonial Dames took it over in 1913.[25]

John Moffatt's house faces the river, where its owner had his warehouses and a private wharf. The house is perched high above the street that parallels the river; the garden is behind the house. This garden has been so altered and embellished over the years by owners who were ardent gardeners that, without an early survey to look at, no one can say just how it was originally laid out. The ground rises behind the house. Long ago the slope was shaped into four terraces, connected by four sets of steps. The straight central path, on an axis with the main entrances to the mansion, runs three hundred

feet from the house to the rear of the property. Typical of Portsmouth gardens of the late eighteenth and early nineteenth centuries, this walkway has probably always been the spine that held the garden together. Captain Moffatt's countinghouse, his stables, and the coach house were sited so as to enclose the garden and enhance its privacy. A damask rose—the so-called Bride's Rose—is said to have been in the garden since 1764, when Moffatt's daughter-in-law brought it there from her mother's garden in England. Myth attaches also to the great horse chestnut (*Aesculus hippocastanum*) that still stands beside the house. Moffatt's son-in-law, William Whipple, supposedly planted the tree to extol the Declaration of Independence, which he had just returned from signing.

· · ·

As the 1798 plan of another Portsmouth property illustrates, the grounds of a merchant's town house involved much more than pleasure and display. Many functions had to be fitted onto the site. The distinguished Wentworth-Gardner house still fronts on the river, as it has since 1760; like Captain Moffatt's, this house once overlooked its owner's busy wharves. Behind the house were sheds, wood houses, and offices, as well as gardens. A linden tree, said to have been planted by the first owner, stood in front of the Wentworth-Gardner

house into the 1980s. The trunk measured fifteen feet around when the tree was more than two hundred years old.[26] Sarah Haven Foster, a talented nineteenth-century Portsmouth painter who recorded with her tiny brushes many marvelously detailed views of the city and its environs, made a watercolor of the Wentworth-Gardner house a century ago, when the linden was in its majestic prime.

· · ·

James Rundlet's name does not figure in history books. His present-day claim to fame rests on the strong probability that his garden is the oldest in Portsmouth to survive in its original configuration on its original site.

When Rundlet arrived in Portsmouth in 1794 at the age of twenty-three, he had nothing but his wits and his ambition to sustain him. Having grown up on a farm at Exeter, a few miles inland, he knew that the thriving seaport was the place for him to seek his fortune. Like many another brash entrepreneur in the booming ports of New England, James Rundlet started out in a small way as a merchant.[27] Buying on credit, selling on commission, he slowly but steadily increased his worth. He imported manufactured goods—cloth, ribbons, and gloves—from England and Holland in exchange for West Indian sugar, molasses, rum, and coffee. By 1807, after assessing his affairs at his downtown counting-

An 1880s watercolor of the Wentworth-Gardner house, with the great linden tree in front. Sarah Haven Foster painted many scenes in and around her native Portsmouth, New Hampshire. (Portsmouth Public Library)

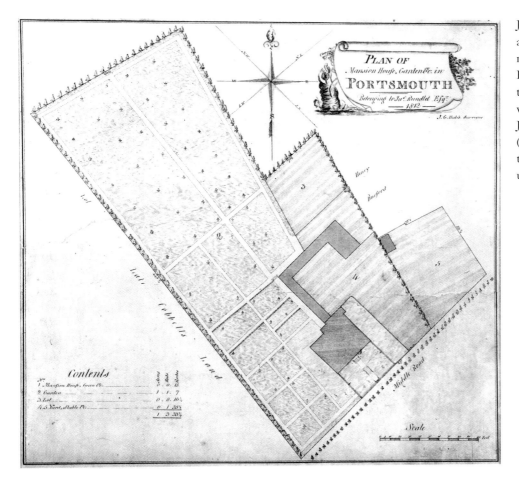

James Rundlet had over an acre of garden, taking up most of his property in Portsmouth. Rundlet is said to have laid out the straight walks and terraces shown in J. G. Hales's 1812 survey. (Society for the Preservation of New England Antiquities)

house, Rundlet decided to proceed with the building of a suitable house for his growing family. He bought thirty acres along Middle Road, then at the outskirts of town.

The house that Rundlet built is imposing, as surely he wanted it to be. It sits seven feet above the level of the street, so that one has to look up and then walk up to the front door, as though approaching the seat of royalty. The monumental, three-storied facade, surmounted by a balustrade surrounding a low-pitched roof, represented the Federal style of the most fashionable houses then being built in Portsmouth, Salem, and Boston.

James Rundlet intended his new estate to be an urban residence. Closely tied as he was to the fortunes of the city, he anticipated Portsmouth's continued expansion. As Portsmouth prospered, so did he. His home was located near the heart of the city and his various mercantile interests. It was perfectly possible then for businessmen or government officials to be part-time farmers and to live surrounded by rural countryside.

New England cities, like the towns from which they grew, were compact, densely settled nodes in an agrarian landscape.

From Rundlet's front door, according to legend, all the land that he could see was his.[28] At that time, when so much of the land had been cleared for agriculture, Rundlet could probably see quite far. He could see the little hill known as "Rundlet's Mountain." Perhaps he was able to glimpse the farm he owned on Sagamore Creek, south of Portsmouth, where his serious farming operations were conducted.[29] Only part of the family's sustenance was raised at their home: apples for cider, vegetables and small fruits for the table, and a few cows for milk.

Surveyor J. G. Hales drew up a plan of James Rundlet's property in 1812. It might have been drawn yesterday. The mansion house still commands its terraced eminence above Middle Road, as it did when Hales made his survey. The barn and stables still enclose the stable yard. Beside and behind the house, gravel paths still follow the regular pattern shown on the plan.

Where the land dropped away behind the house, it was shaped into level terraces that remain to this day.

The regularly spaced rows of trees depicted on the plan in the garden behind the house indicates what was, and still is, an orchard. The small beds nearer the house appear to have had little trees or shrubs at their corners. The whole property was surrounded by trees, according to the plan, closely planted in a single row.

A central axis from the front gate leads straight through the mansion house and on to meet the rear property line at Austin Street. Even though this axial path bends ever so slightly, it *appears* straight. Subordinate walks all cross at right angles or so close to right angles that they seem so. The plan expresses a clear separation of uses, with no visible connections between the stable yard, the lot (or cow yard), and the orchard and garden. The grounds adjoining the house were further separated from the rest of the property by their elevation above it.

Rundlet apparently laid out his grounds himself, to accord with his wishes and his family's needs. Although strictly compartmentalized, the place is an impressively unified whole, combining utility with family privacy and pleasure. This estate was a showplace for Rundlet, attesting to his success in business and to the refinement of his taste.

Rundlet's taste in landscape design was entirely conservative. Although his house was designed in the newest Federal style, his garden might just as well have accompanied a house built before the Revolution. Based on straight lines—almost a grid in plan—this landscape was old-fashioned even when it was brand-new. But this was what everyone else in Portsmouth was doing at the time. The tried and true, symmetrical, right-angled garden was still the style in Portsmouth. Well into the nineteenth century, conservatism prevailed in the domestic landscapes of Portsmouth, as it did in other nearby port cities. The radical changes in garden design that had occurred in England were slow to make much of an impact on this section of the country. Indeed, until Andrew Jackson Downing produced his popular, trend-setting treatise on landscape gardening in 1841, the number of New England gardeners to adopt the English landscape style was very small. In Portsmouth, the number may have been zero.

James Rundlet's property passed by will through generations of his descendants. The familial attachment to the place seems to have increased rather than decreased. Over the years, peripheral lots were sold off,

but the heart of the property was kept intact. The last family owner, Ralph May, in his ninetieth year gave the house with its contents, outbuildings, and all remaining land to the Society for the Preservation of New England Antiquities. By thus ensuring permanent protection for his historic property, May showed clearly the value he placed on it.

.   .   .

Another Portsmouth garden flourished during the years when Rundlet was developing his property. The plan still survives. Edward Parry, having prospered as a dry-goods merchant, moved in 1799 into a house on Pleasant Street on a narrow lot that extended nearly four hundred feet to the South Mill Pond. From a gate behind the house, a straight path bisected the walled garden. The path led to a unique garden feature beside the pond: a small but massive stone fort, quite different from the more customary summerhouse. The eight-foot-high crenellated walls of his "Fort Anglesea" were surmounted by a flagpole, from which flew a banner bearing a Welsh motto that proclaimed, "I serve." Whom Parry thought he served is unclear. He had two swivel-mounted brass cannons on the fort, which he used to fire off on special days. On July Fourth the cannons were at their noisiest.[30] These armaments, plus the report that his garden walls were studded on top with broken bottles, suggest paranoia in addition to eccentricity. Did Parry fear for the safety of rare plants in his garden? He should have worried about money: financial ruin forced him to leave Portsmouth in 1818. Parry's garden, with its fort as an unconventional folly, was eventually incorporated into a public park.

.   .   .

By 1812 the focus of power in New Hampshire had shifted from Portsmouth, the old port city, to newer inland settlements along the Merrimack River.[31] Portsmouth began its long period of decline. The change had come about gradually and for a variety of reasons. By encouraging settlement of the back country, the last

Opposite: In Portsmouth gardens, roses were often grown on distinctive spiral rose trellises like this one beside James Rundlet's Federal mansion. (Photo by Peter Margonelli)

royal governor, John Wentworth, may have inadvertently helped to nudge Portsmouth toward its eventual slide from glory.

Jefferson's embargo on trade with England had proved so unpopular that it helped put the Federalists—the party of Portsmouth's wealthy merchants—back in control of the state in 1809. Meanwhile, however, the Jeffersonian Republicans, strong in the interior, had succeeded in having the state capital moved from Exeter, near the coast, to Concord on the Merrimack. This was a body blow to the prestige of the old coastal settlements, Portsmouth in particular.[32] The Portsmouth Federalists opposed the War of 1812; the inland Republicans supported it. In the elections of 1816, the Federalists—and Portsmouth—lost control of the state government, never to regain it. Daniel Webster, always a bellwether, promptly moved to Boston, knowing full well that Portsmouth had passed its prime. The city had fallen behind in the trade race, too. Within a few years, an observer from England described the city this way: "The environs are embellished by neat country-seats; but the town itself has nothing striking. It has suffered considerably by frequent fires, and, as its trade has been visibly on the decline, no pains have been taken to rebuild the houses. The old town . . . has such a wretched appearance."[33]

According to Charles Brewster, Portsmouth's chief chronicler, the city may have looked particularly sad in the 1830s, when all its street trees were dead or dying. Governor John Langdon had planted Lombardy poplars in front of his house in the 1790s. Following his lead, others in Portsmouth did the same, until many of the major thoroughfares were lined with the columnar poplars. "Portsmouth for some years was indeed a *popular* place," Brewster quipped.[34] When the poplars began to deteriorate and look ugly, as inevitably they do in old age, they were replaced by long rows of buttonwood trees (*Platanus occidentalis*). Just as they reached maturity, the buttonwoods were ravaged by caterpillars. The trees looked so sick and the caterpillars were such a nuisance that the buttonwoods—hundreds of them—were cut down. A "Tree Society," established to improve the situation, planted elms and maples, which flourished for many years.

Portsmouth did not, of course, simply wither away when the balance of commercial and political power in New Hampshire shifted elsewhere. The cultural and social life of the city continued, although conducted with more restraint. The work of making and keeping gardens continued, too. Captain Moffatt's garden, for one, was considerably expanded and elaborated after 1819, when the ownership of the property passed to Moffatt's great-granddaughter, Maria Haven, and her husband, Alexander Ladd.

· · ·

One ardent Portsmouth gardener left to posterity a remarkable series of diaries and memoirs that open a window onto a nineteenth-century garden world. Sarah Parker Rice, born in Portsmouth in 1805, married Ichabod Goodwin, a successful businessman and later governor of New Hampshire. In 1832, Sarah and her husband moved to the house she was to occupy until her death in 1896. The Goodwin house has been moved now to the Portsmouth museum village of Strawbery Banke. Sarah Goodwin's plans, plant lists, and garden records are so complete that horticulturists at Strawbery Banke have been able to replicate the configuration and planting of her garden, even changing the plants a bit each year, just as Sarah did.

Sarah Goodwin at seventy began a journal that she called "Pleasant Memories." "Oh the comfort, the delight I have had in my garden . . . the greatest, most solid comfort I have ever had," she wrote when she was eighty-three. From her recollections of her childhood, it is apparent that her interest in gardens began early. She remembered her Aunt Flagg's garden, with its tall poplars, billowy snowball bushes, and heaps of crimson peonies.[35] She recalled another garden of her childhood, behind the Assembly House where she used to go to dancing school. A broad central walk led through flower beds filled with sweet red clover to a two-story octagonal summerhouse situated on a little rise. Sarah Goodwin also remembered her own first garden: "When I was a very little girl, my Father gave me a little piece of ground, six feet by one, with what was called an 'alley board' around it. In that I had several small roots of very inferior value, that would now be thought scarcely worth cultivating. Among them a bulb, now rarely seen, called a twelve o'clock. It was a little white flower resembling the chicory in shape, which opened at twelve noon and closed in an hour or so."[36]

While in New York on her wedding journey, Sarah Goodwin seized the opportunity to visit the well-known Thorburn seed store. As soon as she and her husband had settled into their own house in 1832, she began to develop her garden. The tall Federal house was then twenty years old. Mrs. Goodwin wrote later that she found foxgloves, rosebushes, and purple lilacs already established. She loved the lilacs; hardy and pest-free, "they bring new life to me every year."[37] White lilacs came much later to Portsmouth than purple ones, she said. Governor Benning Wentworth, at Little Harbor in the 1750s, was said to have been the first in the vicinity of Portsmouth to plant lilacs. To this day, gnarled descendants of his shrubs surround the venerable Wentworth mansion.

As an old lady in the 1880s, Mrs. Goodwin tried to remember the first plants she put into her new garden. She had brought with her some old favorites, including Canterbury bells, sweet williams, and the pink Provence rose from her grandfather's garden. She had damask roses and an old white one. She described the venerable elderberry bush that bloomed with her roses as "one of the most beautiful things in the world."[38] She planted sweet peas while the ground was still frozen, as she waited for spring, and the double tulips that she loved. Later in the season came "white lilies high and low, yellow lilies, purple lilies, lilies of the valley" and more. "In the early years," she recalled, "I cultivated the marigolds, the African, the French and the velvet, but yellow flowers went out of fashion. Now [1888] they are preferred to any."[39]

Sarah Goodwin loved the flowers she called "old-fashioned," those that had been treasured for generations, passing from gardener to gardener. The term was particularly appropriate during her long lifetime, when the horticultural establishment was being bombarded with newly discovered flowering plants from remote corners of the earth. Plants from tropical climes were introduced to chillier regions, where they had to be started under glass and set outdoors only when summer was at hand. Advances in greenhouse technology made this form of horticulture possible. The result was a new style of flower garden, planted entirely with brilliantly colored tender annuals. One writer-gardener, Anna B. Warner, described the new planting technique in the 1870s: using masses of a single variety of flower in a single color, "the beds are laid out in exact shapes, and with a certain reference to each other, the whole forming a pattern of coloured embroidery upon the green turf."[40] Since the plants, ideally, were all the same height, this style of gardening was known as carpet bedding. Individual blossoms, even individual plants, were less important than the overall effect. The display was best ap-preciated from above; a veranda provided the ideal vantage point.

Mrs. Goodwin eagerly tried the new tender annuals and enjoyed experimenting with new designs for beds, although she never entirely abandoned older planting styles. One summer, with the help of "Old Ragan," her gardener for forty years, she had "a great bed of double asters, verbenas, and stocks." A friend told her "it was the handsomest bed of flowers he ever saw."[41] These annuals—asters, verbenas, and stocks —were new introductions in the 1830s and 1840s, available from good seed merchants such as Thorburn in New York and Joseph Breck in Boston. Early on, Sarah Goodwin had a "little thing called the Azure Blue Gillia" (*Gilia capitata*), a California native that had only been discovered in 1833; its seeds were offered for sale by Thorburn in 1838.[42] Mrs. Goodwin took pride in having been among the first to cultivate the "wigelia" (*Weigela florida*). This pink-flowered shrub was one of plant hunter Robert Fortune's discoveries in China in 1846. By 1851, Cambridge, Massachusetts, nurseryman C. M. Hovey stocked it. Mrs. Goodwin may have obtained one of Hovey's first propagations of the weigela.[43]

By her own admission, Mrs. Goodwin was plagued with the craziness that afflicts some hopelessly passionate gardeners: "I would begin work, suitably dressed, directly after breakfast, & many, many days did not return to the house until it was too dark to work any longer. Then & only then did I discover that my back was broken & leaving my dinner & my tea which had been set up for me I made the best of my way to a bath & my bed."[44]

Mrs. Goodwin died in 1896 at the age of ninety-one, Her vivid memories provide rare views of the lively gardening world of nineteenth-century Portsmouth. Sarah Goodwin lived so long and gardened so long that she touched base with most of the changing horticultural trends of the entire century. In her sentimental fondness for the flowers and gardens of her childhood, she was one with Portsmouth's strong conservative tradition. With her gradual embracing of new plants and new ways of displaying them, she allied herself to the venturesome spirit of midcentury. Toward the end of her life, by her invocations of the virtues and charm of "old-fashioned" flowers, she fitted comfortably into the mood of the Colonial Revival, a movement that was particularly strong in and around Portsmouth.

· · ·

Plan of Sarah Goodwin's garden, by A. J. Hoyt, 1862. (Strawbery Banke)

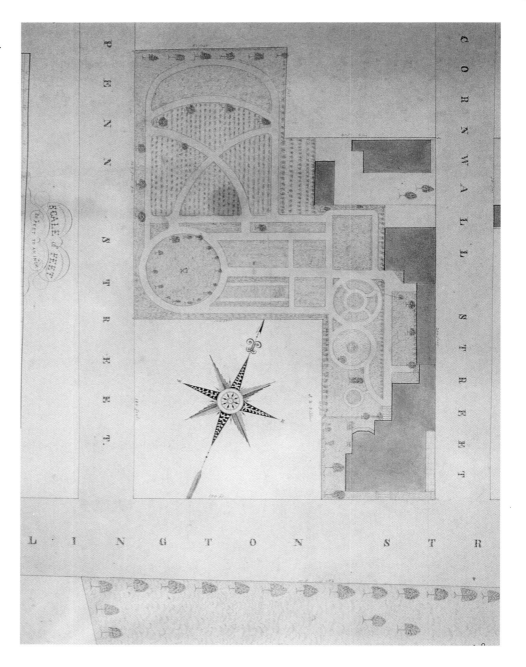

One other Portsmouth garden must be mentioned because of the mystery surrounding its origins. Its design is like no other. It is based on a puzzle. On Pleasant Street, adjacent to the site where Edward Parry once had his fortified garden, is the 1789 house that Jacob Wendell purchased in 1815. Wendell's descendants owned the property from that day until 1990. Barrett Wendell (1855–1921), a grandson of Jacob, spent his honeymoon at the old family home in 1880.[45] In 1910, when he was an eminent Harvard professor, Barrett

Wendell bought his grandfather's house from the estate of a bachelor cousin, who had neglected the place. Neglect can be less inimical to preservation than over-ardent restoration. Fortunately, this was the case at the Wendell property. Professor Wendell found all of his grandfather's furniture and furnishings still in the house. He also found intact the tiny, oddly patterned garden behind the house. Though overgrown and neglected, the layout of the thirty-by-fifty-foot garden was, he said, exactly as he remembered it from his earliest visits to his grandfather's house. In accounts written shortly after Professor Wendell's death in 1921, both his daughter and his biographer were firm in their assertions that the garden predated not only Barrett Wendell's ownership but also the tenure of the cousin who preceded him.[46] But still some say that the professor did it, that it was he who designed the garden, according to his own whim, in 1910.

Beginning in the year of their purchase, Professor Wendell and his wife Edith undertook to clear away the growth of years from the garden. They refurbished the pathways, replaced the rotting boards that enclosed the beds, shored up the old pergola, and planted vines and "such simple flowers as might always have bloomed there," according to their daughter. Considering themselves to be custodians of their historic family property, the Barrett Wendells reportedly preserved the historic pattern of the garden beds and strove to maintain it. This pattern was what made their garden unique. According to family legend, the puzzle from which the garden design was taken was brought home by George Wendell, the captain of a sailing ship, from a voyage to China early in the nineteenth century.[47]

That was all I knew of this garden, but it was enough. I had seen one fuzzy photograph in Alice Lockwood's *Gardens of Colony and State*. In 1987, while in Portsmouth with a friend one autumn day, I said, "Well, let's just *see* if it's still there." I knew the house, which is next

to a little park. We paced slowly back and forth along the high board fence before we decided to try to peek over. On tiptoe, fingertips clinging to the top board, for an instant I glimpsed the garden. "Yes, it is!" I whispered, feeling as though I were shouting.

"Would you like to see my garden?" said a soft voice behind us. We turned, naughty schoolgirls caught in the act. The woman was walking her small dog. She paid not the slightest attention to our apologies and attempts at explanation but invited us into her house and into the garden.

We walked among small raised flower beds, curiously shaped, with narrow brick paths crossing at odd angles. The Wendell garden looks like a crazy quilt, just about big enough to cover a king-size bed. Barrett Wendell's daughter-in-law—for she it was—pointed out the summerhouse, with a carved Chinese figure inside. A sundial bore a carved motto. I bent close to read: "Live Free or Die." Professor Wendell's contribution, I presumed, just so we'd know this was New Hampshire.

The puzzle to which the garden refers is known as a tangram. The tangram originated in China; its popularity spread to the United States and Europe with the China trade. A tangram puzzle consists of seven pieces, including various triangles, a rhomboid, and a square. These pieces can be assembled to form a square, or to conform to an almost infinite number of geometric shapes. Each flower bed in the Wendell garden is

Barrett Wendell's garden was patterned after a seven-piece Chinese tangram puzzle. (From Daniel J. Foley, *The Complete Book of Garden Ornaments, Complements and Accessories*, Crown Publishers, 1972)

shaped like one of the puzzle pieces. This seems an un-usual idea for a garden, an idea that commends itself to other urban gardeners whose space is limited.

As if to confirm the truth of the Wendell legend, the very puzzle that inspired the garden plan was still in the house. Its tiny mother-of-pearl pieces fit neatly into their own little box, the whole not larger than the hand of Mrs. Wendell, as she offered it for our examination. Besides being an heirloom treasure, the puzzle is a more durable guide to the garden than any plan or sur-vey. This may have been kind Mrs. Wendell's last sea-son in her house and her garden. The next year I heard that she had died.

Professor Wendell described the garden in a letter to a friend in November 1915. Even at the tag end of the growing season, he noted that "in our mite of a garden, a few things are still languidly in bloom; white phlox, snapdragons, autumn anemones, roses, and climbing nasturtiums. We have only simple old-fashioned coun-try flowers."[48] The most old-fashioned thing he had was the odd and appealing design of the garden itself.

Notes

1. Elizabeth Forbes Morison and Elting B. Morison, *New Hampshire: A Bicentennial History* (New York: W.W. Norton, 1976), 58. Also Lynn Warren Turner, *The Ninth State: New Hampshire's Formative Years* (Chapel Hill: University of North Carolina Press, 1983).

2. James L. Garvin, "Portsmouth and the Piscataqua: So-cial History and Material Culture," *Historical New Hampshire* 26 (summer 1971): 31.

3. J. P. Brissot de Warville, *New Travels in the United States of America, 1788*, ed. Durand Echeverria (Cambridge, Mass.: Harvard University Press, 1964), 36.

4. William Bentley, *The Diary of William Bentley* (Glouces-ter, Mass.: Peter Smith, 1962), 2:461 (30 December 1802), 3:2 (12 January 1803), 3:268 (24 December 1806); Charles W. Brewster, *Rambles about Portsmouth*, 2d. ser. (Portsmouth, N.H.: Lewis W. Brewster, 1869), 207.

5. Ibid., 219.

6. Ibid., 197.

7. Christopher Hussey, *English Gardens and Landscapes, 1700–1750* (New York: Funk & Wagnalls, 1967), 61.

8. Charles W. Brewster, *Rambles about Portsmouth*, 1st ser. (Portsmouth, N.H.: Lewis W. Brewster, 1859; 2nd ed. 1873), 166.

9. John P. Marquand wrote two books about Dexter: *Lord Timothy Dexter* (New York: Minton, Balch & Co., 1925) and *Timothy Dexter Revisited* (Boston: Little, Brown & Co., 1960).

10. Abbott Lowell Cummings, "Eighteenth-Century New England Garden Design: The Pictorial Evidence," *Eighteenth Century Life*, n.s., 8 (January 1983): 132; James Grant, "A Plan of Piscataqua Harbor, the Town of Portsmouth, etc." (1774), New Hampshire Historical Society, Concord, N.H.

11. *New Hampshire Gazette*, 16 May 1809, quoted in Anne Masury, "Research Techniques and Preservation Solutions for the Historic Landscape" (paper delivered at a conference titled Discover the Historic Landscape of the 1700s, Straw-bery Banke, Portsmouth, N.H., 27–28 January 1984), 16.

12. *New Hampshire Gazette*, 18 June 1816, quoted in Ma-sury, "Research Techniques."

13. *Portsmouth Oracle*, 21 May 1803, quoted in Lucinda A. Brockway, "Land Use and Garden Design in Eighteenth Century Portsmouth" (typescript, n.d., Strawbery Banke, Portsmouth, N.H.), 13.

14. Brewster, *Rambles*, 106. The entire site is now covered by a nursing home.

15. Thomas H. Raddall, *The Governor's Lady* (Garden City, N.Y.: Doubleday, 1960), 74.

16. Morison and Morison, *New Hampshire*, 63–64.

17. James L. Garvin, "Wentworth House: Design, Con-struction, and Furnishings," *New Hampshire Archaeologist* 30 (1989): 27.

18. Ibid., 29; Robert F. W. Meader, *The Saga of a Palace* (Wolfeboro, N.H.: Wolfeboro Historical Society, 1962).

19. "An Inventory of the Estate of John Wentworth, Esq." (1779, after confiscation), reproduced by Peter R. Brunette, *New Hampshire Archaeologist* 30 (1989): 114.

20. Benjamin Franklin Parker, *History of Wolfeborough* (Wolfeboro, N.H., 1901), 85–86.

21. Lawrence Shaw Mayo, *John Wentworth, Governor of New Hampshire, 1767–1775* (Cambridge, Mass.: Harvard University Press, 1921), 94.

22. Peter R. Brunette, "An Historical Overview of the Governor Wentworth Estate," *New Hampshire Archaeologist* 30 (1989): 15.

23. 1770 letter of Frances Wentworth, quoted in Mayo, *John Wentworth*, 92.

24. Gary Hume, state archaeologist, New Hampshire Di-vision of Historical Resources, telephone conversation with author, 1 November 1988. The entire issue, vol. 30 (1989), of *New Hampshire Archaeologist*, noted previously, covers the in-vestigation of this site and the findings that resulted.

25. Mrs. A. T. Dudley, *The Moffatt-Ladd House and Its Garden* (Portsmouth, N.H.: Society of Colonial Dames in New Hampshire, n.d.).

26. Helen H. St. John, "Four Witness Trees of Portsmouth, New Hampshire," *Yankee* (February 1967), 121.

27. Ralph May, *Among Old Portsmouth Houses* (Boston: Wright & Potter, 1946), 25. A historian and a great-grandson of James Rundlet, May inherited the property in 1936. His account of Rundlet's life, though brief, is the best I have found.

28. John Mead Howells, *The Architectural Heritage of the Piscataqua* (New York: Architectural Book Publishing Co., 1937), fig. 126.

29. May, *Among Old Portsmouth Houses*, 33.

30. Edward Owen Parry, "Edward Parry of Portsmouth" (New Hampshire Historical Society, Concord, N.H., 1964, bound typescript), 22.

31. Turner, *Ninth State*, 191–92.

32. Ibid., appendix; Donald B. Cole, *Jacksonian Democracy in New Hampshire, 1800–1857* (Cambridge, Mass.: Harvard University Press, 1970), 22–30; Norman B. Smith, "A Mature Frontier: The New Hampshire Economy, 1790–1850," *Historical New Hampshire* 24 (fall 1969): 3–19.

33. C. D. Arfwedson, *The United States and Canada in 1832, 1833, and 1834* (London: Richard Bentley, 1984), 188.

34. Brewster, *Rambles*, 347.

35. Sarah Parker Rice Goodwin, "Pleasant Memories" (Strawbery Banke, Portsmouth, N.H., 1875–1890, typescript).

36. Ibid. I have not discovered what the twelve o'clock was.

37. "Lilacs," 1887, Sarah Parker Rice Goodwin Papers, box 9:15, Strawbery Banke (hereafter cited as Goodwin Papers).

38. Note dated February 1888, Goodwin Papers.

39. Ibid.

40. Anna B. Warner, *Gardening by Myself* (1872; reprint, West Point, N.Y.: Duffield & Co., 1924), 59.

41. Goodwin, "Pleasant Memories."

42. Peggy Cornett Newcomb, *Popular Annuals of Eastern North America, 1865–1914* (Washington, D.C.: Dumbarton Oaks, 1985), 61.

43. Charles Van Ravenswaay, *A Nineteenth-Century Garden* (New York: Universe Books, 1977), 26.

44. Note dated February 1888, Goodwin Papers.

45. M. A. DeWolfe Howe, *Barrett Wendell and His Letters* (Boston: Atlantic Monthly Press, 1924), 207, 270.

46. Ibid.; Edith Wendell Osborne, "The Jacob Wendell Garden," in *Gardens of Colony and State*, ed. Alice G. B. Lockwood (New York: Charles Scribner's Sons, 1931), 1:149–50.

47. Osborne, "The Jacob Wendell Garden," 150.

48. Letter of 15 November 1915, in Howe, *Barrett Wendell*, 270.

Chapter 3

Radishes and Orchids

The Bootts' Garden in Boston

I N   D O W N T O W N   B O S T O N, on a site now covered by a twenty-two-story office building, there was once a small greenhouse containing what may have been the first orchid collection in the United States. The greenhouse, the mansion house to which it was appendant, and an intensively cultivated garden plot belonged to Kirk Boott and his children after him.

A love for growing plants seemed to run in the Boott family. Kirk Boott (1755–1817) took after his father, and later three of his sons took after him, expressing their passion for plants through horticulture and botany. In their widely differing lives, lives that included important accomplishments as well as madness and tragedy, this was one linking strand.

Kirk Boott grew up in the town of Derby, in the English Midlands, where he and his brothers worked with their father on a two-acre garden. They raised vegetables for sale. Their mother and sisters ran a greengrocer shop at the front of their house, from which they sold the produce. Kirk later recalled rising early to bunch radishes (three for a penny) and bouncing along to the family shop in a horse-drawn cart filled with cabbages.

After their father died in 1776, the five sons scattered to seek their fortunes elsewhere. Their mother and two sisters remained in the little house in Derby, dependent thereafter on the young men to send money home.

One of Francis's sons found a position as gardener on an estate, where he soon had three men under him. Kirk, the second son, left home for London in 1783, when he was twenty-seven. He found a lowly job as a porter in a warehouse. To improve his image and further his ambitions, he invested in a fashionable powdered wig. To his sister he wrote: "[F]rom small beginnings I shall rise to be a Merchant, and traverse the Ocean to distant shores, with the merchandise of Britain."[1] Within five months of leaving home, Kirk Boott arranged for passage aboard the *Rosamond* to Boston.

Kirk had found people willing to support him in a transatlantic mercantile venture. They paid for his passage and furnished him with goods so that he could open a shop when he arrived, gambling on his success to recoup their investments. The diverse shop merchandise that Kirk took with him included hats, nails, and barrels of garden seeds.

When he landed in June 1783, Kirk Boott was delighted by the green and beautiful city of Boston. He lamented England's recent loss of such a fine country. His first letter home sounds like a market gardener's

Kirk Boott (1755–1817), painted miniature.
(Private collection)

report: "Peas have been in a week or more and now sold at 4/6 sterling per peck. I took a walk in the garden belonging to my Lodging House, and saw Kidney Beans one foot high and cucumbers more than that long. They are forwarder than with us. I have made some enquiry after gardening, but can get very indifferent accounts. The gardeners are slovens and idle."[2]

His initial optimism waned quickly. The American economy was still in a shambles after the Revolutionary War, and Boott's business went very badly at first. His merchandise seemed all wrong. He wrote his sister that he rued the day he had forsaken the simple life of a gardener in Derby. Before long, however, his straightforward business ethic—a determination to sell better goods at lower prices than his competitors—enabled him to become established. He repaid his debts and began sending money home. Like other brash entrepreneurs in the booming ports of New England, Boott was soon well on the way to success and prosperity as a Boston merchant.

Boott threw away his powdered wig in order to become more American in appearance. Within two years of his arrival he married another newly arrived English émigré, Mary Love, whose father captained the ship that had brought Boott to Boston. The first of their nine children was born in 1786.

Kirk Boott was an urban man. Although his youth had been spent working the soil, his family's home and livelihood were centered on selling produce in the center of town. The business he established in Boston also required an urban location. After his first forays into the hinterland beyond Boston, he was convinced that the city was a pleasanter place to live. Rural New England he found rocky, densely wooded, and far less beautiful than Old England. When, with business success, he was able to build a fine house for his family, an urban site in town, near his place of business, was the obvious choice.

In 1795, Kirk Boott wrote his sister that "Mr. Theodore Lyman, a worthy friend of ours, has lately bought a Farm. He seems to take much pleasure in it."[3] Boott had collaborated with Lyman in such mercantile adventures as sending a ship to the Pacific Northwest in quest of furs. Lyman's estate, The Vale, was located in Waltham, about five miles from Boston. Seeing The Vale, then being developed as one of the first places in the vicinity of Boston to exemplify the English landscape style, Boott may have considered whether he, too, should establish his family in a country seat.

When yellow fever struck Boston in 1798, all who could fled the city. The sparsely settled countryside was generally viewed as a healthier environment. Lyman urged Boott to escape from the unwholesome city, even offering to provide a house for the family and to send a team of oxen to bring them to Waltham. Boott turned down Lyman's offer, but after listening day and night to the sound of hammer and saw at a nearby coffin maker's shop, Kirk closed his store and left Boston—by then nearly a ghost town—until the epidemic had waned. The Bootts rented temporary quarters in outlying Watertown, where Theodore Lyman generously supplied them with vegetables, fruit, and cider.

During Kirk Boott's lifetime, American cities, including Boston, were experiencing the increase in density and area that so changed this country. As Kirk's fortunes grew, his attachment to urban life was tempered by ambivalence. Although he had chosen to settle in the city, regular escape to the country was necessary, he believed, to one's physical and mental well-being. He bought himself a horse, and early every morning he rode a few miles into the rural environs of Boston. Over the years he repeatedly expressed regret that he had not yet explored "the grand, bold, and picturesque scenery with which this country abounds," but somehow he was always too busy to travel except in winter, when it was too cold, or in summer, when it was too hot.[4]

By 1802, Kirk Boott was at the height of his prosperity. He imported goods from England and elsewhere and ran a store near the waterfront. Neither he nor anyone else foresaw the trade embargo that would severely punish American business a few years later. Confident that his financial success would continue, Kirk decided the time had come to build a town house for himself and his family. His wife worried about the expense, but Kirk was thankful that he was "enabled to provide liberally for [his family's] wants."[5]

The half-acre lot on which Boott built his brick house was then a pasture in Boston's West End, an area that was just beginning to be developed.[6] Boott's three-story Federal mansion, with its tall Palladian windows lighting the staircase overlooking the garden, was very likely designed by Charles Bulfinch, then Boston's leading architect. The Boott house looked much like the mansion in Portsmouth that James Rundlet, another self-made merchant, built for himself in 1809. Kirk's oldest son, Wright, home from school in England, described the new house in 1805 as "larger than I expected, and as much handsomer. The doors on the first floor are all Mahogany and so highly polished as to make the furniture look ordinary."[7] Kirk Boott filled his house with mahogany furniture, Turkish carpets, and a stock of wine. Like several other prosperous Bostonians, he had Gilbert Stuart paint his portrait.

The Bootts mingled socially with Boston's leading families, Lymans and Cabots, Higginsons and Parkmans. At that time their wealth alone admitted them to the social elite. The Bootts invited their acquaintances to a cotillion to show off their gleaming mansion. They were invited often to the town house of Gardiner

Greene, "the most splendid residence in the city," according to one observer.[8] The Greenes' terraced gardens, noted for rare trees and a greenhouse, rose steeply above Tremont Street to provide a sweeping harbor view. "In those primitive days . . . the gardener, like the plants, had to be imported expressly from the old country," according to Greene's daughter. Their gardener was Scottish; he tended the fruit trees and the quaint box-edged beds, where "every hardy flower and odoriferous shrub bloomed and shed its fragrance."[9] At the back of the garden, the stable and cow shed were guarded by the "fierce mastiff, Pedro," whose fur Miss Greene made into mittens. From the windows of the house, this garden looked, as Greene's daughter put it, "so quiet and beautiful in its repose and verdure and yet so social with the neighboring grounds and homes." Greene's two-and-a-half acres made his place much larger than Boott's, but both were urban dwellings set in the midst of the populous city.

. . .

Kirk Boott added to the new house one amenity that may have meant more to him than any other: his greenhouse. Having been raised as a gardener, one aspect of English life that Boott missed particularly was the long growing season. As he wrote in 1804, "[F]rom the severity of the winter, no garden seeds could be put into the ground before April."[10] Inside his greenhouse, Boott could feel that he had defeated winter.

In December 1805, his first season with the green-

The Boott mansion at Bowdoin Square, with the stable on the right. The house sat near the front of a deep, narrow lot. Possibly designed by Bulfinch, the house stood from 1804 until 1847, when it was incorporated into a hotel, Revere House. The Saltonstall state office building now covers the site. (Boston Athenaeum)

house, Boott wrote that he had "Roses, Jassamines, Geraniums, and Stocks in blow [bloom]" and that bulbs sent to him by an English gardening friend were already "shooting above the earth." Boott knew nonetheless that "ere January shall be passed Jack Frost will give us trouble eno' to resist. If this bold intruder can be kept out, I promise myself much pleasure during . . . Feb'y, March, and April, at which time we have but little vegetation. I have taken great pains to keep Lettuce alive thro' the winter."[11]

By April, sure enough, "Winter yet bears sway," he wrote; but happily, "my Greenhouse has flourished beyond my expectation, and what pleases me much, I have found my skill equal to the care of it. Lettuces in abundance I have preserved, and have had fine Sallads thro' the Winter. Yesterday I gathered about a Bushel and gave it to my friends."[12] Lettuce was equal in importance to flowers in Kirk Boott's greenhouse; his family's health depended on it.

Boott's horticultural skills are apparent from his greenhouse successes: bulbs and plants forced into mid-

The House of Gardiner Greene, Cotton Hill, now Court Square, Boston. Henry Cheever Pratt painted this view, ca. 1834. Elaborate terraced gardens climbed the hill behind the mansion, providing a panoramic view of Boston Harbor. (Boston Athenaeum)

winter bloom, roses in December. The greenhouse itself was a long lean-to, its roof only partially glazed. Heat was supplied by a wood fire, the smoke of which was conducted through a horizontal brick flue, past the growing benches, to a chimney at the far end. Theodore Lyman's first greenhouse, one of the oldest survivors in this country and probably built not long before Boott's, can still be examined at The Vale in Waltham, Massachusetts.

Kirk Boott had seen "glasshouses" (greenhouses) in England in his youth. When his older brother began seeking employment as a gardener in 1783, Kirk had observed astutely that "amongst professional gardeners no place is esteemed a good one without Hot House

The earliest greenhouse at The Vale, Theodore Lyman's estate in Waltham, Massachusetts, probably dating from 1804. This view shows the firebox and the horizontal flue for heating. Kirk Boott's greenhouse may have been quite similar. (Society for the Preservation of New England Antiquities)

and Green House."[13] Although the technology was further advanced in England, greenhouses were not uncommon by 1800 on the estates of well-to-do New Englanders. Those of Abraham Redwood in Newport were described by a visitor in 1767; Redwood had "Hot Houses where things that are tender are put for the winter, and hot beds for the West India Fruit."[14] Redwood's gardener produced oranges, lemons, limes, pineapples, and tropical flowers, all under glass.

The Reverend William Bentley, the inveterate sightseer, noted in his diary in 1791 the hothouse at Joseph Barrell's fancy Charlestown estate.[15] Andrew Faneuil was supposed to have had the first greenhouse in Boston. Boott was probably inspired by the greenhouses of Theodore Lyman at The Vale, as well as by the example of Gardiner Greene, his Boston friend and neighbor. Greene's Scottish gardener labeled his greenhouse plants in Latin, and he raised fruits as well as

tomatoes and eggplants, vegetables that the Greene children considered weird and inedible.[16]

In 1806, Bernard M'Mahon published in Philadelphia the first edition of *The American Gardener's Calendar*. In this widely read book, M'Mahon explained the differences in construction and use between a greenhouse and a hothouse. The former had only enough artificial heat to "keep off frost and dispel damps," whereas the latter had an inside stove and more glass.[17] The flowers that Boott grew would suggest that his was actually a hothouse. Loathing the long New England winters and still homesick for England, Boott created his own artificial climate.

Boott had had a garden almost ever since he first landed in Boston. Each year he raised all the vegetables his family could eat and some for the neighbors. He once boasted that "I have not had occasion to buy a cucumber or onion this year, and Mary has had a fine show of annual flowers, Balsam, China Asters, etc." He had his sister send him some gooseberry bushes from England, but they did not flourish for him in Boston. He also had her send him vegetable seeds, specifying such favorites as "the best green, purple, and white Brocolli."[18]

Kirk Boott made use of every square foot of his half-acre lot. The house was set close upon the street, with the greenhouse attached to the back. There was also a stable for a horse and a cow. (That the lot was crowded is indicated by a domestic tragedy of 1809, when Bossy, the milk provider, died after tumbling down the cellar steps.) Boott's garden occupied every remaining inch of land. His description, written to his sister in 1809, reveals as much about the gardener as about the garden:

Our chief pleasure is in our family, and among our flowering plants. Flora has decked our parlour windows for four months past in the most gay and beautiful manner. She is now about transferring her beauties to the open garden. I have more than one hundred Rose-trees of the best kinds just bursting into bloom, from the moss down to the Scotch Mountain—the cluster Monthly red, the Cabbage province, pompon De Meaux, Burgundy, Blandford, Violet, White musk, etc., etc.

From the first dawn of vegetation I have a succession of flowers, the modest snowdrop, the golden Crocus, Daffodils, Narcissus, Hyacinths, Cowslips, Tulips etc. Those from Derby never blow [bloom] but with the most pleasing association of ideas. The common weeds

of my garden are the greenhouse Geraniums, Balsams, Coxcombs, Botany-Bay Xeranthemums, Palma-Christi, China Asters, Lavitera, Convolvulus, Mignonette, etc. and yet a common observer would think there was hardly anything worth looking at.

The Hawthorne—the White Hawthorne is now in full bloom.[19]

Kirk Boott asked for the seeds of more English flowers, London-Pride (*Saxifraga umbrosa*) and "Bird's Eye" (*Primula farinosa*), since "there are none in the country hereabouts. Daisies are such a rarity that they are kept in greenhouses, as well as Cowslips."[20] Even to his taste in wildflowers, Boott remained an Anglophile.

One son, Francis, reminisced years later about his father's devotion to gardening: "He was often in his Garden and about his frames by four o'clock, and I love to believe that my fondness for plants was caught from him. . . . [His garden] had no ostentation about it, and the familiar 'weeds' . . . were his delight. His roses, stocks, Persian Iris, and Lily of the Valley were the pride of his Garden, as the Heath and Geraniums were of his greenhouse. His salads and cucumbers were the height of his pride as a vegetable grower."[21]

These accounts are the only contemporary descriptions of Kirk Boott's garden. Author Marshall P. Wilder, writing in 1881, recalled foreign grapevines and tender fruit trees flourishing there in the open air, fruits that would usually succeed only under glass.[22] The annuals

Engraving of the Boott mansion from the garden side, by an unknown artist between 1840 and 1847. The lean-to greenhouse had hot-beds below it. Trellises for plants ran along the brick walls of the house. A board fence enclosed the garden. (Boston Athenaeum)

Boott grew had been introduced into America before or soon after the Revolution. All appear on the plant lists of such noted contemporary American gardeners as George Washington and Thomas Jefferson. They too grew lavateras, or tree mallows, and the everlasting *Xeranthemum* and *Celosia*, which hold their color when dried. As for Boott's roses, most were the many-petaled centifolias and damasks or small-flowered single varieties such as the fragrant Scotch (*Rosa spinossima*). The pompon rose "de Meaux"—a small pink cabbage rose painted by Redouté—was probably one of Boott's newest varieties, having made its first English appearance at Kew Gardens in 1789.

In 1812, Kirk Boott and his wife at last made their long delayed American sightseeing trip. They were particularly enthralled by the scenery of the Hudson River valley. The fields of wild buttercups observed from the boat reminded Kirk of "the dear and delightful meadows of England," the highest praise he could bestow. Kirk died in 1817, leaving his wife, who survived him by forty years; four daughters; and five sons. Mrs. Boott and her children continued to occupy the family home.

431

Rosa spinosissima, Edwards' Botanical Register, 1819. Kirk Boott called this the Scotch Mountain rose in 1809. It was one of many roses in his garden. (Library of the Gray Herbarium, Harvard University)

. . .

The Bootts of Boston never lost their strong attachment to England, evidenced in their house, the clothes they wore, and the plants they grew. When it came to educating his oldest sons, Kirk Boott sent them to school in England in 1799. Upon his return to Boston in 1805, Wright, the oldest, distressed his father by refusing to go to college. Kirk Jr. and one younger brother, Francis, attended Harvard. Their father considered Harvard the best place for them to receive an American education, but neither one was happy there. Francis graduated in 1810, but Kirk Jr. left without a

degree. These three oldest brothers each took a turn helping in the family store, but only Wright stayed on to become a partner.

Wright Boott, showing no signs of the housebound hermit he was to become, developed an enthusiasm for exploring the country. In 1806, when he was seventeen, he journeyed by carriage into New Hampshire and Vermont, jolting over log roads through mud, rocks, snow, and unending forests. "God deliver me from such a country," he wrote.[23] But two years later he and a cousin set off on a longer trip, to Niagara Falls, Montreal, and Quebec.

Wright's travels developed a focus after his brother Francis returned to Boston in 1814, following four years of study in England. Francis had devoted himself to science, particularly botany. He became interested in collecting New England plants, an interest he shared with Dr. Jacob Bigelow, a young professor of medicine at Harvard. Botany and medicine, two closely related sciences, drew them together. Bigelow asked Francis Boott to help him prepare a comprehensive work on the

Mary Love Boott (1766–1856), the mother of nine children. (Private collection)

J. Wright Boott (1792–1845) in the only known likeness of him, a silhouette made after 1805, when he began working for his father. (Private collection)

a group of grasslike plants—for which he is still known. Harvard honored Francis Boott in 1834 by offering him a professorship in natural history, but Boott was too humble to accept, saying that he knew only botany, not other related disciplines such as horticulture and zoology.[26] Francis Boott gave his herbarium of White Mountain plants to Sir William Hooker, the director of the Royal Botanic Gardens at Kew. Hooker named a goldenrod after Francis Boott, whose name is also attached to one of the sedges he identified and to an Asian water plant, *Boottia cordata*.

Having introduced Wright to botanical exploration and study, Francis went on to inspire their younger brothers, James and William, to follow suit. William studied medicine in Paris and Dublin and also gained a reputation as a botanist. After Francis's death in 1863, William continued his brother's work. Boott's shield fern, *Dryopteris Boottii*, was named for William.

Of the five brothers, only Kirk Jr. had little apparent interest in plants. Instead, he devoted his life to business, achieving renown as one of the chief architects of the industrial revolution in America. As agent and treasurer of a newly formed textile corporation, Merrimack Manufacturing Company, Kirk Boott Jr. was the organizer, overseer, and resident autocrat responsible for the building of the mills, the canals, the housing, and the entire urban fabric of Lowell, Massachusetts, this country's first planned industrial city. Any gardens around his Greek Revival mansion in Lowell were, for him, merely ornamental adjuncts to the home of a man of distinction, no more significant than the tall white columns of his portico.

The botanist brothers, Wright, James, William, and Francis, were elected to membership in the Boston Society of Natural History soon after its founding in 1830. Members of this society were all proud amateurs in the days before professionalism tarnished the amateur image. They were committed to the expansion of knowledge for its own sake. As the forerunner of Boston's Museum of Science, the society undertook to educate not only its members but the general public as well.[27]

Wright Boott and later his brother William joined

flora of New England.[24] To that end, Bigelow, Francis Boott, and three others explored and collected plants in the Berkshire Hills of Massachusetts and in New Hampshire's White Mountains in the summer of 1816. At the summit of Mount Washington the men left their names in a bottle. Their names have been more permanently tagged to certain topographic features of the mountain: Boott Spur and Bigelow's Lawn. Francis took his brother Wright to Mount Washington the following month, and Wright himself returned on several botanical and ornithological expeditions. In 1829, Wright discovered an unknown alpine plant that was later named for him: *Prenanthes Boottii*, rattlesnake root.[25]

Francis Boott returned to England in 1820, where he remained for the rest of his life. He earned his M.D. at Edinburgh in 1825 and entered into practice in London. He was made a fellow and later secretary of the Linnaean Society, at whose London headquarters his portrait now hangs. In 1858 he published the first part of a major botanical work on sedges—the genus *Carex*,

The Haight Family, by Nicolino Calyo, ca. 1844. The greenhouse linked to Kirk Boott's Boston mansion, filled with flowers in winter, provided him with pleasure and was a source of pride. The Haight family apparently felt the same attachment to the flowery conservatory that opened off their parlor. (Museum of the City of New York; bequest of Elizabeth Cushing Iselin)

another important new organization for sharing and spreading knowledge, the Massachusetts Horticultural Society, established in 1829. Both the horticultural and the natural history societies drew their members from the Boston intelligentsia and included many of the Bootts' neighbors, friends, and business associates.

The Horticultural Society held annual shows at which members exhibited fruit, flowers, and greenhouse plants. In the 1834 exhibit at Faneuil Hall, along with Joseph Coolidge's pears and Judge Lowell's orange trees, were three tropical plants from the collection of J. Wright Boott, Esq.: *Plumbago capensis*, blue-flowered leadwort from southern Africa; *Begonia discolor*, a red-foliaged import from Asia with fragrant pink flowers; and a white-flowered *Pancratium*, a "particularly beautiful" member of the amaryllis family.[28]

Wright withdrew from the Horticultural Society immediately after the 1834 show. He never exhibited his plants again. Someone or something must have offended him, but Wright never said. Long before that, however, he had become a moody, difficult man of marked peculiarity.[29]

Soon after his father died in 1817, Wright had begun a gradual retreat from business and society. Eventually, he stopped going out altogether and spoke to almost no one. His troubles apparently began, as troubles often do, with money and a will. Wright was the executor of his father's will and was responsible for supporting his mother in the family mansion, hers for her life. He was also obligated to support his minor siblings, of whom there were four at the time of their father's death, as well as the orphaned children of a cousin. Furthermore, all of Wright's brothers and sisters were entitled to equal shares of the residue of the estate.[30] Unfortunately, even before division, the family fortune was not as large as Kirk's children believed it to be. In a stagnant economy, the Bootts' grand life-style had drastically reduced the fortune from its peak at the century's start. Even by 1810, Kirk Sr. had foreseen that "my property will be but little for each when it comes to be divided."[31]

Wright's brothers joined him in their late father's import business for a few years, hoping in vain to make a go of it. By 1822 all but Wright had withdrawn. In 1826, Wright invested in an iron foundry started by two of his brothers-in-law. Before he pulled out of that disastrous enterprise he had lost a good part of his own and his siblings' inheritance. They later reminded him of this with some frequency. From then on, despite efforts by Kirk to give him an important role in the Lowell tex-

tile industry, Wright never engaged in business again. He stayed at home with his mother and worked with his plants.

Even though Wright Boott had resigned from the Horticultural Society, his rare tropical plants and his success at coaxing them into bloom caused his name to recur often in the society's annals. In 1837, for example, it was noted that Boott's West Indian *Cactus triangularis* had blossomed. This may have been the night-blooming cereus (*Hylocereus undatus*) that opened its spectacular white flowers only one night a year. Boott was also recognized for having imported the novel *Chorizema henchmanni*, an Australian evergreen with bright red flowers.[32] He became known for imported greenhouse plants, particularly orchids.

His plants came from England. The Atlantic Ocean did not seem wide to the Bootts, brought up as they were in the import business and maintaining close ties with their English relatives. Before he became a recluse, Wright himself had traveled to England. His brothers,

Cactus triangularis, Curtis's Botanical Magazine, 1817. Wright Boott had a night-blooming cereus in 1837; it blossomed for only one night each year. (Library of the Gray Herbarium, Harvard University)

Chorizema Henchmanni, Paxton's Magazine of Botany, 1836. Another of Wright Boott's greenhouse plants, with brilliant red flowers. (Library of the Gray Herbarium, Harvard University)

owned the Covent Garden Market in London, on which he built two unique rooftop conservatories in 1827, where plants were grown, shown, and sold in a stylish setting.[35]

Orchids became a refined passion for many gardeners as the nineteenth century progressed, and orchid hunters began stripping them from their native habitats to meet the demand. Appalling numbers of plants gathered in the wild succumbed to the treatment they received from unwitting gardeners, who had no idea how to care for them. There were only fifteen species at the Royal Botanical Garden at Kew in 1790; but by 1812, Loddige's Nursery near London was propagating orchids for sale.[36] Before long there were several professional orchid growers.

The orchid craze came later to the United States. As of 1818, Harvard's Botanic Garden listed only one orchid, *Phaius grandifolius,* or *Bletia Tankervilleae,* a terrestrial orchid, as distinguished from the epiphytes, which grow in trees. The plant explorer John Fothergill had first brought *Phaius grandifolius* to England from China in 1778. This may have been Wright Boott's first orchid, according to accounts by Wilder and another Horticultural Society member, Edward S. Rand Jr.[37]

The epiphytic orchids were more difficult to grow than the terrestrial species, but Wright Boott apparently learned to give them the light and air they needed. His collection included *Dendrobium* orchids from Asia, *Oncidiums* from Central America, and, from Brazil, the *Cattleyas,* whose large blooms of corsage fame are sometimes the color now known as orchid.

Wright Boott's life ended in sadness and bitterness. His mother finally left the family home in 1836 to spend the remainder of her life in England with Francis and his family. Kirk Jr., after years of trying to help Wright improve his own and the family fortunes, died suddenly in Lowell in 1837. James made a permanent move to England a year later. William, who had always been close to Wright and helped him in the greenhouse, left suddenly after Wright unexpectedly threatened him with bodily harm and drove him from the house. According to Caroline Gardiner, a contempo-

particularly Francis, knew all the leading English botanists and plantsmen. Any of these people could easily have carried or sent plants to Wright in Boston.

At an 1874 meeting of the Massachusetts Horticultural Society, Marshall P. Wilder, a former president of the organization and later its historian, reminisced about the "exqusite manner in which the amaryllis was formerly cultivated by J. W. Boott . . . who received from England bulbs of new and rare varieties worth two or three guineas each."[33] Wilder also remembered Boott's as the *only* orchid collection in the country in the early 1830s. "They were cultivated in an ordinary greenhouse, occasionally closing a door [for temperature control], and grew without piling up bricks and charcoal about the stem."

In his article on the history of horticulture in Boston, Wilder wrote that some of Wright's choicest plants had been obtained by his brother Francis from the duke of Bedford.[34] The sixth duke of Bedford, proprietor of Woburn Abbey and an avid naturalist and botanist, rary observer of the Boston social scene, Wright had fallen desperately in love with a young Boott cousin, one of his wards under his father's will.[38] Could it be that his brother William was Wright's more successful rival in love?

For a few years, Wright was the sole occupant of the Boott mansion. Then, in 1844, his youngest sister, Mary Boott Lyman, newly widowed and in straitened circumstances, moved into the family house, as she felt she was legally entitled to do. She lived there for an entire year reportedly without ever sharing a meal with Wright, or indeed even speaking to him: all according to conditions outlined by Wright before she moved in. Two young nephews also lived in the house for a time—in idleness, according to their aunt, who wrote Francis that the young men rose at noon and lounged about for hours, continually smoking cigars.[39]

The family, not surprisingly, became sharply divided. Those in England, including Mrs. Boott, could only feel sorry for Wright. Removed as they were, their image of him was blurred by fondness for the man he once had been. Francis wrote in 1843 to his friend Asa Gray, the eminent botanist, newly arrived in Cambridge to direct the Harvard Botanic Garden, that he hoped Gray would call at the Boott family's Bowdoin Square mansion. Francis was sure Wright would be pleased to show Gray his greenhouse and his plants.[40] In fact, it is unlikely that Gray would have been cordially received. Most of those who had to deal with Wright became convinced that he was insane.

The atmosphere of the Boott establishment must have been distinctly unsettling. One sister, Eliza Brooks, described an 1842 visit to see Wright. She looked for him in the house and then in the garden, but "the plants were so high I did not see him." Eventually, she discovered him "picking dead leaves off a plant." "Your dahlias are very fine," said she. Wright, without a word, retreated among the dahlias, while his sister walked along the gravel path. "I could see Wright watching me through the high plants."[41] In 1845, Wright shot himself in an upper room.

Wright Boott's suicide unleashed a long and tiresome battle, waged in public and in endless print, between his brother-in-law, Edward Brooks, and his executor, John Amory Lowell. Lowell reportedly blamed Brooks for hounding Wright to his death, to which rumor Brooks responded by accusing Lowell of trying to influence Wright to change his will. Both men claimed their only interests were to clear their own good names and to see that justice was done in the matter of inheritance.[42]

After obtaining his mother's consent, Wright had sold the mansion just three months before he died.[43] The bricks in one wall were incorporated into Revere House, a grand new hotel soon erected on the site, but the Boott house, greenhouse, and garden vanished entirely.

John Amory Lowell, the executor of Wright's estate, did benefit from the terms of the will. Wright had bequeathed to Lowell the one possession he truly cared about, his orchid collection. Lowell, a third-generation Boston horticulturist, tended his plants at the family estate in Roxbury. He exhibited some of the orchids at Horticultural Society shows. One year he entered a *Dendrobium calceolaria*, formerly Boott's, that was four feet high and three feet in diameter, covered with fragrant blossoms of delicate rose shaded with yellow. In 1853, Lowell sold his *Oncidium* orchids to the Misses Pratt of Watertown, but most of the orchids went to Edward S. Rand of Dedham, whose collection was later said to be the finest in the country.[44] In 1876, Rand's son still owned the huge *Dendrobium* that had belonged to Boott, as well as another of his, a *Cattleya crispa* "as large as a small washtub," with white petals and a frilled lip of velvety purple.

When the Rand estate was sold, most of the best plants were given to Harvard. Asa Gray himself divided Wright's venerable *Dendrobium* and kept half for Harvard's Botanic Garden. Probably the scattered offspring of Boott's orchids are delighting their growers today. In the end, they were his legacy.

Overleaf: Dendrobium calceolaria, William Jackson Hooker, *Exotic Flora*, Edinburgh, 1827. Wright Boott grew this Himalayan epiphytic orchid in Boston in the 1830s. Long after Boott's death the plant was given to Harvard's Botanic Garden. (Library of the Gray Herbarium, Harvard University)

Page 45: Cattleya crispa, William Jackson Hooker, *A Century of Orchidaceous Plants*, London, 1851. First published in *Curtis's Botanical Magazine*, this plate depicts another of Wright Boott's epiphytic orchids, this one of Central American origin. (Photo by Clive Russ; Massachusetts Horticultural Society)

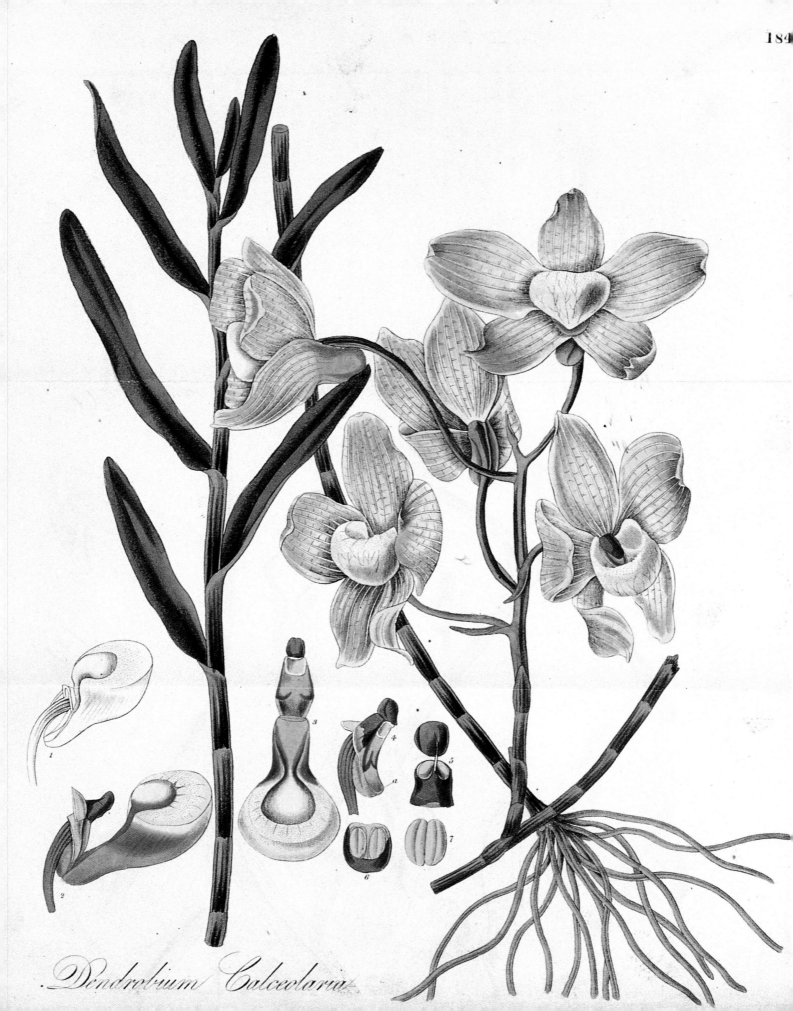

Dendrobium Calceolaria

Plate 32.

Fitch, del. et. lith.

Reeve, imp.

Cattleya crispa.

1. Kirk Boott (hereafter cited as KB) to Eliza Boott (hereafter EB), February 1783, MR (microfilm reel) 1, vol. 1, Massachusetts Historical Society (hereafter cited as MHS).

2. KB to EB, 13 June 1783, MR 1, vol. 2, MHS.

3. KB to EB, 22 July 1795, MR 1, vol. 6, MHS.

4. KB to EB, 13 June 1804, MR 2, vol. 2, MHS.

5. KB to EB, 17 November 1802, MR 2, vol. 1, MHS.

6. Suffolk County Deeds, Boston, 185:82, 208:90.

7. Harold Kirker and James Kirker, *Bulfinch's Boston, 1787–1817* (New York: Oxford University Press, 1964), 80; J. W. Boott to EB, 30 September 1805, MR 2, vol. 2, MHS.

8. Francis Lowell Cabot, *A History of the Gardiner Greene Estate*, ed. Winthrop S. Scudder (Boston: reprinted from the Publications of the Bostonian Society, 1916), 18–19.

9. "Letter of Martha B. (Greene) Amory to Charles Amory, re Gardiner Greene estate, Pemberton Square, Boston," Boston Athenaeum, 1869, typescript.

10. KB to EB, 13 June 1804, MR 2, vol. 2, MHS.

11. KB to EB, 16 Dec. 1805, MR 2, vol. 2, MHS.

12. KB to EB, 15 April 1806, MR 2, vol. 2, MHS.

13. KB to EB, February 1783, MR 1, vol. 1, MHS.

14. Alice G. B. Lockwood, ed., *Gardens of Colony and State* (New York: Charles Scribner's Sons, 1931), 1:217.

15. Marshall Pinckney Wilder, *The Horticulture of Boston and Vicinity* (Boston: privately printed, 1881), 12; William Bentley, *The Diary of William Bentley* (Gloucester, Mass.: Peter Smith, 1962), 1:264 (1791).

16. "Letter . . . to Charles Amory."

17. Bernard M'Mahon, *The American Gardener's Calendar*, 7th ed. (Philadelphia, 1828), 86.

18. KB to EB, 30 October 1787, MR 1, vol. 4, 16 December 1795, MR 1, vol. 6, p. 16, MHS.

19. KB to EB, 10 June 1809, MR 2, vol. 3, MHS. Palma-Christi was the tropical castor-bean tree, *Ricinus communis*, grown for its foliage.

20. J. Wright Boott to EB, 16 May 1807, MR 2, vol. 3, MHS.

21. Note by Francis Boott, MR 2, vol. 3, p.102, MHS.

22. Wilder, *Horticulture of Boston*, 15. This essay was also published in Justin Winsor's *The Memorial History of Boston Including Suffolk County, Massachusetts, 1630–1880* (Boston, 1881), 4.

23. J. Wright Boott to EB, 16 April 1806, MR 2, vol. 2, MHS.

24. Francis Boott to Jacob Bigelow, 25 June 1817, Countway Library, Harvard Medical School.

25. George E. Gifford Jr., "Sedges and a Spur," *Harvard Medical Alumni Bulletin* 42 (winter 1968): 23–26.

26. Asa Gray, "Botanical Necrology for the Year 1863," *American Journal of Sciences and the Arts*, 2nd ser., 37 (May 1864): 289.

27. Boston Society of Natural History records are at the Boston Museum of Science. See Sally G. Kohlstedt, "The Nineteenth-Century Amateur Tradition: The Case of the Boston Society of Natural History," in *Science and Its Public*, ed. Gerald Holten and William A. Blanspiel (Dordrecht, Holland, 1976), 173–87.

28. Massachusetts Horticultural Society, *Transactions* (1834), 23.

29. Wright's sister-in-law, his brother Kirk's wife, was the only Boott to enter any subsequent Horticultural Society show. According to the *Transactions* for the year 1837 (p. 42), she had submitted that year a "curious Cucumber" eight feet long; "its form reminded many of a serpent."

30. *A Correspondence between Edward Brooks and John A. Lowell* (Boston, 1847).

31. KB to EB, 1810, MR 2, vol. 4, MHS.

32. Massachusetts Horticultural Society, *Transactions* (1837–38), 23, 27.

33. Ibid., 1874, pt. 1, 25, 34.

34. Wilder, *Horticulture of Boston*, 15.

35. John Hix, *The Glass House* (Cambridge, Mass.: MIT Press, 1974), 92–93.

36. Gordon P. DeWolf Jr., "Kew and Orchidology," *American Orchid Society Bulletin* 28 (December 1959): 877–80.

37. Massachusetts Horticultural Society, *Transactions* (1874).

38. Caroline Gardiner Curtis, *Memories of Fifty Years in the Last Century* (Boston: privately printed, 1947), 25.

39. *Correspondence between Brooks and Lowell*, 115.

40. Francis Boott to Asa Gray, 1 May 1843, Francis Boott letters, Harvard Herbaria.

41. *Correspondence between Brooks and Lowell*, 113.

42. Ibid. Also Edward Brooks, *Answer to the Pamphlet of Mr. John A. Lowell* (Boston, 1851).

43. Suffolk County Deeds (Boston, Mass.), 544:78.

44. Edward Sprague Rand Jr., *Orchids* (New York, 1876), 131–36.

Chapter 4

Ghosts in the Garden

Vaucluse, Portsmouth, Rhode Island

THAT PART OF Rhode Island where the estate of Vaucluse is located reminded Henry James of "some dim, simplified ghost of a small Greek island, where the clear walls of some pillared portico or pavilion, perched afar, looked like those of temples of the Gods . . ."[1] This describes Vaucluse, that classically inspired, romantically decaying, empty ruin of a country house. The demesne of Vaucluse, a few miles from busy Newport, has always had a mythic aura. Always it has captured the imaginations of those who know it or who have merely heard of it. Generations of children have explored the place at dusk and in secret, running with pounding hearts, stumbling, climbing, peering, fleeing. The legends of Vaucluse have been amplified, treasured, and passed on as something apart from the pragmatic world that was and is New England. Still the place is haunting.

The Rhode Island coastline is so deeply indented that almost every part of the state is connected to the sea. Not long ago one traveled by ferry from one part of the state to another. Nowadays great bridges link the islands and peninsulas of Rhode Island, but even so, the trip from, say, Kingston in the South County to Newport is not to be taken lightly.

Narragansett Bay, the largest extension of the sea, cuts deep into the state, embracing the island of Aquidneck. Henry James used the appealing metaphor of "a little, bare, white, open hand" to describe the charms of this "dainty isle."[2] From fingertips held out to the open ocean, through Newport and Middletown, the island tapers to the narrow wrist of Portsmouth, the town that includes Vaucluse.

The soil lies deep and rich upon the gentle slopes of Portsmouth, between the bay on one side and the broad Sakonnet River on the other. The water has a moderating effect on the climate; growing conditions are ideal. Since early in the eighteenth century there have been vast agricultural estates and famous gardens all up and down both shores. The legends that pertain to some of these places are themselves legendary; but however exaggerated, they paint a compelling picture of a vanished golden age.

In 1931, Miss Alice Brayton, herself a great gardener, compiled an account of significant Rhode Island gardens, extant as well as lost. Miss Brayton had taken over from her father the garden she called "Green Animals," a topiary zoo of clipped privet on the bay side of Portsmouth; so she knew well what a garden *could* be when she described the long gone wonders of the past.

She wrote of the fabled garden on the six-hundred-acre estate of Godfrey Malbone, a Newport slave trader. Though the mansion burned to the ground in 1766, Malbone's garden continued to flourish. People paid for the privilege of strolling along box-edged walks, surrounded by choice fruits, flowers, and "romantic" artificial ponds, "with the silver fish sporting in the water."[3]

Miss Brayton described merchant Abraham Redwood's country seat, begun in the 1740s on the Sakonnet shore of Portsmouth. Redwood employed a German landscape gardener, Johann Ohlman, who was supposed to have worked for the king of Poland. Presumably, it was Ohlman who tended the hothouses—among the first in New England—where oranges, lemons, and pineapples were brought to fruit.[4]

Possibly the most splendid Portsmouth garden before the Revolution, according to Miss Brayton, was that of Metcalf Bowler, at his farm on the Sakonnet River. Late in life, Bowler strove to pass on his knowledge and love of husbandry by writing a little treatise on agriculture, among the first of many penned by New England's Virgil-quoting gentlemen farmers.[5] But Metcalf Bowler is honored chiefly for having introduced the Rhode Island greening apple.[6] The first tiny sprig had been delivered to Bowler by one of his ship captains, in tribute from a Persian prince whose son the captain had saved from a shipwreck. This was no ordinary tree: it was held to be a direct descendant of the Tree of Knowledge, straight from the site of the Garden of Eden.[7] Despite some climatic differences the tree flourished in Portsmouth. Cider made from the fruit was so good that Bowler called it "Eden Champagne." At an apocryphal dinner party toward the end of the Revolutionary War, Bowler is said to have served the champagne to General George Washington, Count Rochambeau, and the marquis de Lafayette. They all loved it; everybody sang; everybody cried.

Hoping to save his estate from the ravages of the British troops, Bowler penned secret appeals to the officers. To no avail; all the Aquidneck Island farms, including his, were ruined. According to Brissot de Warville, a French observer writing in 1788, "The English destroyed all the fruit trees as well as all the other trees; they enjoyed devastating everything."[8] But happily, it was not long after this sad time that Vaucluse was built and its gardens laid out. In Miss Brayton's opinion, Vaucluse was the "last and loveliest of the old country houses of Rhode Island."[9]

. . .

Soon after the Revolution, Gervase Elam, a Quaker merchant of Newport, established the demesne of Vaucluse when he bought fifty arable acres along the Sakonnet, adjacent to Metcalf Bowler's estate. Elam had just planted his apple orchard and built a house when he died in 1785. A "for sale" notice in the *Newport Mercury* advertised the estate's setting: "an Eminence which Commands a pleasingly varied and extensive Prospect over a beautiful wooded Country bounded by the Ocean."[10] Gervase's nephew, Samuel Elam, purchased the property.

The duc de La Rochefoucault, traveling through New England in 1795, visited Samuel Elam at Vaucluse. La Rochefoucault described Elam as "the best of Quakers, and the worthiest of men. He is a bachelor, rich, fond of trade, and of rural life."[11] He was also, according to the duke, "the only farmer in the island who does not personally labour upon his own ground." Elam's stone walls were higher and tighter than those of his neighbors, his livestock more flourishing.

The "snug small house" admired by La Rochefoucault was too modest for Elam, who embarked on an ambitious building program in 1803. He added a majestic pedimented portico with four Doric columns and a pair of pavilion wings that flanked the house. Elam spent $80,000 in three years, enlarging his house and developing his grounds and gardens. The house, in its classical temple guise, was something new in New England at the time, closer in spirit to the taste of Thomas Jefferson in Virginia.

Samuel Elam, a banker and a state legislator, traveled between Vaucluse and his Newport house in a yellow English phaeton, with a postilion and a footman behind.[12] He dressed as a Quaker despite the apparent contradiction between his religion and the opulence in which he lived.

There was, however, a melancholy side to Elam's life. He had been rejected by the love of his life, Newport's beautiful Miss Redwood. For solace he turned to the sonnets of Petrarch, a fellow sufferer from the anguish of unrequited love. In the fourteenth century Petrarch wrote hundreds of poems over more than thirty years to Laura, a mysterious woman he barely knew. Even after she perished in the plague of 1348, he still wrote to her. In his grief Petrarch retreated to the Fontaine de Vaucluse, near Avignon in Provence, where a remarkable spring bubbled from the rocks in a wooded vale. Here all he did was meditate and write of his longing for Laura.[13]

Samuel Elam took more than the name Vaucluse for his country retreat; he succumbed with apparent pleasure to the sentimental grieving that he derived from reading Petrarch. The romantic melancholy that Petrarch cultivated for so long and his apparent faith in the restorative powers of nature in a rural setting had found favor with certain eighteenth-century writers, notably Rousseau. Elam's library pavilion contained the works of Rousseau and Petrarch, of course, as well as those of Virgil and other classical writers.[14] One imagines marble busts of Elam's literary idols standing before his shelves of leather-bound volumes. Elam could sympathize with Rousseau's rejection of worldly sophistication in favor of a simpler life in the country. Ermenonville, near Paris, featuring the tomb of Rousseau, was one of the newly fashionable melancholy and picturesque gardens that Elam read of and probably visited.[15] The literary, elegiac quality of Ermenonville obviously appealed to Elam, even if one were to judge simply by the name and the associations he chose for his own country seat.

Jane Austen made fun of the cult of gloom in her 1818 novel, *Northanger Abbey*. Her naive heroine, Catherine Morland, visits Northanger Abbey, the home of General Tilney and his daughter. While touring the elaborate grounds, Miss Tilney leads her guest down a narrow winding path through a thick grove of firs. Catherine, "struck by its gloomy aspect, and eager to enter it," then "began to talk with easy gaiety of the delightful melancholy which such a grove inspired. 'I am particularly fond of this spot,' said her companion, with a sigh. 'It was my mother's favorite walk.'"[16]

Just a hundred yards from the house at Vaucluse was a steep and deep ravine, at the bottom of which ran a little stream that flowed into the Sakonnet River. Elam had a miniature Roman temple built at the edge of the precipice, where, in moods of melancholy, he may have felt particularly akin to Petrarch. Six miles of serpentine walks threaded the grounds of Vaucluse, where seventeen acres were devoted to Elam's pleasure garden. Marble nymphs stood at turns of the paths. The garden contained a boxwood maze, inspired by the Cretan Labyrinth where Ariadne led Theseus to slay the Minotaur. In the opinion of a contemporary, Elam had developed at Vaucluse exactly the sort of "charming and picturesque scenery" that one would expect from a per-

son of his "highly cultivated mind." Here sentiment, beauty, and utility were joined to form an idyllic *ferme ornée*.

Elam imported plants from England and France. Roses were his craze, reported Miss Brayton; "the borders were full of the roses of France."[17] He planted a pepper tree (perhaps *Vitex agnus-castus*) from Elba, Napoleon's isle of exile.[18] His elms grew to great heights. The famous Vaucluse buttonwood (*Platanus occidentalis*) that fell in 1857 long predated Elam. In the tree's prime, it was said, "a bird resting on its topmost branch could not be reached with an ordinary fowling piece."[19] From a lower branch, a mere seventy feet above the ground, someone, perhaps Elam, had hung a swing, sweet symbol of frivolity.

Elam's life at Vaucluse was not entirely given over to reading and pensive contemplation, nor to agriculture. His entertainments, it was said, were princely. He himself partook freely of wine, cognac, and "sangaree," as his friends could not help but notice. One guest remarked that his tumblers and wineglasses were "highly ornamented and bore his initials."[20] In 1813 he took to his bed, where beside "that low window veiled in yellow brier" he died at sixty-three.

On Elam's death, Vaucluse was purchased by Charles De Wolf Jr., scion of a prominent Rhode Island family. De Wolf kept the place for fifteen years, his sojourn best remembered for one brilliant garden party: "Mr. De Wolf hung two hundred kerosene or whale oil lamps from the trees and the shrubs in those gardens, hired a singing orchestra which concealed itself in a honeysuckle arbor, served absolutely unlimited champagne, and gained a reputation as host which has endured. The beauty of the women who attended the party was not strictly to his credit, nor did he plant the 'winding avenues' in which the 'fair ones, votaries of Venus,' walked. Nevertheless he did well, and increased the glory of Vaucluse."[21]

Charles De Wolf went bankrupt in 1833. He fled to his brother's coffee plantation, Noah's Ark, in Cuba.

·　·　·

For Vaucluse, a new chapter began with its purchase in 1838 by Thomas Robinson Hazard for himself and Frances Minturn, his bride. Hazard, then forty, had grown up in the southern part of Rhode Island, where his family had held large tracts of land for generations. Thomas Hazard, intelligent and well educated, had

Plan of the gardens at Vaucluse, Portsmouth, Rhode Island, according to Miss Alice Brayton, early twentieth century. The ravine is at the bottom of the sketch, below the summerhouse. The Sakonnet River is off to the right. (Original photograph in the collection of the Newport Historical Society)

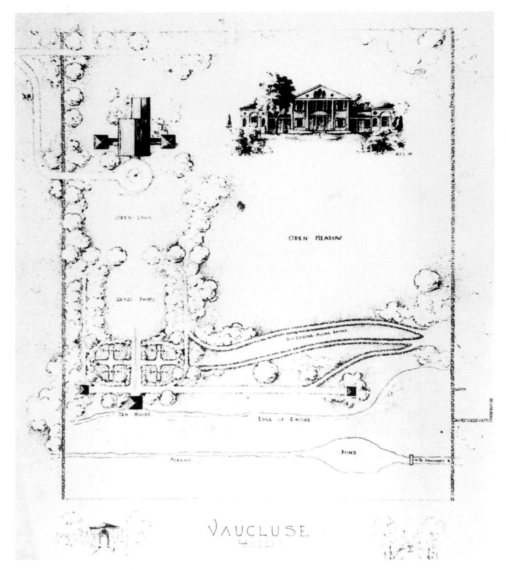

worked in the family woollen manufactory. By the time he acquired Vaucluse, however, having made a great deal of money, he decided to devote himself most actively to sheep farming.[22]

"Shepherd Tom," as he was soon commonly known, nearly doubled the size of Vaucluse by purchasing adjacent land, including the old Metcalf Bowler farm. He brought the mansion and the grounds to polished perfection, adding his own embellishments. The triple Gothic window he inserted in the pediment lent a slightly eerie touch—appropriate, as it turned out—to the mansion's classical facade. Hazard's days were divided between the management of his place and the writing of reformist tracts on causes close to his heart,

such as more enlightened care of the insane and the abolition of slavery. For a time, Shepherd Tom, his adored Frances, and their five children led what seems a charmed existence of domestic bliss in an idyllic setting, tempered by selfless concern with improving the human condition.

Vaucluse Farm, already famous for its natural and cultivated beauty, soon became more celebrated. In the decade before the Civil War, Newport and its vicinity were "discovered" by literary and artistic Bostonians, who came to spend their summers in the pursuit of simple rural pleasures.[23] Only later was Newport invaded and transformed by "fashionable vulgar" New Yorkers. An 1852 guidebook to the region gave Vaucluse the

Thomas Robinson Hazard (1797–1886), "Shepherd Tom"; portrait attributed to Jane Stuart, daughter of Gilbert Stuart. (Private collection)

sensory description of the garden, including the extraordinary flourishing of a southern magnolia in this sheltered corner of Rhode Island.

> Down the long alley, between the high walls of box, the children dawdled, tired out by their run. They passed the turf circle before the house, centered by the old moss-covered sundial around which grew coral honeysuckle. They lingered under the *Magnolia grandiflora*, whose huge white blossoms shone mysteriously against the glossy dark leaves of the tree, and whose overpowering perfume made the senses swoon. They passed the middle summerhouse to the place where the Alpine strawberries grew thickest. The blue-starred myrtle grew here, too, but we came for the strawberries—just ripe, sweet and spicy as the berries that grow beside the Lake of Nemi in far-off Italy.[26]

At the sound of the gong the children ran to the dining room, with its long mahogany table so highly polished that the very spoons were reflected in it. For tea there would be "airily thin" bread with butter from the Vaucluse herd and delicate brown Jonny cakes, to be sprinkled with cinnamon and sugar from a porcelain pineapple. The repast concluded with thinly sliced peaches served in cut-glass saucers with thin old silver teaspoons. "At the feast sat Mr. Hazard, a big man with a loud voice, light blond hair in tight little rings, and blue eyes—the eyes of a mystic. . . . 'Have some cherry bounce, Mrs. Howe?' he booms."

Eyes of a mystic? Shepherd Tom *was* a mystic. After these tea parties the grown-ups would gather on the porch behind the white columns to talk about spiritualism, a popular fad at the time. Spiritualism was intensely serious for Shepherd Tom Hazard; it brought his wife back to him.

Hazard had four daughters—Fanny and Gertrude, twelve in 1854 when their mother died; Anna, who was eight; Esther, six; and a two-year-old son, Barclay. Their father wanted his children to know the spirits who haunted Vaucluse, insisting that they go with him to visit a medium. According to Maud Howe Elliott, the Hazard children were "curious and wild," entirely bored by spirits. Shepherd Tom, however, was convinced that his children had entered the "spirit world."[27]

Fanny took on her mother's role, becoming a "domestic saint and martyr" and humoring her autocratic father.[28] Anna, the middle child and the handsomest of the girls, succumbed to consumption when she was

equivalent of three stars for its picturesque beauty. Sightseers were urged to try to procure from its owner, a "keen appreciator of art, . . . the permission of a peep" at this "very Paradise of Painters."[24]

The Hazard family suffered a tragic loss in 1854, when Frances Minturn Hazard died suddenly, leaving five children under twelve and a husband who went nearly mad with grief. At first, as a widower, Shepherd Tom wanted Vaucluse to be filled with people, just as always. One of Julia Ward Howe's daughters, Maud Howe Elliott, recalled happy summer afternoons with the motherless Hazard children, "the dearest, the most romantic, the most tenderly remembered" of her playmates. The Howe family had purchased Oak Glen, a scenic farm not far from Vaucluse, across a checkerboard of stone-fenced fields.[25] With other friends and cousins, the children played hare and hounds through the fields, the "hounds" following a trail of shredded scraps of the *Boston Advertiser* scattered by the "hares." After the game they all wandered back to the garden at Vaucluse. Here Maud Howe Elliott treats us to a vivid

Thomas Robinson Hazard and his children, ca. 1858. Anna and Esther, standing; Fanny, seated beside her father; Gertrude and Barclay on the left. (Courtesy of the Rhode Island Historical Society)

only twenty-two. Esther, the youngest daughter, was the only one to marry. Her marriage at twenty-one to a man more than twice her age took place beneath a great elm at Vaucluse. In 1877, a few months after Fanny died of consumption at thirty-five, her bereft twin sister Gertrude drowned herself, Ophelia-like, in the dark pool in the glen below the house. Maud Howe Elliott never forgot Gertrude's funeral and the sight of the few remaining Hazards, all dressed in white and bearing white flowers.

Shepherd Tom grew increasingly eccentric, single-minded in his concentration on spiritualism. A quarter of a century after his wife had died, she was still visiting him in spirit form "for hours together" at Vaucluse. Gertrude and Fanny, too, reappeared to him. Hazard's descriptions of these otherworldly manifestations were published in the *Providence Journal.*[29] He had a medium, Mrs. Mary Hall, staying at Vaucluse for weeks of seances. The results of her efforts surpassed anything Hazard had yet experienced.

The garden at Vaucluse was the scene of four seances during the summer of 1879. While writing about his wife's ghostly visits, Hazard gave a vivid picture of his moonlit garden, even to its dimensions. One night, he had watched his wife emerge from the summerhouse, a structure that he claimed was kept locked day and night, its key securely hidden in his desk. The summerhouse was situated at the foot of a broad gravel walk, 320 feet from the house, near the steep edge of the glen. One could re-create the summerhouse from his description: an octagon, twenty feet on a side, with two piazzas, four doors (always bolted), and no windows. Hazard watched his beloved Frances appear at one of the bolted doors, a lace veil over her head and white kid slippers on her feet. She walked thirty-three feet west to a long arbor. She plucked a leaf from the English sycamore and a twig from the weeping willow, then silently handed them to her husband. Wandering to the end of the garden, she gazed pensively down the glade, where tall, ancient trees overarched the deep pool into whose dark depths sad Gertrude had flung herself.

Another evening, Hazard walked beside his spirit wife the whole length of the long arbor—135 feet—trailed by a black kitten and the old Newfoundland dog "Sailor." Then Hazard and Frances sat side by side in the "old familiar seat" at the end of the arbor.

The last seance that Hazard described also began at the octagonal summerhouse. On this occasion, Frances walked seventy feet east, toward the Sakonnet River, to a point where a "narrow, densely shaded serpentine path led off . . . to the long, winding avenue on the outskirts of the shaded grounds, skirting apple, pear and peach orchards, protected on all sides by tall forest and ornamental trees." Frances Hazard paused now and then to admire a cherished view but uttered not a word. "To all appearances, my wife was the very same being who had so often rambled with her infant family when in earth-life through the picturesque grounds of Vaucluse, laid out and planted by an Englishman of great taste a century ago." Frances had been dead for twenty-five years.

The Englishman referred to by Hazard was Samuel Elam, whose trees reached majestic size in Hazard's lifetime. The plan of the grounds remained the same. The walks near the house were broad and straight; farther away, paths had been laid out to take advantage of the natural topography. Irregularities had been turned into picturesque assets. The walks were winding, trees and shrubs planted at random, and scenic views highlighted by informal framing. The shaded perimeter walk described by Hazard in the last seance had become a typical feature of French and English landscape gardens before the end of the eighteenth century. The walk at Vaucluse was perfectly suited to an ideal *ferme ornée*, incorporating glimpses of cultivated orchards and free-growing trees with views of the landscape beyond. If only the medium had stayed longer, Hazard wrote, his spirit wife could have walked to "every part of the picturesque park containing seventeen acres, diversified with hill and dale and scores of pleasing surprises and accompaniments."

Shepherd Tom died in 1886, leaving all his property to Barclay, his only son.[30] Barclay encouraged the circulation of a rumor that conveniently absolved him of any responsibility for the upkeep of his family estate. It was commonly and wrongly believed in Portsmouth that Shepherd Tom's will had directed Barclay to leave Vaucluse *exactly* as it was at his father's death. Barclay chose not to live there and may well have had more gloomy than fond memories of his childhood home. The result was that Vaucluse, "haunted to the end by its gentle ghosts," was abandoned to decay, the noble old house standing "vacant and untended, a dim white phantom among the close-pressing tangle of the overgrown box maze and the forgotten garden."[31]

In its neglected state, Vaucluse still fascinated those who knew its legends. Some who saw it were reminded of a moldering antebellum southern plantation, Tara, in Rhode Island. One traveler wrote of her expedition to Vaucluse: "[W]e scare up many a wild rabbit from the wayside tangle of the sweet brier lane, where one aged homestead appears as if it might topple over should the wind shake the embracing tree at its stoop."[32]

Historian Van Wyck Brooks described a visit to Vaucluse in the 1920s. "This great gray relic of the past," its long-closed window shutters covered over with vines, "surrounded with its gardens and arbours and hedges, where the rose and the myrtle ran riot, was a picture of decay and desolation."[33] Brooks followed the weedy gravel walk that led to the family graveyard. In the garden ivy-covered bowers and ruined summerhouses stood at the intersections of paths that were nearly smothered by ancient overgrown boxwood. A solitary gardener struggled in a neglected flower bed to reclaim the peonies and lilies amid the jungle. Neighboring farmers, according to Brooks, still remembered the old days, the parties, the music, and the dancing.

Later visitors recall picnicking upon a carpet of sweet-scented white violets. The old-fashioned double pheasant-eye narcissus had gone wild at Vaucluse; everyone who coveted its fragrant camellia-like flowers brought spades to dig up clumps of the bulbs for themselves.[34]

Those who explored Vaucluse as children have different memories. Tales of ghosts and seances were all too true for them and deliciously terrifying. Not so terrifying, however, as to prevent their prowling and spying. Daniel Congdon, the son of a farmer in Portsmouth, remembers Sunday school picnics at Vaucluse shortly after World War I.[35] He and his friends would sneak through a window into the dining room of the old mansion, where the caretaker's wife still kept the table laid for twelve, with plates, napkins, silverware,

Vaucluse, photograph by Strelecki, New York, early twentieth century. (Original photograph in the collection of the Newport Historical Society)

Vaucluse by moonlight, oil painting by Durr Freedley, ca. 1925. (Bequest of Alice Brayton, Redwood Library and Athenaeum, Newport, Rhode Island)

and wineglasses ready for the imminent return of the Hazard ghosts. Then, in their breathless rush to escape the haunted house, the children would run to the ravine, scrambling down brushy paths to the dammed-up pool beneath the most enormous trees they had ever seen.

A woman who grew up nearby used to run "cross lots" to Vaucluse with her pals in the 1920s. They would swim in the river, clamber through the glen, and explore the enchanted garden. Scampering through the dense tangle of boxwood, they dared each other to penetrate further into the dark heart of the maze. And then they would all creep into the house, starting at the creak of a door, trembling lest they encounter a ghost or,

more prosaically, fall through the rotting floorboards. The octagonal summerhouse poised at the edge of the ravine was falling into ruin, too. Even after repeated forays inside "the Seance House," as they called it, the children still felt that frisson of fear each time they crept in.[36]

The mansion at Vaucluse was painted as an eerie moonstruck ruin by Durr Freedley, a Newport artist commissioned by Alice Brayton. The painting hung in Miss Brayton's Portsmouth house until she died, leaving the painting to Newport's Redwood Library. The Metropolitan Museum of Art considered the Greek Revival facade of the house at Vaucluse to be of such architectural significance as to warrant its purchase by the museum. This was in 1927, when curators were busily rescuing fragments of buildings for display in museum settings. The crumbling columns, pediment, door, and windows of Vaucluse were hauled off to New York, leaving a pile of mere rubble behind.[37]

Meanwhile, during the first decades of the twentieth century, while Vaucluse was reverting to wilderness, neighboring farms along the Sakonnet shores were being turned into fancy country estates by Vanderbilts and other rich families. The names these new owners gave these places have a topographical ring: Black Point Farm, Greenvale, Sandy Point Farm. Their owners raised horses, sheep, cattle, or all three, with small armies of estate workers to look after things.

The aptly named Rhode Island Estates Corporation, set up by Barclay Hazard, sold off half the Vaucluse property in 1931.[38] The remainder, including the wreck of the house, the garden, the glen, and the farm buildings, was purchased in 1937 by a couple whose fortune, still intact despite the Depression, came from automobiles.[39]

The new owners built a twenty-six-room mansion of whitewashed brick near the site of the old house. In homage to the past, they kept the name Vaucluse and managed to retrieve the original front door from the Metroplitan Museum. Established local families looked down their long noses at these particular nouveau riche with their mock–Mount Vernon mansion, their loud parties, and their brand-new formal garden. Even their prize herd of Jersey cows was mildly derided as being too showy; as a member of old Newport society said of these new people, "One kept away."

The ghosts were banished for a time, when all was bright, noisy, and polished. But then that era ended. There was no one left. The sleek cows were sold at auction. Twenty years later the "new" house at Vaucluse stands empty, rusting around the edges. As a ruin it is not romantic. Or is it only snobbery that leads one to say it lacks the charm of the "real" Vaucluse? The garden that was new fifty years ago is now an impenetrable thicket of yew, through which, here and there, you can spy a murky pool that once held a fountain. Every trace of the original garden, boxwood and all, was banished long ago.

The mysterious deep glen is still there, of course, but the paths are so choked with undergrowth that it is impossible to see the pool or the trunks of the great trees. No animals graze the pastures, but the fields are open to the river's edge. The bucolic scene is sadly deceptive, however, for nothing edible or potable comes from this land nowadays. The fields of Vaucluse are devoted to the growing of sod, that quintessentially suburban product, instant green. Vaucluse belongs to a real estate consortium; before long, perhaps, it will become a con-

dominium community, like so many other former farms in Portsmouth.[40]

No one could casually chop down the old trees at Vaucluse. Giant beeches, locusts and lindens still survive from Shepherd Tom's day. The sycamore in the glen may have been planted by Samuel Elam. The trees will linger, but for ghosts, for poetic melancholy, for the memory of Petrarch's Laura, there may be no room.

Notes

1. Henry James, *The American Scene* (New York: Harper & Bros., 1907), 216.

2. Ibid., 203.

3. Rev. Edward Peterson, 1853, quoted in Alice G. B. Lockwood, ed., *Gardens of Colony and State* (New York: Charles Scribner's Sons, 1931), 1:211.

4. Alice Brayton, "The Gardens of the Planters" and "The Gardens of the Merchants," *Gardens of Colony and State* (New York: Charles Scribner's Sons, 1931), 1:159, 217–21.

5. Metcalf Bowler, *A Treatise on Agriculture and Practical Husbandry* (Providence, R.I.: Bennett Wheeler, 1786).

6. Brayton, *Gardens of Colony and State* 1:216.

7. Thomas Robinson Hazard, *The Jonny-Cake Papers of "Shepherd Tom,"* ed. D. B. Updike (Boston: Merrymount Press, 1915), 90–92.

8. J. P. Brissot de Warville, *New Travels in the United States of America, 1788*, ed. Durand Echeverria (Cambridge, Mass.: Harvard University Press, 1964), 128.

9. Brayton, *Gardens of Colony and State* 1:229.

10. Quoted in "Architectural Details of Vaucluse," *Bulletin of the Metropolitan Museum of Art* 22 (November 1927): 72.

11. Francois de La Rochefoucault Liancourt, *Travels through the United States of America, the Country of the Iroquois and Upper Canada in the Years 1795, 1796 and 1797* (London: R. Phillips, 1799), 1:495, 502.

12. Edward Peterson, *History of Rhode Island and Newport* (New York: John S. Taylor, 1853), 136.

13. *Encyclopedia Britannica*, 1971 ed., s.v. "Petrarch"; Roderick Cameron, *Gardens of the Golden Riviera* (London: Weidenfeld & Nicolson, 1975), 118–25.

14. George C. Channing, *Early Recollections of Newport, Rhode Island, 1793–1811* (Newport, R.I., 1868), 217.

15. R. G. Saisselin, "The French Garden in the Eighteenth Century: From Belle Nature to the Landscape of

Time," *Journal of Garden History* 5 (July–September 1985): 284–97; David Watkin, *The English Vision: The Picturesque in Architecture, Landscape and Garden Design* (New York: Harper & Row, 1982), 161–69; Dora Wiebenson, *The Picturesque Garden in France* (Princeton, N.J.: Princeton University Press, 1978).

16. Jane Austen, *Northanger Abbey* (Oxford: Oxford University Press, 1933), 179.

17. Brayton, *Gardens of Colony and State*, 1:232.

18. Maud Howe Elliott, *This Was My Newport* (Cambridge, Mass.: Mythology Co., 1944), 132.

19. "The Vaucluse Buttonwood," *Magazine of American History* 4 (1880): 455–56.

20. Channing, *Early Recollections*, 217.

21. Brayton, *Gardens of Colony and State*, 1:232.

22. Rowland Gibson Hazard, "Biographical Sketch," in T. R. Hazard, *Jonny-Cake Papers;* Patrick T. Conley, *An Album of Rhode Island History, 1636–1986* (Norfolk, Va.: 1986), 94.

23. Elliott, *This Was My Newport*, 79–86; Thomas Wentworth Higginson, *Malbone: An Oldport Romance* (Boston: Fields, Osgood & Co., 1869), 78, 128.

24. John R. Dix, *A Handbook of Newport and Rhode Island* (Newport, R.I.: C. E. Hammett Jr., 1852), 147.

25. Julia Ward Howe, *Reminiscences, 1819–1899* (Boston: Houghton Mifflin, 1900), 238–39. The Howes transformed a wooded gorge, or glen, similar to the one at Vaucluse into part of their garden. Another Portsmouth glen, called simply "The Glen," was a famous place of resort in the nineteenth century. A public teahouse at the site provided refreshments for tourists, according to Charles C. Mason, in *Newport and Its Environs* (Newport, R.I.: C. E. Hammett Jr., 1848).

26. Elliott, *This Was My Newport*, 66–70.

27. Thomas Robinson Hazard, "Life Immortal," in *Miscellaneous Essays and Letters* (Philadelphia, 1883), 329.

28. Elliott, *This Was My Newport*, 67–68.

29. T. R. Hazard, "Re-Materialization of the Soul" (1878), and "The Angels Are Coming to Stay" (1879), in *Miscellaneous Essays*, 336–62.

30. Portsmouth, R.I., Town Records, 7:349, will of Thomas Robinson Hazard, probated 10 May 1886.

31. Elliott, *This Was My Newport*, 69.

32. Katherine M. Abbott, *Old Paths and Legends of New England* (New York: G. P. Putnam's Sons, 1904), 434.

33. Van Wyck Brooks, *New England: Indian Summer 1865–1915* (New York: E. P. Dutton, 1940), 71.

34. Richard Champlin, interview by author, Newport, R.I., 2 February 1987; Marguerite Peckham, telephone conversation with author, 2 February 1987.

35. Daniel Congdon, interview by author, Portsmouth, R.I., 22 June 1988.

36. Ruth Earle, telephone conversation with author, 21 June 1988.

37. "Architectural Details of Vaucluse," *Bulletin of the Metropolitan Museum of Art* 22 (November 1927): 71–73.

38. "Barclay Hazard Dead at Age of 85," *Providence Journal*, 20 August 1938; Portsmouth Town Records (Deeds), 28:91.

39. "Estate Opened at Portsmouth," *Providence Journal*, 7 July 1937; Portsmouth Town Records, 35:314, 36:540, 38:143, 41:290.

40. "Prize Cows Go on Block Tomorrow," *Providence Sunday Journal*, 2 May 1976; "Vaucluse Farm Sold to Housing Developer," *Providence Journal-Bulletin*, 18 November 1978; Portsmouth Town Records, 89:498.

Chapter 5

Brief Dynasty

John Perkins Cushing's Bellmont,

Watertown, Massachusetts

JOHN PERKINS CUSHING'S house and garden are gone now, but for fifty years in the middle of the nineteenth century his country estate, Bellmont, in Watertown, Massachusetts, was among the most splendid in all New England.

. . .

Cushing was only sixteen in 1803, when his uncle, Thomas Handasyd Perkins, sent him out to China to help organize a trading office in Canton for Perkins and Company of Boston. Cushing's companion on the long voyage was an older Perkins employee, Ephraim Bumstead. Unfortunately, Bumstead fell ill and died on the ship, leaving his youthful assistant to carry on alone.

Cushing (1787–1862) had been left an orphan at an early age. He had been brought up since the age of five by his Perkins aunt and uncle. When Thomas Handasyd Perkins learned that his nephew was alone in Canton, trying on his own to conduct the firm's business, he was alarmed. The Perkins firm had an enormous financial stake in the still new and fiercely competitive China trade. Only since 1785, following the peace treaty signed by John Jay, had American ships been permitted to trade with the Chinese. Thomas Handasyd Perkins himself had first sailed to the Orient in 1789. He was wonderfully successful in selling furs, silver, rum, and tobacco to the Chinese and had then gained a fortune from marketing the silk, porcelain, and tea that his loaded ships brought back to America.

Cushing's first letter from Canton apparently allayed his uncle's fears. Cushing was astute, self-confident, and in the end immensely successful.[1] As a Perkins partner, he stayed in China nearly thirty years, far longer than most foreign traders. A key element in his success was his friendship with Houqua (1769–1843), the Chinese merchant who dealt almost entirely with New Englanders and one of the richest men in the world at the time. Cushing became like a son to Houqua and often visited his friend's princely retreat, with its extensive gardens, open pavilions, and rows of plants in porcelain pots. Houqua helped Cushing in business, both of them making more and more money all the while.

By 1820 most of the Pacific seals and otters had been slaughtered for their valuable pelts. Traders had to seek commodities other than furs to sell to the Chinese. Cushing found American rice to be profitable in 1825, during a time of famine in China, especially as he persuaded the Chinese to admit it duty-free. But it was opium that for many years provided the surest route to riches for Cushing and other American and British traders. Opium was illegal in China, but that only enhanced its trade value. The traffic in opium from Turkey and India involved smuggling and the bribery of corrupt Chinese officials. Houqua and Cushing were among those who reaped huge profits from catering to the spreading drug addiction they helped to foster.

Cushing, known to the Chinese as "Ku-shing," lived like an oriental potentate in Canton, in the style of Houqua. When young John Murray Forbes arrived in Canton in 1828 to work under Cushing for the Perkins firm, he expected to be awed by the great man. As he wrote home, "You know we have always looked upon him as many degrees higher than the pope in all his glory." But he found Cushing quite approachable, and the two became friends.[2] Cushing returned at last to Boston in 1831, forty-four years old and immensely wealthy. He continued for the rest of his life to live in regal splendor.

. . .

In Boston, Cushing settled into a white stone house on Summer Street. He had a wall built of Chinese porcelain tiles around his property. A visitor recalled this "enchanted place," filled with Chinese screens, silks, carvings, and a myriad of Chinese servants clad in gowns of blue crepe.[3] At home, Cushing himself often wore a Chinese silk dressing gown and cap. Soon after establishing himself in Boston, Cushing, aged forty-six, married Mary Louise Gardiner, the daughter of a prominent Boston clergyman.

Following the example of his uncle Perkins, who had a spacious country estate in Brookline, Cushing began to look for a rural retreat for himself and his family. He purchased 117 acres of farmland in Watertown, five miles west of Boston.[4] Cushing and his wife, with their infant son, moved to Watertown in August 1834. Cushing soon sold the Boston house and spent the rest of his days at the place he called Bellmont. He chose the name for his new property in reference to a gentle eminence at its center that provided views toward Fresh Pond and the Mystic River valley.[5]

The very day that Cushing moved to Watertown he recorded the event on the first page of a new diary. From then on he meticulously recorded the development of his garden and grounds, together with the weather and all the major and minor events of his and his family's lives, in daily diary entries. The seven surviving volumes of his diary cover twenty-three of his years at Bellmont.[6] Cushing's life seems oddly flattened in the diary. Both major and minor events are compressed into similar lines of unaccented, often illegible, inky script. He might note on one day the direction of the wind, the cutting of the first asparagus, and the birth of a new baby, with all three occurrences given apparently equal weight. Only rarely do Cushing's true feelings escape onto the pages of his diary. Occasionally, he explodes at the faithlessness of a lazy servant or the perfidy of a nurseryman who sent him bad stock. A reader learns far more about the weather and the development of his house and grounds than about Cushing's relationships with Mary Louise and their children.

Once settled at Watertown, Cushing seldom left home. A ride around Fresh Pond, a trip to a nearby nursery, or a visit to a friend's greenhouse: these outings sufficed for Cushing. His wife, however, with the children and their nurse, journeyed into Boston in the barouche *every* afternoon, health and weather permitting, to visit her mother. Cushing never accompanied her. He sent Ahoo, his Chinese coolie, to tend to errands of business or to deliver greenhouse grapes to sick friends. Cushing never attended parties given by others; he went to weddings and funerals only when he believed it would be rude not to. He even absented himself from his own babies' baptisms in Boston. Pardoxically, however, Cushing regularly welcomed visitors to Bellmont. After his long sojourn in China, Cushing felt detached from the social bustle of Boston. His life was now centered entirely on his home.

. . .

At first he and his family lived in a relatively modest cottage at Bellmont, but Cushing had grandiose plans for his estate and began work immediately. He had great confidence in his own taste. He felt quite able to design his own house and lay out the grounds. When he finally acknowledged the need for technical expertise in the construction of a grand mansion, Cushing hired two architects, not entirely trusting either to please him. Richard Upjohn, a prominent architect, well known for his Gothic-style houses and churches, drew one set of house plans, based, as Cushing had instructed, on illustrations of villas in a book by J. C. Loudon. While still dealing with Upjohn, Cushing consulted Asher Benjamin, one of New England's most influential architects. At length, Cushing dismissed Upjohn and signed a contract with Benjamin. In 1840 an old house on the property was demolished, and construction of the new house began at last.

Benjamin also designed five greenhouses for Cushing and probably planned the new stable, barn, and farmhouse, as well as the cottage where Cushing and his family were living while the mansion was under construction. Cushing was less the passive patron of his architect than the dominant partner. Benjamin would draw plans for the mansion. Cushing would then return them with sketches of his own, insisting that Benjamin be governed by these. This happened repeatedly over several years. Before the house was completed, Cushing conspired with a carpenter to change the front entrance. In 1846, Cushing commissioned John Notman, a Philadelphia-based architect known for picturesque Italianate villa designs, to redesign the roof of the still-unfinished mansion. In the end, Cushing rejected Notman's drawings as "too showy." It was fifteen years before the imposing new mansion was finally completed and the Cushings were at last able to move in.

Cushing had one parlor hung with Chinese wallpaper, hand-painted with plum trees, bamboo, and peonies. Many of the furnishings came from China. But Cushing had diverse interests and tastes, wanting only the best. He bought a complete set of Audubon's *Birds of America* directly from Audubon himself.

. . .

Compared to the building of his house, the planning of Cushing's grounds was less fraught with conflict because he did it all himself. In 1835 he laid out his driveways and staked out locations for planting trees. He selected a wooded knoll as the site of the new house. To open a view to Fresh Pond, Cushing regretfully had a dozen huge trees cut down.

The four-square plan of an old three-acre walled garden at Bellmont survived Cushing's mania for redesigning. This garden dated from the first decade of the nineteenth century, when Ebenezer Preble, a prominent pioneering horticulturist, had owned part of the land that became Bellmont.[7] Cushing knew that the high brick walls would provide a perfect setting for his fruit trees, flower gardens, and greenhouses. He commissioned a local sculptor to make a marble fountain basin and pedestal, which were placed at the intersection of the garden paths. The paths themselves were

The fountain at the center of Cushing's garden; his house can be glimpsed beyond the trees; stereograph, 1870s. (Massachusetts Historical Society)

surfaced with brown gravel from Medford, Massachusetts. Before the end of 1834, Cushing had planted more than two hundred roses from the Winship nursery in nearby Brighton.

The entrance avenue curved gently up a gradual rise to the front of the new mansion. During the fall and winter months, gardeners were kept busy pounding and spreading tons of crushed oyster shells over the surface of this drive. To one side of the avenue was a vast lawn of some twenty acres, with a small pond nestled in a hollow. The lawn ran right up to the house itself. Behind the house were the walled garden and a fenced deer park. A winding path led toward open glades that overlooked fields, farms, Fresh Pond, and, in the distance, the gold dome of the State House in Boston. Another footpath circumnavigated the grounds near their perimeter.

From the outset, Cushing planted trees and hedges as windbreaks and to conceal his stables and farm buildings. He also laid out irregular belts of trees along the main road and on either side of his entrance avenue. Around the great lawn he planted evergreens and deciduous trees in mixed clumps. During the autumn of 1834—his first year at Bellmont—Cushing planted more than six hundred ornamental trees, in addition to over a hundred fruit trees in an orchard and against the garden walls.

In laying out his grounds, Cushing followed local examples and English precedents. He had no interest in re-creating a Chinese garden, as one might have expected. He was strongly influenced by the design of the Brookline estate of his uncle, Thomas Handasyd Perkins. Colonel Perkins's garden dated from early in the nineteenth century. Its greenhouses, high brick walls, and oval, tree-bordered lawn were precedents for Cushing.[8] Cushing was familiar with other established estate gardens in the neighborhood of Boston, as well. The Roxbury garden of John Lowell, a founder of the Massachusetts Horticultural Society, was noted for its belt of majestic trees planted by Lowell himself in 1800.[9] Cushing also knew Theodore Lyman's place, The Vale, in nearby Waltham, which had been laid out in accordance with the precepts of Humphry Repton. Just across the road from Bellmont was the Pratt estate, with a broad lawn and old trees. But Cushing's grounds and gardens were grander and more polished than most. His estate was widely admired by his contemporaries.

In 1841, Andrew Jackson Downing's first book was published. Ponderously titled *A Treatise on the Theory and Practice of Landscape Gardening Adapted to North America*, it was immediately successful and often reprinted. This book, together with Downing's other writings, had enormous influence on American domestic taste. Downing wrote that he found in the environs of Boston many "tastefully laid out" country seats, among them that of J. P. Cushing, Esq. Downing had first visited Bellmont in 1838. Bellmont, like the other gardens Downing praised, quickly achieved national prominence via the pages of his book.

Downing popularized a landscape style based on English prototypes, a style that had seldom been adopted in this country and only by a few cosmopolitan, or merely rich, landowners. Landscape gardening, according to Downing, was an art allied to painting. Its aim should be an "expressive, harmonizing, and refined imitation" of nature.[10] Downing spelled out exactly how to achieve such a goal, quoting often from John Claudius Loudon. Loudon, an Englishman, had preceded Downing in disseminating the principles espoused a few decades earlier by Humphry Repton. Like Loudon, Downing was an interpreter rather than an originator of design theory. In painstaking detail, he advised those of modest means on how to improve their home grounds. Cushing's estate and others were held up as models for middle-class Americans to visit and study, with an eye to replicating them in miniature at their own suburban residences.[11]

According to an 1850 article in Hovey's *Magazine of Horticulture*, Cushing's grounds were "laid out on the plan of modern European gardens, and appear to be an exact counterpart of the style of the late Mr. Loudon."[12] Humphry Repton himself might well have admired Bellmont, where most of his principles were incorporated. The flower garden was near the house, whereas the more remote parts of the estate were assimilated into the natural landscape, as he would have advised.[13] Cushing provided for distant views but planted to conceal his farm buildings and the public road. Cushing's great lawn, like his entire estate, conformed more to the harmonious, polished style known since the eighteenth century as the Beautiful style, than to the rough intricacy of the Picturesque style. These terms, as used by the nineteenth-century popularizers Loudon and Downing, harked back to Repton and the aesthetic theorists of the eighteenth century. The rolling lawn at Bellmont, with its well-placed clumps of beeches and other trees, avoided the twin anathemas of admirers of the Beautiful; it was neither bare and bald nor dotted over with single trees. Cushing's gently curving approach road, too, was closer to the precepts of the Beautiful than one that snaked in meaningless twists.[14]

Bellmont became one of the showplaces in the vicinity of Boston, a spot that many were anxious to visit. As its fame spread, the number of visitors increased well beyond Cushing's circle of friends and family. During the spring and summer the gardens were open once a week to the public. Prepared with letters of introduction, people came from all over the United States and Europe to inspect the gardens and greenhouses at Bellmont. Downing was only one among many visitors who had a professional interest. Nicholas Biddle's gardener came from Philadelphia; J. G. Teschemacher, a garden writer and editor, visited, as did nurseryman James Hogg of New York and Dr. Asa Gray, Harvard's famous botanist. Former President Martin Van Buren came to call. "A Russian lady and gentleman," a Polish count, the French consul, two gentlemen from South Carolina—the famous as well as those now nameless—all wanted to see Cushing's garden.

· · ·

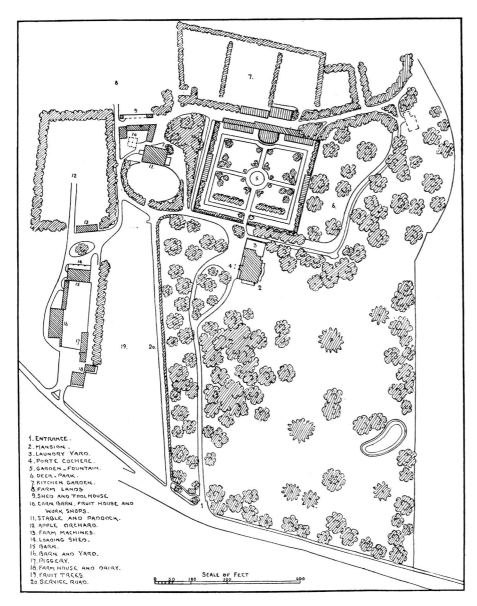

A plan of Bellmont, published in *Garden and Forest*, vol. 2, 10 July 1889. Cushing's view toward Fresh Pond and Boston was to the northeast, beyond the top of this plan. (Frances Loeb Library, Harvard University)

1. ENTRANCE.
2. MANSION.
3. LAUNDRY YARD.
4. PORTE COCHERE.
5. GARDEN - FOUNTAIN.
6. DEER - PARK.
7. KITCHEN GARDEN.
8. FARM LANDS.
9. SHED AND TOOLHOUSE.
10. CORN BARN, FRUIT HOUSE AND WORK SHOPS.
11. STABLE AND PADDOCK.
12. APPLE ORCHARD.
13. FARM MACHINES.
14. LOADING SHED.
15. BARN.
16. BARN AND YARD.
17. PIGGERY.
18. FARM HOUSE AND DAIRY.
19. FRUIT TREES.
20. SERVICE ROAD.

SCALE OF FEET

Boston was a hive of horticultural experimentation during the middle years of the nineteenth century, as were Philadelphia, New York, and Rochester. Cushing's greenhouses and gardens contributed to and benefited from the rich ferment of ideas and techniques. Although competition was rampant, so was the sharing of information. Many of Cushing's callers came to learn as well as to admire his gardening triumphs. His occasional forays to nearby nurseries and private gardens were aimed at acquiring knowledge as well as plants.

Cushing obtained seeds and plants from all over the globe. Commercial nurseries were proliferating around Boston, and so was the range of their stock. Amateurs like Cushing encouraged the professionals to try new plants and to import others. Cushing, in turn, would share his own successful importations with local growers. From Cunningham's of Liverpool, Cushing bought roses, camellias, and "forest trees" by the hundreds. Vilmorin-Andrieux in France sent him carnations and fruit trees. Cushing repeatedly bought fruit trees from Rotterdam and Strasbourg, as well as from local Massachusetts nurseries such as Manning's of Salem and Kenrick's of Brighton. He wrote to Amsterdam for bulbs. Friends and mere acquaintances provided plants and,

A view up the great lawn at Bellmont toward the house. Specimen trees were grouped on the lawn, and a belt of trees encircled the estate. (Massachusetts Historical Society)

more often, seeds. Dr. Francis Boott, the Boston-born botanist, sent flower seeds from London; travelers brought seeds from Manila, Trinidad, and the Rocky Mountains. Someone from Kentucky brought Cushing a cutting of the new "Michigan rose."

Houqua, Cushing's Chinese associate and friend, shipped plants to Cushing from Canton, as well as tea and household furnishings. The plants included peonies, loquats, mulberries, orange trees, and evergreens. Cushing was pleased in 1835 when "only" a quarter of the Chinese plants were dead on arrival in Boston. The sea voyage at the time usually took five months.

Cushing's more local horticultural purchases were not always successful, either. In April 1841 his wrath was aroused when he received twenty-four pear trees from the Downings' nursery in Newburgh, New York. All the trees, Cushing complained, were "destitute of roots and consequently worthless; this is inexcusable in a regular nurseryman and it is the last transaction I shall ever have with said person." The admiring notice that Downing accorded to Bellmont in his book, published that same year, may have cooled Cushing's wrath, for he eventually engaged in several more transactions with the Downing nursery. In 1843, Cushing even lent Downing seven French books on fruit.

The Cushing greenhouses ensured that visitors had plenty to see even in winter. Cushing kept abreast of the publications, mostly English, that offered advice on greenhouse construction, heating, and ventilation. The technology was developing during the 1830s and 1840s. Horticultural writers advanced new theories on the best angle of slope for glass roofs. The lean-to greenhouse, hitherto the norm, was rendered old-fashioned by free-standing structures that admitted light from all sides. Iron construction made greater dimensions possible; curvilinear shapes allowed for fantasies in design.

The showpiece at Bellmont was a sixty-foot conservatory with a domed circular room at its center. The conservatory and adjoining greenhouses were built against the high brick garden walls that predated Cushing. Robert B. Leuchars, who published the first American book on greenhouse design in 1851, had visited Bellmont. Of Cushing's lean-to greenhouses, Leuchars wrote, "call them old-fashioned if you like," but he admired the healthy, well-grown plants therein.[15] Cushing had taken advantage of the known benefits to plant growth of reflected heat from masonry, and had incorporated the latest advances in construction technique.

C. M. Hovey, a local nurseryman with whom Cushing often dealt, described the Cushing conservatory in 1844 as "a blaze of beauty." Its primary purpose was the display of plants. Two circular stages held showy pelargoniums. Hovey admired particularly the splendid crimson spikes of Victoria stock, which he thought should be in every greenhouse.[16] Wisteria and *Rosa Banksia* had "spangled the whole space" with blossoms. Exotic flowering vines trained to trellises were a feature. Hovey noted an Australian bower plant, *Pandorea jasminoides*, thirty feet tall and dappled with panicles of pale pink. A chalice vine from the West Indies, *Solandra grandiflora*, bore big white tubular flowers.

Another climber that impressed Hovey was the nightblooming cereus, *Hylocereus undatus*, a cactus from Jamaica. The Massachusetts Horticultural Society noted in 1838 that Cushing in his enormous conservatory and J. Wright Boott in his tiny greenhouse were the first in Boston to bring this plant to flower. The enormous white blossoms were rare as well as beautiful, because they opened only one night in a year.

Cushing began exhibiting fruit and greenhouse plants at Massachusetts Horticultural Society shows

during his first winter at Bellmont. The annals of the society recorded with regularity the triumphs of Cushing's conservatory.[17] Camellias were well grown there, as they were in other greenhouses around Boston, being at the time very popular. Cushing also grew rhododendrons under glass: the rosy-purple sweet azalea (*Rhododendron pulchrum*) from China and a white one from Java were two of the limited number then available. In 1838 the Horticultural Society noted that Cushing's Himalayan *Rhododendron arboreum* had seventy trusses of scarlet blossoms. In late March, gardenias blossomed in the conservatory, as did roses. The yellow Noisette rose "Cloth of Gold," a favorite of Downing's, arched high overhead.[18] Visitors also commented on the flowering vines: *Ipomea horsfalliae*, a West Indian twiner with pale purple flowers up to three inches across; fragrant passion flowers; and a high-

The garden, gardeners, and central greenhouse at Bellmont; stereograph, 1870s. The brick wall, visible behind the greenhouses, was erected about 1805 and may have been similar to the peach wall that still stands at Theodore Lyman's Waltham estate, The Vale. (Society for the Preservation of New England Antiquities)

climbing, scarlet-blossomed *Tropaeolum tuberosum* from the Andes. Behind Cushing's flowering plants were palms from around the world, such as the sago palm from Japan and a tall-growing fan palm from the island of Reunion.

Flowers were but one product of the Bellmont greenhouses. Cushing eventually had fourteen greenhouses besides the conservatory, each with temperatures adjusted to suit a different sort of plant. In addition to the houses devoted to raising specific ornamentals such as palms, orchids, or azaleas, there were greenhouses for grapevines, figs, strawberries, peaches, nectarines, and early vegetables. Strawberries in March must have seemed a miracle in Massachusetts in 1836. Pineapple and banana plants came from Cuba and Java, some via England and others sent directly to Boston. It was a challenge to bring them to fruit, but in 1837, Cushing's head gardener was the first to exhibit ripe pineapples in Boston.

Cushing was more than a rich amateur in his gardening. He had an unquenchable desire to grow plants well, a great zest for experimentation, and boundless curiosity. He read widely and avidly on horticultural and agricultural matters. At first, most of his books and periodicals on these subjects came from England, because few were published in the United States. He ordered almost everything the prolific John Claudius Loudon wrote. When American publications finally began to appear, Cushing bought them too. In 1837 he described *The Cultivator*, published in Albany, New York, as "the best agricultural periodical in this country." Some of the new magazines that Cushing read were edited by professional Massachusetts nurserymen, including Robert Manning, Thomas G. Fessenden, and Charles M. Hovey. Cushing found American writers, such as Downing and S. B. Parsons, to be more helpful than the English writers to a gardener struggling with the harsh New England climate.

The weather was of unending interest to Cushing. Every day he meticulously recorded in his diary the extremes of temperature, the direction of the wind, and any precipitation or unusual meteorological occurrences. Early frosts, late thaws, hailstorms, periods of drought—all of these he noted as to their effect on his gardens and crops. He scientifically compared one year to another in terms of, for example, the day when the buds on his peach trees first showed color. Sometimes he just enjoyed a day at Bellmont of what he called, in a favorite phrase, "charming weather throughout."

Cushing's earnest record keeping and comparisons were based on observations and on his own horticultural experiments. He conducted long-range tests of different sorts of hedging plants—arborvitae, beech, Osage orange—to see which would flourish and which could best contain livestock. Once he divided a grass plat into four quadrants, applying a different fertilizer to each to ascertain which was most beneficial. He applied tobacco water, chloride of lime, or "a decoction of

Potash" to different roses to see which would stop the worms from eating them. He was forever trying new techniques to foil insects in his fruit trees. In 1836 he found to his chagrin that the peach trees on his wall were dead—killed, he decided, by the ashes he had applied to protect them from borers! In 1835 he determined that spring-planted trees and shrubs were more likely to survive than those planted in the fall. Two years later he decided that *fall* planting was better after all.

With an eye to improving his garden and farm, Cushing frequently sought the advice of experts. Once he hired a geologist to appraise the soils at Bellmont. Cushing was fascinated by machines. He had an ironmonger build him a watering machine like one he had seen pictured. A Shaker came from New Hampshire one day to show Cushing how to use a new Shaker-designed horse-drawn rake. Cushing also studied a new greenhouse heating system at his uncle Perkins's before deciding that he should have one like it.

Farming occupied Cushing almost as much as horticulture. He kept close track of his annual crop of hay, essential as it was to his horses and cattle. In 1852 he expanded his tillage by purchasing a two-hundred-acre farm in Wayland, a few miles from Bellmont. Always seeking out the best, he imported livestock just as he imported plants: cows from Scotland and the Austrian Alps and pigs from China.

. . .

Cushing attentively managed all aspects of his estate but was completely dependent on his head gardener to see that the work was done. Cushing hired David Haggerston to fill this role even before the move to Watertown. Securing the services of Haggerston was quite a coup. As the proprietor of the Charlestown Vineyard, a commercial nursery of small fruits, flowers, and greenhouse camellias, Haggerston had been among the founders of the Massachusetts Horticultural Society in 1829.[19] In 1832 he had been chosen to manage the Horticultural Society's experimental garden at the new rural cemetery of Mount Auburn in Cambridge. Haggerston's selection for this prestigious position reflected well on him. As to how Cushing had managed to lure him from Mount Auburn only two years later, the record is silent.

At Bellmont, Haggerston was in charge of at least a dozen full-time workers and others hired for seasonal tasks. Cushing told Haggerston what he wanted done, and Haggerston then directed the work crews. Cushing noted in his diary just what the various crews had done each day. He paid Haggerston once a month and gave him the money to pay the monthly wages of the workers under him. At the end of November 1834, for example, Cushing handed over $378 to cover the wages of Haggerston and fifteen men. This averages $23.60 per worker for the month, although Haggerston doubtless received more than those under him. Working six days a week, the gardeners earned perhaps $.80 a day in addition to room and board. At the same time, Cushing was buying trees four inches in diameter for $1.25 each and nectarine trees for $.50. Although these prices, like the gardeners' wages, may seem low, the scale of Cushing's operation sheds a different light. A single order of Dutch fruit trees, for instance, cost Cushing $764, more than twice what he paid to sixteen people for a month's work.

Cushing respected David Haggerston, whose horticultural expertise far exceeded his own at first. Several times Cushing sent Haggerston to New York or Philadelphia to visit greenhouses and gardens, to secure different plants, and to "make note of any improvements he may see," with an eye to adopting them at Bellmont. Cushing shared his horticultural books and magazines with his head gardener. Haggerston had books of his own, too. His copy of *The Hot-House and Greenhouse Manual* by Robert Sweet, published in London in 1831, is in the Massachusetts Horticultural Society library.

The Horticultural Society bylaws made a special provision for admitting professional gardeners to membership.[20] Such members were assessed an annual fee of $1, whereas amateur gardeners had to contribute $30 each year. Haggerston was an active member of the society, helping to arrange and judge shows and regularly exhibiting his own handiwork in the form of fruits and flowers. While working for Cushing, Haggerston strove to outshine the displays of other professionals. In 1836 he entered "a large pot containing a living [grape] vine, coiled and beautifully decorated with flowers," including dahlias, "thus blending and uniting the handmaids of Flora and Pomona."[21] At the first annual show in the society's new Horticultural Hall in 1845, Haggerston's prize-winning entry was a domed floral temple fifteen feet high, in the Grecian style, with six wreathed columns and an entablature with the words "Dedicated to Flora" inlaid in purple everlastings.[22] Colonel Perkins's gardener, William Quant, countered with a Gothic pyramid of moss, asters, and marigolds "so well executed as to have the appearance of mosaic." The next year someone else entered a fuchsia-covered Chinese pagoda with a Chinese tea merchant inside it, "politely bowing his head," as well as attesting to the popularity of the Orient as a design source.[23]

In addition to these dazzling displays of horticultural opulence and artifice, Haggerston and his gardening rivals also exhibited more practical and edible examples of horticultural skill. In 1840, for example, Haggerston entered thirty-one varieties of turnip. He was competitive: he won the grape competition for many years. And consider the episode of the rose slugs. Haggerston wrote a letter in 1840 suggesting that the Horticultural Society offer a $100 prize to the discoverer of an antidote to the despised rose slug. His employer, Cushing, responded by donating the prize money. Two years later the Horticultural Society announced that a cure for the rose slug had been found: whale oil soap, which would also kill canker worms, aphids, and red spiders. The winner of the prize was—David Haggerston![24]

As time went on, Cushing began to feel that his gardener was overstepping the limits of his authority. Cushing also discovered that Haggerston was dishonest and had not lived up to his trust. Bills and employee wages had not been paid. In 1846, Haggerston was summarily dismissed after thirteen years, and Cushing set himself to keeping a closer eye on the outdoor affairs of his estate.

Haggerston was succeeded at Bellmont by a team of two German immigrants, Gustave Evers and Heinrich Schwimming, both of whom were experienced estate gardeners. Cushing, more cautious now, did not allocate managerial duties to Haggerston's successors but took care of hiring, firing, and the payment of wages himself. Horticulturally, Cushing's new head gardeners kept Bellmont up to the mark, although their relationship to their employer was never as close as their predecessor's had been. Schwimming was responsible for the greenhouses, in which he raised several plants new to Cushing and to Boston. His *Nepenthes distillataria*, a pitcher plant, attracted much attention at an 1852 tent show in Boston's Public Garden. Evers, an expert on fruit trees and roses, established a successful commercial nursery in Brighton after he eventually left Bellmont.[25]

Cushing attended to certain garden tasks himself, which was unusual for one in his situation at that time. He often pruned his espaliered fruit trees, for example.

This was a pleasant and manageable task and one at which he considered himself adept. His gardeners, Cushing felt, did not sufficiently appreciate the importance of pruning in order to admit more sun as an aid to ripening the fruit. Cushing thinned out his trees himself, at least to the extent of marking those that were to be removed. His diary entries record exactly what he did, as well as just what tasks his gardening crews were engaged in each day of the year.

. . .

Cushing devoted his days in Watertown to improving his garden and farm and to building and furnishing his house. He and Mary Louise had five children, with whose well-being Cushing was much concerned. In his diary he chronicled the events of the children's lives, their illnesses, their tutors, their music and drawing lessons, the Chinese governess he hired for his only daughter, and the sculptors and painters he employed to do their portraits. The garden was the scene of many memorable children's parties. When his oldest son, John, turned six, Cushing had a tent erected in the center of the walled garden, with a marquee beside it for the musicians. Chinese lanterns, banners, and kites were put up around the fountain. Three hundred children came for refreshments, games, hot-air balloons, and, at dusk, a show of Chinese fireworks. The entire garden staff spent all the next day cleaning up.[26]

Cushing had celebrated John's first birthday more simply—but with an eye to the future—by planting a clump of linden trees on the lawn. As it turned out, none of Cushing's heirs were living at Bellmont when these trees reached maturity.

Cushing and Mary Louise both died in 1862. His fortune had increased all during his life; when he died, his estate was appraised at $2.5 million.[27] Cushing left

The mansion at Bellmont in the 1860s, near the end of Cushing's life. (Society for the Preservation of New England Antiquities)

everything to his four surviving children. His daughter sold her share of the Bellmont property to her brothers. In 1866, four years after their father died, his sons sold Bellmont in its entirety for $100,000.[28]

All Cushing's efforts to provide an established rural seat for his family came to naught in the end. Apparently, none of Cushing's sons felt much fondness for the place where they had grown up. It is unlikely that financial necessity drove them to the sale, the return on which was so modest. In the absence of primogeniture, the transition from one generation to the next was unclear. As so often in the United States, even in the years before income and inheritance taxes, a country estate built up over a lifetime went out of family ownership as soon as its maker died.

Another family bought Bellmont. Samuel R. Payson, owner of a woollen mill, lived there happily with his family for twenty years, until his business failed. Fortunes were often lost more quickly than they were made in the years following the Civil War. Bellmont was sold at auction in 1886. Over the next forty years the estate was subdivided, piece by piece, into modest house lots. For a time the mansion became a dormitory for a boys' boarding school. In 1927, deprived of its setting, the house that Cushing built was demolished in a day.[29]

Walking now along the winding streets of the suburban subdivision that once was Bellmont, it is difficult to conjure up images of Cushing's great lawn and gardens, his many greenhouses, or his deer park. Yet something is special about this neighborhood. At intervals along these hilly roads enormous trees loom up, towering above the houses. Giant purple beeches, weeping beeches, shagbark hickories, oaks, gingkos, and spruces are survivors from another era. Behind one house a section of Cushing's eleven-foot brick wall still stands. Then, suddenly, I picture the man himself, secateurs in hand, carefully pruning his peach trees.

Notes

1. Cushing's years in China are discussed in Francis Ross Carpenter, *The Old China Trade, 1784–1843* (New York: Coward McCann, 1976); Tyler Dennett, *Americans in Eastern Asia* (New York: Macmillan, 1922); and Carl Seaburg and Stanley Patterson, *Merchant Prince of Boston* (Cambridge, Mass.: Harvard University Press, 1971).

2. Sarah Forbes Hughes, ed., *Letters and Recollections of John Murray Forbes* (Boston & New York: Houghton Mifflin, 1899), 1:57.

3. Caroline Gardiner Curtis, *Memories of Fifty Years in the Last Century* (Boston: privately printed, 1947), 12.

4. Middlesex County Deeds, 321:20, 334:264, 349:121–23.

5. In 1859, when the present town of Belmont was formed to include part of Watertown, Cushing, the largest taxpayer, saw to it that the new town bore the name of his estate. See *Belmont, Massachusetts: The Architecture and Development of the Town of Homes*, prepared for the Belmont Historic District Commission (Belmont, Mass.: 1984), 16.

6. John Perkins Cushing diary, 7 vols., Manuscript Collection, Boston Athenaeum. Unless otherwise noted, all information on Cushing's life at Bellmont was derived from his diary.

7. Ebenezer Preble, a founder in 1792 and later president of the Massachusetts Society for Promoting Agriculture, experimented with imported fruit trees. See Justin Winsor, *The Memorial History of Boston Including Suffolk County, Mass. 1630–1880* (Boston, 1880–81) 4:633, and Robert Manning, ed., *History of the Massachusetts Horticultural Society: 1829–1878* (Boston, 1880), 42, 255.

8. "Plan of land belonging to Col. T. H. Perkins, Esq., Brookline, Mass., from actual survey by E. C. Cabot," ca. 1849, Manuscript Collection, Boston Athenaeum. See also Alice G. B. Lockwood, ed., *Gardens of Colony and State* (New York: Charles Scribner's Sons, 1931), 42–45. According to R. B. Leuchars, Perkins's poultry house was built to resemble a Chinese pagoda; *Magazine of Horticulture* 16 (February 1850): 59.

9. Andrew Jackson Downing, *A Treatise on the Theory and Practice of Landscape Gardening*, 8th ed. (New York: Orange Judd, 1859), 38.

10. Ibid., 51

11. Andrew Jackson Downing, *Rural Essays* (New York, 1853; reprint, New York: Da Capo Press, 1974), 110–18.

12. R. B. Leuchars, "Notes on Gardens and Gardening in the Neighborhood of Boston," *Magazine of Horticulture* 16 (February 1850): 50.

13. John Claudius Loudon, *The Landscape Gardening and Landscape Architecture of the Late Humphry Repton, Esq.* (London: Longman & Co., 1840), 87, 91, 183, 208, 464, 531.

14. Landscape architect Charles Eliot later criticized this drive, writing that since its destination was revealed at the outset, it had better have been straight; "Some Old American Country Seats," *Garden and Forest* 2 (10 July 1889): 326.

15. Ibid.

16. *Magazine of Horticulture* 10 (1844): 244.

17. Massachusetts Horticultural Society *Transactions* (1829–65). See also Manning, *History*.

18. Downing, *Rural Essays*, 33.

19. Manning, *History*, 93.

20. Massachusetts Horticultural Society *Transactions* (1829–38), Article 3 of the bylaws.

21. Ibid., 23.

22. Ibid. (1843–46): 86.

23. Ibid., 159.

24. Manning, *History*, 256.

25. Ibid., 52. The successes of Evers's nursery are recorded in Massachusetts Horticultural Society *Transactions* (1857–1863).

26. Curtis, *Memories of Fifty Years*, 12.

27. Henrietta M. Larson, "A China Trader Turns Investor," *Harvard Business Review* 12 (April 1934): 345–58.

28. Middlesex County Deeds, 985:35.

29. *Belmont, Massachusetts: Architecture and Development*, 10, 31.

Chapter 6

Boxwood and Bunting

Henry Bowen's Roseland,

Woodstock, Connecticut

" AS ONE APPROACHED the house, the park in front of Roseland Cottage and the entire lawn appeared to be a mass of light with the Japanese lanterns of every conceivable shape hanging from the trees and every object that would support them, and colored lanterns supported upon sticks intermingled with them."[1]

In 1887 a local paper described Henry Chandler Bowen's garden in Woodstock, Connecticut, at the height of its glory, his annual Fourth of July fete. Each year for twenty-five years, from 1870 to 1895, Bowen invited the great and the near-great to celebrate the national holiday in his small Connecticut hometown. More often than not his invitations were accepted. On five occasions he succeeded in attracting a United States president, two of them during their terms of office. President Grant came in 1870 and ex-President Rutherford B. Hayes in 1883. Senator Benjamin Harrison made an appearance in 1887, returning two years later as president and planting a tree on the Roseland lawn as a memento. William McKinley, soon to be president, attended the gala event in 1891.

The grounds of Bowen's Gothic Revival Roseland Cottage were planted, raked, clipped, and weeded to perfection for the two or three hundred guests who strolled the winding, tree-shaded walks at dusk on the eve of July Fourth. The strains of Strauss waltzes by Mose's Orchestra drifted out from the conservatory. As darkness fell, the pink roses and foxgloves lost their color, and creamy spires of yucca and white madonna lilies gleamed in the dusk. The sharp scent of boxwood assailed those who brushed against it along the narrow gravel paths of the parterre garden. On the verandas, guests sipped lemonade—nothing stronger—and nibbled ladyfingers and homegrown strawberries. The fragrance of late roses was temporarily overwhelmed by the whiff of sulfur, as hundreds of colored paper candle lanterns were lit. The grounds were magically transformed into a "scene of brightness . . . an enchanted scene," according to a *New York Times* reporter.[2] In contrast to this elegant evening reception, the next day's public celebration—also organized by Bowen—, with a mile-long parade, orations, and fireworks, attended by thousands, was hot, noisy, and exhausting.

An upper corner of the barn at Roseland is crammed now with Japanese lanterns, lanterns on stakes, paper parasols, huge banners proclaiming "Roseland Park," and faded signs for "carriage parking." There are flags of the states, tiny American flags on sticks, enormous flag banners, and yards of bunting. These memorabilia of Henry Bowen's sumptuous receptions and grandiose July Fourth commemorations have been stored since he died in 1896, hoping to the last that "proper celebrations" would be continued.

. . .

Bowen's summer house in Woodstock and the landscape he shaped over a century ago survive to show what manner of a man he was. The pattern of his elaborate geometrical flower garden has survived since 1850. The garden quite appropriately still attains its blooming zenith by July Fourth, when the old roses open, and continues until the first frosts.

Henry Bowen zealously pursued a circular trail during his life, first breaking away and then gradually moving ever closer to his ancestral roots. Born in Woodstock in 1813, Bowen left his hometown and a job in his father's store when he was twenty-one, heading for greener fields of commerce in New York City. He made money as a silk merchant, dealing in fabric and threads, and made a name for himself as the founder of an influential antislavery weekly, *The Independent*. In 1844 he married Lucy Tappan, whose father was also an outspoken opponent of slavery. After ten years in the city, Bowen returned to Woodstock with his bride to establish a summer residence. He bought land across the town common from his ancestral home, built a house, and began to develop the grounds of his new country estate. Although Bowen never intended his Woodstock menage to be more than a summer retreat, his commitment to the town was energetic. He flung himself and his fortune into civic and cultural improvements that would enhance the rural image of his town. His enthusiasm lasted for the rest of his life.

When Bowen commissioned Joseph Wells, an architect who specialized in Gothic Revival churches, to design his house in Woodstock, he knew what he wanted and what to expect. The house has churchly compo-

Roseland Cottage, Woodstock, Connecticut, from the tree-shaded entrance drive; stereograph, 1860s. The lattice fence, left, encloses the flower garden. A gardener stands at the front entrance to the house. (Society for the Preservation of New England Antiquities)

nents, particularly the stained glass in the conservatory windows. The color of its board and batten siding, however, gives the house a singularly unecclesiastical look. According to local legend and recent paint analysis, the house has always been painted a vivid pink. In 1883 a *New York Times* reporter, describing Bowen's "comfortable mansion," wrote, "Mr. Bowen, keeping just a little ahead of his neighbors, has painted it a brilliant crushed strawberry."[3] Considering the name he gave to his place, Bowen himself may have thought of the color as rose pink. He loved roses.

Wells designed not only the house but the barn, "ten-pin alley," privy, ice house, wood house, and the fence along the road. The wooden fence was ornamented with the same quatrefoil design used on the ve-

Henry Bowen's flower garden was adjacent to his pink Gothic Revival cottage in Woodstock, Connecticut. The bowling alley is at the left. (Photo by Felice Frankel)

randas of the house. All the work was done in 1846–47 by local contractors.[4] The bowling alley is one of the earliest private, indoor facilities. In 1870, President Grant rolled a ten-strike there with his first ball. Immediately afterward he went outside, at the request of his antismoking host, to light up a cigar.[5]

· · ·

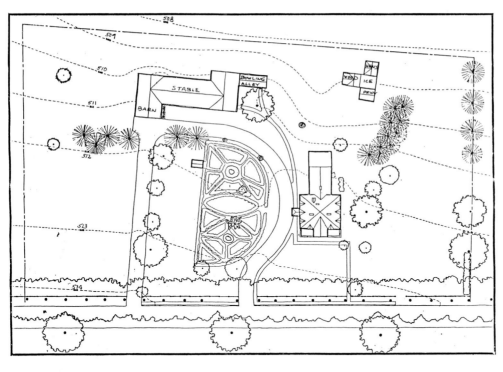

Plan of Roseland. The elaborate boxwood parterre has survived since 1850. (Drawn by Stan Clauson, Harvard Graduate School of Design, 1978)

Bowen started planting trees on his property even before the house was built.[6] In 1847 he placed the first of several orders with Henry A. Dyer, a landscape gardener and proprietor of Raspberry Hill Nursery in the nearby town of Brooklyn, Connecticut. In his enthusiasm, Bowen bought some of everything advertised by the nursery in *The Homestead*, a Connecticut farmers' weekly of which Dyer was an editor. Trees supplied by Dyer included Scotch larches, tulip trees, willows, and fir trees. Bowen's dream of establishing an idyllic rural life in his native town included the growing of fruit, for he developed his orchard with an ardor that never abated. He raised apples, peaches, cherries, pears, plums, nectarines, and quinces, as well as grapes and currants.

Practical advice on how to grow fruit and which varieties to select was not hard to come by in the late 1840s. Andrew Jackson Downing, already well known for his popular writings on home landscapes and architecture, published *Fruits and Fruit Trees of America* in 1845. Patrick Barry, whose Rochester, New York, nursery was nationally famous, also wrote a book on fruit culture. In 1849, George Jaques of Worcester, Massachusetts, published *A Practical Treatise on the Management of Fruit Trees Adapted to the Interior of New England*. Worcester is not far from Woodstock and has a comparable climate.

Many of the fruit varieties Bowen chose received Jaques's blessing.[7] The apple names are pure poetry: Honey Greening, Ramsdale Sweeting, and Gloria Mundi. Bowen raised yellow-, green-, and blue-gage plums and cherries called White Heart and Black Eagle. His peaches were particularly successful. He grew Red Rareripe, French Mignonne, and George the Fourth, among others. Bowen's wife Lucy sent some to her sister, saying, "They will taste better, perhaps, coming from here."[8] Many years later, after Bowen died, one friend had a favorite memory of Bowen contentedly eating his own peaches with cream from his own dairy.[9]

In 1848, Bowen ordered two dozen shrubs from the famous old Parsons Nursery of Flushing, Long Island. A note on the sales slip reads: "The above are all of the choicest kinds of flowering shrubbery and I hope [gardener's name?] will show much taste in setting them out and taking care of them. Those marked with X go in front of the house around grass plot near walk and front fence. Others go around garden fence outside."[10]

Henry A. Dyer supervised the work at Woodstock and continued to furnish trees and plants. Starting in 1850, he supplied bulbs, perennials, and shrubs, including hundreds of arborvitae, and—most significantly in terms of design—six hundred yards of dwarf boxwood

The parterre garden at Roseland, ca. 1890s. (Society for the Preservation of New England Antiquities)

edging.[11] Dyer used the box edging to outline the twenty tiny beds comprising the semicircular flower garden he laid out adjacent to Roseland Cottage. The garden, which covers an area considerably larger than the house, was enclosed by a lattice fence that afforded protection for the boxwood. The flower beds are laid out geometrically. The definition of the word "parterre" describes the Bowen garden: an ornamental arrangement of beds divided by paths. Although no early plans have survived, tradition, a few old photographs, and the box edging itself—still six hundred yards—testify that this may be the oldest surviving boxwood parterre in New England.

"Here all is gay and smiling. Bright parterres of brilliant flowers bask in the full daylight."[12] Bowen's flowers, inevitably, have not survived. He made changes continually, as all gardeners do. Sales receipts indicate many of the plants he used. Most of the bulbs and perennials were suggested by a well-known seed dealer and nurseryman of the day, Joseph Breck, in his popular 1851 book, *The Flower-Garden*.[13] Breck described some of the plants Bowen purchased as charming but old-fashioned: pheasant-eyed pinks (*Dianthus plumarius*), Canterbury bells, sweet william, and madonna lilies. Bowen grew Turk's-cap and "wilding" lilies (*Lilium su-*

perbum and *L. canadensis*), which Breck recommended highly. Bowen tried at least one new plant, the dahlia. Dahlias are native to Mexico, and Breck, for one, wished they had stayed there. Not only are dahlias ugly, wrote Breck, but "you could not catch an old rat even to smell of them the second time."[14]

The names of the roses at Roseland are as lost as their petals and their fragrance. From the literary rose fanciers of Bowen's day, we know which ones he may have grown. Two important American rose manuals were published in the 1840s. Robert Buist, a Philadelphia seed and plant dealer, imported from England and France many of the roses he introduced to his readers and customers in the United States. Nurseryman

Overleaf: Hollyhocks and geraniums in the garden at Roseland; boxwood edging has defined the pattern of the flower beds ever since 1850. The barn and stable, ornamented with a Gothic bargeboard, predate the summerhouse. (Photo by Peter Margonelli)

William Robert Prince included in his book a catalog offering 1,630 different roses for sale. Of the astounding number of roses Bowen had to choose from, many are no longer extant, but others—arguably the best—are still available from specialized nurseries.

The rose has been cultivated and admired since time began. Its fragile blossoms and fleeting fragrance lasted but one June week at best. Gardeners of old had dreamed of a rose that would bloom and bloom again "from the dawn of spring to the frosts of winter."[15] By the middle of the nineteenth century the ancient dream was apparently coming true. New rose varieties, readily available, tempted and tantalized gardeners with the promise of "perpetual" flowering. Nurserymen simply stopped growing many older roses as hybridizers developed supposedly superior varieties, irresistible chiefly by being new. Obviously, many roses were entirely lost by this continuous replacement process.

The new China and Noisette roses were not hardy enough for northern Connecticut, but the Bourbons, imported from France and widely hybridized, proved tougher. With luck and plenty of winter cover, Bowen may have succeeded with one of Andrew Jackson Downing's favorite Bourbons, Souvenir de la Malmaison, a rose of "pale incarnate hue . . . delicate blush with a hint of cream," miraculously still grown.[16] Better than the Bourbons for hardiness and recurrent bloom were the hybrid perpetuals, a new tribe in the 1840s and 1850s. Baronne Prevost, with clear pink flowers of the old flat shape, came on the market in 1842 and may still be growing at Roseland. Others that Bowen may have had are Stanwell Perpetual, with its "large double pale blush flowers of exquisite fragrance," and General Jacqueminot, whose brilliant crimson made it for years the standard by which red roses were judged.[17]

Bowen probably grew moss roses, too, with their delicate downy charm: the old pinks, the new blush-tinged whites, and Crested Moss, all still in commerce. He surely had a tall shrub of Maiden's Blush, the ancient *alba* with its blue-green leaves, and Madame Hardy, of Damask ancestry, whose white flowers have a clear green eye. Bowen probably had Harison's Yellow, too, a big shrub rose of brief early bloom, the first good yellow.

Climbing roses were deemed a garden essential, but few were reliably hardy. Elegans, a purplish-crimson Boursault rose, and the Michigan rose, Queen of the Prairies, with a white stripe along each pink petal, were two climbers recommended by Downing for northern gardeners.[18] Climbing roses covered the trelliswork archway that linked Bowen's garden to the house.

Edward Sayers, in *The American Flower Garden Companion* (1838), recommended placing pillar or standard roses at the centers of beds of low-growing flowers. Downing concurred; roses grown this way would give a "wonderfully brilliant" effect when in bloom. A famous dark crimson rose of 1830, Rivers's George the Fourth, was one of Downing's favorite standards. Susan Fenimore Cooper, daughter of the well-known novelist and herself the author of an 1851 book of rural nostalgia, took an opposite tack. She could not abide the fad for perverting the natural character of the rose by trying to turn it into a shockingly naked little tree: "this stripping the modest rose of her foliage. . . . One could sooner forgive the clipping of a yew-tree into a peacock, according to the quaint fancy of our forefathers."[19] Bowen, traditionalist though he was, probably tried a few tree roses in his garden.

Henry Bowen's garden linked past and present, as all his ventures did. He was much influenced by Andrew Jackson Downing, who was issuing his precepts on landscape design at the time when Bowen was developing Roseland. Downing's talent lay in his ability to disseminate ideas; he did not originate all the theories he promulgated. His reputation is based on his advocacy of "an expressive, harmonious, and refined imitation" of nature, a blend of art and nature—the English landscape style adapted to the needs of middle-class American homeowners.[20] His specific recommendations for flower gardens are less familiar.

Downing did not entirely abandon what he called the ancient or geometric style of gardening. Indeed, he wrote, when a flower garden is adjacent to an "elegant villa," an architectural style is preferable.[21] The flower beds—circles, octagons, or arabesques—could be cut out of the smooth green turf made possible by the recent invention of mechanical lawn mowers. Alternatively, and more traditionally, the beds could be surrounded with "edgings of verdure," such as boxwood.[22]

Downing adapted several geometric flower garden plans from J. C. Loudon, the popular English garden writer. Each bed was to be planted with a single sort of flower, Downing suggested, preferably those that would bloom all season long, to provide "the same pretty effect as a handsome and gay carpet."[23] In one garden he admired, "[t]he beds are surrounded by low edgings of turf or box, and the whole looks like some rich oriental pattern of carpet or embroidery."[24] It is

Bowen's granddaughter, Sylvia Holt, beside a rhododendron in full bloom at Roseland, 1901. Roses on a lattice arbor overarched the entrance to the garden. (Society for the Preservation of New England Antiquities)

refreshing to read of carpet bedding, which present-day gardeners are conditioned to despise, as an ideal of novelty and beauty. Perennials were not suitable for these gardens. Only annuals and ever-blooming roses could provide the desired mass of bright color all season long. Among Downing's choices were pink verbenas, purple petunias, scarlet geraniums, blue lobelia, and white alyssum.

Colorful parterres with traditional box edgings and gravel walks were so common at midcentury that garden writers scarcely mentioned them. Joseph Breck, in *The Flower Garden* (1856), stated unequivocally, "[N]othing makes so neat and trim an edging as box."[25] An 1859 article in *The Gardener's Monthly* suggested that box edgings may be easier to maintain than turf, and a letter writer described how he had clipped 2,400 feet of box—slightly more than Roseland had—in "less

than two days."[26] The Roseland parterre exemplified the standards of its day.

William Ranlett, a partner of Bowen's architect, Joseph Wells, compiled a book of plans for cottages and grounds in a variety of styles, ranging from "Rustic" to "Persian." His "English Cottage" scheme had all the landscape features of Roseland: the grounds laid out in imitation of nature, with curving walks and clumps of trees. Surely, wrote Ranlett, the mere sight of such a garden would elevate public taste and morals.[27] Its owner would be a public benefactor, a role that Bowen certainly fancied. Gervase Wheeler, another author-architect to offer advice on the laying out of grounds, disagreed with Ranlett as to the amount of privacy required for a stylish villa. Wheeler believed a villa should be retired from the public road, screened by shrubbery or a fence.[28] The curving drive and low fence at Roseland struck a balance between privacy and publicity. Both writers agreed on the desirability of having a *lawn*.

The original definition of a lawn was an open space or a glade among forest trees. Nowadays we might think of a lawn as an open stretch of turf maintained by fertilizers, pesticides, sprinklers, and unending hard labor. In the 1850s, however, lawns were hardly open at all. Until croquet became popular in the 1860s, the only uncluttered area was the "bleaching lawn," where clean laundry was whitened by the sun. All other lawn areas were dotted with trees and shrubs. Edward Kemp, an English landscape gardener whose 1860 book purported to advocate simplicity, spoke for others when he wrote, "The general lawn would, of course, be clothed with masses of shrubs and specimen plants with a few flower beds."[29] The impropriety of an *unclothed* lawn would not have appealed to Henry Bowen.

The shrubs on the Roseland lawns were placed so that their flowers could be sniffed and admired from the curving walks. Bowen planted many shrubs that had been grown in the United States since colonial times, including althaea, or Rose of Sharon (*Hibiscus syriacus*); *Daphne mezereum;* sweet shrub, or Carolina allspice (*Calycanthus floridus*); and double-flowering almond (*Prunus glandulosa 'Alboplena'*). Bush honeysuckles (*Lonicera tartarica*) lined the garden fence. Along the front walk were pink and white tree peonies. The 1844 Prince nursery catalog offered forty-two varieties of that majestic plant first imported from China not long before. The number of shrubs available to American and European gardeners exploded in the second half of the century, as plant explorers introduced from Asia such eventual standbys as forsythia, weigela, and a host of rhododendrons. The Roseland garden would in time include the finest of the new, just what Bowen always wanted.

Vines, wrote Downing, "express domesticity and the presence of heart."[30] In addition to grapes and climbing roses, Bowen planted the purple or Chinese wisteria that grows there still. The garden house—a tiny wooden Greek temple—is draped with the akebia that may have been there a century ago.

Bowen kept records of his garden and farm expenses at Woodstock: plants, tools, wheelbarrows, lawn mowers, croquet sets, and a hammock. For fertilizer he purchased bone meal and phosphate, as well as guano imported from certain "bird islands" off the coast of South America. Peruvian guano in particular was said to work miracles in the garden. Bowen had a greenhouse. He raised cattle, pigs, prize horses, and hens. To the rear of his combination woodshed, ice house, and privy, he added the latest in poultry houses. As Downing advised, the hens had generous south-facing windows, good cross ventilation, and a dovecote above.[31]

. . .

Bowen's house and garden express the same mixture of the conservative and the avant-garde that characterized his entire life. His patriotism and his strong attachment to home, family, and his small-town roots were expressed in some ways that were startlingly new. The newly revived Gothic style, exemplified at Roseland, was hailed by writers at that time as more natural and homelike than the prevailing Greek Revival architecture with its "cold, long-legged columns holding up a useless pediment."[32] In *Rural Homes* (1853), Gervase Wheeler dismissed most existing houses as "white boxes" and praised the "common sense" Gothic with its verandas and asymmetrical bay windows.[33]

Gothic architecture was fashionable, but at the same time historic and conservative, a winning combination as far as Bowen was concerned. As a faithful Protestant churchgoer, he approved of the religious tone of the Gothic style. It was also, he felt, an *honest* style in its use of materials, unlike the wooden Greek Revival structures that attempted to imitate stone. Furthermore, good taste was held to be intimately linked to Christian morality.[34] Promoting beauty helps to spread Christianity, wrote William Ranlett, thus justifying Bowen's efforts to improve his town as well as his own homesite.

In his life, Henry Bowen both exemplified and promoted the concept of "home" as an attainable ideal. The very word itself, with all the peripheral images and connotations that gradually attached to it, became an important totem during the second half of the nineteenth century in America. For Bowen, home was more than simply where one lived. It meant house, hearth, family, morals, grounds, garden, and roots—ancestral as well as arboreal. It included church, community, and country.

Many popular writers of Bowen's day dwelt on the fundamental importance of home. "A perfect home [is] the apotheosis of love," wrote George William Curtis in 1853 in his introduction to Andrew Jackson Downing's *Rural Essays.*[35] A perfect home was a moral home; morality could best flourish in settings of "good taste." Downing was the most influential arbiter of just what that taste was. His books—best-sellers for years—taught people how to make an ideal family home.

Downing gave voice to Bowen's conviction that the proper setting for the ideal home was in or near a small town. Economic and social changes were affecting New

England well before the Civil War. The truth was that now most fortunes and even livelihoods were made in cities or in the expanding mill towns. Rural areas and villages were losing population. Like Bowen, however, the bright and ambitious young who left the countryside often continued to yearn for the homes of their childhoods. Their native villages were idealized with halos of sentiment. Currier & Ives engravings of impossibly idyllic homesteads played on this nostalgia. Writers such as Susan Fenimore Cooper (an exact contemporary of Bowen's) romanticized country life and old customs. In 1855, in its first issue, the Connecticut farmers' journal edited by Henry A. Dyer, the nurseryman who planned and planted Bowen's grounds, extolled the significance embodied in the word chosen as the title of the new publication: "The Homestead! What son of the farm, whether still upon its soil, or struggling for wealth in the fierce competition of the city, or battling with the waves for his bread, has not the dear old spot enshrined in his heart, a place of nightly pilgrimage in dreams for life?"[36]

Not everyone, of course, had that paternal home that drew them back. Charles Eliot Norton, for example, editor of the *North American Review* and a distinguished scholar and art historian at Harvard, and his friend, *Harper's* editor George William Curtis, each bought an old house on a farm that adjoined the other's, near the little western Massachusetts town of Ashfield in 1865. Neither of them had roots there. Norton, a believer in the value of small-town community life, had simply driven around in search of a pleasant village in the hills.[37] He stayed in Ashfield for forty-four years. Like Bowen in Woodstock, the Nortons and the Curtises attached themselves to the town they had chosen and worked actively to improve it. Others, like dilettante Ogden Codman Sr. in Lincoln and poet William Cullen Bryant in Cummington, Massachusetts, repurchased family farms that had been sold years earlier. Bryant had lived and worked in New York City for forty years before he was financially able to regain the homestead for which he had apparently been pining.

The new owners of country places were alike in that all were tied economically and intellectually to the city. They spent only summers or vacations in their rural homes. Often referred to by the natives as "city folks," these newcomers depended on the railroad for transportation to and from their urban bases. Henry Bowen had to encourage the Norwich and Worcester Railroad to extend its line toward Woodstock—but not actually quite *into* Woodstock. The town of Putnam, five miles away, was convenient but sufficiently remote to avoid disrupting Woodstock's bucolic peace and quiet. Downing, referring to estates along the Hudson, had noted that "*accessible* perfect seclusion" was "one of the most captivating features in the life of the country gentleman."[38]

To Bowen and others like him who were putting down rural roots, their grounds and gardens were as sacred as the family hearth. "To the home of your youth you may return with gathered wealth to replant it with with flowers." Thus expounded Bowen's close associate, the preacher and editor Henry Ward Beecher.[39] In a treatise on gardening and agriculture, Beecher offered practical advice, but his real purpose was to promote public and private virtue. He and Bowen shared Downing's conviction that handsome houses in beautiful landscapes strengthened the family and developed better citizens.

In his novel *Norwood, or Village Life in New England*, Beecher extolled the virtues of planting trees, not only on home grounds but along town roads. If townspeople worked together to plant trees, he wrote, "New England might be made a magnificent park."[40] Voicing the typically Victorian obsession with nudity, Beecher claimed that "an unclothed road would become a reproach." Another writer rejoiced that the "taste for nakedness is passing away" as he saw people beginning to plant trees around their homes.[41] Ancient forests had been cut down inexorably for decades to create farmland and to provide fuel and timber. At midcentury the landscape of New England was still far more open than it has ever been since. To thoughtful people, especially "city" people like Bowen, trees took on a mythic significance for their beauty and the sense of permanence they engendered. No longer viewed primarily as obstacles to farming, trees became symbols of civic morality. Books, articles, and nurserymen advised people on what trees to plant and how. In 1853 an energetic Miss Hopkins organized a group of Stockbridge, Massachusetts, residents to make their town more beautiful by planting trees. This was the first "village improvement society," the beginning of a movement that gradually swept the country and transformed the appearance of towns.[42] Only later did people begin to lament the loss of the open pastures and mowings.

Henry Bowen was in the vanguard of the community tree-planting mania, as he was in many matters of taste and civic improvement. An undated newspaper clipping in a scrapbook made by Bowen's son Clarence claimed that, even as a boy, Henry Bowen had voluntarily weeded and mowed the town common.[43] Among Henry Bowen's papers are an 1853 contract, warranty, and bill from a Brooklyn nurseryman for five hundred trees. A penciled notation by Bowen states, "This bill is for the first trees set out on Woodstock Common," indicating his justifiable pride in his gift to the town. The trees were all to be at least ten feet tall when delivered. Over half were to be evergreens; the deciduous species included elm, maple, larch, linden, tulip, and horse chestnut.[44] Bowen had a fence installed around the common and continued to provide maintenance. His house overlooked the common, which became almost an extension of his own grounds. The enormous number of trees and shrubs Bowen planted throughout the town enhanced the leafy rural landscape of Woodstock to accord with contemporary taste. Perhaps the enhancement of Bowen's patriarchal image was merely incidental.

In the 1870s, Bowen bought fifty-five wooded acres about a mile from his house, ostensibly to prevent the land from being clear-cut for timber. Bowen began by improving the land he had purchased to make it into a public park. He had fill hauled in by ox-drawn carts to make a level space by the pond. He ornamented the park with thousands of rosebushes and exotic trees, bronze fountains, cast-iron hounds and a stag, and fancy rusticated wooden gates. He provided facilities for concerts, picnicking, bathing, and boating. Roseland Park opened in celebration of the nation's centennial in 1876 and continues as a public park today.[45]

· · ·

Bowen made Woodstock famous. He attracted tourists and summer boarders to the town. The permanent population, however, declined steadily after 1850, thus preserving its quaint village quality. Bowen's wife died in 1863 after bearing their tenth child. Bowen married again. He and his second wife had one child, Bowen's eighth son. Henry Bowen's long life ended in 1896, when he was eighty-three. He left Roseland to his wife. Two sisters, granddaughters of Henry Bowen, were the last family members to live at Roseland. The Bowens continued to be a strong presence in Woodstock, with seven of the eight surviving children of Henry and Lucy Tappan Bowen continuing to summer in Woodstock in houses of their own. The Society for the Preservation of New England Antiquities purchased Roseland from the family in 1971. A gardener who had worked there for forty years stayed on.

Bowen was a complex man. Surely he was motivated in part by self-aggrandizement. How else can we account for the sheer gall of Bowen's annual invitations to the nation's political, judicial, religious, and literary leaders? He was entirely confident that they would come to his small town and to his house, as indeed they did. Who else would hang bunting from all the trees along several miles of road approaching his house? One wonders whether the pyrotechnic displays honored the country's birth more than they touted Bowen's worldly success.

Roseland Park, newly laid out and planted as a public park, the gift of Henry Bowen, ca. 1880. (Society for the Preservation of New England Antiquities)

The vine-draped summerhouse beside Roseland's parterre garden is a Greek temple in miniature. (Photo by Peter Margonelli)

Bowen's family and friends surround six honored guests on the piazza steps of Roseland Cottage during the Fourth of July celebration, probably in 1890, a year when the president did not attend. Henry C. Bowen, looking contented, stands at the center of the back row. (Society for the Preservation of New England Antiquities)

Only late-twentieth-century cynicism can doubt the sincerity of Bowen's idealism. His generosity and his patriotism were as deeply felt as his faith in the possibility of improving the human condition. His ardent commitment to eliminating the evil of slavery continued for thirty years. He publicly defended his principles even when his business suffered for it. He used his wealth to express his sentiments and to bring about lasting change. He intended to bring permanent improvements to his native town and to the lives of its citizens. Free concerts in the park would have the same ennobling value as the trees planted on the town common. The opportunities he provided to hear the great orators of the day were uplifting, but so was the privilege of walking among several hundred rosebushes in the park or gazing at them over the fence at Roseland.

At every July Fourth celebration, Bowen had his honored guests and members of the family assemble on the veranda steps at Roseland for a group photograph. Bowen himself is always in the back row. His narrow face, with full beard, strong nose, deep-set eyes, and bald crown, rises above his wing collar. His chin is lifted. He is smiling. Henry Bowen looks entirely satisfied with himself, his companions, and his setting.

Bowen's life nearly spanned his century. He was buried with his ancestors in the local cemetery, just across the common from Roseland. His grave is marked with the same simple, upright slab as his eighteenth-century forebears'. Henry Bowen is at home.

Notes

Roseland Cottage is regularly open to the public during the summer and early fall.

1. *Putnam (Connecticut) Patriot*, 8 July 1887.

2. *New York Times*, 12 July 1883.

3. Ibid.

4. 1846 ledger and contracts, boxes 1, 7, Bowen Papers, Society for the Preservation of New England Antiquities (SPNEA).

5. Clarence Winthrop Bowen, *History of Woodstock* (Norwood, Mass.: Plimpton Press, 1926), 1:479.

6. Ledger, 10 April 1845 and 13 May 1846, SPNEA.

7. George Jaques, *A Practical Treatise on the Management of Fruit Trees* (Worcester, Mass., 1849).

8. Lucy Tappan Bowen to Ellen Tappan, July 186?, scrapbook 7, Clarence W. Bowen Papers, American Antiquarian Society.

9. Undated clipping, obituary of Henry C. Bowen, scrapbook 11, Bowen Papers, American Antiquarian Society.

10. Parsons & Co. receipt, 18 April 1848, box 2:10, SPNEA.

11. Ledger, November 1850, box 1; receipt, 4 Nov. 1850, box 2:10, SPNEA.

12. Andrew Jackson Downing, *Horticulturist* 2 (October 1847): 157.

13. Joseph Breck, *The Flower-Garden* (Boston, 1851).

14. Ibid., 51.

15. Robert Buist, *The Rose Manual* (1844; reprint, New York: Earl M. Coleman, 1978), 88.

16. Andrew Jackson Downing, *Rural Essays* (New York, 1853), 8; Samuel B. Parsons, *The Rose: Its History, Poetry, Culture and Classification* (New York, 1856), 250; William Robert Prince, *Manual of Roses* (New York, 1846), 130. Roy E. Shepherd's *History of the Rose* (New York: Macmillan, 1954; reprint, New York: Earl M. Coleman, 1978) describes many roses and their introduction into commerce.

17. Buist, *Rose Manual*, 158.

18. Andrew Jackson Downing, *A Treatise on the Theory and Practice of Landscape Gardening*, 8th ed. (New York, 1859), 284.

19. [Susan Fenimore Cooper], *Rural Hours* (New York, 1859), 284.

20. Downing, *Treatise*, 51.

21. Ibid., 372–73; Andrew Jackson Downing, *Cottage Residences* (1842; reprint, Watkins Glen, N.Y.: American Life Foundation, 1967), 149; William W. Valk, "Design for a Geometric Flower Garden," *Horticulturist* 2 (May 1848), 558.

22. Downing, *Treatise*, 373; Downing, "Design for a Small Flower Garden," *Horticulturist* 2 (May 1848): 503.

23. Downing, *Cottage Residences*, 189, and similar proposals, 140, 180, 187; see also Downing, *Treatise*, 375.

24. Downing, *Horticulturist* 2 (October 1847): 157.

25. Breck, *Flower-Garden*, 22; Edward Sayers, *The American Flower Garden Companion* (Boston, 1838), 15, 145.

26. *Gardener's Monthly* 1 (May 1859):76, (October 1859): 154.

27. William H. Ranlett, *The Architect* (1849; reprint, New York: Da Capo, 1976), 1:3–4; 2:43.

28. Gervase Wheeler, *Rural Homes* (Auburn and Rochester, N.Y.: 1853), 70, 110.

29. Edward Kemp, *How to Lay Out a Garden* (New York, 1860), 24.

30. Andrew Jackson Downing, *The Architecture of Country Houses*, 9th ed. (1850; reprint, New York: Da Capo, 1968), 79.

31. Ibid., 237–39.

32. Henry Ward Beecher, *Star Papers or Experiences of Art and Nature* (New York, 1855), 291.

33. Wheeler, *Rural Homes*, chap. 6 and p. 289.

34. Ranlett, *The Architect*, 1:3.

35. Downing, *Rural Essays*, xxxiii.

36. *The Homestead: A Weekly Journal for the Farmer, Gardener and Fruit Grower, The Manufacturer and Mechanic Devoted to the Interests of Producers, on the Farm, in the Work-Shop and at the Fire-side* 1 (20 September 1855).

37. Frederick G. Howes, *History of the Town of Ashfield, Franklin County, Massachusetts* (Ashfield, Mass.: 1910), 377.

38. Downing, *Horticulturist* 2 (Oct. 1847), 153.

39. Beecher, *Star Papers*, 301, and *Pleasant Talk about Fruits, Flowers and Farming* (New York, 1859), 136.

40. Henry Ward Beecher, *Norwood, or Village Life in New England* (New York, 1868), 302–3.

41. *North American Review* 56 (January 1843): 6.

42. Sarah Cabot Sedgwick and Christina Sedgwick Marquand, *Stockbridge, 1739–1939* (Stockbridge, Mass.: Berkshire Courier, 1939), 243.

43. Scrapbook 6, Bowen Papers, American Antiquarian Society.

44. Contract and bill, 21 June and 1 November 1853, box 2:10, SPNEA.

45. Scrapbook 6, Bowen Papers, American Antiquarian Society.

Chapter 7

Family Trees

Wellesley, the Hunnewell Estate

THE YEAR is 1868. Horatio Hollis Hunne-well, planning for the future as always, makes a ceremony of planting a tree for his first grand-child. From his mother's arms, the four-month-old infant looks on, as do a dozen aunts, uncles, and great-aunts, while his grandfather plants a tiny evergreen, *Chamaecyparis pisifera 'Aurea'*, with a silver spoon and waters it with a glass of champagne.[1]

Beginning in 1844, even before he built the mansion house at Wellesley, his country estate near Boston, Mr. Hunnewell had each of his nine children plant a special tree, which was to be his or her own. From the begin-ning, trees were the most important feature of a garden that has flourished for almost a century and a half under the care of one family. In the absence of a tradition of primogeniture, the smooth transition of a family prop-erty through four generations is relatively rare in the United States. Considering changing tastes, shifting mores, and rising taxes, the survival of such a place as Wellesley seems improbable.

From the road a visitor sees the Hunnewell house at the far end of a wide lawn, with big trees picturesquely disposed along the edges of the grass. From the en-trance gate, past a gate lodge embowered in tall ever-greens, the drive curves toward the house, revealing just one aspect of this remarkably comprehensive estate. Only later does a visitor get to see the Italian garden, the lake, the pinetum, and the azalea garden. Also hid-den from the casual viewer are all the working elements of the Hunnewell place: the grape, peach, and orchid houses; the deep pits for storing tender azaleas in win-ter; the vegetable gardens.

The house was built in 1851. Adjoining it is the hip-roofed conservatory, once a separate building. In front of the house two trees stand out, even in this arboreal Eden. One of these turns out not to be a single tree af-ter all but a whole family, the rooted offspring of the trailing branches of a weeping beech, probably planted when the house was new. The original tree is long gone, leaving a circular domed temple, a baptistry of beech, formed by a tracery of interlaced gray trunks and branches. In autumn a veil of yellow leaves filters the sunlight from high overhead in this vast secluded space. One imagines the cycle continuing forever, a new circle of young trees forming around each existing beech, on and on ad infinitum. But this is enough, says Walter Hunnewell, the present owner, who trims the tips of the branches just enough to prevent their forming roots.

The great white oak that stands nearby is the oldest

Horatio Hollis Hunnewell's house, Wellesley, Massachusetts; sterograph, ca. 1870. The conservatory is on the right. (Society for the Preservation of New England Antiquities)

tree on the place. It was the *only* tree in the 1840s, when Hollis Hunnewell began to turn an "old dried-up pasture" into a garden.[2] The oak was thought then to have been standing a century or even two. Still healthy now and more regal than ever, this tree forms the backdrop for many of the framed family photographs covering the brown matchboarded walls of trunk rooms and former servants' bedrooms in the attic story of the house, behind the parapet. In these pictures, generations of young Hunnewells bend over croquet mallets, while their sisters, aunts, and mother sit perched and alert on twig chairs. Behind the women, the mustachioed menfolk are stationed, a protective rear guard. The great oak tree seems to shelter them all.

. . .

Hollis Hunnewell, born in 1810, was in low spirits when he had to start life anew at the age of thirty.[3] In 1840 he had just returned to Boston after fifteen years in Paris, where he had lived with his stylish Welles cousins and worked for Samuel Welles's banking firm. Hollis had married Isabella Welles, Samuel's niece, in 1835. He had hardly settled with his bride into their own Paris house when a swiftly gathering international financial crisis nearly wiped out the Welles bank. The young Hunnewells had no option but to go home to Boston, heartsick over leaving France.

Hollis Hunnewell did not mope for long. From real estate and banking he "drifted into railroads," as he put it, a fairly sure route to riches in those days. He became a director of the Old Colony Railroad, the Illinois Central, and many others. Very soon he built a house for himself and his family on the desirable water side of Beacon Street in the new Back Bay section of Boston. A country estate was an essential adjunct to the life of a Bostonian of his status. In 1843, just three years after their return from France, he and his wife began spending the summers in Natick, a few miles from the city, on part of the old Welles farm, Isabella's inheritance. Hollis Hunnewell plunged into rural life. He planned, planted, expanded, and improved the property, never stopping until he died in 1902 at ninety-two.

The estate, often referred to as "the Hunnewell place" or "the Hunnewell arboretum," does have a name. "We seldom use the name now," explains Walter

Hunnewell, "since both the college and the town are called by it." Wellesley, the name chosen for his estate by Hollis Hunnewell in honor of his wife's family, has also been the name of the college since its founding in 1875 by Mr. Hunnewell's cousin and neighbor, Henry F. Durant. The town took the name in 1881 as a tribute to Mr. Hunnewell, its chief benefactor.

Both Wellesley College and the Hunnewell place overlook lovely Lake Waban, the principal advantage of the site when Hollis and Isabella acquired it. With natural aptitude and aplomb, Mr. Hunnewell himself laid out the grounds of his country house. As an amateur landscape designer working to enhance his own property, Mr. Hunnewell was already something of an anomaly among wealthy Americans.

From the beginning, Hollis Hunnewell wanted his estate to epitomize contemporary fashion. He was inspired in part by the formality and eclectic internationalism of some elaborate new gardens in England, many of them laid out by landscape gardener William Andrews Nesfield (1793–1881), often in collaboration with the prominent architect Sir Charles Barry. Mr. Hunnewell owned a copy of E. Adveno Brooke's outsize 1857 book *The Gardens of England*, which depicted in glowing color nineteen of the most splendid early Victorian gardens.

The history of gardening has seen a continual swing of the pendulum between the claims of art and the emphasis on nature. The eighteenth-century English landscape park represented one extreme of apparent naturalism, with the manor house set amid acres of open pasture from which all elements of regularity and structure had been banished. The widespread popularity of the ha-ha as a hidden device to prevent the livestock from actually peering in at the drawing room windows symbolized the extent to which landowners were seeking to eliminate all signs of human intervention, even one as traditional as a fence. Humphry Repton and his follower John Claudius Loudon had argued successfully for the return of ornament and art to the immediate surroundings of the house. By the 1840s, England was entering what has been called "the heroic age of gardening."[4] Nature, no longer particularly revered, was now considered as merely the canvas upon which human genius could work wonders of artifice.

The new English gardens of the 1840s and 1850s were indeed amazing creations, filled with fountains and sculpture and displaying remarkable feats of horticultural virtuosity. Many of these gardens featured parterres composed of rococo scrolls of clipped boxwood and an infill of colored gravel. Nesfield, their designer, became famous for these. His midcentury design for Eaton Park included topiary *W*'s in honor of the owner, the marquis of Westminster. Brilliantly colored annual flowers, including yellow calceolarias and purple verbenas, filled in the pattern.[5] Parterres such as this drew their inspiration from French designs of an earlier century.

Still other sections of these large gardens invoked different national models. Biddulph Grange in Staffordshire, for example, had an Egyptian court and a Chinese garden, replete with a miniature Great Wall.[6] At Elvaston Castle there was an Alhambra garden. Nearly every grand English estate came to include an Italian garden; indeed, as Brent Elliott noted, the term "gradually became an umbrella label for the revivalist styles."[7] These so-called Italian gardens were characterized by their use of terracing, balustrades, statuary, and clipped evergreens.

English formal revival gardens inspired few imitations in the United States. At that time the gospel according to Andrew Jackson Downing continued to reign supreme. In Downing's view, "it was only after the superior interest of a more natural manner was enforced by men of genius, that natural beauty of expression was recognized, and Landscape Gardening was raised to the rank of a fine art."[8] Downing's efforts to popularize modest translations of the eighteenth-century English landscape park as suitable home grounds for average Americans were strikingly successful. The so-called natural style prevailed throughout most of the nineteenth century. André Parmentier, a French landscape designer who emigrated to this country in 1824, gave an informal character to the grounds of a number of New York estates much admired by Downing.[9] Downing's successors, including Jacob Wiedenmann, Frank J. Scott, and Frederick Law Olmsted, all advocated designs supposedly based on nature, as exemplified in countless rural cemeteries, urban parks, and private estates all across the country. Geometric parterres such as Henry Bowen's at Roseland stood out in otherwise naturalistic gardens.

Hollis Hunnewell may have been the first American to follow English prototypes in reviving the formal garden. His Italian garden at Wellesley, the subject of many articles and admired by hundreds of visitors, was never copied; it remained a phenomenon rather than a model.

Italian Garden and Lake at Wellesley near Boston, ca. 1850, drawn by James D. Smillie for A. J. Downing's *A Treatise on the Theory and Practice of Landscape Gardening*, 8th ed., 1859. (Frances Loeb Library, Harvard University)

Hunnewell began to build his Italian garden in 1854 on the steep bluff below the house. He shaped a series of terraces—six, eventually—with a flight of seventy steps descending to the edge of the lake. On the terraces he planted evergreen trees, which were closely clipped into geometric shapes. Writing later about the Italian garden, Mr. Hunnewell made it seem the inevitable solution to a landscaping problem. The slope was too steep for flowers, he said, and unpruned trees would soon have hidden the lake from view. He attributed his inspiration to the gardens of Elvaston Castle in Derbyshire, an unexpected analogy since the grounds there were entirely flat.[10] The owner of Elvaston, the reclusive earl of Harrington, had shown his place to almost no one for two decades while his head gardener, William Barron, labored to create a topiary tour de force of unparalleled exuberance. Only at the earl's death in 1851 was the public allowed to view the wonders Barron had wrought.[11]

Topiary—the art of clipping trees into predetermined shapes—had been out of fashion in England since the seventeenth century. In the 1850s, with the opening of Elvaston, the ancient art underwent a resurgence of popularity. Hunnewell, in patterning his horticultural exploits after those so freshly revealed at Elvaston, was quick at the starting line. He helped to rescue the art of topiary from a century of scorn and ridicule. In shaping his trees, Hunnewell followed the prevailing preference for the severe geometry of cones, spheres, or pyramids rather than the representations of birds and animals that had been popular in an earlier time.

In Hunnewell's Italian garden, nature was firmly restrained in favor of artifice.

Sarah Parker Rice Goodwin, an avid gardener from Portsmouth whose husband was governor of New Hampshire, visited Wellesley when Hollis Hunnewell's garden was still new: "the most tasteful private grounds I have ever seen," she wrote; "everything that could delight the eye was there."[12] She admired the terraces. the steps, the balustrade along the water's edge. "On the balustrade, at short intervals, were Italian vases and the terraces were adorned with small evergreens and flowers embedded in the emerald grass." Many of the "small evergreens"—no longer small—are still there.

The terraces in the Italian garden once held as many as 250 trees. When English and Irish yews did not prove hardy, Mr. Hunnewell and his head gardener developed their own crosses with tougher yews from Japan. They sheared larch, hemlock, arborvitae, and other trees into shapes that looked as smooth as marble. The Hunnewells may have been the first to clip the native white pine.[13] The pines are now the tallest and most striking of the trees, with fat horizontal disks of soft, glaucous green foliage encircling their trunks. Five men used to spend two months each year on long hand-held ladders clipping the trees. Nowadays, with a rented cherry picker and all the family pitching in, the job is done in a week.

After visiting the villa gardens at Lakes Como and Maggiore in 1864, Hollis Hunnewell imported a gondola—and a gondolier—from Italy. A photograph in the house shows this unexpected craft emerging from a

Geometric topiary in Hunnewell's Italian garden; stereograph, ca. 1870. (Society for the Preservation of New England Antiquities)

The boathouse was built in 1865 to house an Italian gondola; stereograph, 1872. (Society for the Preservation of New England Antiquities)

boathouse below the garden. When the gondolier propelled the boat with reclining passengers around the pond, perhaps even singing as he did so, Lake Waban took on a distinctly Italian character. The lakeside scene at Wellesley, however, was probably inspired principally by Trentham, in Staffordshire, where Sir Charles Barry had just completed an Italian garden for the duke of Sutherland. One of the plates in Brooke's laudatory book on the formal gardens of England por-

trayed the romantic lake shore at Trentham with a gondola prominently featured.[14]

In accordance with the eclecticism so prevalent in English gardens of the day, Hunnewell invoked the spirit of France in another portion of his grounds. In an 1855 article in the *Magazine of Horticulture* on Mr. Hunnewell's new country seat, Charles Mason Hovey, a local nurseryman and writer, described the French-style parterre immediately behind the house: "an architectural flower garden, of the same width as the building, laid out very neatly, with all the beds edged with iron basket work, and gay with the finest roses, verbenas, fuchsias, &c."[15] The rustic teahouse with its stained glass reminded Hovey of those he had seen in England: "The design is by Mr. Hunnewell, and is executed with

The rustic twig teahouse designed by Horatio Hollis Hunnewell; stereograph, ca. 1885. Some of the windows were of stained glass. (Society for the Preservation of New England Antiquities)

larch and cedar poles. It is octagonal, with a projecting roof and rustic posts, over which climb roses, honeysuckles, woodbine, &c. The panelling of the interior is finely executed, and the windows, of different colored panes of glass, afford some of the finest views, both of the water and lawn front, in all the varied hues of purple, gold, and crimson. In front is a small grotto, from which gushes a fountain of crystal water."

The Hunnewell garden leapt to national prominence in 1859, when Henry Winthrop Sargent cited it as a model country place in a new edition of Downing's popular *Treatise on the Theory and Practice of Landscape Gardening.* Sargent (1810–1882) was a first cousin of Hunnewell's wife, Isabella. He gardened at Wodenethe, his estate on the Hudson River at Fishkill Landing. Hollis Hunnewell and Sargent exchanged horticultural advice as well as nursery stock in frequent visits to each other's places. In the course of enumerating all that Hunnewell had accomplished in only seven years to transform a "flat, sandy, arid plain" at Wellesley, Sar-

gent described the amazing Italian garden: "The effect, especially by moonlight, of the lake seen through the balustrades of the parapet, and among the vases and statues which surmount it—with the splashing of the fountain, and the very unique features, at least in this country, of the formally clipped trees and topiary work, quite lead us to suppose we are on the lake of Como."[16]

The fountains at Wellesley were fed with water pumped from the pond by a steam engine that Hunnewell installed in 1854. Innovative technology played an important role in making and keeping the gardens the way he wanted them. He was pleased with the appearance of the great lawn in front of the house, for example, after it had been mowed with a new "Swift's lawn-mower" in 1854. Hunnewell built twelve glasshouses between 1851 and 1885, each one designed for a specific purpose. There were peach houses, graperies, a palm house, a stove house for tropical plants, and a cool greenhouse for oranges. These structures were constantly undergoing enlargement or renovation or being fitted with new boilers. The underground pits to keep the Indian azaleas through the winter were often modified, too.

Hollis Hunnewell's favorite section of his grounds, as the years went by, was his pinetum. He had begun importing trees from England by the hundred even before he built his house. Before long he was focusing most of his attention on cone-bearing evergreen trees. In one area of the Wellesley estate are two steep ridges known as eskers, left behind by the last glacier. The eskers form a narrow curving vale, the banks of which proved ideal for Mr. Hunnewell's pinetum. His aim, he noted in his diary in 1867, was to collect and plant every conifer, native and foreign, that could survive the cold New England winters. He obtained trees from all over the world, keeping careful records of his plantings and how they fared, in his search for hardy strains. Some of the trees now in the pinetum may be the oldest of their kind in the United States.

Pinetums had found favor in England by the 1850s and soon thereafter in the United States. Their popularity was a response to the challenge of utilizing and propagating the vast number of tree and shrub varieties that had been newly introduced into cultivation. While plant explorers like David Douglas, best known today for the Douglas fir (*Pseudotsuga menziesii*), were combing remote mountain ranges for unknown rarities, the owners of country estates were setting aside areas in which to try out new trees. In England the exotic imported trees at first were planted in straight avenues. Soon, however, it became apparent that a systematic arrangement was more useful educationally and that an informal planting scheme was better suited to a varied collection. The pinetums at Bowood and Chatsworth set precedents in this regard.[17]

Mr. Hunnewell worked closely with the leading botanists and dendrologists of his day. Before Harvard's Arnold Arboretum was established in 1872, Hunnewell had one of the most comprehensive collection of coniferous trees in the United States. Charles Sprague Sargent (1841–1927), the first director of the arboretum, learned from Mr. Hunnewell's experiments. Hunnewell respected and liked young Professor Sargent. Together they pooled their knowledge of trees and cooperated on experimental plantings for many years, establishing a bond between the Hunnewell family and the arboretum that persists to this day. Sargent incorporated information based on Hunnewell's experiments in his seminal fourteen-volume *Silva of North America* (1891–1902).

Horatio Hollis Hunnewell (1810–1902). (Photographic Archives of the Arnold Arboretum of Harvard University)

Hollis Hunnewell liked rhododendrons. As he put it, one could no more have too many rhododendrons than too many diamonds.[18] In the 1850s he was the first in the United States to obtain rhododendrons and azaleas from China and the Himalayas. He bought many of his varieties from the prominent English nurseryman, Anthony Waterer, who named some of them after members of the Hunnewell family. Mr. Hunnewell continually tested the effects of climate on each of his plants. Tender azaleas, stored underground through the winter, were put out in the spring under an immense canvas tent.[19] Every year he opened his grounds at Wellesley to the public for the peak bloom of the azaleas and rhododendrons. In a grand gesture to introduce people to his favorite shrub, Mr. Hunnewell, entirely at his own expense, arranged the great rhododendron exhibition of 1873 on Boston Common. During a three-week period in June, forty thousand people marveled at hundreds of Hunnewell's rhododendrons in full bloom. To illustrate how the shrubs would look in a garden, they

The Lake, Trentham Hall Gardens, E. Adveno Brooke, *The Gardens of England*, London, 1857. Hollis Hunnewell owned a copy of Brooke's large, lavishly illustrated volume. He may have been inspired by this view of the duke of Sutherland's estate in Staffordshire to import his own Italian gondola and gondolier to the shore of Lake Waban in Wellesley, Massachusetts. (Photo by Clive Russ; Massachusetts Horticultural Society)

were sunk directly into the ground on the Common, as if growing naturally. The usual flower show custom had been to display the plants in pots. All proceeds from the show were donated to the Massachusetts Horticultural Society for prize money to encourage the growing of rhododendrons. The rhododendron show illustrates

Hollis Hunnewell's continuing efforts to transfer to the public sector the fruits of the expansion of horticultural knowledge made possible by his wealth.[20] His close lifetime involvement with both the Arnold Arboretum and the Massachusetts Horticultural Society reflect his dedication to social improvement, a dedication not necessarily characteristic of others who were amassing great fortunes during his lifetime.

Late in his life, Hollis Hunnewell tried to ease the burden on his heirs at Wellesley by simplifying maintenance wherever he could. After fifty years of putting out tender bedding plants in the French parterre in late May, he finally gave it all up. The effort spent there for one transitory season of bloom, he reasoned, could be better devoted to shrubs and trees that would last for several generations. He forced himself to remove some precious old trees in order to preserve a view or to allow other trees to develop fully. Even while thinning, he continued to plant more and rarer trees: cryptomerias, torreyas, *Thujopsis dolobrata.* He struggled to develop a hardy strain of the blue Atlas cedar (*Cedrus atlantica glauca*). Mr. Hunnewell was in his late eighties when he made his last botanical expedition to the White Mountains. "Have seen nowhere here in the mountains among the numerous white pines and spruces any to be compared with those at Wellesley in beauty or size," he wrote.[21] He loved his trees and was pleased with what he had been able to accomplish over fifty years.

At the century's end, Hollis Hunnewell realized that the "topiary exploits" of his unique Italian garden had once again passed out of fashion. He had read the books of William Robinson (1838–1935), the impassioned English advocate of naturalistic or "wild" gardening, and he knew the vitriol with which Robinson ridiculed formality. (Robinson had visited Wellesley in 1870 and praised the pinetum. He afterward sent his host an inscribed copy of his latest book, *The Wild Garden*.) Even Mr. Hunnewell's good friend Charles Sprague Sargent expressed doubts in the journal he edited as to "whether such a garden is a thing to be desired in a rural situation in America."[22] An architecture critic condemned Hunnewell's topiary in 1904 as "a senseless perversion."[23] But Hollis Hunnewell continued to defend his Italian garden as the best treatment for that steep site. He was affected not a little by the enthusiasm of thousands of visitors who never had seen and never would again see anything like it.

· · ·

The Italian garden; stereo view, ca. 1890. (Society for the Preservation of New England Antiquities)

Ever since Hollis Hunnewell died in 1902, the place has continued to be tended to chiefly by the men of the family. Hollis's son Walter took over from his father, followed in turn by two more successive Walters, four generations of Hunnewells so far. All of them carefully recorded their successes and failures and every year measured their trees with the help of their sons. Family members continue to be involved in the garden.

The strong sense of stewardship that Hollis Hunnewell felt toward the land and the trees at Wellesley has continued to inspire his descendants. The strength of this ongoing familial tradition is awe-inspiring. It is also unusual. Consider the opposite fate that befell Bellmont, for example, the place to which John Perkins Cushing devoted himself with a fervor equal to Hollis Hunnewell's at Wellesley. Cushing intended to establish a dynastic tradition there; yet as soon as he died, his sons sold the property. We can only wonder why the Cushings behaved so differently from the Hunnewells.

One important factor in the continuing survival of the garden at Wellesley may be the family's long-standing commitment to the advancement of horticultural knowledge. Hollis Hunnewell did not garden in private or purely for personal glory. He was always involved in the community, in working with the Massachusetts Horticultural Society and the Arnold Arboretum, and in helping to disseminate information to the public. He served on the committee to oversee Harvard's Botanic Garden in Cambridge. Further afield, Hunnewell embarked on an expensive effort to ascertain the best wood for railroad ties. He employed a forester to plant four hundred acres of Kansas prairie in catalpa trees. Although the catalpas were not a success, continuing experiments proved that white oak made the best ties.[24]

Hunnewell made major financial contributions to the arboretum and the horticultural society. When the society needed a new hall in 1865, he donated $2,500, a sizable sum at the time. He gave the statue of Flora that ornamented the building's facade. For many years, the prestigious Hunnewell prize, established by Hollis in 1868, encouraged ornamental horticulture by rewarding those who, over a three-year period, had done the best job of "embellishing and improving" their home grounds.[25] Hollis Hunnewell served for years on the finance committee of the horticultural society. His sons, grandsons, and great-grandsons have served on the society's board of trustees, several of them as presidents.

Hollis Hunnewell instilled his sense of mission in his children, who passed it on in their turn.

With a continuity remarkably parallel to the family succession, there have been only four head gardeners since 1850. Walter Hunnewell attributes the long-term dedication of the professional gardeners to the active involvement of the owners in caring for the garden. Everyone can take pride in the successes of a shared enterprise.

The ambitious scale and increased complexity of estate gardens during the nineteenth century demanded skilled professional gardeners. The position of head gardener required managerial skills to oversee a large staff, as well as horticultural expertise to cope with the diversity of new plant material and of the ways in which plants were grown. The head gardener, or superintendent, usually exercised enormous authority and was much respected, as in the case of David Haggerston at John Perkins Cushing's Bellmont.

F. L. Harris, the first head gardener at Wellesley, was with Mr. Hunnewell from the bleak beginnings in the 1850s until 1900. Late in his life he recalled with pride the progress he had done so much to foster.[26]

A dense and hardy yew, often planted today, memorializes its originator, T. D. Hatfield, the second superintendent at Wellesley. Hatfield began his career working at a nursery in his native Britain. He advanced to employment at the Royal Botanic Gardens at Kew, where he received training in botany and horticulture that was second to none. He came to work at Wellesley in 1887, where he remained for forty years. In Hollis Hunnewell's last years, Hatfield was entrusted with almost unlimited authority. "I have been given every opportunity to carry on experimental work," he wrote near the end of his career.[27] He developed crosses and experimented with the propagation of rhododendrons from seed. The Hunnewells gave away so many plants that Hatfield operated the equivalent of a trade nursery. He introduced the raising of chrysanthemums, carnations, begonias, and dahlias at Wellesley and published many articles on his horticultural findings. During the 1890s he wrote frequently for *Garden and Forest*, an important weekly journal established by Charles Sprague Sargent with the support of Hollis Hunnewell and Frederick Law Olmsted.

The third superintendent, John Ellis, also held the post for some forty years. John C. Cowles, the current superintendent, may supervise a smaller staff than his predecessors did, but it is a staff that is less rigidly stratified. Where once the "inside" men worked only in the greenhouses and the "outside" men were highly specialized, those who work at Wellesley now are more versatile and can take on one another's tasks when necessary.

Walter Hunnewell thinks that, in at least one respect, maintenance is now better than ever. In the old days, when walks and parapets in the Italian garden were lined each season with tender trees in tubs and century plants in pots, the terrace banks were mowed with scythes. Now a rotary mower makes a far smoother greensward, as the gardener, using a rope, guides the machine along the steep banks, just as though he were walking a dog on a leash.

Grapes and peaches grown under glass used to be a luxury but a justifiable luxury when fresh fruit was unavailable for months on end. The Hunnewells still raise fruit in their greenhouses, but now, without artificial heat to speed its ripening, it is ready to eat just when local nursery stands are heaped with fruit grown outdoors. But one cannot buy Muscat of Alexandria grapes. Pale green, nectar sweet, and translucent as alabaster, great tapered bunches gleam in the autumn sunlight, hanging ready for the brush and canvas of an eighteenth-century Dutch painter. The vines fill one long greenhouse. The peach and nectarine house is patrolled by a sleek Siamese cat who tries to slip out the merest crack of an opened door despite what would seem to be an idyllic existence.

Orchids are Walter Hunnewell's favorites among the potted plants. Having lived and worked in Mexico and South America for many years, he and his wife, Luisa, collected orchids in the mosquitoey wild. *Stanhopea oculata*, a large-flowered creamy white orchid with the sweet fragrance of cheap candy, grows in a warm greenhouse. The cattleyas flourish at cooler temperatures in an adjacent house.

The brick wall of another greenhouse is covered with the dangling pink and white bells of *Lapageria*, the Chilean bellflower that Walter Hunnewell's father particularly liked. Walter himself brought these plants from Chile. Along one bench, tender Malaysian rhododendrons offer clustered blooms of delicately shaded yellow and salmon. There are pots of clivia, oleanders, chrysanthemums, and fig trees. A search for a ripe fig is fruitless. Everyone loves them.

Other members of the Hunnewell family continue to live on or near the Wellesley estate, as Hollis Hunne-well hoped they would when he built houses for each of his seven surviving children. Only one of the houses is no longer lived in by Hunnewells, serving instead as a research facility for Wellesley College.

The Hunnewells have always been able to adapt to changing conditions without sacrificing the garden's integrity. They have modified the garden whenever it seemed prudent to do so. Family members contribute to the upkeep in different ways. Walter's brother Willard has a special interest in the camellias that occupy one greenhouse. Willard Hunnewell does not claim sole credit for the plants; some are far older than he. One venerable treasure, a *Camellia alba plena*, ten feet tall, is covered with snowy blooms by late November. Walter Hunnewell's son Francis made a different sort of contribution when he found in China some new tiles of the same size and shape as the antique tiles in the balustrade above the Italian garden. He brought three hundred of them home to replace the cracked and broken originals. The continuity at Wellesley is not only in the trees.

Like his great-grandfather before him, Walter Hunnewell plants for the future. In one of his greenhouses hundreds of tree seedlings fill flat after flat. Under a long-standing and mutually beneficial arrangement, Mr. Hunnewell tries out new and untested tree species that Harvard's Arnold Arboretum obtains from around the globe. Many now come from China. If these trees prosper at the arboretum—and ideally, at Wellesley too—and if they can be propagated easily, they will eventually be available commercially. The Dawn Redwood (*Metasequoia glyptostroboides*) is one recent example. Known to botanists only as a fossil until the 1940s, it was then discovered alive, and the Hunnewells were among those who grew it from collected seed. Now any of us can buy one.

The conservatory at the house is simpler now. No longer are potted plants banked up, tier on tier, as they were years ago. But the tall acacias and slow-growing palms still frame massed pots of chrysanthemums or azaleas, depending on the season.

The house reflects the same continuity that the garden does. In the parlor the painted furniture that was

Overleaf: Topiary in the Hunnewells' terraced Italian Garden. The tallest trees are native white pines, clipped once a year. (Photo by Mick Hales)

An interior view of the Hunnewell conservatory; stereograph, ca. 1880. The statue of Flora by Martin Milmore
(1844–83) still occupies the same spot. (Society for the
Preservation of New England Antiquities)

brought from France in 1811 by Isabella Welles Hunnewell's father is covered in emerald silk, just as it always has been. An 1868 oil painting on the stair landing portrays the same marble Flora who still presides over the garden. The wide central hallway has scenic wallpaper dating from the 1870s. Many of the books in the sunny Blue Room, where Hollis Hunnewell wrote each day in his diary, and in the library across the hall bear his signature or inscriptions by their authors. Not surprisingly, the book collection leans toward natural history and horticulture. On a top shelf in the library, beside bound nineteenth-century gardening magazines, are Hollis Hunnewell's garden ledgers, listing what plants he bought and from whom.

The chief glory of Wellesley is the pinetum. Walter Hunnewell walks along a winding lane among the magnificent trees, his well-thumbed plan in hand, checking on his favorites, picking up a broken branch here, uprooting an unwanted seedling there. As a boy he worked here with his father. The trees are old companions, whose habits and idiosyncrasies he knows well. All are different in their shades of green, their textures, the colors of their bark, and the way their branches grow. The greens in each single tree vary, too, from the pastels of new growth to the black-green of some mature needles. Some trees show white undersides when a breeze lifts their branches. Now and then one walks into a sweet needle fragrance; could it be *Abies cephalonica*? Or is it *Picea pungens Hunnewelliana*?

Most of the trees are labeled—an unending task—and Walter Hunnewell knows their ages. One of the largest and oldest is an uncommon fir from Asia Minor, *Abies cilicica*. A tall swamp cypress grows here at the northern edge of its range, shedding yellow needles in the fall and remaining bare until June. Mr. Hunnewell wonders why the majestic cedar of Lebanon (*Cedrus libani*), with its cones upright like little candles, is so seldom seen in the northern United States. His has grown from the seed of a cold-hardy strain found in the mountains of Asia Minor by an Arnold Arboretum expedition in 1903.

After walking around the Hunnewell place for several hours one chilly day, I thought of a remark Hollis Hunnewell made in 1899, in reference to his trees. "No Vanderbilt, with all his great wealth, can possess one of these for the next 50 years, for it could not be grown in less time than that."[28]

Notes

1. Horatio Hollis Hunnewell, *Life, Letters, and Diary*, ed. Hollis Horatio Hunnewell (Boston: privately printed, 1906), vol. 2, 6 June 1868.

2. Ibid., 1:195.

3. Volume 1 of Hunnewell's *Life, Letters, and Diary* includes a biographical sketch by the grandson who edited his papers. An account of Hunnewell's early years is in Gertrude Montague Graves, *A New England Family and Their French Connections* (Boston: privately printed, 1930).

4. Brent Elliott, *Victorian Gardens* (Portland, Ore.: Timber Press, 1986), 79.

5. Ian C. Laurie, "Landscape Gardeners at Eaton Park, Chester: 2," *Garden History* 13 (autumn 1985): 126–55; and "Nesfield in Cheshire," *Garden History* 15 (autumn 1987): 145–56.

6. Geoffrey Jellicoe and Susan Jellicoe, *The Oxford Companion to Gardens* (New York: Oxford University Press, 1986), 54.

7. Elliott, *Victorian Gardens*, 77.

8. Andrew Jackson Downing, *A Treatise on the Theory and Practice of Landscape Gardening*, 8th ed. (New York: Orange Judd, 1859), 47.

9. Ibid., 24–25.

10. Hunnewell, *Life, Letters, and Diary*, 3:101.

11. Elliott, *Victorian Gardens*, 83–87, 118–20.

12. Sarah Parker Rice Goodwin Papers, Strawbery Banke, Portsmouth, N.H.

13. Charles Mason Hovey, "Suburban Visits," *Magazine of Horticulture* 21 (August 1855): 381.

14. E. Adveno Brooke, *The Gardens of England* (London: 1857), plate 2.

15. Hovey, "Suburban Visits," 379.

16. Henry Winthrop Sargent, "Supplement to the 6th edition," in Downing, *Theory and Practice of Landscape Gardening*, 444.

17. Elliott, *Victorian Gardens*, 115.

18. Hunnewell, *Life, Letters, and Diary* 3:82, excerpt from a letter to *Garden and Forest*, May 1895.

19. Marshall P. Wilder, *The Horticulture of Boston and Vicinity* (Boston, 1881), 52.

20. Albert Fein, "A Garden for the Public: H. H. Hunnewell's Rhododendron Show," *Horticulture* (July 1978): 52–55.

21. Hunnewell, *Life, Letters, and Diary*, vol. 2, 1 August 1894.

22. Charles Sprague Sargent, *Garden and Forest* 2 (27 February 1899): 98–99.

23. Herbert Croly, *Architectural Record* 15 (March 1904): 195.

24. Peter Del Tredici, "The Great Catalpa Craze," *Arnoldia* 46 (spring 1986): 5–7.

25. Albert Emerson Benson, *History of the Massachusetts Horticultural Society* (Boston: Massachusetts Horticultural Society, 1929), 157.

26. Bryant Fleming, "The Hunnewell Estate at Wellesley," *Country Life in America* 3 (November 1902): 27.

27. Theophilus D. Hatfield, "My Work," undated typescript, Wellesley College Archives.

28. Hunnewell, *Life, Letters, and Diary*, 3:118.

Chapter 8

To Bring Back the Past

The Codmans at The Grange,

Lincoln, Massachusetts

THE EIGHTEENTH-CENTURY country estate in Lincoln, Massachusetts, so cherished by John Codman (see chapter 1) took on new life in the 1860s, when a subsequent generation of Codmans took it over. Although they viewed their ancestral demesne with reverence, often stating their intention to restore the place to its former glory, these later Codmans put their own stamp on the property. The new character they gave to the place reflected contemporary trends and technology as well as the peculiar personalities of family members and their attitudes toward the past.

The Codman estate had its origins in the eighteenth century, a hundred years before H. H. Hunnewell began gardening at Wellesley. In the 1790s, when John Codman instituted his improvements, his 450-acre family property was already half a century old. His planned alterations to the ornamental landscape were merely parts of a grand scheme. He had upgraded the farming operation with new barns, outbuildings, walls, and wells and the draining of wet fields. As a founding member (in 1792) of the Massachusetts Society for Promoting Agriculture, he was open to new techniques. He hired an excellent farm manager, who boosted the raising and sale of livestock and field crops. The mansion house was enlarged and transformed in the style of Charles Bulfinch, possibly *by* him. John Codman was pleased and proud when, in 1800, his friend and neighbor Mrs. Christopher Gore called his Lincoln estate "the handsomest place in America."[1]

Despite John Codman's expressed wish that his descendants carry on the rural estate, his son divided and sold the property without apparent remorse soon after his father died in 1803. In 1815 an advertisement for the sale of "A Valuable Farm" of 280 acres made it sound a magnificent place still.[2] Subsequent owners, however, stored farm tools, rakes, and spades in the house itself, a hint of greatly diminished grandeur. Sale notices and tax records reveal a steady decline in livestock, crops, and real value. In 1844 the Fitchburg Railroad secured a right-of-way through the estate, and the train ran, as it still does, less than two hundred yards from the house. To Henry David Thoreau, walking the country near Walden Pond in the 1840s, the estate was still "the Codman place" after it had been out of the hands of that family for nearly forty years.[3]

In 1862 it had always been "the Codman place" in the mind of Ogden Codman, John's grandson. Born in 1839, Ogden Codman married Sarah Bradlee in 1861.

The Grange, Lincoln, Massachusetts, 1872. Ogden Sr.'s newly planted trees and rhododendrons dot the lawns under eighteenth-century elms. A tamarack, the American larch, stands in front of the house. Ogden Jr. and Alice pose with their ponies; Tom sits on the grass. (Photo by Barton Sprague, Codman Family Photograph Collection, Society for the Preservation of New England Antiquities)

A year later, according to Sarah's diary, Ogden proposed his "Lincoln plan," a dream since boyhood, to buy back and restore the estate his father had sold in 1807.[4] Ogden imagined his grandfather John as being like the lord of some English manor. The grandson idolized the grandfather he had never known and took him as a role model.

Over the years, Ogden's wife and eventually their five children came to share Ogden's ancestor worship. Even the "stump and last branch of grandfather's mulberry" were preserved into the 1890s as living eighteenth-century artifacts, long past the time when the tree was an object of beauty. In 1908, after having the woods thinned out, Sarah Codman wrote her son Ogden that "it looks now as I think it must have looked in Grandfather John's time."[5] Both Ogden Jr. and his brother Tom were lifelong admirers of the taste of "the Honorable John," their great-grandfather, as exemplified in the family house and its landscape setting.

When Ogden Sr. acquired the estate in 1862, he named it The Grange. A grange is by definition a country house with associated barns and other farm buildings, indicating that Codman intended to develop the place for farming. He purchased at least seventy-five books on agriculture and horticulture during the 1860s. The Grange symbolized Codman's ambition to assume what he saw as his rightful role as a member of the landed squirearchy.

Even before he moved in, Ogden Codman invited his brother-in-law, architect John Hubbard Sturgis, to look over the rundown property. Sturgis seemed the perfect choice to remodel the house. His wife, Fanny, Ogden's sister, shared the family's sentimental attachment to The Grange. Sturgis was interested in eighteenth-century Georgian architecture long before the American Colonial Revival swept the country.[6] Sturgis designed a new farm cottage at The Grange and recommended replacing the deteriorated 1790s stable. He added window pediments and corner quoins to the mansion house, making it look more as it may have done before John Codman's redesign in the 1790s. For all Ogden Codman's professed admiration for his grandfather's taste, the changes he and Sturgis made in the 1860s removed some of the Federal period details while adding elements of the earlier Georgian style. At the same time, the house and its landscape setting began to accommodate mid-nineteenth-century taste and sensibility.

The grounds were the scene of feverish activity by 1863. The retaining wall that formed a ha-ha in front of the house was reconstructed. New walls were built; roads and walks were improved. Codman embarked on reclaiming the wet octagon meadow for a hayfield and an ornamental pond. At the same time, he plunged into diverse and extensive farming. A new barn, connected to the old one, formed a farmyard inspired, perhaps, by *The Book of Farm Buildings: Their Arrangement and Construction* (Henry Stephens and R. Scott Burn, 1862), one of Ogden's many useful English books. He kept workhorses, sporting ponies, hens, pigs, and a dairy herd. He grew corn and hay for feed. All vegetables for the family and tenant employees were raised on the place, a custom that was to continue through the 1940s. Early vegetables were forced in a greenhouse or sun-heated pit, following directions in Codman's well-worn copy of John Claudius Loudon's comprehensive manual, *The Horticulturist* (1860).

Codman planted apple and pear trees, raspberries, strawberries, blackberries, and currants that he ordered from a nursery in Dorchester, Massachusetts. He ordered a wheeled Whitcomb rake, a "garden engine," and tools for pruning and weeding. In 1866 he began buying an exotic fertilizer for which there was a great craze, Peruvian guano, touted by author John Wilson in another of Codman's books, *British Farming* (1862).

The books Ogden Codman consulted were oriented more toward practical matters than to ornamental horticulture and design. He probably felt that the landscape of The Grange was entirely satisfactory in its plan, having been so since the time of Grandfather John. Andrew Jackson Downing's writings on domestic landscape design were so influential that even twenty years after Downing's death Ogden Codman could scarcely have avoided a familiarity with his precepts. In

the end, the only change Codman made to the pleasure grounds near his house was the addition of new trees and shrubs, surely in response to Downing's advice.

All the Codmans were great savers; hardly a scrap of paper seems to have been thrown away. As a result, the garden is as well documented as are other aspects of the family's existence. Surviving sales receipts show the enormous number of trees that Ogden Codman set out during his first years in Lincoln. His choices reflect Downing's influence: many different species, both evergreen and deciduous, and a number of weeping varieties. In 1872, Sarah Codman noted in her diary that her husband had gone to see about some trees sent from England. Practicality won out over his Anglophilism, however, and most of his purchases were from American nurseries. He ordered from local growers as well as from the important Ellwanger & Barry nursery in Rochester, New York. It was quite the thing at the time for a landowner to collect trees to form a private arboretum. Codman's efforts along these lines were modest compared to those of H. H. Hunnewell at Wellesley. Hunnewell was both serious and well informed about raising trees, whereas Codman planted solely for ornamental effect. The lawns at The Grange were soon dotted with trees. By the 1890s, however, many of the young trees had already been cleared away, marking another change of taste in favor of open sweeps of lawn.

A 1939 letter from Thomas Codman to his brother Ogden Jr. refers to a "big English elm the pater must have planted when he set out most of the trees some 75 years ago," or about 1870.[7] Even bigger were several eighteenth-century elms, one of which lasted until 1922. Two venerable larch trees, or tamaracks, memorialized in a pencil sketch by Sarah, stood in front of the house in the 1860s.

Ogden Codman ordered climbing vines—wisteria, honeysuckle, and clematis—from nearby nurseries. Although herbs are not usually associated with Victorian-era gardens, Codman purchased ninety-four assorted herb plants in 1867. His annual seed order always included the fragrant mignonette, a well-loved flower at the time. As one would expect, given its popularity then, the Codmans had some gardens of floral carpet bedding. An 1872 sales slip includes red and blue verbena and lavender heliotrope in quantities sufficient to make a stylish show when planted en masse. Tall cannas marked the centers of circular beds on the terraces in front of the house. Ogden ordered tender fuchsias, carnations, and "assorted plants for vases." He established shrubberies of Japanese quinces, *Spiraea* in varieties then newly introduced from Japan, and *Philadelphus*, or mock orange, then called syringa. Rhododendron borders were established in 1872, according to Sarah's diary.

Sarah Codman's diary, kept meticulously during the years from her engagement to her death in 1922, provides a vivid picture of family life at The Grange.[8] Despite her cryptic style, lacking punctuation and modifiers, her account is detailed and continuous. With their small son, Ogden Jr., the Codmans had moved to Lincoln from Boston for the first time in July 1864. The cistern promptly gave out, and persistent servant troubles began. "The cook wretched"; "new cook comes"; "the chambermaid leaves"; "servants fight about church"—the phrases form a litany throughout all the Codman years in Lincoln.

The outdoor staff proved equally difficult: "The farmer and the coachman quarrel"; "the farmer leaves"; "a fuss with the farm men about their board, and they all leave." Meanwhile, more babies are born, Sarah's younger sister Alice spends the summers there, and they all go out for drives in the buggy. They take walks; they take picnics to Walden Pond, a mile away. The children learn to ride ponies; they fall off. Sometimes they all ride in the yellow wagon or the sleigh. Every year they attend the Concord Cattle Show and sometimes a fair at Lowell. Ogden goes steeplechasing, and one year he lays out a race course at The Grange. They play croquet, a newly fashionable lawn sport. Almost every day there are guests for lunch or tea. Mr. Hunnewell comes from Wellesley to dine. Sarah, sounding like Marie Antoinette in her pastoral guise, makes butter in a glass churn. She makes her first modest planting efforts and begins to study and collect wild plants.

In a continuous counterpoint to this rural idyll, Sarah and Ogden make frequent trips to town—to balls, to the theater, to the opera. They travel: to the mountains, to the sea, to Europe. Every autumn, the Codmans move to Boston, where they maintain another house. Suddenly, the tenor of their luxurious lifestyle was threatened. The great Boston fire of 1872 destroyed Ogden's extensive real estate holdings in the city, almost ruining him financially. On the strength of reports that it was cheaper to live in France, the whole family sailed in 1874 for a ten-year exile among the American colony in the little town of Dinard on the Brittany coast. The quasi-eighteenth-century pastorale at Lincoln was over.

While the Codmans were away, the mansion, pleasure grounds, garden, and pasture were leased out. Ogden's older brother James rented the farm on the property. In his increasingly gloomy letters, James kept Ogden abreast of the deterioration of The Grange and urged his brother either to resume living there or to sell the place. The tenant farmer was quarreling with the caretaker, he reported, and both were undoubtedly cheating Ogden. The horses were "abused," most of the cows "not worth their keep," the grassland "much run out," and the orchard trees "old and worthless."[9] Even Ogden's old dog had become "a thief and a chicken killer." Only the recently planted trees and shrubs were doing well.

Ogden Codman did bring his family home at the end

The last generation of the Codmans of Lincoln on the steps of their ancestral home, ca. 1895. Ogden Codman Sr. stands beside his wife, Sarah Bradlee Codman; Lady Grey-Egerton is standing at the right. Seated, left to right, are Thomas Newbold Codman, pensive Alice Newbold Codman, Violet Grey-Egerton, and Ogden Codman Jr. (Codman Family Photograph Collection, Society for the Preservation of New England Antiquities)

of 1884, although his financial situation was still precarious. He had to lease out the farm and in summer the mansion house, too. The family's relationship to their estate was oddly tentative into the 1890s, when they again lived in Europe for several years. Finally, in 1897, they settled permanently at The Grange.

. . .

The oldest of the five Codman children, Ogden Jr., born in 1864, had returned to Boston from France in 1882. He lived with his aunt and uncle, Fanny and John Hubbard Sturgis, and studied architecture for a year at what is now the Massachusetts Institute of Technology. He then spent two miserable years in Lowell as an apprentice architect, followed by a stint with the Boston firm of Andrews & Jacques. In 1891 he opened his own office in Boston. In letters to his family in France, he continually urged them to return to Boston and The Grange. Like his uncle, James Codman, he too reported on the abysmal state of the family place, where neglect was taking a heavy toll. Ogden Jr. began making his own plans for refurbishing the house to which he felt so strongly attached. His ideas were quite different from those of his uncle John Sturgis, who, he said later, had very nearly spoiled the house.[10]

Well launched on his architectural career, Ogden Jr. left Boston, worked in Newport, and soon opened a New York office. The year of his family's return to Lincoln, 1897, saw the publication of the book, *The Decoration of Houses*, on which he and Edith Wharton had collaborated. The book was a tremendous popular success and had a significant impact on interior design and domestic architecture. The co-authors had tested their theories on the Whartons' Newport house. Ogden Jr. continued to apply his taste and talent to The Grange.

At the time the family reestablished itself in Lincoln, Ogden and Sarah's other children seemed to be developing their talents and reaching out toward life as Ogden Jr. had. Alice, or "Ahla," three years younger than Ogden, was thirty in 1897. She studied painting and had an active social life, frequently attending parties at the Lymans' estate, The Vale, just a few miles from Lincoln. Tom, then twenty-eight, had taken up photography, and Hugh at twenty-two showed great promise on the violin. Dorothy, the youngest, was fourteen when the family settled permanently into The Grange.

Out of his intense interest in his family place, Ogden Jr. drew up plans for alterations to the house and grounds. He proposed a tall, pedimented addition in the classical style for the east side of the mansion, which would have then become the principal facade. Among Ogden Jr.'s surviving drawings are plans for an imposing entrance court adjacent to his proposed ell.[11] One of the sketches, underlying the formal layout he advocated, shows the casual teardrop shape of the drive as even today it loops up to the side door.

Much as he admired his great-grandfather John, Ogden Jr.'s splendid schemes are entirely unlike the English landscape gardens that John Codman had so admired in 1800. Ogden Jr.'s plans, if carried out, would have extended the architecture of the house into the landscape and imposed an entirely new symmetrical plan. Because it was so firmly related to the facade of the house, Ogden Jr. approved of the existing terraced front that his great-grandfather had hoped to eliminate. Ogden's embryonic plans show a geometrical entrance court, a central courtyard enclosed by new flanking

Landscape proposal for The Grange, ca. 1890, by Ogden Codman Jr. The existing house and its front terraces are shown at the top. Courtyard, flanking wings, avenues, *rond point*, and terracing west of the house remained paper plans, but Sarah's Italian garden was soon to be built on the spot marked "sunk garden." (Codman Family Manuscripts Collection, Society for the Preservation of New England Antiquities)

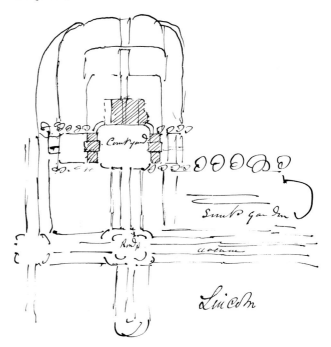

pavilions, and formal terracing down the steep western slope. One drawing proposes a *rond point* on an axis with the north side of the house, with *allées* radiating outward. A Le Notre–like landscape might have appeared in Lincoln had these changes, so reflective of Ogden Jr.'s continental classicism, progressed beyond the drawing board.

In her diary, Sarah Codman mentions the three-day visit in 1892 of "Trix" Jones—Beatrix Jones (later Farrand), a niece of Edith Wharton's and soon to become one of the nation's leading garden designers (see chapter 15). One wonders what impression the grounds at The Grange made on her during her visit and what she would have made of Ogden's schemes.

After 1897, when the family finally settled down in Lincoln, Sarah's diaries continued to refer to her "children," although they were hardly children any longer, three of them soon passing thirty. Yet all of them except Ogden remained at The Grange for the rest of their lives, gradually abandoning their independence and their talents. Ogden was the only one of the five ever to work for pay or to marry. The others continued to live much as they had when they *were* children: snapping pictures of each other, taking nature walks, riding bicycles or horses, playing tennis or tether ball, and looking after their pets. When they went to parties, the Codman girls reportedly danced only with their brothers.[12] Ahla painted charming watercolors of the Lincoln land-

scape until 1912, when the mysterious debility that blighted the remainder of her life kept her from pursuing her real talent.[13]

Their father, Ogden Sr., who died in 1904, seems a shadowy figure in his last years. He was often absent. His wife's pretty younger sister was a frequent companion on his travels, giving rise to speculation as to their relationship. As the Codmans' Lincoln neighbor, Thomas Boylston Adams, put it, "He liked good company and champagne and found occupation elsewhere."[14] Ogden Sr. kept private his modest collection of trick figurines and lewd cartoons. He had apparently decided that farming and gardening were not for him, after all. He still ordered trees, however, and more horticultural books. In 1898 he bought Liberty Hyde Bailey's *Garden Making*, a thoroughly practical manual for ordinary folk with modest means and modest grounds, people who would actually work the soil themselves. Sarah began to do just that. By 1900, as her husband was fading from the scene, Sarah, with advice from her son Ogden, took charge of The Grange.

Near the west corner of the house, in the shade of a horse chestnut tree, the Codmans gathered on summer afternoons at the turn of the century, reclining in canvas deck chairs around a linen-covered tea table, with "Mère Cot," as her children called their mother, presiding over the silver samovar. Other times, the family resorted to the rocking chairs on the side piazza, where

Sarah presides at the tea table, August 1899, surrounded by white geraniums, deck chairs, and a lawn roller in this snapshot from one of Alice's albums. (Codman Family Photograph Collection, Society for the Preservation of New England Antiquities)

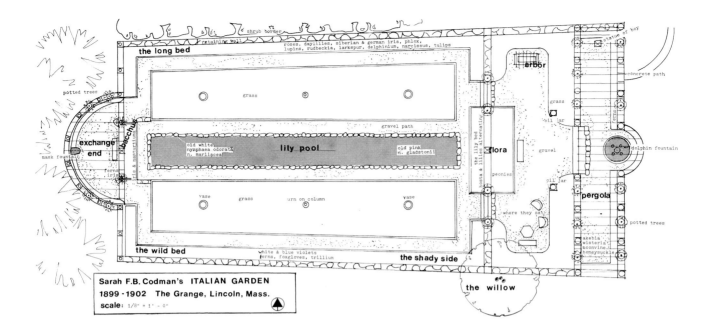

shrub border
retaining wall
the long bed
roses, daylilies, siberian & german iris, phlox, lupins, rudbeckia, larkspur, delphinium, narcissus, tulips
arbor
statue of boy
concrete path
potted trees
grass
grass
oil jar
gravel path
gravel
exchange end
Tobacchum
mask fountain
iris & nasturtiums
old white nymphaea odorata n. marliacea
lily pool
old pink n. gladstonii
flora
the lily bed hosta & lilies alternating
dolphin fountain
ferns iris
peonies
oil jar
vase
grass
urn on column
vase
pergola
where they eat
potted trees
the wild bed
white & blue violets ferns, foxgloves, trillium
the shady side
akebia wisteria moonvine honeysuckle
the willow

Sarah F.B. Codman's ITALIAN GARDEN
1899-1902 The Grange, Lincoln, Mass.
scale: 1/8" = 1' - 0"

rolled awnings of striped canvas sheltered them and the potted palms from the noonday sun.

The English garden writer, Gertrude Jekyll, whose book *Wood and Garden* (1899) was in the Codmans' library, wrote that gardening required a true artist to create a living picture. She scorned the ugly, outmoded "bedding out" of tender plants in parterres of brilliant colors. But Sarah Codman clung to the old practice in front of her house. She had Schlegel & Fottler of Boston, suppliers of seeds to the Codmans since the 1860s, prepare a plan for circular beds on the terraces. *Ricinus*, a tropical foliage plant, was to be planted in the center, surrounded by cannas and phlox, with scarlet salvia, blue ageratum and heliotrope, and yellow marigolds massed around the periphery.[15] Every year, Sarah Codman noted the date of the first hard frost that killed the salvia and heliotrope in these patterned beds. Sarah and Ahla set up their easels in the octagon one afternoon in 1898 to paint the view of their house towering over its verdant terraces. These watercolors show the blazing scarlet of geraniums and salvia, the Italian pots of boxwood, and the vases planted with spiky dracaena.

Sarah Codman oversaw all the landscape maintenance. The pond in the octagon was then larger than it is now, and she insisted that its banks be kept clear of brush. In a 1907 letter, Sarah reported having trees cut so that "we can now see the end of the road from the porch as we used to do."[16]

Plan of the Italian garden at The Grange. Construction extended from 1899 to 1903. The house is to the right of the plan. (Drawing by Alan Emmet)

In 1899, when she was fifty-seven, Sarah Codman embarked on her grandest project at The Grange. Northwest of the house was a low, wet area known to the Codmans as the pond hole. It may once have been an actual pond. Here, over the course of two years, a walled Italianate garden was built. The garden was carefully planned and laid out, probably by Ogden Codman Jr., but his mother's diary, usually so inclusive, is silent as to the planning phase. No drawing of the garden has been found, an indication that the design was measured and staked out directly on the ground. The enclosing pergolas and statuary, the fountain, and the canal are of Italian derivation, used here to make a walled outdoor room—a *giardino segreto*. Lacking any visual links to the house or the countryside, the garden is more medieval than Renaissance. Its sense of enclosure is increased by its location in a hollow. The trees outside the garden shelter it further while softening the transition between the garden's architecture and the natural landscape. The narrowing perspective within the garden, which increases its apparent length, was planned with assurance and skill.

As soon as the site was cleared, even before the walls were completed, Sarah began putting in plants. The

site was so wet that a pool seemed a necessity. Men were digging and pumping all through the spring of 1900. Despite the formality of the long lily pool, Sarah ever after referred to it as "the Ditch." A pergola was built next. Tom, who had learned to work with concrete, made the columns. A year later the curved arbor at the far end was built, using slender marble columns and heavy Corinthian capitals salvaged from a building Ogden Sr. had once owned at Exchange Place in Boston. The building itself was one of those destroyed in the terrible fire of 1872. Timbers were laid across the columns at what the Codmans called "the Exchange end." Statues of Bacchus and Flora, freestanding deco-

In 1898, Sarah Bradlee Codman painted this watercolor of the family home in Lincoln, Massachusetts. Circular beds on the terraces leading up to the front entrance were planted with red salvia and other brightly colored annuals. (Photo by David Bohl; Society for the Preservation of New England Antiquities)

rative columns, and two fountains were in place by 1903. Clematis, wisteria, and honeysuckle soon clambered over the pergolas, giving the garden a look of maturity. Huge oil jars, potted trees, and benches were placed symmetrically. Sarah Codman called this simply

"the garden." Dorothy referred to it as her mother's garden. "The Italian garden" is a more recent appellation.

Outside the garden, the slope from the house is treated poorly. There is no satisfactory approach to the garden. Perhaps the major contribution to landscape art of the great Italian villa gardens lies in their adaptation of sloping sites, whereas the Italianate garden at The Grange entirely ignores the slope. It seems hard to believe that Ogden Codman Jr. allowed this to happen. With his knowledge of the principles of classical architecture, his predilection for coherence and symmetry, and his flair for dramatic design, he surely had a clear

The Italian Garden at The Grange, looking toward the "Exchange end," where only fragments remain of the marble columns that once formed an enclosing arbor. Narrowing perspective makes the garden appear longer than it is. The flower bed against the retaining wall at the right is the "long bed," where Sarah Codman labored day after day until finally her knees gave out. (Photo by Peter Margonelli)

Pergola in the Italian garden, ca. 1903. Pots, statuary, and vines have given the new garden a look of age. (Codman Family Photograph Collection, Society for the Preservation of New England Antiquities)

concept for a suitable entrance to this garden. Was this a matter of money? The Codmans usually felt poor, but that seldom hindered their doing what they wanted if it involved The Grange.

Despite the weaknesses of its relationship to its setting, the Italian garden is sophisticated in its design. Though modest in size and scope, it does not suffer in comparison to some of the more princely gardens that were being built at the time. The Italian villa model and the Beaux Arts style were widely popular at the turn of the century. From Cornish, New Hampshire, or Lenox, Massachusetts, to Greenwich, Connecticut, and throughout the United States, people with newer and larger fortunes than that of the Codmans were developing country estates along formal classical lines. Many people had more European artifacts than the Codmans had—older oil jars, finer statues, longer pergolas, and larger fountains. But not many owners of such places worked in their gardens on hands and knees as Sarah Codman did.

Sarah's garden became her passion. She worked on it continually; and when not working, she sat there at a little table shaded by a willow in a corner near the pergola. She planted many sorts of vines. In the shady border she planted foxgloves, wildflowers, and ferns. From Mr. Pratt's Concord Nursery she bought white lilacs,

forsythia, yellow caragana, and other shrubs to set out above the wall.[17] In the pool were water lilies. Hostas and lilies grew in the bed at Flora's feet. In front of Bacchus, at the far end, bearded iris was succeeded by a border of nasturtiums. Every spring the Italian pots planted with tender trees were set out in the garden.

The "long bed," as Sarah called it, sunny and sheltered by the north wall, required the most work. She was always revising the border, raising it for better drainage, trying new plants, or dividing the old. She grew red General Jacqueminot roses and such other favorite roses as Frau Karl Druschki, Mrs. John Laing, and Dorothy Perkins. She planted many bulbs, including white Roman hyacinths, scarlet Keizerkroon and yellow Pottebakker tulips, *Lilium auratum* and *L. martagon*. She grew dozens of perennials, among them bleeding heart, white phlox, daylilies, lupins, veronica, and several varieties of *Dianthus*.[18] Dorothy worked with her mother in the garden day after day. When the outdoor gardening season ended, they turned to the greenhouse to pot bulbs to force for the following spring.

In 1911, Sarah Codman, almost seventy, was in pain. Her doctor diagnosed her problem as "housemaid's knee." If he knew her well, he should have called it "gardener's knee." After that it was Dorothy who

tended the garden for her mother. Her interest in gardening and her knowledge of it had grown apace with her mother's, but this avocation played an even more central role in Dorothy's life. Thirty-five years after her mother's death, Dorothy was still tending the garden, which she still called "Mother's garden."

Dorothy was a compulsive collector and record keeper. In her own garden next to the stable she tried a whole zoo of plants, some of them not even close to being hardy in Massachusetts. But Dorothy earnestly listed her many failures as well as her successes in her gardening journals. Her meticulous plans, with lists of exactly what grew successfully where, make restoration of her garden relatively simple.[19] Maintaining it is another story. Dorothy Codman devoted her life to it. The Italian garden was continually being photographed from every angle, but there are almost no photographs of Dorothy's garden. This lack is unexpected, to say the least, in a family so driven to record with their cameras every aspect of their lives at The Grange. Dorothy herself filled album after album with snap-

The so-called Exchange end of the Italian garden, ca, 1903, with columns salvaged from a building Ogden Codman Sr. had owned at Exchange Place in Boston. The statue of Bacchus, surrounded by iris, survives, but the frail columns are broken and gone. (Codman Family Photograph Collection, Society for the Preservation of New England Antiquities)

shots of everything except the one thing she seems to have cared most about.

"Dorothy's made over garden has been very successful and she takes a good deal of pleasure in it," wrote Sarah in July 1908.[20] Tom built a pool for his sister in 1909, and Henry A. Dreer, seed and plant merchants of Philadelphia, filled an order for water lilies. Dorothy and her mother made frequent buying trips to local nurseries, usually by car. The Codmans had acquired their first car in 1903. Of a typical outing on a June afternoon in 1905, Sarah noted in her diary, "Ogden, Tom, D[orothy], and I to the Shady Hill nursery [in Bedford] in the auto."

Dorothy's garden was in the style of an English cottage garden, that legendary small, crowded, colorful enclosure that Gertrude Jekyll and other writers were acclaiming. The sunny and protected site of Dorothy's garden was ideal for her purposes, not close to a cottage but to the horses and hens of a simple rural life. Inside a picket fence, small flower beds were geometrically arranged, with quaintly narrow paths. Each bed was edged with homely little plants, such as violets or pinks. Roses and clematis overhung the paths from a series of metal arches set at intervals around the garden. Dorothy grew herbs among her flowers, and grapes on a small arbor.

At the time when Dorothy made her garden, styles of the American colonial period were becoming popular, contrasting oddly with the parallel rage for European formality. As appreciators of Early American decorative arts, the Codmans were in the vanguard. Dorothy and her family drove for miles to look at and photograph old houses. Ogden Jr. made measured drawings of many of the most important eighteenth- and early-nineteenth-century houses in the vicinity of Boston. While many gardeners were attempting to reproduce old-fashioned flower gardens, Dorothy's garden represents the loosest possible interpretation of an actual colonial example.

Dorothy ordered shrubs that were not available through local nurseries from the Yokohama Nursery in

Japan: tree peonies, *Enkianthus*, *Pieris japonica*, *Rhododendron keiskei*, *Styrax japonica*, and others such as *Skimmia japonica* and *Stewartia pseudocamellia*, more suited to the milder climate of hardiness zone 8, far south of Lincoln.[21] One year she planted clematis beneath six locust trees beside her garden, intending to connect the trees with a garland of vines. The following year she lamented in her diary that the locust trees were dying. As often happened, her ambitious plan was a failure.

In 1913 the Codmans had their greenhouse refurbished, with cool, temperate, and hot rooms to meet the cultural needs of different plants. Dorothy ordered unusual bulbs and seeds from Vilmorin-Andrieux, a well-known Paris seed house. From the beautiful catalogs of the Yokohama Nursery she ordered camellias, gardenias, citrus trees, and porcelain pots to put them in.[22] Her banana trees actually produced fruit. Gardening was a year-round occupation for Dorothy.

As a widow, Sarah continued for the rest of her life to try to maintain The Grange as she felt it should be. She and her children treasured their house and its setting. Any changes were intended to enhance the eighteenth-century ambience of the place. The last major structural addition to the landscape was the combination woodshed and carriage house of 1908. Sarah wrote that she, Tom, and Hugh had driven about "looking for an old woodshed to copy."[23]

The Codmans were quick to take to the new sport of

Four of the young Codmans in their new Cadillac, 1903. Ogden Jr. is at the wheel with a map. (Codman Family Photograph Collection, Society for the Preservation of New England Antiquities)

motoring, and in 1903 it was a sport. Their first car was a Cadillac, in which they ventured as far as Marblehead. For Tom and Hugh, their first automobiles were like toys. They photographed each other and their friends seated in Hugh's Hudson and the family's Peerless. With Place, the chauffeur, at the wheel, their mother enjoyed regular outings. "After tea," she wrote in a typical diary entry, "Tom, A[hla], and I take a turn in the motor." Sarah Codman traveled with one or more of her children to gather wild ferns for her garden, to visit favorite nurseries, or, when Ogden Jr. was at home, to look at old houses with him in Beverly or Bolton, anywhere in the environs of Boston.

Ogden Jr. was having great success as a society architect, designing new houses for wealthy and worldly clients—Rockefellers and others—and proposing alterations and opulent interior designs for the houses they already owned.[24] In 1904, to the surprise of some who knew him, Ogden got married. He was forty-one. The bride was Leila Griswold Webb, a rich widow a few years older than Ogden, whom he had met while designing a house for her in New York City. The marriage lasted only six years; Leila died unexpectedly in 1910. There were no children.

Sarah wrote at least once a week to her son Ogden in New York or in France, where he eventually bought a chateau outside Paris. Her letters kept him informed of every aspect of her management of The Grange. Her gardeners, Watson and Charley, refurbished the vegetable garden in 1907. They removed old pear trees and planted new ones. Hugh wrote to nurseries as far afield as California in his search for the Doyenne du Comice pear, a particularly delectable variety that was not raised commercially in New England. In a comment that typifies her and her children's ongoing intentions for their estate, Sarah wrote in 1907, "We are going to put it back as it was in the beginning."[25]

The trees in Lincoln were being defoliated in 1907 by an infestation of gypsy moths. Dorothy, Ahla, and their brothers spent hours crushing the caterpillars, one by one. This was war. "[I]t is a desperate fight," their mother wrote to Ogden the following year. "Hugh killed 147 caterpillars on one tree near the vegetable garden yesterday."[26] The local tree warden sprayed with arsenate of lead but was more enthusiastic about biological pest control. Sarah, too, had hopes that a parasite could be found "who will fight them." She embarked on a program of clearing saplings and underbrush from the woods. This was supposed to discourage the moths, but

the family admired the aesthetic effect as a reminder of how it must once have been.

Hugh played the violin in Orchestral Club concerts in Boston and in private recitals until about 1912, when the onset of Parkinson's disease ended his amateur career. While her younger sister stayed at home on her knees in her mother's or her own garden, Ahla paid visits to relatives and friends in Marblehead or Manchester-by-the-Sea, Newport, Bar Harbor, and Dublin, New Hampshire. She went on a sketching trip to Ogunquit, Maine. Then, in 1912, Ahla's social life came to an abrupt end with a nervous collapse from which she never recovered. She took to her bed, or was put there, with fits of hysteria. Ahla became the family invalid. For years afterward her mother noted in her diary the "good days," when Ahla might be well enough to come down to lunch with her nurse or be taken to the garden by Tom. More frequent were the "bad days," which, one guesses, must have upset the entire household. Sarah recorded Ahla's daily dose of veronal, a powerful sedative that sometimes induced such heavy sleep that it was impossible to waken her. Ahla's incapacitating depression and hysteria had perhaps been kept at bay by her constant traveling, but once she collapsed, her enforced bed rest and isolation, compounded by barbiturates and her ensuing addiction, made recovery impossible.[27] Neurasthenia, then the umbrella label for the ill-defined incapacitating "disease of the age," seemed to afflict intelligent women with particular frequency. Among the sufferers was Henry James's sister, another Alice.

In 1922 the last of the towering elms that dated from John Codman's time had to be removed from the lawn, a symbolic end to the family dream of recovering their imagined golden age. Soon thereafter the pathetic remnant of John Codman's mulberry tree finally collapsed on the front terrace. That same year Sarah died at the age of eighty. A year later Ahla's sad life came to an end. Ogden, living permanently in France, the only one who

Overleaf: The Codmans' Italian Garden, laid out by Ogden Codman Jr. in 1899, was submerged in silt and weeds by the 1970s. Now Bacchus once again watches over the lily pool, the pergola Tom Codman built has been restored, and vines are beginning to provide the leafy roof that once gave shade to Sarah when her garden work was done. (Photo by Peter Margonelli)

had ever left home, made his last visit to The Grange at the time of his mother's death.

Ogden was still tied to the family home, despite being half a world away. Tom's long letters kept him informed, and Ogden replied with gossip and advice. Ogden had a biting tongue and a caustic wit when it came to describing mutual acquaintances or even his parents. He felt that their mother had "let the place run down," a harsh judgment.[28] The farm, still rented out, was a bad investment, he thought. He told Tom that "Père Cot," their father, had once uncovered a sample of the yellow paint that John Codman had used on the exterior of the house. He wondered whether "any of the old elms around the Octagon still remain." The hurricane of September 1938 downed ninety-six trees around the house and the octagon, requiring months to clean up. Tom wrote Ogden that one elm had 167 rings, indicating that it had stood since the time of the Revolution. Ogden never stopped dreaming of a new reforestation project "for the future." He clung to the hope that one day The Grange would "resume its place as the head of the big houses in Lincoln."[29]

With Hugh an invalid, Tom and Dorothy struggled to keep going. As Tom wrote Ogden in 1939, when they were both in their seventies, "Men are busy haying, mowing the lawns, the vegetable garden, and the usual things."[30] These "usual things" had been done every year since their father purchased the place nearly eight decades earlier. After Hugh's death in 1946, Tom moved permanently to France to join Ogden. Dorothy, now all alone, wrote her brothers that the red geraniums were looking very well, as they had each season of the family's years at The Grange.

Dorothy still had some help, her garden still bloomed, and she was able to walk a little in the woods. Hay was still cut by a horse-drawn mower but now baled in the field by machine, to Dorothy's amazement. "Lo the Octagon was sprinkled with bales of hay!" she wrote.[31] In 1956 the Lincoln tree warden informed her that at least two of her elms were afflicted with a new plague, Dutch elm disease. DDT was the recommended remedy.[32]

As a family the Codmans had deliberately tried to live in an imagined past. The five childless members of the last generation had known for years that they *were* the last Codmans to occupy The Grange. Ogden Jr., the most knowledgeable and dedicated antiquarian of the family, arranged as early as 1920 that upon the demise of the last of them the property should pass to the Society for the Preservation of New England Antiquities. After Dorothy's quiet life ended in 1969, the society took over at The Grange. Sarah's Italian garden, by then submerged in a jungle of weeds and vines, buried in silt, its pergolas broken, and its walls tumbled, was excavated and reclaimed like the ruins of Pompeii. Dorothy's garden was little more than a memory. Most of the Codman farmland passed to the town of Lincoln; its use is restricted to farming. Sheep and Devon cattle graze the pastures. Through foresight and good fortune the accumulated efforts of generations of Codmans and their ancestors will not be lost. Cared for and now open to the public, their house is still, as Thomas Boylston Adams once described it, "a silent exclamation point of beauty in a landscape itself as beautiful and arranged as the setting of a precious jewel."[33]

Notes

1. John Codman to Catherine Amory Codman, 24 August 1800, Codman Family Manuscripts Collection, box 118, Society for the Preservation of New England Antiquities (hereafter cited as CFMC).

2. Sale notice, 12 September 1815, CFMC, box 118.

3. Henry David Thoreau, *Walden and Other Writings*, ed. Brooks Atkinson (New York: Random House, 1950), 233.

4. Sarah Bradlee Codman diary, July 1862, CFMC, box 58.

5. Sarah Bradlee Codman to Ogden Codman Jr., 23 June 1908, CFMC, 120: 1933.

6. Margaret Henderson Floyd, "Redesign of 'The Grange' by John Hubbard Sturgis, 1862–1866," *Old-Time New England* 71 (1981): 61.

7. Thomas Newbold Codman to Ogden Codman Jr., 28 May 1939, CFMC, box 86.

8. Sarah Bradlee Codman diaries, 1864–1920, CFMC, box 58.

9. James McMaster Codman to Ogden Codman, 22 September 1878, 18 April 1880, and undated, CFMC, 35:809.

10. Ogden Codman Jr. to Dorothy Codman, 16 June 1927, CFMC, box 142.

11. Ogden Codman Jr., architectural notes, CFMC, 217: 3003.

12. Thomas Boylston Adams, "Lincoln and the Codmans," *Old-Time New England* 71 (1981): 3.

13. Alice Newbold Codman papers, CFMC, 133:2127.

14. Adams, "Lincoln and the Codmans," 3.

15. J. Lawrence Carney to Ogden Codman, 10 July 1902, CFMC, 40:954; Ogden Codman papers, CFMC, 46:1083.

16. Sarah Bradlee Codman to Leila Codman, 18 September 1907, CFMC, 120:1934.

17. F. G. Pratt to Ogden Codman, 25 October 1900, CFMC, 40:953.

18. Shady Hill Nursery to Ogden Codman, 18 October 1902 and 11 November 1902, CFMC, 41:956; F. H. Horsford to Sarah Bradlee Codman, 20 April 1905, CFMC, 59:1293.

19. Dorothy Codman notebooks, CFMC, 197:2972–74.

20. Sarah Bradlee Codman to Leila Codman, 9 July 1908, CFMC, 120:1936.

21. Yokohama Nursery to Dorothy Codman, 26 August 1913, CFMC, 161:2383.

22. Vilmorin-Andrieux et Cie to Dorothy Codman, 9 February 1914; Yokohama Nursery to Dorothy Codman, 2 April 1914, CFMC, 161:2383.

23. Sarah Bradlee Codman to Leila Codman, 18 August 1908, CFMC, 120:1936.

24. See Pauline C. Metcalf, "From Lincoln to Leopolda," and Nicholas King, "Living With Codman," *Ogden Codman and the Decoration of Houses*, ed. Pauline C. Metcalf (Boston: Boston Athenaeum, 1988), 1–47.

25. Sarah Bradlee Codman to Leila Codman, 13 October 1907, CFMC, 129:1934.

26. Sarah Bradlee Codman to Ogden Codman Jr., 23 June 1908, CFMC, box 120.

27. Sarah Bradlee Codman diaries, 1913–1920 CFMC, box 58; T. J. Jackson Lears, *No Place of Grace* (Chicago: University of Chicago Press, 1994), 47–58.

28. Ogden Codman Jr. to Thomas Newbold Codman, 21 June 1923, CFMC, box 87.

29. Ibid., 30 June 1934, 12 June 1935, 4 October 1935, CFMC, box 88; Thomas Newbold Codman to Ogden Codman Jr., 16 July 1939, CFMC, box 86.

30. Thomas Newbold Codman to Ogden Codman Jr., 16 July 1939, CFMC, box 86.

31. Dorothy Codman to Thomas Newbold Codman, 17 June 1949, CFMC, 154:2301.

32. Robert Ralston, Arborway Nursery to Dorothy Codman, 6 February 1957, CFMC, 189:2862.

33. Adams, "Lincoln and the Codmans," 2.

Chapter 9

A Little Taste of Everything

Potter's Grove, Arlington, Massachusetts

DEEP IN THE HEART of the Boston suburb of Arlington, only a block from the town's main thoroughfare but well hidden from public view, there stands a fountain. The cast-iron figure of a child holds an outsize dove, from whose up-turned bill water once spouted. The child stands on a cast-iron boulder, ornamented with iron ferns, in the center of a circular basin. The fountain is rusty now, and the white paint that once made it look almost like marble has flaked off. In 1870 the fountain was a feature of an ornate little landscape that was made, maintained, and opened to the public as Potter's Grove. Commercial photographers marketed stereo views of Potter's Grove, along with views of Bunker Hill Monument, the State House at Boston, and other celebrated sights.

The decade immediately after the Civil War saw many changes in the way Americans lived and in how they perceived their surroundings. In response to increasing industrialization and rapid urban growth, new suburbs peripheral to the cities were being developed at a rapid rate. A parallel phenomenon was the environmental concern that led to the establishment of urban and metropolitan parks. The garden of Joseph S. Potter (1822–1904) manifested some of the changes then occurring in the lives of ordinary Americans.

. . .

The once prominent creator of Potter's Grove has faded now into the same obscurity as his garden. Joseph S. Potter exemplified the entrepreneurial spirit that flourished in the United States of the nineteenth century. Potter was always looking ahead. In addition to his business ventures, Potter took advantage of the opportunities provided by government service to promote himself and his fortunes. Historian Daniel J. Boorstin might have been describing Potter when he defined the late-nineteenth-century businessman, then a new and uniquely American type: "His starting belief was in the interfusing of public and private prosperity."[1]

The recorded histories of the town where Potter made his mark (and his garden) give no clues as to his origins. He turned up there soon after 1850, having already worked in three different cities. He was born in 1822 near Syracuse, New York, the youngest of seven children.[2] When he was seventeen, he and the then-governor of New York started a daily paper in Albany. A year later, Potter went to work for the Baltimore *Pilot*, where he helped to promote William Henry Harrison's

successful candidacy for president of the United States. In 1851 politics worked to Potter's advantage. He was appointed official state printer for Massachusetts, laying the foundation of a business that provided him with a steady income for many years. Ever versatile and ever on the lookout for new opportunities, Potter invented a knitting machine. During the Civil War he secured a government contract to supply socks to the Union forces. A competent organizer, Potter soon had nine factories turning out army socks on his machines.

Meanwhile, Potter was establishing a name for himself in the town where he had chosen to live. West Cambridge, as Arlington was then named, had been lopped off from the town of Cambridge in 1807 to form a separate municipality. Potter was new in town in 1853

when he achieved recognition for his donation of portrait busts of noted patriots to decorate the new town hall. Before long he was elected town moderator, that all-important figure who guides and often controls the conduct of local affairs in New England town meetings. By 1865 and the end of the war, Potter was a man of substance. He won the highest town office as one of three selectmen. Soon thereafter he was elected state representative and subsequently state senator.

By 1867, Potter was of the opinion that "West Cambridge" was not a sufficiently distinctive name for his town. As chairman of the committee to select a new name, he pushed a bill through the legislature to call the town Arlington, a name that "had no previous historical significance in the place," as one local chronicler sniffed.[3] Potter arranged an elaborate celebration of the name change, luring the governor and other state dignitaries to march at the head of a grand parade under a triumphal arch.

Prior to the Civil War, Arlington's chief industry was farming. For a few years after the war this was still true. The town seal, adopted in 1871, features a plow. However, a big change was already under way. With the growing city of Boston providing a convenient market, Arlington's farmers began concentrating almost entirely on producing vegetables and fruit. Railroad and horsecar lines, running every hour, linked Arlington to the city. Land values rose dramatically, tempting farmers to sell off portions of their land to builders.[4] Soon houses were springing up where lettuces and cabbages had grown. The town was becoming that new sort of entity, a suburb. Potter helped provide town water and more roads, the infrastructure for suburban growth.

Rapid growth was not unique to Boston. Throughout the United States, more and more people were flocking to cities. Cities offered employment opportunities but few other amenities. Overcrowding, smoke-laden air, polluted water, and inadequate sewage disposal made city living unhealthy and miserable for many. The middle class felt threatened by the new immigrants and the poor. The long-standing American prejudice against urban life seemed more valid than ever before. The rural ideal, so fervently promoted since the 1840s by Andrew Jackson Downing in his books and articles, became increasingly appealing. With the development of suburbs that ideal became attainable for more people.

Suburbs were a compromise, promising urban convenience with rural advantages. Ordinary citizens could commute to work from comfortable houses, similar in size and cost to those of their neighbors. Each house could have tastefully landscaped grounds, with space, perhaps, for a horse, some hens, or a cow, for a few fruit trees and a vegetable garden. Utilitarian structures would be screened from view, but everyone could admire each other's front lawns, that new space, "not private, but not entirely public either."[5] Life in the suburbs provided opportunities for sociability with a modicum of privacy while avoiding both the overcrowded conditions of city living and the loneliness that often characterized farm life.

As new residential subdivisions were being platted around American cities in the years after the Civil War, designers were telling people how to lay out their grounds. Gervase Wheeler, the architect who had titled his first book *Rural Homes* (1853), named his next one *Homes for the People in Suburb and Country*, as he kept pace with a significant social change. Wheeler included advice on laying out home grounds, treating that as part of an architect's role. Jacob Weidenmann was another promoter of suburban living, whose *Beautifying Country Homes* was published in 1870. Frank J. Scott saw himself as carrying on the mission of Downing, who had died in 1852. Scott's book, *The Art of Beautifying Suburban Home Grounds* (1870), though filled with plans, sketches, and practical suggestions, was primarily a paean to the suburb. "We believe this kind of half-country, half-town life is the happy medium and the realizeable ideal for the great majority of well-to-do Americans," proclaimed Scott.[6] He, like Weidenmann, was writing about lots from a half-acre up to four. Writer Edward Everett Hale touted suburban living for reasons of health, both moral and physical. The air would be better, residents could raise some of their own food, and children would grow up closer to nature. Assuming frequent and rapid train service, men (only the men) could commute easily to their jobs in the city. But above all, people would become self-respecting property owners, rather than mere tenants, and thus closer to the original American ideal.[7]

In his one published speech, Potter proposed radical solutions to the problems then facing Boston, the city with which Arlington was inextricably linked. His proposal was to enhance the city of Boston by enlarging it. He addressed the Massachusetts senate in 1873 in support of his bill, "On the Subject of Uniting Certain Cities and Towns with the City of Boston."[8] Although this bill was defeated, most of Potter's forward-looking proposals were enacted over the next twenty years. He was ahead of his time.

Sensing that development was inevitable, Potter urged the city and surrounding towns to prepare for it. He was a *regional* thinker, seeking to remedy present community ills and to plan in advance for a better future. Some of his ideas had been articulated by the landscape designer Robert Morris Copeland, whose 1872 "Essay and Plan for the Improvement of the City of Boston" Potter had undoubtedly studied.[9] Potter thought the city was still too limited in extent to provide the amenities that people needed. He owed his inspiration, he said, to Frederick Law Olmsted. For "health, convenience, and beauty" there should be open "breathing spaces" throughout the city. A renewed and greater

J. S. Potter's Cottage Homestead—1867. Gardeners attend to the meticulous grounds while the women sit on the piazza. The house survives. (Boston Athenaeum)

Boston should have a web of spacious boulevards like those of Paris and even more acreage in parkland than New York had at Central Park. The beautiful hills, forests, and lakes of the surrounding region should be preserved for the benefit of the public. So Potter pleaded. In 1878, five years after the defeat of his bill, Olmsted was hired by Boston's new park commission to plan a citywide park system. Boston's so-called Emerald Necklace of parks was developed over the next decade. During the 1890s landscape architect Charles Eliot extended the system into the periphery of the city, with parkways and reservations just where Potter had hoped they would be.

Potter's concern with the loss of naturally beautiful areas as they succumbed to development had led him in 1864 to purchase a three-acre tract near the center of Arlington.[10] This land had already been platted for subdivision into quarter-acre lots. It was near but not adjoining Potter's own homesite and the Carpenter Gothic cottage where he continued to live with his wife, Sarah. The terrain that became "Potter's Grove" was dramatic, a mountain glen in miniature. A hill at the center was almost level on top, but on all sides the land fell away sharply. A brook crossed the property, rushing down a rocky bank toward the lowest-lying corner. The steep slopes and the brook would seem to have been unsuitable for building. Potter landscaped his grove so as to accentuate its natural features. When the work was

 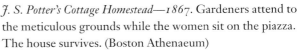

Croquet Lawn, on Grounds of J. S. Potter—1869. (Boston Athenaeum)

completed, Potter encouraged people to visit freely. By allowing (and undoubtedly urging) commercial photographers to purvey stereopticon views of his showplace, he spread word of it to a wider sightseeing public. Visitors were welcome.

Faded photographs of Potter's Grove show how much effort its owner put into shaping his landscape. The top of the hill was graded smooth to make a lawn. "Lawns are of chief importance, and form the basis of the whole ornamental pleasure ground," wrote Weidenmann in 1870.[11] The new availability of small lawn mowers enhanced the popularity of lawn sports, and croquet became a fad. A photograph shows young girls in crinolines aiming for the wickets on Potter's lawn.

Since the area Potter had to work with was small, the components of his garden landscape were small, too. Narrow walks curved closely around the lawn and hugged the terraced slopes. The flights of stone steps were narrow. The brook was forced through a crevice to emerge as a foaming cascade that gushed over a series of rocks into a serpentine goldfish pond. Below the cascade, close enough to catch the spray, was a little Chinese bridge. The meandering edges of the pond were neatly finished off with blocks of cut stone. Water bubbled over the tiers of a cast-iron fountain on an island in the middle. Potter planted dozens of flowering shrubs and young evergreens in this sunken garden. He would have agreed that "an acre lot can have its charming pond or its noisy little cascades with the same propriety as a large park its lakes and brooks."[12]

Potter's Grove did not lack ornaments. On the croquet lawn was a second fountain, the child with the dove; a carved wooden bridge crossed the brook above the cascade. Potter also had stone basins, urn vases, flower baskets on tree stumps, iron arches for vines, a pair of dozing lions, and a statue of a lightly clad goddess.

The site was probably well wooded when Potter bought it, but he added exotic trees, vines, and shrubs. According to newspaper accounts of Potter's Grove, he imported many plants from England.[13] Some old and unusual spruces, firs, and oaks still survive. Potter, like Henry Bowen of Roseland, appreciated trees and undertook the planting of trees along many of Arlington's streets as well. When a storm felled two venerable elms by the town hall, Potter saw to it that their replacements were planted immediately.

The hill at Potter's Grove would have had a fine view of scenic Spy Pond except that trees were growing in the way. To take advantage of the view, Potter built among his pines a prospect tower, by far the largest of his garden ornaments. The three-story hexagonal structure was made of wood and trimmed with a scalloped frieze. A small spire crowned the top of the tower, probably about thirty-five feet in the air. The view from the top of the tower must have been worth the climb. The

View on Grounds of J. S. Potter—Arlington, 1870. Granite steps, vases, cascade, fountain, and serpentine pond. The photographer arranged the people as if they too were garden ornaments. (Boston Athenaeum)

experience, if perhaps not utterly awesome, was the closest approach to a thrill for Potter's visitors.

Prospect towers as landscape features were not uncommon when Potter built his. In England such towers had been adjuncts to landscape gardens since the middle of the eighteenth century. Barbara Jones has described many of them, speculating as to their builders' motives. A tower, she wrote, could "add another county or so" to the owner's view.[14] The first such tower in the United States may have been that of Daniel Wadsworth; it was built in 1810 and was open to the public at Monte Video, his estate near Hartford, Connecticut. A

few years later, André Parmentier, a landscape designer, built a rustic wooden tower in his garden, near Brooklyn, the better to see New York Harbor. Downing admired Parmentier's tower, saying that from its top a spectator could obtain a "charming . . . bird's-eye view of the surrounding countryside."[15] Praise from Down-

The three-story prospect tower offered a view of Spy Pond, with Cambridge and Boston in the distance; stereograph, ca. 1870. (Society for the Preservation of New England Antiquities)

ing almost guaranteed imitation, and imitated it was. One tower that Potter could probably see from his own was that which crowns the famous Mount Auburn Cemetery. Motorists along the Mohawk Trail through the Berkshires are still exhorted to patronize rival viewing towers. Signs promise syrup, sheepskins, and "A View of Four States!"

Towers, both the commercial and the garden variety,

are themselves objects in the landscape. They provide a view, and at the same time, looking the other way, they *are* the view. Potter's tower indicates his concern with pictorial values. The other objects in his landscape were treated as scenery, too. It is no accident that this garden survives as a series of pictures. Between 1865 and 1870, Potter compiled his own album of photographs of Potter's Grove, along with travel scenes and views of Arlington.[16] This album, "Shadows Reflected from the World of Art by Stray Sunbeams," has an ornate title page, hand-painted by Potter, who also used his artistic talents to decorate china. Though photography was an infant art in the 1860s, Potter's Grove might almost have been designed to be photographed. As a landscape garden it was Picturesque in the truest sense of the word.

The landscape style known as the Picturesque had its roots in eighteenth-century England. Three theorists of landscape design—Horace Walpole, William Gilpin, and Uvedale Price—had each attempted his own defin-

ition of the Picturesque style. Their standards of picturesque beauty had been formed in part by the landscape paintings of Salvator Rosa and Claude Lorrain. Picturesque gardens were deliberately composed to look like paintings. Architecture was integrated with scenery; the elements of a picturesque landscape were both natural and artificial. Even animals were considered in forming a composition. Horace Walpole, at his estate, Strawberry Hill, had in 1748 "some Turkish sheep and two cows, all studied in their colours for becoming the view."[17]

The Picturesque style was redefined and elaborated during the nineteenth century. In the 1830s, J. C. Loudon, the prolific English garden writer, coined the unappetizing term "gardenesque" to define those gardens that were planned around the wide variety of exotic trees and shrubs then newly available. In 1860 another writer, Edward Kemp, struggled with definitions, concluding that Picturesque gardens were based on "extreme naturalness." Much more common when

Tea in the Grove—Cottage Homestead—1865. J. S. Potter is seated behind the much-decorated table; his wife Sara and his mother-in-law are to the left. (Boston Athenaeum)

Kemp was writing were gardens in the "mixed style," his catch-all phrase for those gardens where art was blended with nature.[18] Mixed-style gardens were characterized by serpentine lines (the nature part); their art lay in the inclusion of such ornamental features as statues, fountains, and structures of various kinds.

In the United States, Downing interpreted the nature of the Picturesque style to homeowners in the 1840s, contrasting it with the Beautiful. The smooth blandness of the Beautiful style suited residences on level or gently rounded terrain; irregular sites with bold rock outcrops, rushing streams, and abrupt slopes needed only skillful enhancement to be models of the Picturesque.[19] Potter's Grove perfectly exemplified Downing's criteria for a picturesque landscape.

By permitting and even encouraging free access to Potter's Grove, its owner made, in effect, a public park of his own grounds. At least two others in the suburbs of Boston enhanced their own grounds as Potter had done and then invited the public in. Ridge Hill Farms in Needham, the seven-hundred-acre estate of sewing machine magnate William E. Baker, far eclipsed Potter's Grove; by 1877 it had thousands of visitors each week. With its mosaic garden, flower beds in the shape of anchors or hearts, trick fountains, fake animals, and even a bear pit, it could have been a prototype for Disney World.[20] In 1895, Cornelia Warren installed a replica of the Hampton Court maze at Cedar Hill in Waltham. The hedges grew so thick and tall that Miss Warren had to build a watchtower and hire a man to "extricate the bewildered."[21] She, like both Potter and Baker, charged no admission and aimed particularly at attracting children. Most photographs of Potter's Grove include children, particularly adolescent girls. Fountains, bridges, the tower, winding paths and steps, and stone lions to climb on comprised a playground for the imagination, a world in miniature.

Despite the dissemination of commercial photographs of the Grove, most of its visitors were local. The place was nonetheless important and even inspirational to those who frequented it. As the local paper wrote of Potter's Grove in 1876, "The grounds . . . were made beautiful, and for a long time have been a favorite resort for large numbers of our local citizens."[22]

Potter's Grove was in its prime for barely ten years. In many ways, its demise was as typical of the era as its inception. Joseph Potter's rapid rise to relative affluence and his involvement in a series of lucrative enterprises culminated in 1871, when he became president of a brick company. Bricks were vital to the rapid development of Boston, but unfortunately, the industry was susceptible to recession. With the Panic of 1873 and a sudden slowdown in construction, Potter suffered reverses. This may have forced him to sell almost half of the three acres that comprised Potter's Grove in 1873.

It was virtually inevitable that the land would be developed into house lots. Potter, after all, had helped to make Arlington, and his neighborhood in particular, extremely attractive to would-be suburbanites. On the little more than one acre that Potter sold, a builder put up eight houses.[23] Potter had intended to build a substantial house for himself and his wife on his property. For years there was a birdhouse at Potter's Grove that was allegedly a model of Potter's dream house.[24] The dream, however, was permanently postponed. In 1875, perhaps seeking to improve his fortunes, Potter accepted an appointment from President Grant as United States consul to Stuttgart, Germany. Before he sailed, he put the remainder of Potter's Grove up for sale at auction.

Potter abandoned Arlington and Potter's Grove, returning only for occasional visits. Just as his early years had been characterized by frequent moves, so were his later years. When he retired from the consular service, he pursued his hobby of painting on porcelain and bought a plantation in Virginia. Rootless as ever, Potter moved again before long.[25] Arlington, however, was undoubtedly the place to which he felt the strongest attachment for the longest time.

When Potter died in 1904 at the age of eighty, his funeral took place in Arlington. There were few who still remembered him and fewer who came to mourn. The Potters were childless; only his wife survived him.[26] Potter was buried in Arlington's Mount Pleasant Cemetery. One looks in vain among the imposing Victorian monuments for one with his name on it. His grave site is smooth, grassy, and entirely unmarked.

Potter's Grove, diminished in size but still picturesque, passed in 1875 to a new owner, who built a house on the highest point of the property.[27] He announced his intention to leave the remainder of the beautiful grounds intact, rather than subdividing it, as many feared he would. No longer, however, was the public

Opposite: Observatory and Swing on the grounds of J. S. Potter— 1866. Two of many attractions for children and young girls; a photograph from Potter's album. (Boston Athenaeum)

encouraged to make free use of the place. A subsequent owner of the property, Marshall Rice, maintained and improved the garden. He was a recipient of new oriental plants from the Arnold Arboretum. His wife so objected to the continual influx of trees and shrubs that Rice resorted to secreting them about the grounds, hoping she wouldn't look under the bridge in the ravine.[28]

In 1958 the pond and sunken garden were filled in to create two more house lots. The steep granite steps that once paralleled the cascade are intact, though useless. They terminate abruptly at a chain link fence. The cascade no longer exists. Where, we wonder, does the water flow now?

. . .

Potter was a self-made man. Of necessity, he had started early to earn a living. For him there had been no opportunity for advanced education or a cultural Grand Tour. A quest for business success had guided his peregrinations. He was largely self-taught in matters of taste, and his tastes were not the most sophisticated.

Potter adapted the teachings of the contemporary gurus of garden design to suit himself. Even in the Victorian heyday of clutter, Potter crowded too much into a confined space. The editors of the *Horticulturist*, the magazine Downing had started, lamented in 1864 the eclectic mix of garden features such as they might have encountered at Potter's Grove: "crowds of statues, with ludicrous incongruity of subject and fitness; classical vases mingled in with Chinese structures, rustic work with finished work; all sorts of styles mingled in meaningless companionship."[29]

Novelist Maria Edgeworth (1767–1849) poked fun at unsophisticated property owners who, by attempting too much in landscaping their grounds, end with chaos. Her 1812 novel, *The Absentee*, includes this account of a visit to Tusculum, the imaginary Irish demesne of Mrs. Raffarty, the wife of a successful grocer. Before taking her guests around the garden, Mrs. Raffarty offers an apology:

> . . . she had been reduced to having some things on a confined scale . . . ; but she prided herself upon having put as much into a tight pattern as could well be; . . . for she was determined to have at least the honour of having a little *taste* of everything at Tusculum.

So she led the way to a little conservatory, and a little pinery, and a little grapery, and a little aviary, and a little pheasantry, and a little dairy for show, and a little cottage for ditto, with a grotto full of shells, and a little hermitage, full of earwigs, and a little ruin full of looking-glass, 'to enlarge and multiply the effect of the Gothic.'[30]

And, like Potter, Mrs. Raffarty had a little Chinese bridge.

Potter's Grove was not a designed landscape of the highest style. Its busy grounds did not form a great composition of garden art. The place was more cozy than grand. Nonetheless, Potter's Grove follows in the long tradition of the Picturesque that originated in eighteenth-century England. Potter, the self-made business man, the self-taught civic improver, probably did not know just how closely he followed precedent.

Notes

Potter's Grove was located between Pleasant Street and Academy Street in Arlington; Pelham Terrace, a cul-de-sac, was part of the property. The garden steps that once paralleled the cascade can be seen from Academy Street. Potter's Gothic "Cottage Homestead" is at 16 Maple Street.

1. Daniel J. Boorstin, *The Americans: The National Experience* (New York: Vintage Books, Random House, 1965), 116.

2. Charles Edward Potter, ed., *Genealogies of the Potter Families* (Boston: Alfred Mudge & Son, 1888), 29.

3. Charles S. Parker, *The Town of Arlington: Past and Present*, (Arlington, Mass.: C. S. Parker & Son, 1907), 128.

4. Ronald Dale Karr, "The Transformation of Agriculture in Brookline, 1770–1885," *Historical Journal of Massachusetts* 15 (January 1987): 33–41.

5. Robert Fishman, *Bourgeois Utopias: The Rise and Fall of Suburbia* (New York: Basic Books, 1987), 135.

6. Frank J. Scott, *The Art of Beautifying Suburban Home Grounds*, (New York: John B. Alden, 1886), 31. This book was first published in 1870.

7. Edward Everett Hale, *Sybaris and Other Homes* (Boston: Fields, Osgood, & Co., 1869).

8. Potter's speech of 24 April 1873 was published with other legislative proceedings, Massachusetts State Library Archives.

9. On Copeland's plan see John Brinckerhoff Jackson,

American Space: The Centennial Years: 1865–1876 (New York: W. W. Norton, 1972), 129–35.

10. Middlesex County Deeds, East Cambridge, Mass., 855:38, 885:94, 932:553.

11. Jacob Weidenmann, *Beautifying Country Homes* (1870: reprint, Watkins Glen, N.Y.: American Life Foundation, 1978), 8.

12. Ibid., 29.

13. *Arlington (Mass.) Advocate*, 17 June 1876; 17 September 1904; 1 March 1919; 5 November 1936.

14. Barbara Jones, *Follies and Grottoes* (London: Constable, 1979), 35.

15. Andrew Jackson Downing, *A Treatise on the Theory and Practice of Landscape Gardening*, 8th ed. (New York: Orange Judd, 1859), 397–98.

16. Print Department, The Boston Athenaeum.

17. Quoted in David Watkin, *The English Vision: The Picturesque in Architecture, Landscape and Garden Design* (New York: Harper & Row, 1982), 90.

18. Edward Kemp, *How to Lay Out a Garden*, 2nd ed. (New York: John, Wiley, 1860) 123–24.

19. Downing, *Treatise*, 45–68.

20. Gamaliel Bradford, *Early Days in Wellesley* (Wellesley, Mass.: Wellesley National Bank, 1929), 14–15; Leslie G. Crumbaker, *The Baker Estate of Ridge Hill Farms of Needham* (Needham, Mass.: Needham Historical Society, 1975).

21. Charles Calhoun, *Maine Times*, 20 May 1988; Cornelia Warren, *A Memorial of My Mother* (Boston: privately printed, 1908), 140.

22. *Arlington Advocate*, 17 June 1876.

23. Middlesex County Deeds, 1260:534; *Arlington Advocate*, 31 May 1873.

24. Elizabeth Rice, interview by author, 8 May 1981.

25. *Arlington Advocate*, 9 March 1900.

26. Ibid., 17 September 1904.

27. Middlesex County Deeds, 1352:215; *Arlington Advocate* 17 June 1876.

28. Elizabeth Rice, 8 May 1981.

29. "The Use of Ornaments in Landscape Gardening." *Horticulturist and Journal of Rural Art and Rural Taste* 19 (August 1864): 246.

30. Maria Edgeworth, "The Absentee," in *Tales and Miscellaneous Pieces* (London, 1825): 10:118–19.

Chapter 10

On the Isles of Shoals

Celia Thaxter and Her Garden by the Sea

CELIA THAXTER'S garden on Appledore Island, off the southernmost corner of the Maine coast, achieved a renown far greater than its modest size and the simplicity of its design would seem to warrant. Through a fortuitous combination of conditions peculiar to its time and place, Celia Thaxter's cottage and the garden it overlooked became a mecca for American aspirants to culture in the decades after the Civil War. The miracle of a glowing, burgeoning garden, apparently sprung from the wind-swept rock of a tiny, wave-washed island and tended by a charming, beautiful, and talented young poet: this was the stuff of myth. Celia herself, her parlor, her garden, and the island became ever more wrapped in romance from the 1860s, when her first poem was published, until long after she died in 1894 at the age of fifty-nine.

. . .

Celia Laighton was born in Portsmouth, New Hampshire, in 1835.[1] Her father, Thomas Laighton, had his own business for the coastal transport of lumber and freight. He served also as a representative to the state legislature. Immediately after an election defeat in 1839, Thomas Laighton signed on as keeper of the White Island light. He and his wife, with four-year-old Celia and her infant brother, moved to the only house on the barren rock that was White Island, one of the smallest of the clustered Isles of Shoals, ten miles out at sea. Celia and her two brothers grew up on the Isles of Shoals. Even when their father gave up lighthouse keeping in 1841 for a disillusioning and final foray into political life on the mainland, the Laighton family remained on the islands. Mrs. Laighton was a strong, imaginative, and loving mother, to whom her children always remained unusually close. Their father gave them their schooling.

In 1846, Mr. and Mrs. Laighton opened a small summer hotel on the Isles of Shoals. Two years later, with other investors, they started the Appledore Hotel on the island of that name, the largest of the group. They could accommodate 130 guests at first. Later additions to the hotel made room for several hundred more.

Politics and innkeeping are surely among the most sociable of pursuits. Although he clung for over twenty years to a vow he made in 1843 never again to set foot on the mainland, Thomas Laighton was not exactly like Timon, the embittered Shakespearean hermit/hero to whom one writer compared him in 1878.[2] Lord Timon of Athens exiled himself to a life of poverty in a cave by the sea when faced with ingratitude and betrayal at the hands of his former followers. Laighton, in contrast, devoted the rest of his life to attracting the public to his inn and pleasing them when they got there. For his family, however, Thomas Laighton's aberrant choice of a place to live and work truly shaped their lives.

Celia's childhood was lonely but brief. At sixteen she married Levi Thaxter, eleven years her senior. As a Harvard student, he had visited the inn and stayed on over one winter to tutor the Laighton children. Levi loved the bleak, seagirt isles, where the elemental forces of wind and tide ruled the lives of the few hardy residents. The tale of his capture of the willing heart of the innocent, free-spirited maiden of the rock, the beautiful Celia, might have been told by Browning, Levi's favorite poet. Actually, it had been told by Shakespeare, as Nathaniel Hawthorne pointed out. Levi and Celia had been married for a year when Hawthorne made his first visit to the Isles of Shoals in 1852. He found the young couple and their situation truly romantic. After several evenings of conversation, apple toddy, and Celia's singing in the Thaxter parlor, Hawthorne referred to her as "the pretty Miranda."[3] The analogy to the heroine of *The Tempest* was apt. After being banished from his dukedom, Prospero, with his three-year-old daughter Miranda, had been washed ashore on a lonely island. Twelve years later, Miranda—like Celia—

fell in love at fifteen with the first man besides her father whom she had ever seen.[4]

Levi took his bride to live with his family in Watertown, Massachusetts, while he tried to decide on his life's work. He had two degrees from Harvard, one of them in law. He toyed for a time with the idea of becoming an actor. In the end, the high points of his career were his public readings of Browning's poetry. At first Levi's parents provided marginal support for his wife and the three sons she soon bore. Celia had to earn money as well. Although Levi suffered from poor health, he was usually free to travel.

At first the Thaxters returned regularly to Appledore Island. In 1855, however, Levi's romance with the sea ended abruptly. While sailing out to the island in a small boat, he and one of Celia's brothers were capsized by a sudden and violent squall. The two men were tossed onto the rocks of Appledore and were lucky to survive. Levi's love for island life turned to fear and loathing. He returned, it seems, only once. The romance of his marriage began to decline, too, although less suddenly.

Celia was not happy in suburban Boston, even after she and Levi finally had a home of their own, given them by his parents. She was always tired from overwork. In letters and verse she expressed her wistful longing for her island home. She gave her brother a pathetic account of how she had even talked to a dead

Celia Thaxter at twenty-one, with her sons John and Karl, 1856. (Courtesy of Rosamond Thaxter, Dimond Library, University of New Hampshire)

haddock as she cut it up for the family dinner in Watertown: "tell me the last news from the salt sea."[5] Without her knowledge, Levi gave one of Celia's poems to his college friend, James Russell Lowell, editor of the new *Atlantic Monthly*.[6] "Land-locked," Celia's first published poem, appeared in 1861, to her surprise. Considering that her poem described how sad and homesick she was in their new home, Levi's pride in her accomplishment must have been tinged with some ambivalence.

Celia continued to write poetry, and the *Atlantic* continued to publish her work. James T. Fields, the publisher, and his wife, Annie Fields, who had taken Celia under her wing, persuaded her to try prose and to use her own background as her subject matter. In 1869 and 1870, "Among the Isles of Shoals" came out serially in four issues of the *Atlantic* and later as a book.[7]

Celia found herself swept up in the lively Boston cultural scene—and she loved it. Attending lectures, concerts, operas, literary dinner parties, meeting everyone important, and being made much of: this was in heady contrast to her island girlhood. At the same time, she returned to Appledore with increasing frequency, almost always without Levi, particularly after her father died in 1866.

The strong attraction that the islands held for Celia was tempered by her awareness of their depressive effect upon her. She described them in 1869 as desolate, inhospitable, and melancholy, their rocky shores "beaten by the bitter brine for unknown ages." "Very sad they look, stern, bleak, and unpromising," she wrote. She remembered her constant fear as a child of finding some "dreadful token of disaster" washed up on the shore. The sight and sound of the breakers produced in her—and in others, she implied—a "lotus-eating state of mind." She was referring to Odysseus's shipmates, who lost all motivation and all memory of home when they ate the addictive, honey-sweet flower food of the island where they found refuge in a storm. Appledore, too, so peaceful and so strangely beautiful, held a dangerous allure. "It is not good," Celia wrote, "for men to live their whole lives through in such remote and solitary places." She followed her own precept, dividing her time between island and city but always with conflicting emotions.

Celia came early to gardening, according to her own account. She made her first garden when she was five: one square yard devoted entirely to pot marigolds (calendulas) in "fire-colored" shades of orange and yellow.[8]

She planted the crescent-shaped seeds herself. As children, Celia and her brothers noticed and treasured every weed or wildflower that grew on the islands—even every blade of grass, she claimed. The sparseness of the natural vegetation made each tiny plant seem precious.

Mrs. Laighton, Celia's mother, was a gardener. While the family lived on White Island, smaller and even rockier than Appledore, Mrs. Laighton had grown flowers in a pocket of soil between the ledges. She made their house cheerful in winter with potted plants, many of them opening fragrant flowers weeks before spring came. After her marriage in 1851, Celia's younger brother, Cedric, wrote frequent funny, affectionate letters to his sister "on the continent," as they called the mainland, keeping her informed in her absence of happenings on the islands, horticultural and otherwise. He told Celia, for instance, that their mother's calla lily had opened a flower in February 1867.[9] He reported that Mrs. Laighton had coaxed into bloom an oleander, fuchsias, a seven-foot Madeira vine (*Andredera cordifolia*), and some hyacinth bulbs that Celia had sent her.

In 1863, Mr. and Mrs. Laighton built a new house for themselves on Appledore, set a little apart from the vast hotel. This house became Celia's within a few years. As she began to spend more of her summers on the island, she developed her treasured and soon celebrated garden in front of the house.

· · ·

Celia Thaxter became a cult figure early in her adult life, and the magic continued to grow. By intensifying the drama in her own life, her prose and poetry contributed to the mythic aura that surrounded her. Perhaps in no other age would she have become such an alluring icon for so many. Her artistic appeal proved irresistible, particularly when combined with the romantic and tonic quality attributed to life by the sea.

When the dean of Harvard Medical School proclaimed in 1820 that the dyspeptic and the debilitated would benefit from sea air and salt water, he inadvertently helped to promote the establishment of the first summer hotels along the New England coast. The Nahant Hotel, opened in 1823 on a promontory near Boston, may have been the first resort in the region to cater to those in search of health by the sea.[10] The Boar's Head Inn at Hampton Beach, New Hampshire, was started a year later.[11] By promoting the healing quality of seaside life, these inns and others that followed countered the appeal of the mineral springs resorts further inland. Thomas Laighton's Appledore Hotel, started in 1848, was held to possess "the tonic qualities of a sea voyage" because it was ten miles offshore.[12] Visitors were promised equable temperatures, stimulating breezes, and freedom from hay fever. These claims were almost irresistible for those who suffered from "nerves" or from such common and often fatal diseases as tuberculosis, for which no cures were known. More and more people sought to escape, at least briefly, from city life, believing with some justification that their urban environment was unhealthy.

Social life, at first simply a fringe benefit of the quest for physical and mental health, was soon the dominant feature of summer hotel vacations. Common to all the coastal resorts were strolls along the rocky shore, festive evening galas, games of croquet, and rocking, chatting, and courting on the ubiquitous long verandas. Because of its island location the Appledore Hotel offered its guests none of the peripheral commercial diversions available at larger resorts on the mainland. After 1861, when her first poem was published, the chief attraction at Appledore was Celia Thaxter herself.

Celia lived at a time when poetry was popular and poets were revered. Longfellow, Emerson, and James Russell Lowell were famous far beyond the periphery of Boston, where they lived. People all over the country purchased stereopticon views of the houses of famous poets. Audiences flocked to hear poets give public readings. Bostonians gathered to hear Celia's husband, Levi, read from the works of Browning. In his autobiography, novelist William Dean Howells recounted an incident that indicates the adulation accorded to the leading literary lights of that time. When he returned to his Ohio boyhood home in the late 1860s, from Cambridge, Massachusetts, where he was then living, he dropped in on a family friend, James P. Garfield (later United States president). Just as Howells began talking, his host interrupted, crying, "Just a minute!" Garfield then rushed off the veranda to summon all his neighbors, shouting, "Come over here! He's telling about Holmes, and Longfellow, and Lowell, and Whittier!"[13] In the late nineteenth century, poets, essayists, painters, and musicians were often as fawned upon as sports stars and television pundits or evangelists are today.

Boston was the nation's cultural capital in the decades following the Civil War.[14] During the winters, Celia Thaxter became part of the city's literary and artistic milieu. Through her husband she met James Russell Lowell, the *Atlantic*'s first editor, and James T. Fields, the ebullient book publisher. Celia became a close friend of Annie Fields, who introduced her to everyone who mattered. Celia charmed those who met her, including the celebrated Dickens on his American tour and John Greenleaf Whittier, then New England's unofficial poet laureate. Her extraordinary upbringing enhanced her appeal as a person and as an author. In the simplicity of her dress—her only jewels were the periwinkle shells she gathered and strung herself—and the unspoiled enthusiasm of her enjoyment, she seemed, according to her friend Elizabeth Stuart Phelps, as wholesome and fresh as "a breeze from her own island waves."[15]

The Appledore Hotel could not have found a better press agent than Celia. The writers, musicians, and artists she met came to the island to be near her and to partake of the sources of her poetic inspiration. Those who knew her only through her books came, too. According to one admirer, thousands came each summer in the 1870s just to catch a glimpse of the real Celia Thaxter, some of them even pressing noses to her windows or snatching souvenir flowers from her garden.[16]

Her parlor and her piazza were by no means open to any and all hotel guests. Celia's sanctuary was protected by those she favored with her friendship. She had many friends, and her circle was constantly expanding to include younger talents and people whom she found sympathetic. She reached out particularly to other women who wrote. Her parlor became her salon and, for her intimates, the most desirable place in the world to be.

The roster of those who were part of her Appledore circle reads like a literary and artistic *Who's Who* for the country in the second half of the nineteenth century. Celia attracted all the variety of types and talents that William Dean Howells claimed was indispensable to a woman's salon. She even met his cynical condition that it was essential not to include one's husband.[17] Somehow, in Celia's presence, it seemed that musicians played their best, and poets read their best. Whittier, almost a second father to Celia, was a frequent visitor and faithful correspondent. He wrote her in 1874 wondering what the island would be like without her: "a mere pile of rocks, I imagine, dead as the moon's old volcanic mountains."[18]

On a typical day at the height of the summer season, Celia's salon would commence promptly each morning at eleven. The hostess herself would have been working

Celia Thaxter's parlor on Appledore Island, bedecked with flowers and framed pictures; photo by Conner, Portsmouth, New Hampshire, 1880s. (Analesa Adams Collection, Dimond Library, University of New Hampshire)

in the garden and arranging flowers since the early hours. At the appointed time, friends would gather in the airy, flower-decked parlor, on the piazza, or on the steps outside to hear Professor John K. Paine of Harvard play Beethoven sonatas on the upright piano or perhaps Julius Eichberg playing Grieg on his cello. When the music ended, Celia would simply sigh, "Heavenly!" and her guests would echo. In the afternoons, there would be talk or readings; often Celia could be persuaded to read Tennyson or her own latest poems. Of an evening the room would be dimly candle-lit for more poetry or a spiritualist seance, the 1880s craze that engrossed Celia for a time. Or it might ring

with laughter while historian John Fiske sang from *Pinafore* and Charlotte Dana danced.[19] Celia herself, dressed always in white, was the calm center of the life that swirled through her parlor.

Part of Celia's appeal to the popular imagination came from her romantic view of the past. While New England's rural population was moving to the cities or to the West, abandoning farms and leaving whole villages to revert to wilderness, the relics of bygone days were haloed with sentiment. Appledore Island had been densely populated in the seventeenth century by fishing families. The island was covered with old graves and cellar holes. Celia wrote stirringly about this lost settlement in "Among the Isles of Shoals." Hawthorne had written of his fascination with these particular remnants of the past, and Celia claimed that the "traces of vanished humanity" inspired her dreams.[20]

Celia herself seemed to her readers and acquaintances a link to an older New England, to a more elemental life lived close to the land and the sea. This closeness was made vivid in her poems. Her cottage and her parlor seemed simple and retrospective to her visitors, although in photographs the room looks cluttered to modern eyes. The parlor walls were embellished to the ceiling with tier on tier of framed pictures, and every flat surface was covered with shawls, bric-a-brac, and vases of flowers. Childe Hassam's 1894 oil painting, *The Room of Flowers*, conveys the languor of a summer afternoon in Celia's parlor amid the clutter and the flowers. Most of Celia's chairs and tables dated from an earlier era, as can be seen in the painting and in photographs. Many of the flowers in her garden were "quite old-fashioned and out of date in the greenhouses and gardens of good society," according to one admiring friend.[21] Before long, however, with the advent of the Colonial Revival, "good society" gardeners were growing the same old-fashioned flowers as Celia.

Another aspect of Celia's appeal was the popular perception of her as a domestic, motherly woman as well as a poet and an artist. Even though, as many said, she looked like a goddess, one admiring man marveled that she could also cook, knit, garden, nurse the sick, and comfort those in trouble.[22] Her poetry and the painting she did later in her life were thus elevated above the mundane, traditional feminine routine of her days. Celia indeed devoted much of her life to caring for members of her family in infancy, illnesses, and, for her parents, enfeebled old age. All her life, Celia looked after her eldest son, Karl, who caused her endless concern. He apparently had suffered brain damage at birth and was always unstable, subject to violent fits of temper. Karl left a valuable legacy, however, in his photographs of his mother's cottage and her garden.

Celia worked hard and was often overburdened. Levi contributed little financial or other support to the family. Celia truly needed the money she earned from her writing, poetry readings, and painting. Her path was made no easier when her friend Whittier advised her in 1867 not to set herself up as "a strong-minded woman," adding, "I think men are inclined to deprecate the idea of a merely literary woman."[23] Probably a large majority of women at the time would have deprecated the idea, too. They may have been reassured by Celia's "womanliness," with which they could identify. Whittier's paternalistic strictures may be viewed now as limiting to Celia's use of her talents, but her conformation to his ideal indubitably elevated her status as a cult heroine at that time. Whittier was not intentionally patronizing her when he said of her writing, "It is so

pleasant to know that such things can be done by a woman who looks to her own household, and makes her own fire-side circle happy."

．　．　．

Celia depended on her brothers to help her with gardening chores early and late in the season. Unlike her, they lived on Appledore year round, having taken over the management of the hotel from their father. Cedric wrote her at the end of March 1871 that despite severe weather "the flowers have actually begun to start in your garden. Pansies coming up in every direction."[24] A month later he reported that the garden had been spaded and manured, and "I will see that it is planted according to the approved rules of landscape gardening. Don't spend any more of your pome [*sic*] money for seeds; I will fix everything as though you were here."[25] Celia returned to Appledore for the summer, but in the fall she again left Cedric in charge of her garden. In October he reported, "Your flower garden in its palmiest August days never looked as gorgeous as it does now. The flowers sparkle like gems, and . . . the poppies, for color, are wonderful to see. I have saved lots of four o'clock seeds."[26]

Celia, having learned gardening from her mother, soon began to surpass her at it, as Mrs. Laighton observed. Cedric wrote Celia one May that their mother's flowers were ablaze with blossoms. "And no tongue can tell how she enjoys them. She keeps saying, 'I think they beat sister's.'"[27]

Celia's cottage had a covered piazza running all along its front, typical of resort architecture of the period. Her garden was below the piazza. Begun in the 1860s, the garden was twice enlarged. Even at its greatest extent it was only fifteen feet wide and fifty feet long, very small considering its celebrity. Outside the board fence that enclosed the garden and tempered the wind, Celia planted sunflowers and hollyhocks. She covered the banks below the fence with sweet peas and California poppies. By swathing the piazza in vines she further enlarged her garden. The dim, green cavern of her piazza must have been a welcome relief from glare on the almost treeless island. Intermingled honeysuckle, hops, clematis, akebia, wild cucumber, and wisteria looped their way up every post and along the eaves, forming a flower-spangled curtain of green. Openings cut into the greenery provided glimpses of the sea.

At the urging of her writer friend, Sarah Orne Jew-

Celia Thaxter's restored garden beside the rocky shores of Appledore Island, off the coast of Maine. (Photo by Mick Hales)

ett, Celia made a plan of her garden as it was in 1893.[28] On paper it looks formal enough: rectangular beds divided by narrow walkways, and long, straight borders around the perimeter. But judging from pictures and Celia's own account, the garden was the antithesis of formality. It was densely planted; indeed, it was packed with flowering plants. Her plan accounts for fifty-seven varieties, and she mentions at least that many more. It is a wonder that any small or delicate plants could withstand the encroachment of those more vigorous. Celia admitted to having to throw away "enough flowers to stock half a dozen gardens, in order to let the remaining plants have room to grow. . . . It breaks my heart to have to pull up a single one!"[29]

She attributes her acute pain at pulling out a plant to having grown up in a sparsely vegetated island setting. Ever since she was a small child, Celia had treasured the first shoots and blossoms of each tiny plant. She continued to be captivated by the smallest details of a flower, as well as by the massed effects of color. The close-up view and the distant blur characterize myopic eyes. Celia may well have been nearsighted. She used a magnifying glass to peer even more closely. Her porings over "every blossom that unfolds" were transcendental experiences, opening for her "unknown gates into the wonders and splendors of creation."

If one but gazes closely into a tiny flower of the pale blue Forget-me-not, what a chapter of loveliness is there! One sees at a glance the sweet color of the starry, compact cluster, and perhaps will notice that the delicate buds in their cherishing calyx are several shades of rose and lilac before they unclose, but unless one studies it closely, how shall one know that in most cases the *himmel-blau* petals are distinctly heart-shaped, that round its golden centre it wears a necklace of pearls, or so they seem, till on looking closer one discovers that the effect is made by the fluting of the whitened folds of

each petal at the base; it looks precisely as if it wore a string of polished beads.[30]

Celia herself could never choose a favorite among her flowers, but certainly poppies ranked high. She grew every variety and species she could lay her hands on, both annual and perennial. She described with eloquence their infinite tints from "tenderest lilac" to a red that was close to black. To her friend Rose Lamb she wrote that the exquisitely shaded Shirley poppies "make the garden look as if the dawn had fallen into it out of the sky."[31] The "great scarlet flags" of the Orientals had an "angry brilliance," while the petals of the orange Iceland poppies, "wrinkled in a thousand folds" within each calyx, opened to "flutter out on the gentle breeze like silken banners to the sun."[32] Poppies pleased her with their form at all stages of their growth. To her, their seedpods were "supremely graceful urns . . . wrought with such matchless elegance of shape," recalling the mystic power of sleep imprisoned within.

Celia was convinced that flower colors were more brilliant in her island garden than on the mainland. Ordinary garden flowers, usually "decorous, commonplace, and pale," were for her mysteriously transfigured as if by alchemy. Her pansies were "streaked with burning gold," her larkspurs "brilliant as lapis lazuli."[33] She is not the only seaside gardener to have remarked on this phenomenon. Although her heightened sensitivity

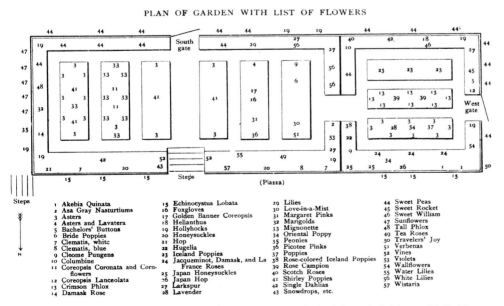

PLAN OF GARDEN WITH LIST OF FLOWERS

1 Akebia Quinata	15 Echinocystus Lobata	29 Lilies	44 Sweet Peas
2 Asa Gray Nasturtiums	16 Foxgloves	30 Love-in-a-Mist	45 Sweet Rocket
3 Asters	17 Golden Banner Coreopsis	31 Margaret Pinks	46 Sweet William
4 Asters and Lavatera	18 Helianthus	32 Marigolds	47 Sunflowers
5 Bachelors' Buttons	19 Hollyhocks	33 Mignonette	48 Tall Phlox
6 Bride Poppies	20 Honeysuckles	34 Oriental Poppy	49 Tea Roses
7 Clematis, white	21 Hop	35 Peonies	50 Travelers' Joy
8 Clematis, blue	22 Hugelia	36 Picotee Pinks	51 Verbenas
9 Cleome Pungens	23 Iceland Poppies	37 Poppies	52 Vines
10 Columbine	24 Jacqueminot, Damask, and La	38 Rose-colored Iceland Poppies	53 Violets
11 Coreopsis Coronata and Corn-	France Roses	39 Rose Campion	54 Wallflowers
flowers	25 Japan Honeysuckles	40 Scotch Roses	55 Water Lilies
12 Coreopsis Lanceolata	26 Japan Hop	41 Shirley Poppies	56 White Lilies
13 Crimson Phlox	27 Larkspur	42 Single Dahlias	57 Wistaria
14 Damask Rose	28 Lavender	43 Snowdrops, etc.	

NOTE. — The garden is 50 ft. long by 15 ft. wide, and is surrounded by a border of all sorts of mixed flowers. A bank of flowers at the southwest corner slopes from the garden fence.

This plan of Celia Thaxter's garden was drawn for her book, *An Island Garden*, 1894.

Celia Thaxter among her flowers; Childe Hassam painted her in similar guise in 1892. (Portsmouth Library Collection, Dimond Library, University of New Hampshire)

shades; a slender rosy glass echoed the pink to coral sweet peas it held.

Celia described herself as worshipping her flowers, but she also felt that they worshipped *her*. She talked to them, greeting them as if they were people—children, actually, dependent on her care. Everything about her garden was thus romanticized and exaggerated. Even the humble act of weeding, as she described it, was glorified as gratifying to the senses. Reclining on a bit of carpet, her face as close as possible to her work, she feels the "potent heats" that cause everything to grow. "Hot, hot, and bright, . . . Oh, the joy of it! . . . delicious scents . . . the glitter of drops on the young green . . . clouds of incense."[34] The flowers bring her to orgasmic ecstasy. The poppies above her "swayed with pleasure," and "one enormous red Hollyhock grew thirteen feet high . . . Oh, but he was superb!" Much could be made of this imagery.

Nature evoked the extremes of emotion from Celia. Impassioned ardor was countered by violent hatreds. In fury she crushes rose beetles and impales cutworms on pins. She keeps a shelf of deadly powders to destroy her garden foes. Slugs she hates most of all. After sleepless nights, she goes to her garden at four in the morning to "make a business of slaughtering them" before breakfast.[35] She blames herself for having inadvertently introduced the slugs to the island. Whether or not this was true, her zeal for exterminating them knew no bounds. She had friends on the mainland collecting toads, natural enemies of slugs. The toads were shipped to her by the boxful and then released to join the battle as auxiliaries in Celia's war.

Her most detested weeds become demonic personae.[36] Stramonium (*Datura*), for one, is "powerful and persistent . . . a poisonous thing with a loathsome odor . . . bat-like leaves . . . wicked luxuriance." Seedlings of dodder, a bindweed, turn into vampires, adhering to their chosen garden victims "with a grip that grows more and more horrible; they suck all its juices, drink all its health and strength and beauty." The result is "ruin and despair."

Celia did not despair, however, but persisted, as avid gardeners always do. She could identify with Charles Dudley Warner, whose 1885 book, *My Summer in a Garden*, chronicled his fight against the aggressive weed "pusley," or purslane. Warner's account, unlike Celia's, was leavened with whimsy, as in his challenge to Darwin (by then deceased) to show him a garden run in accord with the theory of natural selection.[37] Perhaps, as

led her to exaggerate, other, less sentimental observers agree that flower colors are, or at least seem, more vivid by the sea. Thalassa Cruso, an expert gardener who pointed out that she had no scientific evidence for her theory, hazarded a guess that cooler nights and moister air may defer the inevitable bleaching of the petals by the sun.

Early each morning, shears in hand, Celia went among her flowers while the dew was still on them to gather decorations for her parlor. She filled dozens of jars, bowls, baskets, vases of Bohemian or Venetian glass, and one pearly conch shell. She covered windowsills, bookcases, mantelpiece, and tables with her massed arrangements. One table she called her "altar"; another was the "shrine." Worshipping her flowers indoors provided her with more opportunities for close-up observation of their form and color. She placed pale and deeper yellow nasturtiums in a vase of the same one scholar has suggested, her garden represented for Celia the duality she saw in nature. In her constant struggle against the encroachment of evil in the garden she nurtured the good and the beautiful, just as she tried to do in all aspects of her life.[38]

When Celia got around to writing *An Island Garden* in 1893, the year before she died, she intended to proffer practical gardening advice. Most of her readers, however, undoubtedly knew her as a poet, from whom any personal account would be welcome. Her book recounts some of her successful horticultural techniques, but not all of them would have been entirely useful to the average gardener. Celia saved eggshells to start seedlings of poppies and other annuals that did not transplant easily. She set the shells in shallow, sand-filled boxes, tending the seedlings carefully in a cool room through the weeks of winter. In April the boxes of growing seedlings were loaded onto the deck of the steam tug *Pinafore*, together with Celia's houseplants, for the trip over the waves from Portsmouth to Appledore. Celia was charmed by the sight of the little vessel, decked with flowers and greenery, as for a May Day festival.[39]

Celia wrote of the pleasure she took in her gardening tools.[40] She spaded, she hoed, and she raked, making it acceptable for other "ladies" to follow her example. Her book about her garden is, above all, inspirational. Its message undoubtedly lured some women out of their houses and into their gardens, prepared to till the soil themselves.

The other message conveyed by her book had to do with her style, or rather, her antistyle. She advocated by example a luxuriant melange of plants, grown together but appreciated individually, as in a traditional cottage garden. She shot her lethal arrow at contemporary garden fashion with this mild-sounding disclaimer: "I have not room to experiment with rockworks and ribbon-borders and the like, nor should I do it even if I had all the room in the world. For mine is just a little old-fashioned garden where the flowers come together to praise the Lord and teach all who look upon them to do likewise."[41]

This personal philosophy was hammered home to Celia's readers by the book's illustrations. Childe Hassam (1859–1935), a friend and frequent visitor to Appledore, painted twenty-two watercolors for this book. Ten of them were charming close-ups of flowers in bloom or in seed. The others were impressionist views of the garden itself or, in one case, of the flower-decked

"altar and shrine" in Celia's parlor. One reviewer, who found Hassam's illustrations unrealistic in their riotous colors, had to allow that at least they suited the rhapsodic, "excited" style of the text.[42] Hassam's attention to the effects of light on the colors in the garden and the water parallel Celia's own concerns. Two of the paintings include the gardener herself, standing pensive among her flowers and, in another, emerging from the shadowy piazza. The book that resulted from Celia's collaboration with Hassam was extraordinarily beautiful. Even the cover was handsome, in green fabric with a stylized flower design stamped in gold. Author and illustrator were remarkably well suited. Hassam's work—and he made many more paintings of the island—brought greater fame to Celia and her garden, adding luster to her romantic image even after her death.

In 1874, Celia wrote to a friend that she had taken up painting. She painted the botanical subjects that she knew and loved best and occasional seascapes. "I want to paint everything that I see; every leaf, stem, seed vessel, grass blade, rush, and reed and flower has new charms, and I thought I knew them all before."[43] With her watercolors, she often added hand-painted illustrations to printed volumes of her poetry for favored friends or for sale. A painted spider might dangle from his web on the title page, or Celia's own renderings of a scarlet pimpernel might overlap the text of her poem about that flower. She also painted on porcelain. This was a popular hobby and art form at the time, particularly for women. Celia decorated cups, plates, or pitchers of translucent white Haviland china, using special paints and tiny brushes. Her work was an outlet for her considerable talent, and it led her, as she said, to even closer observation of plants, their "every cup and spray and leaf." Many of her pieces were inscribed and given to friends. For James T. Fields, at Christmas one year, Celia painted a tiny cup with a sprig of wild roses and an orange and brown butterfly on the handle. On the saucer, there were more roses, and a verse:

> O cup of the wild rose, curved close
> To hold odorous dew.
> What thought do you hide in your heart?
> I would that I knew![44]

During 1877 alone, Celia, by her own count, painted 114 pieces of china, many of them on commission. She worked year round on pieces for sale to supplement her income, eventually earning more from her painting

than from her poetry.[45] She described herself as working every day all summer. "While the music went on, while the people went in and out and talked and talked, I painted on steadily every minute."[46] She encouraged other guests who painted to work along with her. J. Appleton Brown, Elihu Vedder, Ellen Robbins, Ross Sterling Turner, and Hassam were among the artists who painted Celia's flowers or the rocks and sunsets of Appledore Island.

Celia died in the summer of 1894, a year after completing her book about her garden. Her friend Annie Fields described Celia at the time as a flower herself, who developed to perfection and then, all petals falling in a night, was gone.[47] Appledore lost its magic without Celia. The hotel had already folded when it and Celia's cottage were destroyed by fire in 1914.

In 1973 the Shoals Marine Laboratory was established on Appledore Island under the auspices of the University of New Hampshire and Cornell University. The laboratory's first director, John M. Kingsbury, was inspired to reconstruct Celia's garden on its original site exactly as it was in 1893, using her book as a guide. In

Poppies "make the garden look as if the dawn had fallen into it out of the sky," wrote Celia Thaxter of one of her favorite flowers. (Photo by Mick Hales)

Opposite: The Garden in Its Glory, by Childe Hassam, 1892. One of twenty-two watercolors Hassam painted as illustrations for Celia Thaxter's book, *An Island Garden*. Here the gardener herself heads out into her dooryard garden. (National Museum of American Art, Smithsonian Institution; gift of John Gellatly)

1977 the first seeds and plants were set out. Dr. Kingsbury persuaded Virginia Chisholm to take charge of the garden. She still tends it, with help from members of her garden club. University of New Hampshire horticulturists raise some of the plants. Nowadays, the garden is more of a collaborative effort than it was for Celia, who had only her brothers to help her.

A few of Celia's actual plants are still growing. A couple of old roses and rugged vines, such as the common

hop (*Humulus lupulus*) and "Traveler's Joy" clematis, have managed to survive decades of neglect. To carry the reconstruction forward, the original sequence of the garden's development ought now to be carried on in reverse. The piazza and the cottage itself should be rebuilt to frame and enclose the garden as it was.

Mrs. Chisholm consults Celia's letters and her book about the garden for answers to questions about plant varieties, flower color, and horticultural techniques. The garden is put to bed in the autumn under a four-inch blanket of seaweed, just as in Celia's day. During the winters, Mrs. Chisholm peruses seed and nursery catalogs for antique varieties that would have been available to Celia. The flowers are never exactly the same from one year to another, just as Celia would have had it. American garden books of the period when Celia was gardening have been helpful. Helena Rutherfurd Ely's *A Woman's Hardy Garden* (1903) is filled with advice on planting flower borders and vines around relatively modest, "ordinary" country houses. *The Garden Month by Month* (1907), by Mabel Cabot Sedgwick, who also gardened north of Boston, has proved invaluable, especially as a guide to flower color.

Virginia Chisholm would modestly deny it, but she now stands in for Celia as the guiding spirit of the garden. Like Celia, she has worked in the garden at dawn and has grown to love the setting of sea and sky in all its moods. From poring over photographs, paintings, and books, including Celia's own, she has come to appreciate the difficulties she encountered and overcame. The flourishing reconstructed garden reflects this care and understanding.

In a verse from a poem titled "My Garden," Celia asked hard questions. Her garden gave her no answers, but in it she found the solace that other gardeners often know.

> Where are they all who wide have ranged?
> Where are the flowers of other years?
> What ear the wistful question hears?
> Ah, some are dead and all are changed.
>
> And still the constant earth renews
> Her treasured splendor; still unfold
> Petals of purple and of gold
> Beneath the sunshine and the dews.[48]

Notes

Arrangements to visit Celia Thaxter's restored garden can be made through the Shoals Marine Laboratory at Cornell University.

1. Rosamond Thaxter, *Sandpiper: Life and Letters of Celia Thaxter*, rev. ed. (Francestown, N.H.: Marshall, Jones Co., 1963). This is the only full-length biography of Celia Thaxter (hereafter cited as CT), written by her granddaughter.

2. Samuel G. W. Benjamin, *The Atlantic Islands as Resorts of Health and Pleasure* (New York: Harper & Bros., 1878), 211.

3. Nathaniel Hawthorne, *Passages from the American Notebooks* (Boston: Houghton Mifflin, 1883), 437.

4. The myth continued even after CT's death. Elizabeth Stuart Phelps (1844–1911), a prolific popular novelist, called her "the Miranda of the Shoals" in *Chapters from a Life* (Boston: Houghton Mifflin, 1896), 179.

5. Cedric Laighton, "Letters to Celia Thaxter, 1853–88," typescript, private collection.

6. Thaxter, *Sandpiper*, 61.

7. CT, "Among the Isles of Shoals," *Atlantic Monthly* 24 (August 1869): 177–87; 25 (January 1870): 16–29; 25 (February 1870): 204–13; 25 (May 1870): 579–88.

8. CT, *An Island Garden* (1894; reprint, Bowie, MD: Heritage Books, 1978), v.

9. Cedric Laighton, *Letters to Celia*, ed. Frederick T. McGill Jr. (Boston: Star Island Corp., 1972), 125 (10 February 1867). All references to Cedric's letters are taken from this book.

10. Marie L. Ahearn, "Health Resorts on the New England Coast," in *Victorian Resorts and Hotels*, ed. Richard Guy Wilson (Philadelphia: Victorian Society, 1982), 41.

11. William M. Varrell, *Summer-by-the-Sea* (Portsmouth, N.H.: Strawbery Banke Print Shop, 1972), 37.

12. Benjamin, *Atlantic Islands*, 221.

13. William Dean Howells, *Years of My Youth* (New York: Harper & Brothers, 1916), 204–5.

14. Van Wyck Brooks, *New England Indian Summer, 1865–1915* (New York: E. P. Dutton, 1940), 1.

15. Phelps, *Chapters*, 175.

16. Frank Preston Stearns, *Sketches from Concord and Appledore* (New York: G. P. Putnam's Sons, 1895), 243. According to Keith N. Morgan, Celia Thaxter's picture appeared on cigar boxes, a testament to her celebrity status that she may not have welcomed.

17. William Dean Howells, *The Undiscovered Country* (Boston: Houghton Mifflin, 1880), 87.

18. Samuel T. Pickard, *Life and Letters of John Greenleaf Whittier* (Boston: Houghton Mifflin, 1907), 595.

19. Ellen Robbins, "Reminiscences of a Flower Painter," *New England Magazine* 14 (July 1896): 540.

20. Hawthorne, *American Notebooks*, 439–42. Also CT, "Among the Isles," 185.

21. Oscar Laighton, ed., *The Heavenly Guest* (privately printed, 1935), 137.

22. John Albee, "Memories of Celia Thaxter," *New England Magazine*, n.s., 24 (April 1901):172.

23. Thaxter, *Sandpiper:* John Greenleaf Whittier to CT (29 March 1867), 204.

24. Laighton, *Letters to Celia:* Cedric Laighton to CT (30 March 1871), 141.

25. Ibid.: Cedric Laighton to CT (29 April 1871), 143.

26. Ibid.: Cedric Laighton to CT (6 October 1871), 145.

27. Ibid.: Cedric Laighton to CT (5 May 1872), 155.

28. *Letters of Celia Thaxter*, ed. AF and RL (Boston: Houghton Mifflin, 1895): CT to Sarah Orne Jewett (28 September 1893), 207.

29. Ibid.: CT to Feroline W. Fox (16 June 1874), 57.

30. CT, *Island Garden*, 120.

31. *Letters of Celia Thaxter:* CT to Rose Lamb (25 March 1893), 203.

32. CT, *Island Garden*, 84–85.

33. CT, "Among the Isles," 183.

34. CT, *Island Garden*, 59–60.

35. Ibid., 62.

36. Ibid., 33, 35.

37. Charles Dudley Warner, *My Summer in a Garden* (Boston: Houghton Mifflin, 1885), 79.

38. Perry D. Westbrook, "Celia Thaxter's Controversy with Nature," *New England Quarterly* 20 (December 1947): 511.

39. CT, *Island Garden*, 62.

40. Ibid., 24.

41. Ibid., 71.

42. *Garden and Forest* 7 (16 May 1894): 199.

43. *Letters of Celia Thaxter:* CT to Feroline W. Fox (22 September 1874), 58.

44. The cup and saucer, property of the Society for the Preservation of New England Antiquities, are at the Sarah Orne Jewett house, South Berwick, Maine.

45. Jane E. Vallier, *Poet on Demand: The Life, Letters and Works of Celia Thaxter* (Camden, Maine: Down East Books, 1982), 101. This book is the first to consider Thaxter as a significant figure in American literary history.

46. *Letters of Celia Thaxter:* CT to Feroline W. Fox (10 October 1878), 93.

47. Ibid., Introduction, xi.

48. CT, "The Garden," in Thaxter, *Sandpiper*, 275.

Chapter 11

The Power Landscape

William Seward Webb's

Shelburne Farms, Shelburne, Vermont

ANYONE WHO WALKS through the woods in New England can hardly miss the stone fences. Lichen-covered, often half buried in pine needles, they thread their way uphill and down, now and then meeting each other at odd sharp angles. These fences are such an obvious sign of a drastically altered land use that you begin to wonder how the land once looked. And then you marvel at the sheer strength and determination of the region's first farmers.

The terrain at Shelburne Farms is different. Here, beside Lake Champlain in northern Vermont, you could walk through a thousand acres of woods and pasture land without encountering even a remnant of the typical old stone fences. The landscape is idyllically pastoral, with Brown Swiss cows browsing in verdant rolling meadows. This bucolic setting, unique now in the rapidly developing periphery of Burlington, Vermont's largest city, has long been an anomaly. The truth is that Shelburne Farms was deliberately made to look different from the surrounding countryside. The boundary walls of the old agricultural order were removed, stone by stone, in the 1880s, and the terrain was reshaped on a new and grand scale.

Shelburne Farms is at the opposite end of the scale from Celia Thaxter's island garden. At Shelburne, seemingly endless resources and apparently limitless authority enabled William S. Webb and his wife, Lila, to make a new landscape of nearly four thousand Vermont acres. In a display of wealth and power rivaling that of Louis XIV at Versailles—or closer to home, of Lila's brother George Washington Vanderbilt at Biltmore in North Carolina—the Webbs, with expert guidance, entirely transformed their property to accord with their own vision. Farmhouses, barns, woodlots, fields, and lanes were removed along with the fences. Of the earlier settlers, the only relics to withstand the Webbs' dominating onslaught were a few apple trees and the stark little burying ground that survives to this day. Owing to a continuity of ownership and planning, the landscape of the Webbs has lasted now for over a century.

Ceres, the goddess of farmers and fruitfulness, is poised symbolically above the dome of Vermont's state capitol, providing a clue to what its early legislators thought typified their state. By the 1880s, however, although farming was still the most common occupation in Vermont, it no longer provided a generally satisfactory way of life. At least two-thirds of the land in the state had by then been cleared for tillage or pasture.[1] The original timber had been cut from even the steepest slopes. The high tide of land clearing was already beginning to ebb, however, just when it reached its greatest extent. With increasing frequency, especially after 1880, hill-country farms were being abandoned as unprofitable and left to revert gradually to forest. In southern New England, the shrinkage of cleared land had been observable for at least thirty years before it affected Vermont.[2] New England's farm economy declined in the decades after the Civil War. The reasons for the decline, often analyzed, form a complex web.

The first settlers of the region's hinterland had been subsistence farmers. Nearly everything a family needed was produced at home. Nineteenth-century industrialization changed all that. Farm families could buy factory-made shoes and cloth. They could also obtain factory jobs. People became dissatisfied with the austerity of a rural existence. Farm life was experienced as exhausting and isolated. The young and the energetic moved, in a steady stream, to the mill, to the city, and to the promised land of the West.

Canals and eventually railroads provided transportation. Not only people but produce, too, could be moved. Vermonters could ship their corn and wheat to distant markets, but before long western grain was being shipped east and sold at a lower price. New England could not compete. Sheep raising, touted as a panacea for farmers, became a craze throughout the region during the 1830s and 1840s. Soon the West won out again, however, and wool prices plummeted.[3]

The Civil War drew many young men off the farms. Even those who survived the fighting seldom returned to work the farms on which they had grown up. The Homestead Acts of 1862 and 1864, with especially liberal provisions for veterans, lured many to the West.

Vermont farmers shifted more of their resources into dairying after the war. The number of cows rose steadily. Most of the milk was made into cheese or, later, into butter, products that could be shipped with relative ease to distant markets. In 1869, alarmed by competion from midwestern butter, Vermont farmers organized the nation's first state dairy association.[4] Butter was entirely farm-produced until 1879, when the first cooperative creamery in New England opened in the town of Shelburne. Soon farmers everywhere were taking their milk to a local creamery.

Cooperation offered farmers the possibility of improving their lot by the power of association. The Vermont Grange, New England's first, was organized in 1872, the same year that the state Board of Agriculture was established.[5] These organizations assisted farmers

Steamer off Shelburne Point, oil by Charles Lewis Hyde. This mid-nineteenth-century painting illustrates the view that Olmsted admired in 1845. The typical agrarian Vermont landscape in the foreground later became part of William S. Webb's Shelburne Farms and was subjected to a grand reordering. (Shelburne Museum, Shelburne, Vermont)

by promoting new advances in farm machinery or technique. The "silo system" for storing winter feed, developed in the 1880s, was one advance that caught on quickly.[6] Before long almost every barn had a silo next to it.

Vermont farmers in general were not prospering, however, despite new methods. The Board of Agriculture's report for 1878 included an article probing reasons and remedies for "The Depopulation of Our Rural Districts." One of the author's recommendations was that "the hills that are fit for nothing else . . . be allowed again to become covered with forests."[7] Trees were taking over the land even as he wrote. By 1900, according to census figures, Vermont had only half as many operating farms as in 1880.

The stark reality of farm abandonment caused shock and dismay in Vermont, as it did throughout New England. Those who observed conditions in the back country were appalled. Dozens of heart-rending articles on the phenomenon were published before and after the turn of the century. E. R. Pember's 1884 description is typical: "The observing traveller . . . will notice . . . in the older settled portions many evidences of decay and desertion. The crumbling ruins of the foundations only are left to mark the site, or perchance it may be that the tottering well sweep and perennial lilac bush still stand as mementoes of once happy homes, where families were born, reared, and went forth to do valiant service in the battle of life."[8] Henry James, observing New England with the eye of an expatriate, was appalled in 1906 by the rural poverty and the bareness, all "telling the tale of the difference made, in a land of long winters, by the suppression of the two great factors of the familiar English landscape, the squire and the parson."[9]

Vermont's Board of Agriculture tried to help the owners of unoccupied or unused farms by publishing catalogs that listed and described places for sale.[10] Massachusetts and New Hampshire did the same. The reasons for selling recur: "cannot get help" or "getting old." The selling points often emphasized accessibility: "roads rolled after every storm in winter," "ten minute walk from the station," and significantly, "would be a splendid summer home." Even considering inflation, prices seem strikingly low. In that pre-skiing era one could have purchased a fifty-acre farm at Stratton Mountain for $400, or a house, barn, and 150 acres on the side of Mount Mansfield for $2,700.

People laid the blame for the "tragedy" of farm abandonment on everything from the Homestead Acts to unfair taxes to the laziness and inefficiency of the farmers themselves. A more perceptive view was that farmers gave up after seeing the "dark side," the side so memorably portrayed in Wharton's *Ethan Frome*.[11] Those who left their stony hill farms for the factory or the city generally improved their lot. The fields they had tilled and planted, year after year, were left to grow up once again into forest.

The farmers of the Champlain Valley in northwestern Vermont were more favored than their peers in the uplands. The lake had a moderating effect on the climate, and the soil was deeper. Even those valley farmers who were unable or unwilling to adopt the latest scientific techniques could at least manage to survive. Despite difficulties, they were less prone than the hill farmers to abandon their farms.

The valley farms were also less isolated than those in the hill country. Since 1823 the Champlain Canal had linked the lake to the Hudson River. By 1849, two railroad lines ran to Burlington.[12] For many of the farmers in the town of Shelburne, six miles south of Burlington, the railroad turned out eventually to be the power that changed their lives. The incident that sparked the change was Dr. Webb's first visit to Burlington in 1880 on railroad business.

. . .

William Seward Webb (1851–1926) had grown up in New York City, where his father was the "pugnacious" editor of a New York paper.[13] Seward Webb studied medicine in Europe and at Columbia. He practiced for only three or four years before turning to finance on Wall Street, where he established his own brokerage house. Before long he became involved in railroad business with William Henry Vanderbilt, oldest son and chief heir of "Commodore" Cornelius Vanderbilt.[14]

Dr. Webb traveled to Vermont in 1880 to look at the Rutland railroad with an eye to annexing it to the Vanderbilt empire. Although he did not favor acquisition of the railroad, he liked what he saw of Burlington and the Champlain Valley. He also liked the Vanderbilts. In 1881, Seward Webb married Lila Vanderbilt, the next youngest of William Henry's eight children. Not long after his marriage, Dr. Webb was named president of the Wagner Palace Car Company, suppliers of sleeping cars to the Vanderbilt-controlled New York Central Railroad.

For a wedding present, Lila's father gave her a house

Dr. William Seward Webb, ca. 1890. (Shelburne Farms, Shelburne, Vermont)

view of the blue Adirondack mountains, rising tier on tier, on the far side of the lake. From Lone Tree Hill in Shelburne, three hundred feet above the water, the view to the west was even more impressive.

Webb began negotiating in 1885 to buy up parcels of land in Shelburne. In December of that year, his father-in-law, William Henry Vanderbilt, died, having doubled the fortune that *his* father, Cornelius, had bequeathed to him a mere eight years earlier.[16] Lila's inheritance was only a small fraction of her father's $200 million estate, but added to Seward Webb's own rapidly growing fortune, it made the couple's means seem limitless. The Webbs could have almost anything they wanted. Dr. Webb enlarged the scope of his plans for Shelburne and accelerated the pace of his land purchases. Through an agent he negotiated with local farmers, many of them impoverished, but not all of whom were pleased to learn that they had granted sales options to the same mysterious buyer.[17] By 1891, Webb had purchased all or portions of twenty-nine farms, covering 2,800 acres. The prices Webb paid varied widely, but the average was less than $150 per acre over a six year-period. Existing farm buildings added little if any value; Webb was interested only in land.[18] Still he continued to buy. Eventually he owned almost four thousand contiguous acres.

. . .

Dr. Webb intended all along to reshape the separate farms he was buying into one great unified whole. His first move was to hire an architect to design a suitable house and major farm buildings. His choice of R. H. Robertson was a happy one for both men. Robertson was known to Webb as a designer of railroad stations and as architect of the Gothic Revival Church of Saint James in Manhattan. He worked for Webb for years. With Webb as his patron, Robertson's major work was done at Shelburne.

One of Dr. Webb's first directives to Robertson was to ask Frederick Law Olmsted, then the nation's preeminent landscape architect, to come as soon as possible to Shelburne to confer in regard to the "landscape department."[19] In his June 1886 letter to Olmsted conveying Webb's invitation, Robertson wrote that he had been retained to design "a most important Country house, stock barns—stables etc." for the 1,700 acres that Webb had by that time purchased along the lake. To make sure that Olmsted realized the significance of

on Fifth Avenue at Fifty-fourth Street, just a block from his own mansion and those of other family members. Their Fifth Avenue house was to be the Webbs' primary residence for thirty years. As the location for their requisite country house, they promptly settled on the remote and unfashionable part of Vermont that had appealed to Dr. Webb.

On the shores of Lake Champlain at Burlington, the Webbs built a rustic summer cottage called Oakledge.[15] This was all very well for a young couple, but the Webbs had something grander in mind. Scouting out the area, Seward Webb decided the most desirable land lay along the lake in Shelburne. The farms there may have been worn out, but the topography and the scenery were special. The shoreline was irregular, with rocky promontories and curving bays. From any point along that stretch of shore, one had the extraordinary the project, Robertson wrote that "if justice is done to the situation and conditions it will without doubt be one of the most important and beautiful country places in America and in view of this fact I *hope you can undertake the problem*." Olmsted wrote to Dr. Webb immediately, arranging to make an inspection trip to Shelburne the very next week, adding that his charge for a preliminary visit would be $100 and traveling expenses.[20] Within a month after his first visit, Olmsted had formulated the basis for his proposal, which, as he outlined it to his colleague, Charles Eliot, was to be "a perfectly simple park, or pasture-field, a mile long on the lake, half a mile deep, the house looking down over it."[21]

Olmsted was at the peak of his career when he agreed to advise Dr. Webb. Ten years earlier, having completed his work on the New York City parks, he had moved his office to Brookline, Massachusetts. Since then, his practice had taken him all over the country. He continued to design public parks for cities, including Boston, Detroit, and Washington, D.C. He advised

on campus plans, ranging from Groton School to Stanford University. He collaborated with prominent architects such as H. H. Richardson on designs for private estates. At about the same time that he took on Dr. Webb as a client, he was working for other members of the extended Vanderbilt family in Newport, Lenox, and Bar Harbor. Biltmore, by far his largest undertaking for a private client, was still ahead. Olmsted's connection with the Vanderbilts had even included laying out the grounds for the family mausoleum on Staten Island.[22]

Staten Island, as it happened, had been the site of Olmsted's first contact with the Vanderbilts. In 1848, aged twenty-six and unsure of his life work, Olmsted had attempted to run a farm bought for him by his father. He lasted only two years on Staten Island but did get to know a neighboring farmer, William Henry Vanderbilt (the father, much later, of Lila Webb).[23] Vanderbilt was exactly the same age as Olmsted. He had been rusticated to farming by his father, Cornelius, who at the time considered him "an improvident dolt."[24] Dolt

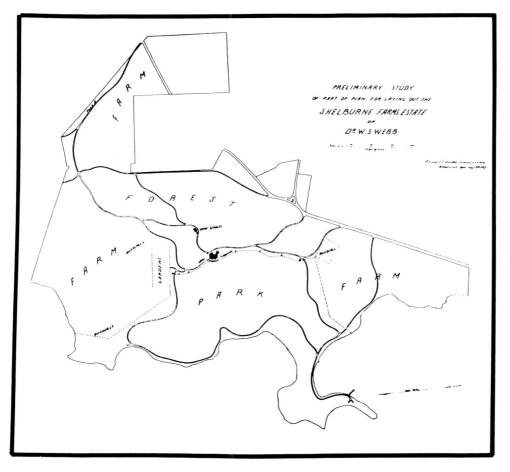

Preliminary Study for Part of Plan for Laying Out the Shelburne Farms Estate for Dr. W. S. Webb, by F. L. and J. C. Olmsted, 1887. The lake shore is at the lower edge of this plan; the house, shown at the center, with its "home grounds" and "home stables" on top of Lone Tree Hill, was actually built close to the lake, contrary to Olmsted's advice. The plan indicates Olmsted's division of the estate into separate areas of farm, park, and forest. (Shelburne Farms)

Frederick Law Olmsted, 1890s, oil by John Singer Sargent. The portrait was painted shortly after Olmsted left Shelburne Farms, while he was laying out the grounds of Biltmore, in the North Carolina mountains, for Lila Webb's brother, George W. Vanderbilt. (Biltmore Estate, Asheville, North Carolina)

Wherever he worked, Olmsted was keenly aware of the character and scenery of the locale. This, to him, was what the word "landscape" meant. He realized that this concern set him apart from others in his field. Most designers, he observed, were unfortunately attuned only to elements, incidents, and features, rather than the landscape itself. This he held to be the direct result of their training as gardeners. "A training which is innocently assumed to be a training in landscape gardening is a training in fact away from it."[25]

At a time when there were no academic programs in landscape design and planning, Olmsted's own education had depended on his remarkable powers of observation. Even as a young man, he had been keenly aware of scenery and well able to describe what he saw. In an 1845 letter to his father he had by chance described the actual setting of what, forty years later, was to become Shelburne Farms. Exploring that part of Vermont on a horse, he had observed the marginal state of the region's agriculture. He rode past burned stumps, patches of mullein, and so little grass that "I should think the poor sheep would find it hard work enough to live, without troubling themselves with growing wool." South of Burlington, standing probably on Lone Tree Hill, the highest point at Shelburne Farms, Olmsted encountered one of the finest views he had ever seen. He admired Lake Champlain with its bays and islands, but the "chief charm" was the mountain backdrop across the lake: "I never saw mountains rise more beautifully one above another the larger ones seeming to cluster round and protect the smaller, nor did the summer veil of haze ever sit on them more sweetly. Back of all rose some magnificent thunderheads and they rose fast too, compelling me at 5 o'clock to take refuge and toast and eggs in a little road-side inn."[26] The setting was certainly no less impressive in 1886, when Olmsted responded to Dr. Webb's summons.

. . .

or not, Vanderbilt's farm, unlike Olmsted's, was quite prosperous.

Throughout his career as a landscape architect, one of Olmsted's primary goals was to improve the environment of the burgeoning cities where more and more people spent their lives. At the same time, he perceived the importance of planning to preserve wilderness areas and places of particular natural beauty. Olmsted worked to protect Yosemite and Niagara Falls, places he deemed to be national treasures, the birthright of all Americans. His work for rich private clients was just as firmly grounded in his belief in the necessity for conserving natural resources.

Relations between Webb and Olmsted were unfailingly polite but not entirely harmonious. Both were men of strong character with firmly held convictions. Despite disagreements, however, their respect for each other never wavered. Dr. Webb, the client, always sought and demanded the best of everything. He employed Olmsted because Olmsted was unquestionably the foremost landscape architect in the country. Olmsted, in turn, was impressed by the breadth of Webb's vision, the grand scope of his scheme, and doubtless, the apparently unlimited extent of Webb's resources for carrying out an idea. When he first embarked on the project for Webb, Olmsted, like Robertson, was convinced that, when completed, the design of Shelburne Farms "would be the most interesting and publicly valuable private work of the time on the American continent."[27]

A major point of disagreement between Webb and Olmsted arose over the placement of the manor house. At first, Webb and Olmsted apparently concurred that the house should be sited on the summit of Lone Tree Hill, to overlook the pasture lands along the lake, half a mile away. Had it been built on this highest point, with its sweeping view, the house would have emphasized dramatically the dominance of the lord of the manor over the surrounding landscape.

Webb's architect, Robertson, sensed early on that Webb's continuing land purchases might change the presumed location of the house, thus necessitating a complete reworking of his plans. The winter of 1886–87 passed with no definite word from Webb to Robertson or Olmsted on a matter that was obviously of vital concern to both designers. In July 1887, Olmsted sent Webb his preliminary plan, which showed the house on top of the hill. Meanwhile, a supposedly temporary cottage was being built for the Webbs on Saxton's Point,

surrounded on three sides by the waters of the lake.

By the spring of 1888, Webb had decided against building on the hilltop. He now favored a lakeside site near that of the temporary cottage. His self-confidence was such that he felt no need of a high visible symbol to crown his dominion. Olmsted was not pleased. He wrote Webb, saying: "I greatly hope that you will come back to the old position for the mansion. You know, perhaps, that since I saw you I have spent a day on the place, having this question particularly in view. I am sure that there is no other site that offers nearly equal advantages. I had thought of three others as promising well but when I came to try to fit a house and grounds to them none proved satisfactory."[28] Webb was not swayed by the best professional judgment of his eminent landscape designer. His Shelburne residence was to remain on Saxton's Point, the site to which he and Lila had become attached.

One of Olmsted's proposals for Shelburne farms, the one he most ardently promoted, was that the estate include an arboretum of all the trees and shrubs native to Vermont. The arboretum was to accord with the guidelines established by Harvard professor Charles Sprague Sargent in planning the Bussey (later the Arnold) Arboretum. To stock this "Arboretum Vermontii," Olmsted urged Webb to take advantage of the distinguished

The Webbs' house at Shelburne Farms, designed by R. H. Robertson; photo by T. E. Marr, Boston, ca. 1900. The rooms on this western side faced Lake Champlain and the Adirondack Mountains. (Shelburne Farms)

nursery of Pringle & Horsford, located just six miles south of Shelburne.[29] After discussing the idea with his superintendent, Arthur Taylor, who would be responsible for planting and care, Webb agreed to proceed with the arboretum.[30]

As envisioned by Olmsted, the arboretum was to follow the curving roadways he had laid out, being set back from the road on both sides. Such a scheme meant that the arboretum would be an integral and very visible part of Shelburne Farms, which was exactly Olmsted's intent. He placed orders with nurseries all across the country for species that Pringle & Horsford were unable to supply in sufficient quantity. Thousands of trees and shrubs were planted under Taylor's supervision, beginning in 1887. For the sake of economy, a vast number were grown to planting-out size in an extensive nursery established on the Shelburne property.

As was his custom, Olmsted had recommended native and hardy plants, based on his analysis of the site. His plant lists included most of the northeastern native trees: ash, basswood, birch, elm, hickory, oak, and willow, as well as the American chestnut and the American elm.[31] Balsam fir, hemlock, and various native pines were ordered in quantity. Olmsted expected Pringle & Horsford to collect many shrub species by the hundred from the wild: alder, swamp azalea, blueberry, buttonbush, elderberry, pussy willow, black and red raspberries, wild roses, viburnum, witch hazel, and others. He also ordered native vines, including bittersweet, clematis, and wild grape. Olmsted asked for wildflowers, such as twinflower (*Linnea borealis*) and trailing arbutus (*Epigaea repens*). The plants ordered for Shelburne Farms were certainly far different from the typical ornamentals with which gardeners and estate managers were decorating most other country places at the time. Olmsted's ultimate aim seemed to be to reproduce the plant diversity that the region might have supported a century or two earlier, before the land was cleared for farming. The only alien plants he ordered were western evergreens from P. Douglass & Sons: Colorado spruce (*Picea pungens*) and Douglas fir (*Pseudotsuga menziesii*).

Webb's ideas for planting began to diverge from Olmsted's as soon as he fully undertood what Olmsted was proposing. Webb *wanted* to include ornamental varieties; the greenery indigenous to Vermont seemed too stark for the Shelburne Farms he envisioned. He began to request tender and exotic species, such as rhododendrons, weeping willows, tea roses, and gardenias. Olmsted pointed out that these would not survive at Shel-

burne and would be entirely out of character with the landscape.[32] He refused to involve himself with the growing of tropical flowers under glass if that was Webb's desire.

A great deal of planting was done according to Olmsted's recommendation, but the Vermont Arboretum was never completed. This may have been Olmsted's greatest frustration at Shelburne. He had believed strongly that Shelburne Farms, although privately owned, would have a public purpose. As he wrote when he submitted his preliminary plan to Webb in July 1887, "I have satisfied myself by personal examination of the feasibility of such an arrangement and that a beautiful, interesting, instructive and publicly important arboretum can be so obtained, the present natural woods forming an appropriate and harmonious background for it and adding directly to its scientific value."[33]

Olmsted lost his enthusiasm for Shelburne Farms when he realized that Webb did not share his belief in the educational and scientific importance to the public of the work they might have accomplished there together. After the summer of 1888, Olmsted's sons and associates attended to the work at Shelburne. The senior Olmsted, meanwhile, was becoming deeply involved with an even larger private project and a much more sympathetic patron. At Biltmore, in the North Carolina mountains, George W. Vanderbilt, Lila Webb's brother, granted Olmsted the trust and the latitude that he had not received from the Webbs.

Despite his opposition to some of Olmsted's ideas for Shelburne, Webb wholeheartedly recommended Olmsted to another brother-in-law, Frederick W. Vanderbilt, who was building a house at Newport. Even though Olmsted—then at the peak of his career and nationally famous—had no need of referrals, Webb indicated his respect by advising others to consult him as a landscape architect.[34] The significant influence that Olmsted had on Webb is, to this day, reflected in the landscape at Shelburne Farms.

Much of Olmsted's preliminary plan was implemented, as were his carefully articulated principles of design and the separation of conflicting uses. Olmsted divided the property into three areas: "1st Tillage and pasture lands in rotation; 2nd Park or permanent pasture lands; 3rd Forest Arboretum Vermontii."[35] He insisted that cattle should be kept from the home grounds, the main roads, and the forest but without the continual nuisance of gates. To this end, Olmsted pro-

A stretch of one of the new roads, here passing between old-growth forest trees interspersed with recent planting; photo by T. E. Marr, ca. 1900. (Shelburne Farms)

posed the use of sunken fences with retaining walls, like the unobtrusive ha-has of the English landscape school, to confine the livestock. Fences, particularly near the house, were to be as inconspicuous as possible. Even the main entrance gates to the estate could generally be left open, under Olmsted's plan. The existing "straight and graceless" roads were to be changed in course and character to suit the terrain and the lush farmland through which they would run.

The new trees and shrubs were to be set back from the roads, with here and there a grouping brought forward in an apparently random way. "Fine specimen trees of the old spontaneous growth are to be preserved," Olmsted wrote.[36] Groups of trees and the undergrowth were to look as natural as possible.

Olmsted emphasized to Webb the importance of having a definite plan before proceeding. Ongoing land purchases made this difficult, if not impossible. In 1889, after purchasing five pasture farms to the south of his original tract, Webb finally agreed to plant the hilly northern part of the estate in trees, as Olmsted had recommended all along.[37]

The English parks that Olmsted had so admired on his first trip abroad as a young man in 1850 were the chief source of his inspiration throughout his long career. The design principles on which he based his pub-

lic and private work came from his interpretation of
English landscape styles. The idyllic pastoral landscape
of Shelburne Farms is typically Olmstedian. The main
road rolls through broad meadowland, then up a gentle
rise into a stretch of deep woods. Upon emerging again
into the open, one glimpses at a distance the lake or, at
another point, the great house. Then the road bends
away, and the distant vision is hidden once again. The
views that seem so accidental were arranged with care.
Transitions from forest to pasture to lawn and flower
garden are smooth and gradual. There is a sense of fitness and inevitability about this landscape.

The buildings at Shelburne Farms express most
vividly the wealth and confidence—even arrogance—
that made this great agricultural estate. The main farm
barn, completed in 1890, is enormous and looks it, even
from afar. Nestled into the hillside, it appears to have
been there for centuries. It might be a French chateau
or an entire medieval village. Conical corner turrets,
tall clock tower, and massive stone walls enclose a courtyard that covers nearly two acres. This was, and is, headquarters, the heart of the Shelburne Farms operation.

In a different part of the estate is the breeding barn,
which has its own set of superlatives. When it was completed in 1893, it contained the largest indoor riding
ring in the world. Close to a hundred box stalls paneled

The breeding barn, completed in 1893; photo by T. E. Marr,
ca. 1900. The brass and varnished mahogany of the interior
are still intact. (Shelburne Farms)

with chevrons of matched pine boards housed the imported hackney mares and the French coaching stallions that Dr. Webb expected to revitalize Vermont's
horse-breeding industry. There were other barns and
other structures, all designed by R. H. Robertson, each
designed for a specific use and each providing the best
possible facilities for that use.

· · ·

Dr. Webb anticipated and intended that his farm would
provide a model for others throughout the state. Unlike
the previous owners of his land and unlike the typical
Vermont farmer, Webb was able to try experimental
methods and invest in expensive machinery.[38] The
costly new and scientific techniques that were employed at Shelburne Farms may have educated and inspired some, but the marginal farmers who most needed
help were least able to emulate the Shelburne model.

Webb had a good estate manager in Arthur Taylor, a
Scotsman trained both as a horticulturist and landscape

Harvesting wheat with a new McCormick reaper; photo by T. E. Marr, ca. 1900. (Shelburne Farms)

gardener. Taylor had been managing a Burlington farm before he was hired by Webb to help shape his new agricultural enterprise.[39] Webb, who at the outset knew nothing of farming, depended on Taylor. But Webb educated himself. He read widely, from the Vermont agricultural reports to the journals of the Royal Agricultural Society. Before long he was named a trustee of Vermont's agricultural college. He traded livestock with Pierre Lorillard, John Jacob Astor, and other rich gentleman farmers of his acquaintance throughout the Northeast.

Webb had a real sense of stewardship toward his land. He followed an established American tradition of those who achieved success in profession or business and then chose to concern themselves with agricultural improvements on their own rural estates. This was the Washington–Jefferson model, exemplified in New England by the founders of the Massachusetts Society for Promoting Agriculture, Theodore Lyman at The Vale, the Codmans of Lincoln, Jeremiah Wadsworth near Hartford, and a host of others. Agriculture had become John P. Cushing's consuming passion after his years as a businessman in China. An influential spokesman for an intelligent approach to farming by those who could afford to experiment was writer Donald G. Mitchell. Mitchell had begun farming as a hobby at Edgewood, his property near New Haven. He then wrote for others like himself in *My Farm of Edgewood* (1863) and other rural essays, offering advice based on his experience. By the end of the century, many of the new American agricultural estates were, like Shelburne Farms, on an amazingly grand scale. One contemporary commentator noted that such estates were usually "of modern growth, the result of great wealth on the part of the owner, who calls together his architects, landscape gardeners and engineers, and has it built to order."[40]

These great agricultural estates may have inspired American farmers, as was often claimed, but they also displayed to advantage the wealth and power of their owners. The acres of smooth parkland were unusual enough to be awesome. Impeccable maintenance set an example that few could match. The ownership of prize

Opposite: The farm barn at Shelburne Farms, built in 1890, spreads over almost two acres. Beyond are Lake Champlain and the foothills of the Adirondacks. (Photo by Clyde H. Smith)

breeding stock conferred fame and prestige. The sheer diversity of these mega-farms was overwhelming. Shelburne raised the best cows, prize horses, choicest sheep and poultry, had game birds in quantity, and also operated a model piggery. By 1903 the estate's orchards were producing five thousand barrels of top-quality apples each year. Flawless roses and sweet violets from the greenhouses were shipped to the Webbs' New York house every week all winter long.[41]

One of Webb's goals at Shelburne was to restore to its earlier prestige the Vermont horse-breeding industry by bringing back a stronger draft horse for farm work. In 1893, Webb wrote a book about his efforts toward this end, which he saw as presenting "a large field for philanthropic endeavor and afford[ing] so many opportunities for the achievement of lasting good to the community."[42] He was sure that he knew better than his fellow Vermonters what they ought to do. His patronizing attitude may have doomed this particular project. Vermont farmers, he wrote, were foolishly interested only in fast trotters. Despite Webb's object lessons proving the inferiority of the typical farmer's "weedy mares" for farm work, Vermonters persisted in their benighted ways. Webb offered his fancy imported stallions for stud service at a nominal fee. So few took advantage of the opportunity that he began offering the service free. Still he had few takers. Webb was puzzled and chagrined by the lack of response from farmers of the area. He never recognized the degree of quiet resentment evoked by his paternalism.

Like other large agricultural estates, Shelburne Farms was run as a business, with a strict hierarchy of personnel. If the estate staff formed something like a family, Webb himself was its father.[43] The establishment might also have been compared to a duchy, with Dr. Webb as the duke.

Shelburne Farms was nearly self-contained, as it had to be. The estate office, manned by four full-time clerks, managed farm business. The place had its own teams of painters, blacksmiths, carpenters, and wheelwrights, each trade occupying a separate workshop. In addition to the farmhands, gardeners, grooms, and house servants, there were workers and technicians to maintain the miles of roads, the water mains and pumping station, the electricity and gas plants, and a private fire department.[44] Upper-echelon employees had their own cottages, models of the genre, but all estate workers were provided with adequately furnished sleeping and living quarters. There were comfortable clubhouses and fully staffed restaurants for all employees. No necessities were omitted.

· · ·

Webb's desire to improve Vermont's farm economy led him to endorse scientific forestry. He saw to it that his own woodlands were managed properly and extended by reforestation. Even though Olmsted had been unable to persuade him to establish a definitive Vermont arboretum, Webb gained from his landscape architect an appreciation for forest management. He was impressed by Olmsted's experience and his achievements in forestry. At the Phillips Farm in Beverly, Massachusetts, for instance, laid out by Olmsted in 1880, the uplands were devoted to forest trees. Ten years later the woods there were beginning to earn a profit.[45]

Webb needed someone to manage his woodlands. He telegraphed Olmsted in June 1889, asking him to recommend a forester. John Olmsted replied on behalf of his father, who was then at Biltmore, studying the forests there.[46] The Olmsteds were unable to suggest anyone to Webb. The only possibility, according to John, would be to import a trained forester from Europe.

There were at that time no schools of forestry in the United States. Gifford Pinchot, an 1889 graduate of Yale, was about to change that. He studied forestry in France for two years and in 1891 went to work at Biltmore, where he met the senior Olmsted.[47] Both Olmsted and George Vanderbilt developed great respect for Pinchot and gave him an opportunity to prove definitively the worth of scientific forestry. Pinchot started the first American forestry school at Biltmore in 1896.

In 1892, during a visit to his brother-in-law at Biltmore, Webb was impressed by Pinchot's work and invited him to Shelburne Farms. Pinchot made several visits and undoubtedly proffered advice, although no written record of this has turned up. Webb had been easily persuaded by Pinchot's assertion that forest management was preferable to mere lumbering. The conservation of woodland resources benefited the whole country, Pinchot pointed out, as well as the individual landowner.[48] Certainly, the abandoned farms of Vermont, where the forests had been destroyed, provided a vivid object lesson.

Webb gave Pinchot more scope than even Shelburne Farms could provide to develop a profitably managed forest preserve. In 1890, Webb had purchased forty thousand acres in the Adirondacks. There, at Ne-Ha-Sa-Ne on the shores of Lake Lila (named for Lila Vanderbilt Webb), the Webbs spent a few weeks each year in relative simplicity at a rustic-style lodge designed by the family architect, R. H. Robertson. Pinchot worked out a detailed plan for Ne-Ha-Sa-Ne's woodlands. With Webb's support, Pinchot completed a book in 1898, *Adirondack Spruce*, on the results of his work there.[49]

. . .

The Webbs considered their mode of life at Shelburne to be informal. And so it was, in comparison with Newport, Hyde Park, or Lenox, where most of their friends and family summered. Even in the remote fastness of Biltmore, Lila's brother lived in palatial splendor. The Shelburne house, while large and far more than merely comfortable, was not palatial according to the standards known to the Webbs. Dr. and Mrs. Webb, their four children, and the ever-present houseguests spent their days riding, hunting, or engaging in other sports. The golf course in front of the house was among the first in the country. A 117-foot steam yacht, the *Elfrieda*, had a crew of fifteen ready for day trips or cruising on Lake Champlain.[50]

The Webb family and their visitors traveled between New York and Shelburne Farms by private rail car, an overnight trip. The depot at Shelburne, designed by architect Robertson, was not far from the estate's main gate. Travelers were taken the last few miles from the depot to the house by horse-drawn carriage. Shelburne Farms was predicated on its accessibility by rail, as were Biltmore and other inland estates and resorts in the years before the advent of the automobile. Horses were essential for local transportation as well as for farm work. Horses were used for pleasure and sport, too, of course. The Webbs enjoyed "coaching," an often competitive sport involving teams of horses. On one memorable occasion in 1894, Dr. Webb and members of his Coaching Club drove from New York City to Shelburne Farms.

Not surprisingly, Webb was an early and enthusiastic fan of the motorcar. He was a founder in 1899 of the Automobile Club of America, which pushed for better roads. At that time, motoring was still little more than a novel and daring sport for the rich.

As one would naturally expect, there was always an ornamental flower garden at Shelburne Farms. There is no indication that the Olmsted office was involved in its design. The earliest garden was laid out in geometrically patterned beds, reportedly modeled after the

Dr. and Mrs. Webb prepared for driving four-in-hand. Horses and equipment were maintained at the coach barn, another Robertson-designed structure, not far from the house; photo by T. E. Marr, ca. 1900. (Shelburne Farms)

From the flower garden, steps descended to a lily pool and a curved parapet overlooking Lake Champlain. Bay trees in Italian pots were set out each summer along the balustrade. Photo by A. A. McAllister, 1916. (Shelburne Farms)

The Webb family in the flower garden, ca. 1916. Dr. and Mrs. Webb flank their grandchildren in the front row. The delphinium display was a feature of the perennial borders. In the background is a long curved pergola. Photo by A. A. McAllister. (Shelburne Farms)

garden at Hampton Court.[51] The beds were planted each year with massed annuals that had been raised in the estate's greenhouses. By 1911, Lila Webb was taking more interest in the garden. She was dissatisfied with what she had. Apparently, she herself planned the Italianate garden on which work began in 1912.[52] The new garden ran the entire length of the house, between it and the lake. Long, low brick walls divided the gentle declivity into shallow terraces. At one end of the upper level, a pergola curved around an oval basin. On the lowest terrace, between the arms of a balustraded double stairway, was a lily pool. The garden ended at a parapet, bowed out above the cliff at the lake's edge. Each season, tubbed bay trees were put out along the balustrade. The scene looked for all the world like Isola Bella at Lake Maggiore or like the Italian-inspired garden of 1850 at Bantry House in Ireland, which overlooked a bay of the sea with mountains all around. In northern Vermont such a garden was definitely unusual.

A garden of this style and magnitude was not uncommon, however, on the estates of the rich in pre–World War I America, when formality was fashionable and European prototypes were valued. The Webbs, on their frequent trips abroad, had statuary and a sundial shipped home. Stanford White allegedly brought them an antique fountain sculpture from Italy.[53] The Webbs had a mason who worked full-time to maintain the walls and stonework while a troop of gardeners managed the flower beds. There were peony beds, a rose garden, and deep perennial borders backed by majestic spires of delphiniums that echoed the shades of blue in the mountains across the lake.

Lila Webb amassed a comprehensive garden library as her interest grew. Her 1847 copy of (Samuel B.) *Parsons on the Rose* is inscribed "Lila from Seward, 1912." She had English books, already classics, by John Sedding and Gertrude Jekyll, as well as the recent works of Helena Rutherfurd Ely, Louise Beebe Wilder, and Mrs. Francis King, among others. Her books included at least three on Italian gardens, those by Charles Platt, Edith Wharton, and George S. Elgood. A tiny 1914 diary by Lila Webb reads as if it were intended to be a calendar of practical hints to other gardeners. If she had filled it with authoritative "do's and don'ts" for each month or week of the year, her book could have followed a time-honored tradition: "Plant Sweet Peas as soon as the frost is out of the ground." Unfortunately,

Lila Webb's literary efforts petered out not long after the frost would have been out of the Shelburne ground that year.

. . .

Seward Webb died at Shelburne Farms in 1926. The following year, by act of God or as an indicator of the insidious onset of neglect, all the potted bay trees along the parapet were killed by an early frost.[54] The glory days were over. Webb had invented Shelburne Farms. He had imposed his own grand plan on the landscape by his authority and the power of his wealth but above all by the power of his personality. When that force was withdrawn, decline and decay soon set in.

If only it were that simple. There were other forces at work. Social change was gnawing away at the exotic fabric of Shelburne Farms and other estates of the country's landed gentry. Income taxes and property taxes, hardly a consideration when Webb first began buying land at Shelburne, were cutting ever deeper. The place was expensive to run, more and more of a luxury. Contrary to Webb's high hopes, his farming operations continued to cost more than they earned. It was increasingly difficult to provide the impeccable maintenance that had given Shelburne Farms its cachet. The labor force was less docile and more demanding, less well trained and more independent.

Shelburne Farms had been built up very quickly. In typically American fashion, it flourished as long as did its creator. Its decline was precipitous—to a point. The survival and rebirth of Shelburne Farms could be a case study in preservation. Dr. Webb's descendants have shown as much determination and as much devotion to Shelburne Farms as did their progenitor. In this they are akin to Hollis Hunnewell's heirs at Wellesley. It takes a special kind of power to adapt gracefully to change.

Notes

1. Howard S. Russell, *A Long, Deep Furrow: Three Centuries of Farming in New England* (Hanover, N.H.: University Press of New England, 1976), 460.

2. Harold Fisher Wilson, *The Hill-Country of Northern New England* (New York: Columbia University Press, 1936), 238–39.

3. Ibid., 81.

4. Russell, *Long, Deep Furrow*, 472–73.

5. Ibid., 475.

6. Wilson, *Hill-Country*, 199.

7. Vermont Board of Agriculture, Fifth Report (Montpelier, Vt., 1878), 138.

8. Vermont Board of Agriculture, Eighth Report (1884), "Our Hill Farms," 362.

9. Henry James, *The American Scene* (New York: Harper & Bros., 1907), 23.

10. Vermont Department of State, *Good Homes in Vermont: A List of Desirable Farms for Sale* (Burlington, Vt., 1893).

11. State of New Hampshire Board of Agriculture, *Catalogue of New Hampshire Farms for Summer Homes* (Manchester, N.H.: Arthur E. Clarke, 1899), 4; Edith Wharton, *Ethan Frome* (New York: Charles Scribner's Sons, 1911).

12. Wilson, *Hill-Country*, 41.

13. "Dr. W. Seward Webb Dead in Vermont," *New York Times*, 30 October 1926.

14. Wayne Andrews, *The Vanderbilt Legend* (New York: Harcourt Brace, 1941), 147.

15. Joe Sherman, *The House at Shelburne Farms* (Middlebury, Vt.: Paul S. Eriksson, 1986), 9–11.

16. John Tebbel, *The Inheritors: A Study of America's Great Fortunes and What Happened to Them* (New York: G. P. Putnam's Sons, 1962), 30.

17. Sherman, *The House at Shelburne Farms*, 16.

18. Land records of the Town of Shelburne; William C. Lipke, ed., *Shelburne Farms: The History of an Agricultural Estate* (Burlington, Vt.: University of Vermont, Robert Hull Fleming Museum, 1974), 16.

19. R. H. Robertson to Frederick Law Olmsted, 17 June 1886, job file 1031, box B-74, Frederick Law Olmsted Papers, Manuscript Division, Library of Congress.

20. Frederick Law Olmsted to William Seward Webb, 18 June 1886, Olmsted Papers.

21. Frederick Law Olmsted to Charles Eliot, 20 July 1886, quoted in Joan Wiecek, "Shelburne Farms" (master's project, University of Massachusetts, 1984), 21.

22. Albert Fein, *Frederick Law Olmsted and the American Environmental Tradition* (New York: Braziller, 1972), 166–69.

23. Laura Wood Roper, *FLO: A Biography of Frederick Law Olmsted* (Baltimore: Johns Hopkins University Press, 1973), 55–66.

24. Andrews, *Vanderbilt Legend*, 25.

25. Quoted in Frederick Law Olmsted Jr. and Theodora Kimball, *Frederick Law Olmsted, Landscape Architect, 1822–1903*, (New York: G. P. Putnam's Sons, 1922), 128.

26. Ibid., 64–65.

27. Frederick Law Olmsted to William Seward Webb, 11 April 1888, Olmsted Papers.

28. Ibid.

29. Frederick Law Olmsted to William Seward Webb, 17 March 1887, reel A1:68, Olmsted Papers.

30. William Seward Webb to Frederick Law Olmsted, 26 March 1887, Olmsted Papers.

31. The Olmsted firm placed orders with Pringle & Horsford and nine other nurseries in the spring of 1887. See Olmsted Papers and "List of Trees and Shrubs Proposed to Be Ordered for Dr. W. S. Webb," 22 April 1887, Frederick Law Olmsted National Historic Site, Brookline, Mass.

32. F. L. Olmsted and J. C. Olmsted to William Seward Webb, 24 January 1889, reel A3:140; Frederick Law Olmsted to William Seward Webb, 7 March 1888, reel A2:249, Olmsted Papers.

33. Frederick Law Olmsted to William Seward Webb, 12 July 1887, reel A1:887, Olmsted Papers.

34. William Seward Webb to Frederick Law Olmsted, 9 March 1887, job file 1036, box B-74, Olmsted Papers.

35. Frederick Law Olmsted to William Seward Webb, 12 July 1887, Olmsted Papers.

36. Ibid.

37. William Seward Webb to Frederick Law Olmsted, 20 February 1889, Olmsted Papers.

38. Lipke, *Shelburne Farms*. The editor's introduction and chap. 2, Sheafe Satterthwaite's "The American Agricultural Estate," provide a good analysis of this phase of American agricultural and social history.

39. Ibid., 18.

40. William Frederick Dix, "The American Country Estate," *Independent* 55 (5 August 1903): 1860.

41. Edwin C. Powell, "Shelburne Farm: An Ideal Country Place," *Country Life in America* 3 (February 1903): 152–56.

42. William Seward Webb, "Shelburne Farms Stud," quoted in Lipke, *Shelburne Farms*, 41–44.

43. Sheafe Satterthwaite refers to the typical estate staff as "a kind of super-family," in Lipke, *Shelburne Farms*, 13.

44. "A. H. G.," 32; Powell, "Shelburne Farm," 155.

45. "A Modern Massachusetts Farm," *Garden and Forest* 5 (30 March 1892): 145–46.

46. J. C. Olmsted to William Seward Webb, 26 June 1889, reel A3:912; F. L. and J. C. Olmsted to Arthur Taylor, 26 June 1889, reel A3:909, Olmsted Papers.

47. Roper, *FLO*, 414; Gifford Pinchot, *Breaking New Ground* (New York: Harcourt Brace, 1947), 48–49.

48. Gifford Pinchot, "The Forest: Forestry for the Farmer," *Garden and Forest* 5 (2 March 1892): 104–5, and "Abandoned Farms and Wasted Forests," *Garden and Forest* 6 (10 May 1803): 201.

49. Pinchot, *Breaking New Ground*, 74–75, and "The Forests of Ne-Ha-Sa-Ne Park in Northern New York," *Garden and Forest* 6 (12 April 1893): 168–69.

50. Joe Sherman describes the life-style in *The House at Shelburne Farms*.

51. Wiecek, "Shelburne Farms," 44.

52. Susan Cady Hayward, "Gardens of a Gilded Age," *Vermont Life* 42 (summer 1988): 6.

53. Isabell H. Hardie, "The Garden of Mrs. W. Seward Webb," *Country Life in America* 32 (October 1917): 62–63, and "The Garden at Shelburne Farms," *Arts and Decoration* 11 (June 1919): 66–67.

54. Sherman, *The House at Shelburne Farms*, 76.

Chapter 12

The Sculptor Makes a Garden

Daniel Chester French's Chesterwood,

Stockbridge, Massachusetts

"OLD BERKSHIRE Honored Again," the headline in a Pittsfield paper crowed in 1898. "Daniel French, the world-renowned sculptor, chooses to make his summer home in the village of Glendale."[1] On the old farm that came to be Chesterwood, French worked over the years to shape the landscape into a work of art almost as though he were working on a piece of sculpture. Chesterwood never failed to delight him. To a friend, French wrote one year in June, "It is as beautiful as fairy-land here now, . . . the hemlocks are decorating themselves with their light-green tassels and the laurel is beginning to blossom and the paeonies are a glory in the garden. I go about in an ecstasy of delight over the loveliness of things."[2]

It was in August 1896 that French and his wife, Mary, acquired the Marshall Warner property, with an old farmhouse and a barn, situated on both sides of a quiet back road in Glendale, the western corner of Stockbridge, Massachusetts. The land, as the elated French wrote his brother, "consists of about eighty acres, a large proportion of which is woodland. . . . I see possibilities in the place that it will be a great pleasure to develop and nature has done much to make it beautiful. The approach is pretty and the view down the valley of the Housatonic, without being very extended, is particularly charming to me."[3] From the farmhouse, open fields served as foreground for a prospect across the valley to Monument Mountain and Mount Everett, "The Dome." A friend of the Frenches showed them a letter that Matthew Arnold, an eminent English man of letters, had written her after his 1886 visit to Stockbridge: "I long to come again and drive with you to the Marshall Warner farm and lean on the fence and gaze long at that beautiful and soul-satisfying view."[4] Not that French needed convincing. This view was one of the chief assets of the property, one that for the next thirty-five years French worked to preserve by trimming or removing interfering trees.

.   .   .

Daniel Chester French was forty-six when he acquired his own country place and embarked on his first foray into landscape design. His father, Henry Flagg French, by profession a lawyer and a judge, was far more than an amateur in his devotion to both practical and aesthetic landscape values and was a strong early influence on Dan's environmental awareness. Judge French worked to enhance town streets and his own farms in Exeter,

The view south as it appeared when the Frenches purchased the Warner farm; looking down the Housatonic valley to Monument Mountain and Mount Everett. Photo by Daniel Chester French(?), 1896 or 1897. (Chesterwood Museum Archives, Chesterwood, a property of the National Trust for Historic Preservation, Stockbridge, Massachusetts)

New Hampshire and later in Concord, Massachusetts, by planting trees. He wrote for Downing's magazine, the *Horticulturist*. For two years he served as the first president of the Massachusetts Agricultural College (now the University of Massachusetts) at Amherst. After the move to Concord, Dan helped out in a family enterprise, the commercial raising of asparagus and strawberries. The Frenches also raised pigs and kept a herd of dairy cows. Judge French's library contained the works of all the major nineteenth-century horticultural writers, books that Dan also read. The judge himself wrote a book, a practical manual titled *Farm Drainage*, published in 1884. Dan's older brother had already embarked on a landscape architectural career in Chicago.

As a boy, Dan French preferred outdoor life to school. He spent one unsuccessful year at Massachusetts Institute of Technology, where he managed to fail physics, chemistry, and algebra. He was happiest roaming the woods around Concord and exploring the rivers with his friends, particularly William C. Brewster (1851–1919). From carefree days of boating, hunting, and observing the habits of birds, the two grew up to share a devotion to plants and trees. Brewster was closely involved with French over many years in forming the Chesterwood landscape.

By the time he was twenty-four, Dan French had already made his mark as a sculptor with his *Minute Man* for the town of Concord. Even before the statue was

dedicated, in 1874, French had left for Florence for two years of study. Italy was Mecca for a young sculptor, as it was for American artists, writers, and seekers after culture, during the second half of the nineteenth century. French lived and worked with the leading American sculptors of the day. Thomas Ball, one of French's mentors, had a house and studio in Florence surrounded by a garden with a fountain playing, a setting that particularly impressed French.[5] A few years later, French again traveled to Europe, this time to Paris and London. He met two of the most important members of the American cultural elite then living in London, John Singer Sargent and Henry James. After lunch at Henry James's apartment one day, James took French to call on the artist Sir Edward Burne-Jones, whose romantic paintings reflected impressions of Italian culture. Burne-Jones, like Sir Lawrence Alma-Tadema, a prominent painter whom French also visited, lived in a house "in a pretty Italian garden with a studio at its foot."[6] Indelibly printed on French's imagination was the image of a successful artist having a separate studio near his house, all within a garden setting. Ten years later he was developing such an environment for himself.

French's growing artistic success brought him into contact with the leading American artists and architects, particularly after his move to New York City and his marriage in 1888 to his cousin Mary (Mamie) French.

At the invitation of fellow-sculptor Augustus Saint-Gaudens (1848–1907), Dan and Mary French spent the summers of 1891 and 1893 in Cornish, New Hampshire, the important artists' colony that had begun with Saint-Gaudens's arrival there in 1885. Gardening as an art was taken seriously in Cornish; many artists there laid out their own grounds.[7] Saint-Gaudens's garden, like the others being made in Cornish, was tied to the architecture of the house. The Cornish gardens were personal and intimate, lacking in grandeur, and French was impressed by them. The Frenches admired the garden of sculptor Herbert Adams for its lack of "display," although, with its columns and amphoras, "one might have been in Italy."[8] Charles Adams Platt's garden seemed to French and his wife "a kind of American Italy." Platt went on to become an important garden designer, as did two others of the Cornish colony, Ellen Shipman and Rose Standish Nichols, the latter best known for her books on European gardens.

French spent his first summer in Cornish working on his sculptures for the World's Columbian Exposition in Chicago. The next summer the Frenches took a house in Chicago while Dan completed and installed his monumental statues, including the sixty-five-foot female figure, *Republic*. The Chicago fair of 1893 was a major American artistic spectacle. It marked the rebirth of the classical style in the United States, inspired a resurgence of patriotism, and seemed to promise a new and triumphant era in American life. American art and architecture were believed to have attained at last their well-deserved niche in the pantheon of earthly glories. For the first time in this country, artists of various disciplines, invoking the spirit of the Italian Renaissance, worked in harmony to produce a dramatic display of civic art.[9] Even Frederick Law Olmsted, in the evening of his career, turned from the "natural" landscape style for which he was famous to employment of a grand geometry, with formal basins, a "Court of Honor," and long vistas terminating in ornate classical buildings and monuments. All this was an abrupt departure from the nineteenth-century fondness for picturesque asymmetry. French's involvement in the fair—the "White City"—and his collaboration with the other artists there affected the design sensibility that was expressed in his sculpture and soon in his landscape design as well.

. . .

For French, the purchase of a farm held particular sig-

nificance because of his upbringing and his respect for his father. He was serious about restoring the farm's agricultural potential, and he worked at making it productive during all the years he lived there. In his efforts to combine use and beauty in his own domestic landscape, French was adhering to a long and illustrious American tradition. Art and agricultural bounty went hand in hand for him; a view of well-tended fields was a valued landscape amenity.

Popular magazines before and after the turn of the century were filled with articles by and about city folk who had scoured the countryside searching for an old farm to buy, a place "where the farmer has ceased to coax his wizened crops from the sterile soil and abandoned it in despair to the wilderness from which his ancestors conquered it."[10] Prices were low and the purchasers more likely to farm as a hobby if they farmed at all. Country life held an attraction for those who earned their living in the city. Trains and the rural trolley network had made once remote spots easily accessible, well before the advent of the motorcar. French's purchase of a summer home in the country aligned him with many others of the upper social stratum who were doing the same thing.

Part of Stockbridge's appeal to the Frenches stemmed from its "atmosphere of respectability and culture," that and the fact that it was only three hours from New York by train.[11] But the Frenches' summer home was distinctive in that it was planned from the outset as the setting for serious creative work. The first thing Dan French did there was build a proper studio. After four seasons of trying to make do in the cramped old farmhouse, the Frenches tore it down and built a new and larger house. The architect of the studio and the house was Henry Bacon, whom French had met in Chicago when they were both working on the Columbian Exposition. French described the new house as "colonial in style if it is anything."[12] He insisted that Bacon incorporate into the house the actual woodwork of a small parlor from the farmhouse. French also had Bacon reproduce the exact architectural features of the parlor in his grandparents' house in Chester, New Hampshire, the town after which French named his own place. For furnishings the Frenches sought out local antiques, still an esoteric pursuit in 1896 but one that soon increased in popularity.[13] French's interest in early American decorative arts was not surprising, considering his loyalty to his own forebears and his innate patriotism. But the so-called Colo-

The south facade of the Frenches' new house, designed by Henry Bacon, ca. 1904. (Chesterwood Museum Archives, Chesterwood, a property of the National Trust for Historic Preservation, Stockbridge, Massachusetts)

nial Revival, fostered in part by several pavilions built for the Chicago fair in 1893, made the styles that French admired widely popular.

An eclectic blend of styles—Colonial Revival and classical Italianate, blending into the agricultural landscape typical of nineteenth-century New England—characterizes the architecture and the garden at Chesterwood. In a pioneering 1893 book that French owned,

Art Out-of-Doors: Hints on Good Taste in Gardening, the influential author, Mrs. Schuyler van Rensselaer, espoused a balance between the naturalistic and the architectural style for gardens. Her chief message was that landscape design is an *art*. French would surely have agreed.

In 1898, French's creative energy turned toward the design and construction of what he called "the studio garden." The site of the garden, once an orchard, still contained several old apple trees and a white mulberry. Mary French quoted the patronizing comment of an unnamed woman: "I hear that your husband has decorated the garden with apple trees. Such an interesting idea!"[14] But Mrs. French knew that the apple trees were there first and that her husband had deliberately incorporated them into the garden. For him the old trees were a link with the thrifty New England farming tradition, another reminder of his father and of a bygone era. Their beauty was enhanced for him by their usefulness; each autumn he recorded the quantity of fruit these trees produced.

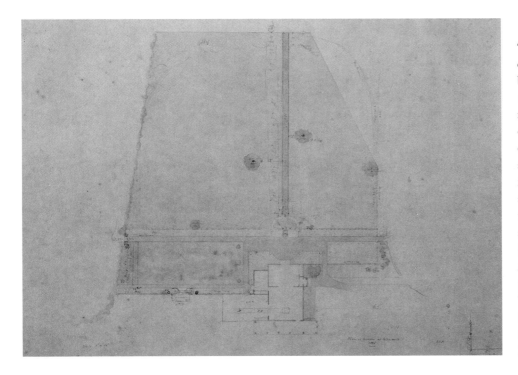

"Plan of Garden at Glendale," designed and drawn by Daniel Chester French, 1898. The garden was organized around French's studio, with a curved exedra opposite the main entrance and straight walks extending in three directions. Old apple trees and a mulberry, treasured by French, are shown in this sketch. (Chesterwood Museum Archives, Chesterwood, a property of the National Trust for Historic Preservation, Stockbridge, Massachusetts. Photo by Doug Munson)

French's sister-in-law, Alice Helm French, made a pastel drawing of the studio garden in 1899. Looking along the walk to the west, French's studio is on the left and the semicircular exedra on the right, surrounded by perennial borders. Two columns mark the end of the formal garden and an entrance into the woods. (Chesterwood Museum Archives, Chesterwood, a property of the National Trust for Historic Preservation, Stockbridge, Massachusetts. Photo by Isabel Chenoweth)

As his own sketch plans show, French intended, as he told his sister, a "formal garden in connection with the studio."[15] The original design, which never changed, was based on an axial relationship to the new studio. From a spacious graveled terrace outside the main entrance to the studio, straight walks bordered by flowers extended right and left; a third path, which French often referred to as the "vista," ran straight north from the entrance and into the woods. In its plan and its planting the Frenches' garden bore some similarities to other gardens of the period. A unique feature of the stu-

dio garden enclosing the terrace was the semicircular seat, the exedra, designed by French and cast from his own formula for "marble cement."

French's lifelong friend Will Brewster, well known by then as an ornithologist and writer, came from Concord, Massachusetts, in July 1898 for the first of many visits. French relied on Brewster for advice on the garden and on improving and enhancing the entire Chesterwood landscape. Brewster sent him boxes of larkspur, phlox, lily of the valley, and roses from his own garden, which French put in the ground "with my own hands within an hour."[16]

At the far end of the garden, where the path entered the woods, French installed a pair of white-glazed terracotta columns that he had salvaged from a sculpture exhibition in New York.[17] He added a pergola, marble benches, and a pedestal to support the bust of a young woman, which had been given him by fellow sculptor Herbert Adams. A tiny square pool in the lawn, filled to the brim, was stocked with goldfish and planted with yellow water lilies. The garden wall was topped with flat marble slabs that French, who was careful with money, had purchased cheaply from a local quarry because they had been rejected as gravestones for the military.[18]

The Frenches usually moved from New York City to Chesterwood in May, staying on most years through October, a good five months. French entered all that happened there in a notebook that he kept every year from 1897 until his death in 1931. His two-volume "Notes on Chesterwood" is not a diary but rather a detailed record of events. He reported on the comings and goings of family, employees, relatives, and friends and on social events. His chief emphasis was on the work that was done, both by him in his studio and on the construction, plantings, and maintenance of the grounds at Chesterwood, the place he often referred to as Glendale after the village in which it was located. He recorded the sources from which he ordered plants or seed. He kept track of everything that was planted, dates of bloom or harvest, successes and failures. He noted weather conditions: late frosts, droughts and storms, and the first killing frost each autumn. His daughter Margaret later compared her father to George Washington and Thomas Jefferson, two farmers and gardeners who also kept notebooks over many years.[19]

French had made a scale model of the new house and was, as he told his brother in 1900, "laying out the grounds, the grading, planting &c in wax in the studio. It is very entertaining and practical."[20] This was the first instance of French's chief method of landscape design, a technique he used for at least two other gardens he designed later. As a sculptor, he was accustomed to envisioning three-dimensional shapes and to making maquettes prior to fashioning the sculpture itself. Indeed, that was French's genius. Flat drawings were of limited use to him. The creation of a scale model enabled him to envision with his hands as well as his eyes the physical shape of the land with which he was working. At Chesterwood, as one admirer put it, "Mr. French has shaped the woods and fields to the form of his ideal as readily as he shapes marble and clay with chisel and thumb."[21]

French ordered bulbs, perennials, and vines for his garden from nurseries near and far. One of his regular sources was the F. H. Horsford nursery in Charlotte, Vermont, whose slogan was "Hardy Plants for Cold Weather." Among French's favorite plants were iris, clematis, and lilies. He planted dozens of roses over the years, many of them from the Rosedale Nursery of Tarrytown, New York. A particular favorite was the white Frau Karl Druschki, a rose still available.[22] His daughter remembered the roses, "which my father al-

ways pruned and sprayed himself."[23] On either side of the vista walk, French planted standard hydrangeas and peonies, interplanted with auratum lilies, a combination that provided almost a full season of bloom. Annuals—larkspur, mignonette, heliotrope, snapdragons, sunflowers, zinnias, and more—filled in the perennial borders. French's friend, fellow artist, and neighbor, Newton Mackintosh, described the terrace in the early years as "gaily decorated with morning glories and nasturtiums, and severely ornamented with eight privet trees and two hydrangias [sic] in Italian pots."[24] French had purchased thirty terra-cotta pots while he and his wife were in Florence in 1900.

French's zest for gardening increased rapidly, together with his interest in plants. He expanded his palette of perennials year by year and soon learned about staking tall plants and pinching back to make them bushier. Mary French, too, worked in the flower garden in the early years. Her husband would write in his garden notebook that "Mary has been setting out many asters lately" or that she had planted montbretias and dahlia tubers for summer bloom.[25] She was somewhat reclusive and suffered from occasional bouts of what may have been depression. French wrote in 1905 of his "hope that being out of doors and digging in her garden will make her well."[26]

"I clipped the lilac hedge last week," French wrote in June 1902, his first reference to an aspect of garden maintenance that he chose to reserve to himself over the years.[27] He planted a variety of hedges as structural elements in the studio garden and elsewhere on the grounds. He himself clipped—often several times a year—hemlock, privet, and barberry hedges, as well as the lilacs, which he trimmed to a "box shape" after they bloomed.[28] French also pruned the grapevines on the arbor by the kitchen garden, a skill he had learned when he lived in Italy.[29]

But French did not lack for help. By 1904 he was writing to his brother that he was, "I hope temporarily . . . , employing three men, with the result that the place is kept in apple-pie order."[30] His chief groundskeeper was James Kelly, a farmer and woodsman, who worked at Chesterwood under French's keen supervision for twenty years. Other outdoor help often came and went after a season or two. The Frenches always had a coachman and later a chauffeur. French had been concerned right from the beginning that, with all his ambitious improvements, Chesterwood was becoming too elaborate. "This old farm seems to be developing into a gentleman's estate in spite of me," he told his sister, but "I can't help trying to make its natural features more beautiful any more than father could."[31] The place "looks much too fine for a mere artist," as he styled himself in a letter to his brother.[32]

He could not have felt the same twinges of guilt about his farming activities. He kept a few cows and a flock of hens. He had horses for the farm work—plowing, harrowing, planting, and harvesting the fields of oats, corn, buckwheat, and barley. The extensive lawns —to French perhaps another shameful but indispensable luxury—were cut with a horse-drawn mower. Not until 1909 did the Frenches own an automobile; before that their two-horse phaeton met them at the train and took them everywhere around Stockbridge.

In addition to all the pear and apple trees that were on the farm when French bought it, he set out many more, plus cherry, plum, and peach trees. One year he planted eleven varieties of apple, ones that we seldom see now, such as Sweet Bow, Grimes, Golden Russet, Rhode Island Greening, Northern Spy, Pumpkin Sweet. His orchard adjoined the kitchen garden near the barn and stable, the working side of Chesterwood. Will Brewster advised French on pruning and feeding his fruit trees and on spraying them with lead arsenate. The area around the fruit trees was made into a lawn, contrary to Brewster's recommendation, but as French put it, "I care more about looks than utility in this case."[33] In fact he always cared about looks as much as if not more than about utility. He improved his farm not only by making it more productive but also by making it more beautiful in all its aspects.

The Chesterwood household included Dan and Mary; their daughter Margaret, born in 1889; French's two or three studio assistants; a cook, a butler, and a maid; and a continuous stream of houseguests. All the fruit and vegetables for the house were raised in the kitchen garden. In steady succession came rhubarb, asparagus, strawberries, currants, gooseberries, and grapes. "First peas!" French would note each year in late June.

French was constantly planting ornamental trees and shrubs or rebuilding walls and steps. In 1901 he wrote his brother that the garden was looking as pretty as the pastel that William's wife, Alice Helm French, had made of it. "It is a relief to go through a high wall and into a place that is finished," French wrote while much of the place was in a "chaos" of construction and reconstruction.[34] The Chesterwood garden was not at all chaotic when Guy Lowell, the Beaux-Arts–trained architect of Boston's classical Museum of Fine Arts, gave it his ultimate seal of approval by including four photos and a plan in his 1902 book, *American Gardens,* an influential work featuring many of that era's grandest new estates.

· · ·

Nineteen eleven was the Year of the Fountain. French had been long dreaming of a fountain outside the studio, in front of the exedra. Making and installing it was a major project. He had decorated the fountain's circular pedestal with a frieze of *bambini,* as he called the little frolicking figures. When the installation was finally completed in July, French described it for Brewster as "the realization of a dream . . . a fountain! . . . it's the prettiest thing you ever saw,—if I do say it as shouldn't!"[35] Now French could feel that his studio garden was complete.

Like many another great landscape gardener, French "saw that all Nature was a garden."[36] He cared about *all* of his land, as well as the views beyond his boundaries. Over the years he purchased adjoining parcels until the farm included 163 acres, about doubling his original purchase. With his friend Brewster, French extended his "garden" into the woodland, clearing selectively to highlight a noble tree here or a curious rock formation there. Together they carved out paths that led to special viewing spots. They shaped openings in the woods, places of destination. French was the sculptor in his woods.

Brewster spent three weeks or a month at Chesterwood almost every summer. "We have been improving the woods . . . cutting out openings and views," French noted in 1903.[37] They worked across the road but even more ambitiously behind French's house and studio. One project was the "Circle." From the studio the vista walk ran straight toward the woods and eventually to a majestic sugar maple. Here French and Brewster made a circular clearing, with hemlocks around it. French designed a seat for the Circle, with sphinxes on the arm rests. He wrote Brewster that the seat was "the pride of my heart."[38] He shared a bird sighting from the Circle with Brewster in 1913: "My great boast is a family of barred owls whose stamping ground is in the vicinity of the seat upon which you sat last year."[39]

From the Circle, French and his friend cleared and thinned trees to reveal the handsome cliff face that rose

to the summit of the hill behind Chesterwood. With help from James Kelly, paths were extended through the woods to two "outlooks" on the hill, from which one could see Monument Mountain and the spires of Stockbridge. French designed wooden seats on which to rest from the climb and enjoy the view.

With Brewster French also created the "Glade," another grassy opening in the woods, bordered with hemlocks, mountain laurel, and narcissus. Kelly and his helpers did much of the work, as usual, including the laying of broad stone steps that link the Glade to the woodland walks.[40] The Glade was the setting for a family reunion in 1913, with fifteen relatives gathering there to hear French's older brother, Will, read from their father's letters. Dan French had set out chairs to face a bust of their father, placed there just for this occasion.[41]

On the lawn above the flower garden, French had laid out a tennis court in 1903. "I think I shall enjoy it," he told his brother then, "also Margaret for whom it is built."[42] In her teens, Margaret was more gregarious than her mother, giving and going to parties, playing

Daniel Chester French, in 1915, beside the fountain he had decorated in bas-relief. From the exedra a straight walk, bordered by peonies and hydrangeas, extended toward and into the woods. (Chesterwood Museum Archives, Chesterwood, a property of the National Trust for Historic Preservation, Stockbridge, Massachusetts. Photo by A. B. Bogart, New York)

tennis and croquet at Chesterwood. At sixteen she noted in her diary, "Dick and I went out & sat on the marble seat in the garden (in the moonlight) & talked till so late that Poppa had to call us!"[43] A local weekly described one "delightful" garden party that Mrs. French gave at Chesterwood: "It was given on the edge of the woods . . . a charming setting."[44] The Frenches were part of Stockbridge's summer social set. They knew Edith Wharton, whose Lenox garden they sometimes visited. Margaret noted one day in her diary that "Mrs. Wharton and nine other people and three dogs came to call."[45]

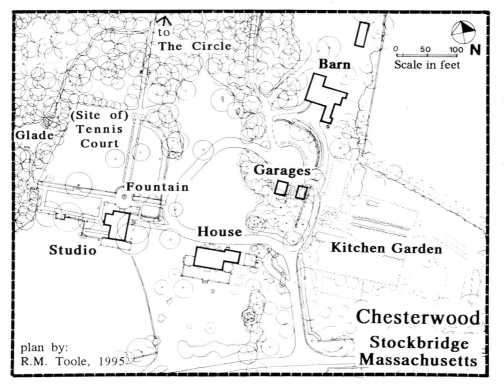

Plan of the core of French's estate of Chesterwood. The view was to the south; French cleared paths through the woods to "the Circle" and up the hill to two overlooks. (Drawing by Robert M. Toole, LA, Saratoga Springs, New York)

French's daughter Margaret, at top left, beside her mother, with three of her cousins on the stone steps leading from the woodland "Glade." Photo by Daniel Chester French, 1906. (Chesterwood Museum Archives, Chesterwood, a property of the National Trust for Historic Preservation, Stockbridge, Massachusetts)

Opposite: Daniel Chester French, left, and his lifelong friend ornithologist William Brewster in the studio garden at Chesterwood, 1915. Brewster spent several weeks each summer working with French to clear paths and openings in the woodland. (Chesterwood Museum Archives, Chesterwood, a property of the National Trust for Historic Preservation, Stockbridge, Massachusetts. Autochrome photo by Thomas Shields Clarke)

The Frenches had other literary and artistic friends in or near Stockbridge who were intimately involved with their own gardens. Richard Watson Gilder, a poet and editor of the *Century Magazine*, a widely read voice for art and culture, and his wife, Helena deKay, a painter, were close friends of the Frenches. Gilder himself cleared pastures and tended sheep on their farm, Four Brooks, where they also had a classically inspired garden with a marble fountain and lavish flower borders. Tea in their garden was served under an arbor, with an old millstone serving as a table.[46] The Gilders' garden, like Chesterwood, was modest compared to others in the neighborhood. Naumkeag, the high-perched summer home of Mr. and Mrs. Joseph Choate, friends of the Frenches, had far more extensive gardens, even before Fletcher Steele expanded them further after 1926. Begun in 1885, the Naumkeag gardens, designed by Nathan Franklin Barrett, were among the first to impose a classical regularity upon the bucolic Berkshire hills. Barrett's design featured an *allée* of sixty linden trees, a brilliant floral display, and a hemlock hedge clipped into fortresslike battlements.[47] Bellefontaine, the Giraud Fosters' estate, had perhaps the most pretentious of the Berkshire gardens—pools, fountains, Roman temples, statues of goats and goddesses, twirly marble columns, and possibly more urns than plants.[48]

. . .

In 1915 the Frenches, feeling limited by farmer James Kelly's lack of expertise in the flower garden, asked him to look out for an experienced assistant. "It makes it rather hard for Mrs. French to keep the flower garden in good order without someone she can call on who really knows something about flowers."[49] She was not to have that someone for another several years. French, meanwhile, was turning to designing gardens for other people. "I seem to have finished mine," he wrote, "so that there is nothing for me to do."[50] For pleasure and without pay he designed and helped to install six other gardens in Stockbridge between 1915 and 1929, one of them for his daughter at her marriage. He made clay or wax models for at least two gardens, as he had at Chesterwood.[51] All of French's designs included one or more of the features he had used in his own garden: a lily pool, an exedra, a pergola, broad stone steps. "I am getting lots of fun out of laying out Mrs. Lamond's gardens," he told Brewster. "I am not sure that I shall not retire from sculpture and take to landscape gardening."[52]

French's enthusiasm for his own garden was rekindled during the last eight years of his life, after Charles Dupuy came to Chesterwood as "head man," replacing Kelly. It was a match made in heaven. French got along perfectly with Dupuy, respected him, trusted him, and

French, at the right, on a slat seat of his design beneath one of the old apple trees he cherished. Peonies bloom along the walk, looking south to the fountain and the main door of the studio, 1914. (Chesterwood Museum Archives, Chesterwood, a property of the National Trust for Historic Preservation, Stockbridge, Massachusetts)

grew to depend on him more and more. French's daughter wrote that French lent Dupuy books on pruning and fruit culture and taught him how to "clip a hedge as straight as an arrow with no line to guide him."[53] Dupuy was paid $100 a month at first and had two men under him. The Frenches provided him with a house across the road, near a second studio, the "little studio" that French had had built. Dupuy wrote his employer long detailed letters during the winter months, keeping French abreast of all that went on. French, in turn, wrote Dupuy with suggestions and requests, once even advising him on how to clean the Frenches' polar bear rug—by taking it outside and rubbing it with snow.[54] "You always work much too hard," French told Dupuy in 1927.[55]

Dupuy took over one part of the role that William Brewster, who died in 1919, had played in French's life. Together he and Dupuy tended the paths and clearings in the woods, despite the heart attack that afflicted French in May 1925.[56] Together they struggled to prop up and save the venerable apple trees in the studio garden, trees that had been there when French bought the property in 1896. When one finally collapsed, French

mourned; "I feel as if one of the chief glories of Chesterwood has departed."[57] He had endured the loss of all the chestnut trees in the woods in 1917–18, when they succumbed to the epidemic chestnut blight that changed all New England woodlands. But he suffered the loss of individual trees. When a battered but familiar old butternut between the house and the studio had to be taken down in 1925, French wrote his daughter that the place looked "as if it had lost its front tooth."[58]

Dupuy was likely to have shared French's fury in July 1927 when a woodchuck burrowed under the wall in the studio garden, wrecking the delphiniums then at their peak.[59] That fall they embarked on a major revamping of all the flower beds. Dupuy had the arduous task of digging up and resetting every plant. French made lists of what they had, drew detailed plans for each bed, and ordered dozens more perennials from the Horsford nursery. The flower colors were pink, white,

French drew plans for each of his flower beds in 1927, when he and his "head man," Charles Dupuy, entirely replanted them. (French Family Papers, Library of Congress, Washington, D.C.)

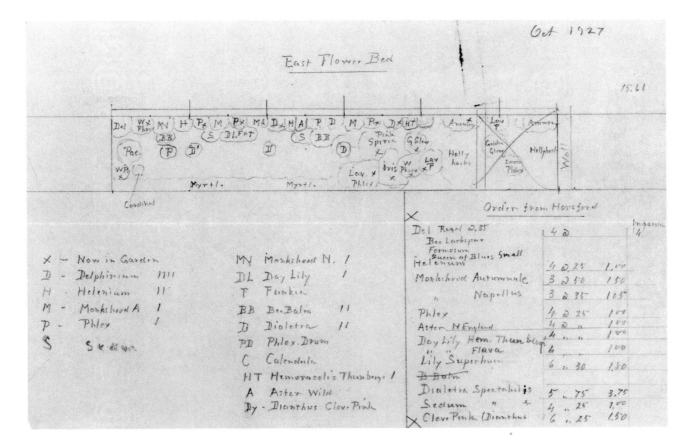

yellow, and blue and included a fresh supply of delphiniums.[60]

. . .

Years later, French's daughter Margaret remembered how her father had likened garden design to sculpture: "[I]f you got your essentials right, . . . if your skeleton and bones were in the right place, then the chances were that you would have a statue—or a garden—that would stand up and look well throughout the years."[61] French himself wrote, "I think the test of a garden is whether you like to be there, and whether you feel like staying and enjoying it, instead of wondering at its magnificence."[62] These complementary principles were at the heart of French's garden making.

With the hindsight of a century it seems remarkable that a sculptor without enormous inherited wealth could achieve the material success that would enable him to fashion a country estate and to live in the commensurate style. The Frenches also maintained a New York town-house with a studio, had ample indoor and outdoor staff, and were able to travel as they pleased and to fill their houses with visitors. But this was the time of the American Renaissance. Artists were esteemed for their contributions to the monuments that glorified the nation's past and seemed to assure its destined place in world civilization.[63] French's garden at Chesterwood and the entire landscape that he shaped there manifested his background, his artistic talents, and the flourishing cultural climate of the time in which he lived.

A cousin, Marguerite Jameson, described for Margaret the arrival of her father, then eighty years old, at Chesterwood in May 1930:

> We caught a glimpse of the house from the train . . . , and your father was so thrilled! . . . we all three . . . inspected the garden. The bleeding hearts are out—so are the little white narcissus and the Virginia cowslips. The cherry tree outside of the studio gate looks as it did last year—a solid mass of white. . . . Your father and I walked out to the view in the pasture where the seat is, and the birch is gone that interfered with the view. It was too lovely! Your father was so happy. He came along behind me whistling and breaking off dead branches and having such a nice time. Your ma and I cut rhubarb and asparagus.[64]

French started off 1931 as usual, unaware that it would be his last season at Chesterwood. He showed his typical optimism in a letter written early that year to Newton Mackintosh, the friend of his youth: "The days are getting longer and, though this is the only reminder of approaching spring, it sets me thinking of Glendale,—of the new paeonies that I planted last fall and of all sorts of exciting things."[65] French drew plans that spring for remodeling the barn and had Dupuy repairing fences and planting more perennials. He tried as usual to persuade Dupuy to cut down on the size of the vegetable garden. As always, French delighted in his gardening successes. On July 4 he wrote in his notebook: "seven blossoms on the Clematis Henryi, diameter 7″; Delphinium 8′ 3″ high; Jack-in-the-pulpit 2′ 8″ high. Paeonies are past. A great crop of Sweet Williams."[66]

Telling Mackintosh about a tall tulip tree that had blown down, French wrote as though prophesying his own demise: "Apparently the clock at Glendale was wound up to run down at about this time."[67] On the seventh of October, 1931, French died at Chesterwood.

Notes

Chesterwood has been a property of the National Trust for Historic Preservation for more than twenty years, a gift and bequest of French's daughter, Margaret French Cresson. The house, studio, and grounds are regularly open to the public between April and October.

1. *Pittsfield (Mass.) Sunday Morning Call* 20 March 1898:1.

2. Daniel Chester French (hereafter cited as DCF) to Newton Mackintosh, 13 June 1911, French Family Papers (hereafter cited as FFP), Library of Congress, MR 1:781.

3. DCF to William Merchant Richardson French, 16 August 1896, FFP, MR 41:375.

4. Margaret French Cresson, "The Strength of the Hills," typescript, n.d., Chesterwood Archives.

5. [DCF], "Ball's Studio at Florence," newspaper clipping, *Chicago Tribune*, 1876?, FFP, MR 29:297.

6. DCF to William Merchant Richardson French, 10 November 1886, FFP, MR 40:652–56.

7. *A Circle of Friends: Art Colonies of Cornish and Durham*

(Durham: University of New Hampshire Art Galleries, 1985), 107–10.

8. Mrs. Daniel Chester French, *Memories of a Sculptor's Wife* (Boston: Houghton Mifflin, 1928), 182.

9. See *The American Renaissance: 1876–1917* (New York: Brooklyn Museum, 1979), esp. 11–25; Henry Hope Reed, *The Golden City* (New York: Doubleday, 1959), 77–80.

10. William Dean Howells, *The Undiscovered Country* (Boston: Houghton Mifflin, 1880), 134. One typical magazine article is A. Chamberlain, "The Ideal Abandoned Farm," *New England Magazine*, n.s., 16 (June 1897): 473–82.

11. Mrs. D. C. French, *Memories*, 200.

12. DCF to William Merchant Richardson French, 30 December 1900, FFP, MR 41:422.

13. DCF to William Merchant Richardson French, 23 September 1894, FFP, MR 41:281–82; William B. Rhoads, *The Colonial Revival* (New York: Garland, 1977), 384 ff; *American Renaissance*, 57–61.

14. Mrs. D. C. French, *Memories*, 182.

15. DCF to Harriette French Hollis, 1 July 1898, FFP, MR 41:397–98.

16. DCF to William Brewster, 26 May 1898 and 29 May 1899, William Brewster Papers, Museum of Comparative Zoology, Harvard University.

17. Cresson, "Strength of the Hills," 7.

18. "Notes on Chesterwood" (hereafter cited as NOC) 1, 30 October 1900, photocopy, Chesterwood Archives.

19. Cresson, "Strength of the Hills," 19.

20. DCF to William Merchant Richardson French, 30 December 1900, FFP, MR 41:422.

21. William Merriam Rouse, "A Sculptor's Ideal Realized among the Berkshire Hills," *Countryside Magazine* 20 (February 1915): 75.

22. NOC 1, 11 May 1906.

23. Cresson, "Strength of the Hills," 10.

24. Newton Mackintosh, longhand mss., n.d., Chesterwood Archives.

25. NOC 1, 7 July 1901 and 1 June 1905.

26. DCF to Major B. B. French, 22 April 1905, FFP, MR 41:495.

27. NOC 1, 8 June 1902.

28. NOC 1, 7 Aug. 1904.

29. Margaret French Cresson, interviewed by Jonathan Gray, 27 July 1971, typescript, Chesterwood Archives.

30. DCF to William Merchant Richardson French, 19 June 1904, FFP, MR 41:472.

31. DCF to Harriette French Hollis, 16 October 1898, FFP, MR 41:395.

32. DCF to William Merchant Richardson French, 3 June 1906, FFP, MR 41:498.

33. DCF to William C. Brewster, 19 September 1911, Brewster Papers.

34. DCF to William Merchant Richardson French, summer 1901, FFP, MR 41:427.

35. DCF to William Brewster, 16 July 1911, Brewster Papers.

36. Horace Walpole, "On Modern Gardening," referring to early-18th-century English landscaper William Kent, quoted in Geoffrey Jellicoe et al., *The Oxford Companion to Gardening* (New York: Oxford University Press, 1989), 310.

37. NOC 1, 13 September 1903.

38. DCF to William Brewster, 5 July 1908, Brewster Papers.

39. DCF to William Brewster, 23 June 1913, Brewster Papers.

40. NOC 1, 7 June 1899, 14 and 27 October 1906.

41. DCF to William Brewster, 22 August 1913, Brewster Papers.

42. DCF to William Merchant Richardson French, 11 October 1903. FFP, MR 41:462–63.

43. Margaret French (Cresson), Diary, 15 June 1905, Chesterwood Archives.

44. *Berkshire Resort Topics*, 25 July 1903, 117.

45. Margaret French (Cresson), Diary, 3 July 1905, Chesterwood Archives.

46. Rosamund Gilder, ed., *Letters of Richard Watson Gilder* (Boston: Houghton Mifflin, 1916), 331, 448–50.

47. Guy Lowell, *American Gardens* (Boston: Bates & Guild, 1902), plate 96; *Country Life in America* 18 (August 1910): 433–36; Louise Shelton, *Beautiful Gardens in America* (New York: Charles Scribner's Sons, 1915), plate 29; *Landscape Architecture Quarterly* 10 (1920): 109–13.

48. Lowell, *American Gardens*, plates 29, 30, and 31. French's copy of this book is still in his library at Chesterwood.

49. DCF to James Kelly, 8 December 1915, FFP, MR 3:263.

50. DCF to John E. Burdick, 4 October 1926, FFP, MR 9:445.

51. DCF to Newton Mackintosh, 1 April 1918, FFP, MR 4:527; DCF to William B. Terhune, 26 February 1929, FFP, MR 10:750.

52. DCF to William Brewster, 26 September 1915, Brewster Papers.

53. Margaret French Cresson, typescript on Charles Dupuy, n.d., Chesterwood Archives.

54. DCF to Charles Dupuy, 11 February 1930, Chesterwood Archives.

55. DCF to Charles Dupuy, 11 April 1927, Chesterwood Archives.

56. NOC 2, 11 May 1925.

57. DCF to Margaret French Cresson, 16 February 1927, FFP, MR 9:585.

58. DFC to Margaret French Cresson, 15 November 1925, FFP, MR 9:016

59. NOC 2, July 1927.

60. NOC 2, 12 October 1927; DCF sketch plans, 11 September and October 1927, FFP, MR 126:338–40.

61. Margaret French Cresson, "The Chesterwood Garden," *Garden Club of America Bulletin* 44 (March 1956): 21.

62. DCF to Ruth MacFarland Furniss, 29 November 1924, FFP, MR 8:338.

63. *American Renaissance*, 11–15.

64. Marguerite Jameson to Margaret French Cresson, 11 May 1930, FFP, box 51.

65. DCF to Newton Mackintosh, n.d., FFP, MR 12:453.

66. NOC 2, 4 July 1931.

67. DCF to Newton Mackintosh, 23 April 1931, FFP, MR 12:188.

Chapter 13

Of Time and the River

The Gardens at Hamilton House,

South Berwick, Maine

COLONEL JONATHAN HAMILTON deserves to have his name permanently attached to the house he built for himself and his family in 1785. His elegant mansion, set so spectacularly above a bend in southern Maine's Piscataqua River, is a sublime monument to the colonel's taste as well as to his success in the West Indies trade.

The setting is remarkably serene. Just as Sarah Orne Jewett described it a hundred years ago, it is still "a quiet place, that the destroying left hand of progress had failed to touch."[1] Two hundred years ago, however, noise and bustle resounded at the adjacent Lower Landing, on the east branch of the Piscataqua in the old town of Berwick. This was the upstream terminus of the navigable portion of the river. Here ships were loaded with timber from the piles on the shore. When these vessels dropped anchor again, on returning from the West Indies or farther, their cargo of sugar, cotton, iron, or rum would be piled on the great wharves and stored in long warehouses. Before the coming of the railroad, the river was the town's highway.

Jonathan Hamilton, born in Berwick in 1745, grew rich in retail trade. Eventually, as a shipowner, he acquired enough prestige to call himself Colonel.[2] In 1783 he bought thirty acres at this landing on the river, where his ships would tie up at his wharves.[3] There was no house; a previous dwelling had burned. Colonel Hamilton built a grand but chaste Georgian mansion atop the hill known as Pipe Stave Point. The house had views from three of its beautifully proportioned facades—up, down, and across the river to the hills beyond. The mansion, in turn, could be seen from all directions, a consideration surely of equal importance to a man who had achieved all the social and economic eminence to which he had ever aspired.

No plans or account books have turned up to describe the landscape of the house in Hamilton's day; deeds reveal nothing. Landscape fashion at the time when Hamilton built his house often meant a house set, as his was, on a rise of land to gain "prospect." The slopes were then often shaped into terraces, but as recent archaeological excavations prove, Colonel Hamilton never took that extra step. The grassy terraces that now surround the house are of a later date. The elms that dominated the site in 1880s photographs were probably familiar to Hamilton. He may have planted the poplars that ran along a fence just below the house. Lombardy poplars were offered for sale in New England before 1800 and distributed widely.[4] Usually

Hamilton House, South Berwick, Maine, seen from the south, ca. 1880. The barn standing near the house covers the site that became the garden after the Tysons purchased the property. (Society for the Preservation of New England Antiquities)

planted in rows, their stiff upright shape was much admired.

Colonel Hamilton died in the house in 1802 at the age of fifty-seven. The property changed hands three times before Alpheus Goodwin bought it in 1839 as a farm.[5] Schooners and brigantines no longer loaded and unloaded goods at the landing; now sheep grazed the pastures while the Goodwin men mowed the upland fields and set out apple trees on the riverbank. By 1877 the price of wool had fallen, and things were not going well. Goodwin's sons mortgaged their late father's farm and struggled to make ends meet. Their difficulties reflected the social and economic changes that swept New England after the Civil War. The steep, stony hill farms could not compete with the flat fertile fields of the Midwest. The Goodwin farm was just one of many sad relics, despite its still majestic house.

When the Hamilton house was put up for sale in 1895, Sarah Orne Jewett took it upon herself to save it. Hearing that a developer planned to tear down the old house and divide the property into new house lots, she determined to use all her Boston connections to find a sympathetic buyer.

Sarah Orne Jewett, born in South Berwick in 1849, had known Hamilton House since, as a child, she had accompanied her doctor father on rides through the countryside. Hamilton House continued to be one of her favorite destinations. In 1869 she noted in her diary: "Took Mrs. Gordon to ride in the morning to the Hamilton House and Guptils Woods. Listened to the thrushes."[6] She described the setting in an 1881 essay published in *Atlantic Monthly:* the house "stands on a point below which the river is at its widest. The rows of poplars and its terraced garden have fallen and been spoiled by time, but a company of great elms stand guard over it."[7] The "terraced garden," according to the archaeologists, was a figment of her imagination, but it reflects what she thought the house deserved. Jewett's historical romance, *The Tory Lover,* published in 1901, was more fantasy than history. Key scenes of the novel were set at Hamilton House and in the garden she felt it should have had: balustrades, clumps of hardy box, rosebushes, and peach trees.[8]

Sarah Orne Jewett, like many of her friends, was drawn to old houses, old furnishings, and old gardens. She had grown up and lived for the rest of her life in an eighteenth-century house in the village of South Berwick, a house that, like its neighbors, had "its four lilac bushes and its white fences to shut it in from the rest of the world."[9] Jewett remembered her grandmother's French pinks, larkspur, honeysuckle, Canterbury bells, London pride, peonies, and "blush roses, and white roses, and cinnamon roses all in a tangle in one corner." She lamented the passing of these old-fashioned front yards, where picket fences were being removed and the lawn mower taking over, depriving women of one precious outlet from their constricted lives. Jewett and her sister undertook to refurbish their own garden in 1888, with flagstone walks and a trellised arbor wreathed with honeysuckle. They planted snowberry and flowering currant bushes, box hedges, and all the perennials they had loved since childhood.[10]

In the 1880s, Jewett began spending half the year in Boston with Annie Fields, whose husband, publisher James T. Fields, had recently died. Jewett made many friends and literary connections, including Whittier and Celia Thaxter, who frequented Annie Fields's apartment on Charles Street. On visits to Appledore Island, Jewett traded cuttings with Celia Thaxter.

In 1896, while staying at Annie Fields's summer cottage in Manchester-by-the-Sea, Jewett described for her sister the intensity of her efforts to find a buyer for Hamilton House:

> Mrs. Dexter said that she thought Mr. McCagg would go down with his wife to see the house, and asked me if any others . . . had been in Berwick. They, she said, were her last hope but I thought I might as well speak out and I said I supposed she had quite given up her plans now, and then she confessed that it didn't seem to be practical. I thought Katherine [Mrs. Dexter's daughter] still clung to the idea but I have made up my mind there is an end to it now—and yet I am glad that so many more people know about the house and so something will come out of it perhaps.[11]

The Dexters and the McCaggs disappointed Jewett, but she had not exhausted the possibilities. As early as 1894 she had thought of Mrs. George Tyson and her stepdaughter as potential purchasers. She wrote her sister then, "I thought of Elise Tyson at her houseparty—but they wouldn't be so cramped inside Hamilton House even if it were bad weather outside."[12]

Emily Tyson, a rich widow then in her early fifties, and her twenty-six-year-old stepdaughter, Elise, lived in Boston's Back Bay, where they mingled with the city's cultural elite. Mrs. Tyson was known for aesthetic private literary readings that held her hearers spellbound.[13] In 1898 she and Elise took over the mortgage and bought the house plus 110 acres, paying the Goodwin family $4,000.[14] Even before the deed was drawn, Mrs. Tyson wrote Miss Jewett a warm and appreciative letter: "All our roads seem to lead us toward Hamilton House, though it has taken some time to find it out. Now you see what trouble a first kind step leads to." Her gratitude to Miss Jewett was intertwined with her fondness for the house: "one good and compatible whole and I like it and thank you a thousand times."[15] The Bangor *Daily Commercial* noted in 1901 that Ham-

ilton House "has been taken and made recently into a duplicate of its former stately splendors by Mrs. George Tyson of Boston and the North Shore, who is making an ideal country place of the home."[16]

The friendship continued until Sarah Orne Jewett's death in 1909. Her letters record visits, luncheons, and occasional train rides together between South Berwick and Boston. In the spring of 1903, Jewett wrote to her sister, "This is a lovely day for the Hamilton House ladies to move. It gives anybody a real sense of comfort to think they are back again."[17] Elise Tyson told Jewett, "It seemed like getting home to see the river and the dear old house again."[18]

.   .   .

Emily Davis Tyson was born in Philadelphia in 1846. Her father was in the sugar business and served a term in Congress. Photographs taken in the early 1900s at Hill Top, the Davis family place near Philadelphia where

Sarah Orne Jewett, right, and Mrs. Tyson amid delphiniums and foxgloves at Hamilton House, 1905. (Society for the Preservation of New England Antiquities)

Emily grew up, show acres of lawn, towering trees, a long wisteria-draped arbor, and an old stone house. Emily married George Tyson, then a widower with three small children, in 1875.[19]

George Tyson, born in 1831, joined the Boston-based trading firm of Russell and Company as a young man.[20] In 1860 he became a partner and was well on his way toward the fortune that, long after his demise, made possible the renaissance of Hamilton House. In 1863, Tyson set sail for China with his first wife, Sarah. He was attached to Russell and Company's office in Shanghai, where they spent four years. The Tysons became part of a small, close-knit group of Americans. The firm provided comfortable living quarters in a compound, personal servants, meals, wine, and cigars. The letters of J. Murray Forbes, a colleague of Tyson's, describe cross-country paper chases on ponies and crew races between the American merchants and the English.[21] The Tysons' first child was born at Shanghai in 1867. The Russell partners all made money, dealing no longer in opium but in tea, silk, or cotton goods. On returning home they invested in growing American industries, especially railroads. Former Russell partners ran the Chicago, Burlington, and Quincy Railroad, during years of fierce wheeling and dealing over routes in the upper Midwest. The railroad's head office was in Boston, where Tyson served as auditor and later comptroller of the C.B. & Q.[22]

George and Sarah Tyson had two more children after they left China: a second son in 1869 and a daughter Elizabeth (Elise) in 1871. The Tysons settled into a new house at 314 Dartmouth Street in Boston, where Sarah Tyson soon died.[23] George Tyson promptly married again, but his second marriage, to Emily Davis, lasted only five years before he died in 1881.[24] Thirty-five-year-old Emily, with no children of her own, was now solely responsible for three young stepchildren. In his will, Tyson expressed his "earnest desire" that his wife and children would continue in their "affectionate relations." The four of them shared equally in his estate, which provided more than they needed to live in perfect comfort. Emily Tyson built a large house in Pride's Crossing, north of Boston, soon after her husband's death. The Boston house remained their winter home.

When Emily Tyson and Elise together bought Hamilton House in 1898, they restored it, added to it, and cherished the house and its surroundings. Elise recorded their early years there with her camera. They

chose Herbert W. C. Browne as their architect. He and Arthur Little were partners in a well-known Boston firm that had established its reputation with designs for houses in the Colonial Revival style. The 1876 Centennial Exposition in Philadelphia had sparked a resurgence of patriotism and a pride in America's history. There was a general sense in the years after the Civil War that things were getting out of hand. With cities burgeoning, immigrants pouring in, and industrialization taking over, a return to an idealized national past, simpler and more stable, was very appealing.[25] One patriotic promoter of the Colonial Revival, Sydney George Fisher, hoped he was seeing the end of the "vulgar worship of everything foreign which so long has been our bane."[26] After decades of eclectic plundering of ever more esoteric European models, American architects in the late nineteenth century often turned back to invoke in new construction the straightforward order of the eighteenth century. Although Colonial Revival houses were usually far more elaborate than their prototypes, the search for architectural roots was sincere.

Writer Thomas Nelson Page used the Tysons' Hamilton House as the basis for a romantic short story, calling it "a perfect example of the Colonial architecture which seems to have blown across the country a century and a half ago like the breath of a classical spring."[27] All the Tysons had to do was refurbish the house and the grounds, following their architect's lead, in an effort to bring the place up to the pitch that they all felt Colonel Hamilton *should* have reached.

Herbert Browne's surviving account books record his work for the Tysons. In 1899 he listed "[a]lterations to house at South Berwick - work done by local contractors."[28] To make the house suitable for luxurious, hospitable country living, a new kitchen wing was added and the dining room enlarged. On the south side, overlooking the river, the Tysons' added a partially enclosed piazza. Browne faced both additions with trellising, a popular Colonial Revival motif. The trellises made the new wings look less like excrescences upon the pristine mansion and more like additions to the garden, especially when they were covered with vines. The Tysons liked the trellis theme so much that they chose a wallpaper of rose-hung trellises for their back parlor and had wooden trellising applied to the inside wall of the piazza.

A "colonial" garden was by then considered an essential adjunct to a colonial house. This generally meant a garden with a straight walk down the middle, other

Enclosed porches were added to the west end of the house, and vines were encouraged. Marble urns by the granite steps had belonged to Sarah Orne Jewett's family. Photo by George Brayton, 1923. (Society for the Preservation of New England Antiquities)

walks at right angles, and rectangular beds of flowers. As early as 1876 an article in *Lippincott's Magazine,* "Fashions in Gardens," reacted to the prevailing informality espoused by Downing, asking, "Is a rigid formality worse than a premeditated and elaborately manufactured irregularity?"[29] The Tysons had the Jewett garden as a local model and were surely familiar with other people near Boston who were planting "old-fashioned" gardens. Mary Caroline Robbins was the author of a popular book, *The Rescue of an Old Place* (1892), about the Massachusetts farm she had bought. She revived a flower garden made long ago by "two dear old ladies" and treasured "an old Box arbor" and the "simple and homely" flowers that still survived. Beneath her old pear trees she planted beds of hardy perennials.[30] Her account and her description are typical of a genre that flourished around the turn of the century, when the Tysons began their developing their garden.

Since Hamilton House did not have an old garden to restore, Mrs. Tyson and Elise depended on Browne to provide the structure of a new one. They decided early on that the big Goodwin barn, standing close by the house in the New England tradition, must be moved to provide a level site for the garden. The level of the ground around the house was raised and shaped into the terraces that they all agreed belonged there.

Browne had a large and carefully cataloged library of garden books as a resource when it came to designing the architecture of the Tysons' garden. His accounts itemize landscape work at some twenty-five other estates between 1894 and 1929. A *Harper's Monthly* article proclaimed a new trend in 1899: "Instead of employing an architect to design the [house] and a gardener to fumble over the [garden], we are intrusting both to the architect."[31] In 1899, architecture was still the only formal discipline that taught the skills necessary to design the type of formal garden that Mrs. Tyson and many others wanted.

Formality in a garden depended on the use of straight lines, geometric curves, symmetry, and the frequent inclusion of structural elements. Rest and harmony were only to be found in gardens that were related to the architecture of the house, according to one critic; the formal garden was seen as a necessary transition between the house and its setting.[32] Herbert Browne was familiar with Charles Adams Platt's influential 1894 book on Italian gardens, and he undoubtedly met Platt when both were working in Brookline, Massachusetts, during

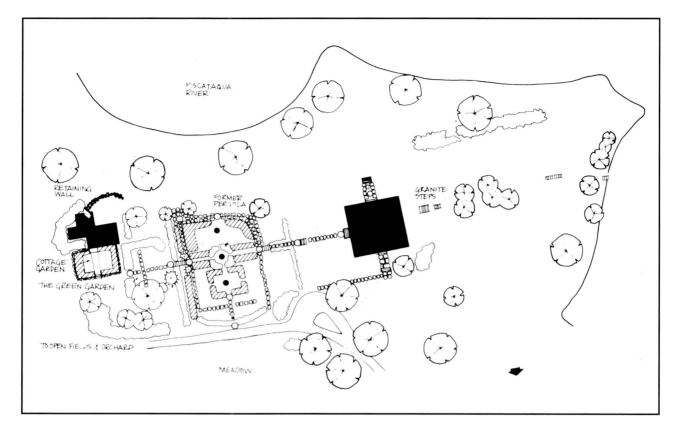

Plan of the garden at Hamilton House. (From a sketch by Alan Emmet)

the 1890s. The Tysons' new garden, modest compared to most of Platt's designs, clearly springs from the same assumptions. Its outdoor rooms, together with the two new wings, extended the balanced architecture of the house onto a larger landscape.

The main flower garden was aligned with the east door of the house. At the foot of the steps from the house an arched gateway covered with vines opened onto a central path and a vista through the garden and beyond. To the left of the garden, looking from the house, was a long, low garden house of Browne's design. Crowned with finials, trimmed with latticework, and draped with honeysuckle, it served as part of the garden's enclosure. To the right, a long pergola of white-painted wood extended from the entrance gate along the edge of the river bluff to the far corner of the garden. There the flagstone paving widened out to form a small open-air sitting room, where, under a roof of vines, Mrs. Tyson poured tea for her guests. It was

probably there that Edith Wharton sat when she and Teddy dropped by one July afternoon in 1905, driven by Cook, their chauffeur. In a chapter titled "The Social Side of Gardens," Hildegarde Hawthorne described a small tea party in the garden at Hamilton House in 1910, the guests listening to bird songs and the trickle of the fountain and discussing "the joy of a sundial, the vagaries of certain bulbs."[33] Hawthorne was of the opinion that in a garden people could associate more intimately than anywhere else.

Photographs taken in 1903, when the garden was only three years old, show fences, arches, and arbor almost smothered by greenery: wisteria, trumpet vine, akebia, grapevines, and ivy. Constant clipping of vines and hedges preserved openings to the river view. The house, too, was festooned with verdure.

The garden at first opened onto a long slope of meadow and orchard. In 1907 the Tysons had a little cottage built beyond the garden at the edge of the river bank. They had rescued beams and paneling from an eighteenth-century house that was slated for demolition. The antiquarian interest in collecting old furnishings and artifacts was part and parcel of the Colonial Revival movement. William Dean Howells, that astute

Under the pergola were pots of blooming white hydrangeas; at its far end the pergola opened out to form an outdoor sitting room, a place for intimate tea parties, 1905. (Society for the Preservation of New England Antiquities)

chronicler of fads and fashions, described in an 1888 novel a cottage newly furnished with a spinning wheel, an "ancient crane found in the scrap heap at the black-smith's," and a table with turned legs "picked up in the hen-house of a neighboring farmer for a song."[34] Like the Tysons, Daniel Chester French, too, was "picking up a lot of old things" and reusing antique wood panel-ing in the building of Chesterwood. Incorporating the old woodwork into the Tysons' new cottage, Herbert Browne added an incongruously large arched window that replicated the stair windows in the mansion. The Dollhouse, as it was called, home of Elise's collection of antique dolls and miniature furniture, was given a little walled cottage garden of its own, made quaint with brick paths and overhung with lilacs. Box-edged beds were filled with humble flowers: foxglove, hollyhock, sweet william, and forget-me-not. Between the Doll-house and the main garden was a cool and shady green garden, more sophisticated, enclosed by a clipped hedge of arborvitae and punctuated by white birches and white statues.

The big flower garden—"the heart of the garden"—

was centered on a sundial, an icon of the Colonial Revival garden. Mrs. Tyson soon added a marble fountain and classical statuary. The flowers were primarily varieties that were considered to be old-fashioned. Although it was a brand-new creation, the garden was, after all, supposed to represent the ancient garden that the house should once have had. The Massachusetts exhibit at the 1893 World's Columbian Exhibition in Chicago had featured an old-fashioned garden of herbaceous perennials, attracting considerable attention. Arthur Shurtleff wrote in 1899 of his regard for gardens of "olden times"; no matter how decayed, they had for him a glory and a glamour that new gardens lacked.[35] Old gardens could, however, be reproduced, as he pointed out—a good thing, since so few of them survived.

Louise Shelton, who wrote books and articles on gardens, visited Hamilton House in 1909. She described the garden as "to all appearances . . . a part of the past," even though she knew it was not.[36] The flowers may have been old-fashioned, but they were assembled with consummate artistry. The garden's glory began in June, wrote Shelton, when blue flowers, "slightly relieved by white and yellow, had a monopoly." Delphinium spires provided the blue, with white madonna lilies in front of them. Soon afterward pink peonies and roses predominated, and Shelton sighed, "One feels that the fairest garden ever grown was dressed all in pink." Hildegarde Hawthorne wrote of the garden's green arbors and the beds "gay with corn-flowers and canterbury-bells, sweet with heliotrope and lily, separated each from each by grassy paths edged with box and given seclusion by rose-hung wall and pergola."[37]

Shelton described the "artist-owner" as being the head gardener, toiling daily among her plants. The reference is to Mrs. Tyson, but her stepdaughter Elise became as great a gardener. Between them they filled in the strong structural framework that Browne had laid out. The Tysons had no greenhouse, but each season pots of oleander, a fig tree, and clipped bay trees appeared on steps and in corners. Great tubs of white hydrangea illuminated the shadows underneath the arbor.

Grandmother's Garden, Lydia Field Emmet, oil on canvas, ca. 1912. This garden, with its vine-covered arbor, trim hedges, fountain basin, delphinium spires, and pots of flowers, shares much of the ambience that Mrs. Tyson and her daughter Elise created at Hamilton House in South Berwick, Maine.(National Academy of Design, New York, New York)

The Tysons maintained cutting gardens, vegetable gardens, and reserves of replacement plants, all of which required much labor. Strangely, however, in four fat albums of photographs taken by Elise, no pictures show anyone working in the garden. Not one of a hired man weeding or raking, not one of Mrs. Tyson snipping off a deadhead.

When visitors arrived at Hamilton House, they pulled up at the end of a lane onto a stone-paved circle. Both paving and hitching posts came from a small local quarry, according to Burton Trafton Jr., whose grandfather cut and laid the stone for the Tysons.[38] At the approach to the house, Lombardy poplars and Dutchman's-pipe concealed the kitchen wing. Clumps of tiger lilies glowed beside the path to the front door. A host of flowering crabapples and pears, underplanted with daffodils, replaced the old orchard of Alpheus Goodwin on the slope toward the river.

Passing through the wide central hall and out the south door, one emerged onto a sitting area beside the vine-draped house. Giant elms filtered the sun. Chairs stood around an old grinding stone from a local mill. Venetian marble urns, two of a set of four that had belonged to the Jewett family, stood by the granite steps, adding a typically Tyson touch of the exotic to Colonial Revival New England.

Mrs. Tyson, right, by the fountain with a friend, 1904. (Society for the Preservation of New England Antiquities)

There were plenty of visitors. Mrs. Tyson and Elise had luncheon guests and guests who stayed for a weekend or a week. Sometimes Elise had nine or ten of her "crowd," including William Sumner Appleton, the antiquarian activist who was soon to found New England's first and still preeminent preservation society. In summer the friends canoed on the river, taking their picnic in wicker hampers. Elise's photographs show young women in long skirts and men wearing knickers and tweed caps. In autumn they would all work in the woods, clearing paths or building rustic seats. The Tysons and their friends also came to "Souta B," as they called it, in winter.[39] Elise's friends would skate on the river or pile onto toboggans for a run down the meadow slope. On snowshoes or long wooden skis, they tromped through the snow or crowded, laughing in the frosty air, into a sleigh behind two horses.

Elise's photographs convey her love for the place and her keen sense of natural beauty. She caught the early morning mist over the garden from her bedroom window or high-piled clouds over the river at sunset. She captured the sunlight shining through silken poppy petals, as well as milkweed pods poking through the first snow. Isaac Gilliland, the Tysons' caretaker and farmer, is seen mowing with his scythe, Father Time silhouetted against the sky, or hastily loading hay onto the wagon as thunderheads gather overhead, the eerie light conveying a sense of urgency.

The caretaker lived on the place year round. When the Tysons were in residence, they had a housekeeper, three maids, and a liveried chauffeur in a tall silk hat. The Tysons were richer than anyone in South Berwick, and their style ensured that they were noticed. But they were generous and well liked. Elizabeth Goodwin, a neighbor, remembers Mrs. Tyson as an old lady dressed always in white.[40] Emily Tyson died in 1922.

Elise took over at Hamilton House. She had been married in 1915 to Henry Goodwin Vaughan, a lawyer and a leader in the world of fox hunting, whose Maine antecedents linked him to the very Goodwins who had once owned Hamilton House. The Vaughans built a house in Sherborn, Massachusetts, their architect none other than Herbert Browne. In the new house, Browne included tall arched windows like those at Hamilton House; millstones similar to those in the grounds at Hamilton House were laid in the Sherborn garden. The Vaughans had no children. During the 1930s, Vaughan served in the Maine state legislature, and they spent more and more time at Hamilton House.

Previous page: Delphiniums and stone *putti* in the garden at Hamilton House. (Photo by Peter Margonelli)

Elise Tyson took over the garden after her mother died. Among her additions were these pineapple-topped posts, seen in a view through the garden toward the house. Photo by Paul Weber, Boston, 1929. (Society for the Preservation of New England Antiquities)

Elise Vaughan was active in the Garden Club of America. She served as an officer at different times of both the national and the local organizations. In 1934, while she was president of the Piscataqua Garden Club, the national organization held its annual meeting in Maine, spending three days at York Harbor, not far from South Berwick. Elise's penciled notations indicate the complexity of the arrangements for the five hun-

dred attendees: thirty buses, thirty minutes to see Hamilton House, two busloads for lunch, twenty minutes at another garden, on and on. In other years, Elise Vaughan would travel to distant cities, often by special private train, to attend the club's annual meetings. Touring other members' gardens, she would write marginal comments in her guidebook on the fancy places she rushed through: Mrs. Torrey's garden was "ugly and

Hamilton House and its gardens overlook the Piscataqua River, more serene now than when the house was built and seagoing ships were unloaded nearby. Much of this land is now a state park, the bequest of Elise Tyson Vaughan. (Photo by Peter Margonelli)

very grand and formal"; Mrs. Taylor's Boxley had "almost too much fat Box!"

Neighbor Elizabeth Goodwin still remembers an occasion when the local garden club met at Hamilton House, and members were shocked to learn that gardeners had stuffed new plants in full and perfect bloom into the garden that very morning. But Mrs. Vaughan was a serious gardener, according to Burton Trafton, who knew her in her later years. He treasures a pot of agapanthus, blue lily-of-the Nile, started thirty years ago from a slip of her plant.

Elise Vaughan's reserve gardens provided a constant supply of plants. Her garden was not old-fashioned in the sense that her mother's was. Whether daylilies or roses, she always had the latest hybrids. She paid more attention to her color scheme; a garden club bulletin called hers a "blue and white garden," but she had pink and pale yellow flowers, too.[41] She grew many rare plants, according to Mr. Trafton, including some not considered hardy in southern Maine. A silverbell tree (*Halesia carolina*), for example, grew to thirty feet along a south-facing wall. Unusual perennials, such as plume poppy (*Macleaya cordata*) and a rare double form of the old August lily (*Hosta plantaginea*), flourished in her garden. She, more than her mother, saw that vines and hedges were always neatly trimmed. Her additions to the garden included a series of white-painted posts topped with finials and a circle of arborvitae around the sundial.

After her husband's death in 1938, Elise Vaughan grew frail. On one occasion she was brought to Hamilton House from Boston by ambulance. She died there in 1949. Two hundred acres of her woods were set aside under her will as a state park.[42] Hamilton House and its gardens were bequeathed to the Society for the Preservation of New England Antiquities (SPNEA). Elise had planned ever since her mother's death in 1922 to leave the "wondrous old place" to SPNEA, whose founder, William Sumner Appleton, had visited there so often.[43]

In 1950 a fierce windstorm almost entirely demolished the long wooden pergola, already weakened after fifty Maine winters. With only a modest endowment from Mrs. Vaughan, SPNEA was unable to rebuild the pergola or any of the other rotting wooden structures in the garden. All the posts, arbors, and lattice fences were removed. For simplicity and ease of maintenance, some of the hedges and flower beds were eliminated; certain plants were replaced by others more rugged. The fountain, the old millstones, and a patterned array of flower beds and hedges still surround the sundial. Quite unlike the enclosed garden of Mrs. Tyson and Elise Vaughan, the garden is now open to the magnificent view of the river. And the river, after all, was what led Colonel Hamilton to build his house there in the first place.

Notes

Hamilton House and its gardens are regularly open to the public during the summer and early fall.

1. Sarah Orne Jewett, "River Driftwood," *Atlantic Monthly* 48 (November 1881): 505.

2. Burton W. F. Trafton Jr., "Hamilton House, South Berwick, Maine," *Old-Time New England* 48 (January–March 1958): 57–65.

3. York County Deeds, Alfred, Maine, 47:80.

4. U. P. Hedrick, *A History of Horticulture in America* (New York: Oxford University Press, 1950), 42, 146; the poplars are shown in an undated sketch, signed "Mary O. Hayes," that belongs to Burton W. F. Trafton Jr. and was reproduced in *The Magazine Antiques* (May 1960), 488.

5. York County Deeds, 86:108, 91:219–20. Subsequent deed references include 165:81 and 358:457.

6. Sarah Orne Jewett diary, 28 June 1869, Jewett Papers, Houghton Library at Harvard University.

7. Jewett, "River Driftwood," 504.

8. Sarah Orne Jewett, *The Tory Lover* (Boston: Houghton Mifflin, 1901), 32, 34–35.

9. Sarah Orne Jewett, "From a Mournful Villager," in *Country By-Ways* (Boston: Houghton Mifflin, 1881), 135.

10. Paula Blanchard, *Sarah Orne Jewett: Her World and Her Work* (Reading, Mass.: Addison Wesley, 1994), 197; Elizabeth Silverthorne, *Sarah Orne Jewett: A Writer's Life* (Woodstock, N.Y.: Overlook Press, 1993), 129.

11. Sarah Orne Jewett to Mary Jewett, 18 September 1896, Jewett Papers, Society for the Preservation of New England Antiquities (hereafter cited as SPNEA).

12. Sarah Orne Jewett to Mary Jewett, 30 August 1894, SPNEA.

13. Robert Grant, *Fourscore* (Boston: Houghton Mifflin, 1934), 283.

14. York County Deeds, 493:34, 486:320.

15. Emily D. Tyson to Sarah Orne Jewett, 22 March 1898, Jewett Papers, Houghton Library.

16. *Bangor (Maine) Daily Commercial*, 20 December 1901, clipping, Houghton Library.

17. Sarah Orne Jewett to Mary Jewett, 23 April 1903 and 25 April 1903, SPNEA.

18. Elise Tyson to Sarah Orne Jewett, undated box 2, folder 4, SPNEA.

19. Suffolk County Probate Records, Boston, docket 59410, and 1922 death certificates, vol. 2:7.

20. Robert Bennet Forbes, *Personal Reminiscences* (Boston: 1882, 1892), appendix.

21. J. Murray Forbes, letters (typescript), Peabody-Essex Museum, Salem, Mass.

22. Boston directories, 1876, 1877, 1879, 1880.

23. Suffolk County Deeds, 1088:51.

24. Philadelphia Department of Records, Vital Statistics, death certificate, 8 January 1881.

25. See Alan Axelrod, ed., *The Colonial Revival in America*

(New York: W. W. Norton, 1985); William B. Rhoads, *The Colonial Revival* (New York: Garland, 1977.).

26. Sydney George Fisher, *Men, Women and Manners in Colonial Times* (Philadelphia: J. B. Lippincott, 1898) 7–8.

27. Thomas Nelson Page, "Miss Goodwin's Inheritance," in *Under the Crust* (New York: Charles Scribner's Sons, 1907), 15.

28. Herbert Browne, account books, SPNEA Archives.

29. E. C. G., "Fashions in Gardens," *Lippincott's Magazine* 18 (August 1876): 257–59.

30. Mary Caroline Robbins, *The Rescue of an Old Place* (Boston: Houghton Mifflin, 1892), 79–80.

31. Charles H. Caffin, "Formal Gardens and a New England Example," *Harper's Monthly Magazine* 99 (September 1899):565.

32. Jessie M. Good, "The Art of Formal Gardening," *Country Life in America*, 1 (1902): 209; Wilhelm Miller, "An Italian Garden That Is Full of Flowers," *Country Life in America* 7 (1905): 492.

33. Hildegarde Hawthorne, *The Lure of the Garden* (New York: Century, 1911), 102.

34. William Dean Howells, *Annie Kilburn* (New York: Harper & Bros., 1888), 107.

35. Arthur A. Shurtleff, "Some Old New England Flower Gardens," *New England Magazine*, n.s., 21 (December 1899): 422–426.

36. Louise Shelton, "The Garden at Hamilton House," *American Homes and Gardens* 6 (November 1909): 422–25.

37. Hawthorne, *Lure of the Garden*, 101. Hawthorne also described the garden in "A Garden of Romance: Mrs. Tyson's at Hamilton House, South Berwick, Maine," *Century Magazine* 80 (September 1910): 778–86.

38. Burton W. F. Trafton Jr., interview by author, 1 July 1981.

39. Isabella Halsted, interview by author, 15 November 1981.

40. Elizabeth Goodwin, interview by author, 8 July 1981.

41. *Garden Club of America Bulletin* (September 1934), 30. Photographs of Elise Vaughan's garden were published in "The Garden in Good Taste," *House Beautiful* 65 (March 1929): 313–16.

42. Suffolk County Probate, docket 350538, will of Elizabeth R. Vaughan.

43. Elizabeth R. Vaughan to William Sumner Appleton, 29 June 1923, SPNEA property files.

Chapter 14

The Italian Inspiration

The Garden at Faulkner Farm,

Brookline, Massachusetts

BROOKLINE, MASSACHUSETTS, adjacent to Boston, was a pace-setting town in American garden design during the second half of the nineteenth century. Perhaps it was the climate, the intellectual climate. Many lively and intelligent people in all fields of endeavor lived in Brookline. Andrew Jackson Downing, in his popular, often-reprinted 1841 *Treatise on the Theory and Practice of Landscape Gardening*, selected two Brookline estates as exemplars of the taste he advocated. Both Thomas Lee's estate and Colonel Thomas Handasyd Perkins's Pinebank embodied Downing's ideal combination of "the Beautiful and the Picturesque." By the 1880s, John Lowell Gardner and his wife, Isabella Stewart Gardner, the flamboyant art collector, had filled a part of their elaborate Brookline garden, Green Hill, with Italian artifacts, long before hosts of other moneyed Americans began doing the same thing. Frederick Law Olmsted, already famous as a landscape designer, established his home and office in Brookline in 1883. At the same time, Charles Sprague Sargent, director of Harvard's new Arnold Arboretum, was expanding and developing his family estate, Holm Lea, into 150 acres of idealized natural landscape. And then, in the last three years of the century, the Honorable and Mrs. Charles F. Sprague oversaw the transformation of their Brookline estate, Faulkner Farm, into something entirely new in America. Their garden, in situation and in plan, was patterned directly after the Renaissance villa gardens of Italy.

William Fletcher Weld of Boston owned the largest fleet of sailing ships in America just before the Civil War.[1] He later invested in steamships, railroads, and real estate. From his country seat on a hilltop in Brookline, Weld could see his vessels coming into Boston Harbor on a clear day. His granddaughter, Mary Bryant Pratt, inherited a fortune and a large part of Weld's Brookline estate prior to her marriage in 1891 to Charles Sprague. Her property included a twenty-acre farm that had once belonged to Charles Faulkner, whose name was applied by the Spragues to their entire property.

Charles Sprague, thirty-four at the time of his marriage, practiced law in Boston, but like his father and grandfather before him, his primary interest was politics.[2] On his mother's side, Sprague was descended from the Lawrences, a family of successful Boston merchants and mill owners. Sprague ran for political office and was elected state representative, then state senator, and ultimately, in 1896, representative in Congress. In all his elective offices, Sprague pushed for reform measures. According to one account, Sprague found his two years as a Boston park commissioner the most satisfying period of his public life.[3] The park commission had been established for nearly twenty years when Sprague began his service in 1893. Frederick Law Olmsted's active involvement in planning Boston's parks was drawing to a close. In 1894 the links in Olmsted's citywide plan—the Emerald Necklace—were finally completed, making it possible to ride or drive on parkland through almost the entire city.[4] Sprague participated enthusiastically in the development of Boston's park system. At the same time, he and his wife embarked on the development of their own private park into a trend-setting garden.

Mary Sprague, fourteen years younger than her husband, was known for her interest in art. After her marriage she became a collector of treasures for her house, many of them purchased on their frequent trips to Europe. Their first house was situated on the highest part of their inherited land.

In 1893 the Spragues retained architect Herbert Browne of the Boston firm of Little, Browne & Moore to build them a new and larger house. At the same time, Charles Sprague asked Frederick Law Olmsted's son John to site the house and plan its driveways. It was natural for Sprague to turn to the preeminent Olmsted firm, whose office was nearby and with whom he was working closely on Boston's parks. The relationships between client, architect, and landscape architect were distant and difficult, however. Sprague seems to have tried deliberately to keep Browne and the Olmsted firm from working together. He continually countermanded his own previous instructions while alternately expanding and contracting the scope of his designers' authority.[5]

Herbert Browne often went beyond simply designing houses for his clients. He frequently planned gardens, too, as he had done for Mrs. Tyson at Hamilton House. But most of his landscaping was done to complement the Colonial Revival houses of his own design. Browne apparently wanted to plan the Spragues' entire landscape but was permitted to design only the entrance court. Even that effort was fraught with dissension, and his design for the court was later changed.

The office of Olmsted, Olmsted & Eliot was not allowed to do much either. Among the firm's least satisfied clients, Charles Sprague must rank high. Before work on the site had even begun, Sprague complained

that the Olmsted designers had exceeded their scope by indicating on their preliminary plan the terracing they deemed necessary for the steep site.[6] A year later the firm informed Sprague of its dissatisfaction with Browne's design for the approach road and court, which, according to the Olmsted designers, should be symmetrical and formal.[7] The firm objected above all to the conflict of responsibility.

By 1895, Charles Eliot of the Olmsted office was in charge of the Faulkner Farm job. That spring marked the high point in Sprague's often strained relationship with Olmsted, Olmsted & Eliot. In April, Sprague wrote: "I desire to have your firm attend to the general treatment and laying out of my place and wish to consult you in regard to any improvements which you may think it desirable for me to make. . . . In general my idea is to have the surroundings of my house and the crest of the hill like a garden. The lower portion I wish to keep like a farm."[8] He seemed to be giving the firm broad authority to make a "general plan," as he called it, which would include drainage and placement of outbuildings as well as planting.

Charles Eliot went to work promptly. One of his first proposals was to treat Sprague's agricultural lowland as a *ferme ornée*, with a narrow circuit drive through the prettiest parts. Apparently still unsure about the latitude Sprague had actually granted them, the Olmsted firm wrote Little, Browne & Moore: "If Mr. Sprague has definitely agreed to any suggestions of yours respecting the flower garden and the arrangement of the great terrace west of the house, we should [like] to receive copies of the accepted plans."[9] At the same time, the Olmsted office asked Sprague to please let his friends know that Olmsted, Olmsted & Eliot were in no way responsible for the driveways and carriage court that had already been built.[10] Although not anxious to step on the toes of architects Little, Browne & Moore, the Olmsted firm did not wish to be blamed for someone else's poor work.

Sprague was furious. From Europe he wrote that he had not and would not adopt Olmsted, Olmsted & Eliot's plans for his avenues. Everything the firm had already done had to be changed, he wrote, but would they please hurry and finish the planting plan for the steep slopes. Sprague's final words to the Olmsted firm were "If your plan contemplated the treatment of the bank after the fashion of banks in the public parks, with bushes alone I should not want to adopt it."[11] Bitter words from an ex–park commissioner.

The Sprague house in Brookline, Massachusetts, 1901. Architect Herbert Browne designed the house, the walled forecourt, and the gateway. Photo by T. E. Marr. (Courtesy *Architectural Record* and Frances Loeb Library, Harvard University)

In the spring of 1896 the Spragues moved into their new house. According to the architect's account book, the Spragues spent $182,000 on their house, courtyard, terrace, and stable and on the wrought iron gates and marble floors that they added a year later.[12] Of white clapboard, with dark shutters and a balustrade around the low hip roof, the house paid stylistic tribute to the New England tradition. With its elliptical pediment, carved urns, and arched windows, it was, like most country houses of its period, more elaborate than any American prototype.

Charles Sprague had expressed his dissatisfaction with the Olmsted firm by reducing the scope of their work for him to almost nothing. Yet he was unwilling to entrust the design of the garden to Herbert Browne. Fortunately, in 1896, Sprague and his wife were introduced to Charles Adams Platt. Platt impressed the Spragues as the garden designer they were seeking.

Platt (1861–1933) had studied art in New York at the National Academy of Design and in Paris at the Académie Julian.[13] While in Europe during the 1880s, he traveled in Italy. He soon gained renown for his etchings and his paintings. When he returned to the United States, he joined the colony of artists in Cornish, New Hampshire. He built a house for himself there in 1890 and began designing houses and gardens for others— without any formal training. A turning point in his life was the 1892 trip he took to Italy with his younger brother, William. William Platt was employed at Olmsted's office, which was then, in effect, a school of landscape architecture when there were as yet no formal academic programs. Charles Platt, thinking that Olmsted's training deemphasized the architectural aspect of garden design, took it upon himself to fill this gap in his brother's education.[14] The two brothers toured at least twenty-five of the best-known Italian gardens, Charles sketching and taking photographs as they went. Sadly, soon after they returned to the United States, William was drowned at the age of twenty-four.

Charles went on to publish two articles on Italian gardens in *Harpers' Monthly Magazine.* In 1894 he expanded the articles into a book, which he illustrated himself with drawings and photographs. Platt's book appeared at a fortuitous time—for him and for the Spragues. Their architect, Herbert Browne, owned a copy, and Charles Eliot, with whom Sprague dealt at the Olmsted office, reviewed the book in the *Nation.*[15] Although critical of Platt's omission of historical background, Eliot felt the Italian villas described and illustrated in the book could provide valuable lessons for

American garden designers. Charles Platt's *Italian Gardens* struck an immediate response in Mr. and Mrs. Sprague. They turned away from Browne and from the Olmsted firm and entrusted the design of their garden to Platt. The site the Spragues had selected for their own "villa" was, after all, just such a one as an Italian Renaissance prince or cardinal might have chosen.

The design of the Spragues' garden was Platt's first major landscape project for clients beyond the circle of his friends in Cornish. His only previous work outside Cornish was a house with a garden in Needham, Massachusetts, which he designed in 1895 for Dr. Elliot, Sprague's physician, who had introduced the Spragues to Platt. Although they were taking a chance when they commissioned someone with so little practical experience to undertake such a complex project on their steep hillside, they trusted Platt and allowed him the latitude so necessary to an artist. Platt must have been delighted with the Spragues' site and with the long view over the *campagna* stretching out to the southwest far below. In 1897 work began on the garden. In September 1899, *Harpers' Monthly Magazine* published Platt's plan, nine photographs of the completed garden, and a rave re-

view.[16] This was the first of dozens of articles and books describing the garden at Faulkner Farm.

Platt eventually became famous for his ability to integrate the design of a house and its gardens into a unified whole. His stylistic models were the villa gardens of Italy, of which he wrote, "The evident harmony of arrangement between house and surrounding landscape is what first strikes one in Italian landscape architecture."[17] The garden, he said, should be treated like another apartment of the house. Platt was able to do this when he designed both simultaneously, but at Faulkner Farm he had to work with an existing house. (As it happened, as soon as the garden he designed was

Charles Platt's plan of the grounds surrounding the house at Faulkner Farm. High ground above the house, at the top in the plan, was laid out as a grove. At the bottom of the plan the land falls steeply; the view from the terraces and the flower garden extends over the farmland below. Photo from *American Country Homes and their Gardens*, John Cordis Baker, 1906. (Boston Athenaeum)

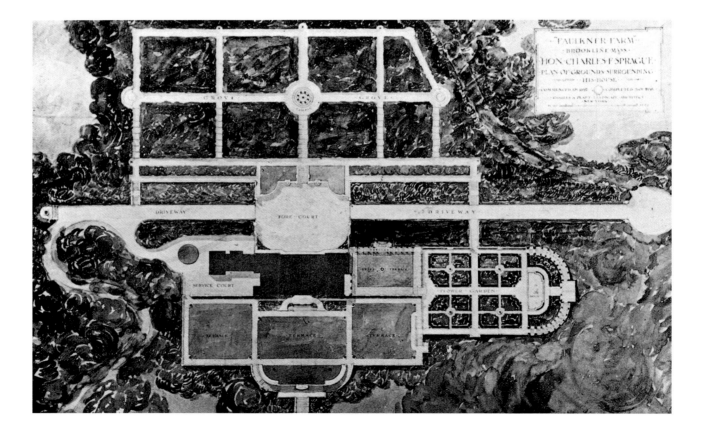

The temple in the grove at Faulkner Farm stands on the property's highest point, providing a commanding view. (Photo by Peter Margonelli)

completed, the Spragues remodeled and enlarged their new house!)

One of the least photographed parts of the garden was the hillside above the house. By one account, Mrs. Sprague herself had made a sketch of a formal *bosquet* for this hilltop prior to consultation with Charles Platt.[18] Platt's plan for the grove, as he called it, may have been based on her sketch. Steep steps led from the entrance drive and forecourt to the grove, which, with its closely planted trees and wide, straight paths, looked very like the one at the Villa Portici, as portrayed in Platt's book. At either end of the grove were round, unadorned basins of water. A central circular temple marked the highest point in the garden. From the temple one had a view of Boston to the east, as well as over the countryside to the west.

Platt's scheme called for changing the newly completed curving driveway and the entry court. The straight drive, as he laid it out, passed between huge gates of Browne's design into the forecourt, with its twelve-foot brick walls. Through another gateway the drive continued straight toward an outsize statue of Juno. When the colossal goddess arrived from Italy in 1904, it took twelve oxen to haul her into place.[19] The long vista across the facade of the house, with Juno as the focus, was reminiscent of some of the strongly axial perspective views Platt had chosen to illustrate his book.[20]

The pergola on the upper terrace was removed when the Sprague house was enlarged in 1902. Guy Lowell included this photograph in his 1902 book, *American Gardens*. (National Park Service, Frederick Law Olmsted National Historic Site)

Charles Platt's most important work at Faulkner Farm was on the slopes south and west of the house, where he developed a series of walled terraces and steps leading to the farmland a hundred feet below. The uppermost terrace, adjacent to the house, was grass, with an Italian wellhead at its center. Along the uphill side a long Corinthian-columned pergola included an outdoor sitting room. This pergola was removed after a few years, when the Spragues had the house enlarged. A lower grass terrace ran along the entire west side of the house. The terraces overlooked woods, fields, and pond to distant hills and evening sunsets. From the entrance drive the view was hidden by a wall and closely set trees. Platt typically withheld a view until it could be appreciated to the fullest, a device he had used even in his first commission, at High Court in Cornish.[21]

At one side of the house, and down a few steps, was the flower garden, rectangular in plan with a semicircle at the far end. A central path led through the garden to a tile-roofed pavilion, the "casino," which had two curving pergola arms enclosing a pool. The main part of the garden was divided into four squares, each of them again quartered and each with a font or wellhead at its center.

The beds were full of flowers. Photographs from the early years show dense plantings of spring and summer bulbs, perennials such as phlox and poppies, and masses of lilies. The garden bore a marked resemblance to the Italian flower gardens Platt had used to illustrate his book. He admired many of those he had seen and noted sadly those villas that had "lost" their flower gardens. He praised the simple arrangement of flower beds at the Medici Villa at Castello, and he appreciated the profusion of flowers at Villa Colonna. A decade after Platt's book was published, Edith Wharton stated firmly that flowers were merely occasional and incidental grace notes in Italian gardens. "Marble, water, and perennial verdure" were, to her, the important elements.[22] Her opinion was influential, shaping the common American perception of Italian gardens as primarily green. For Platt, however, as for most of his clients, flowers were essential.

The pergolas at Faulkner Farm were hung with grapevines. Bay trees in tubs were placed between the stone columns and in corners throughout the garden.

The casino overlooks a pool at the end of the garden. Bay trees and antique pots were placed along the walls and steps. Photo by T. E. Marr, 1901. (*Architectural Record;* Frances Loeb Library, Harvard University)

Every autumn these tender trees were moved by wagon down the hill to "bay pits," where they spent the winter underground, safely below the frost line. Along the garden balustrades stood oil jars, ancient vases, and a Roman sarcophagus. The Sprague garden had fewer statues than many later Italianate gardens. Other than the colossal Juno, there were only two pairs of terms (pillars adorned at the top with carved heads) flanking the steps from the house and from the casino.

The casino, as Keith Morgan has pointed out, resembled a pavilion at the Villa Lante, a photograph of which Platt had used in his book. The interior of the casino was decorated with frescos, probably of Platt's own design, in an antique style. From the casino, elevated as it was, one had a view of the garden and the surrounding countryside.

The flower garden and the grass terraces were supported by a massive retaining wall of rough stonework topped by a brick parapet. Twin flights of steps curved down from the central bowed exedra of the terrace to a shallow grotto with a slowly dripping fountain. Below, more steps and a path led through groves of oak, rhododendron, and mountain laurel to a pond and the farm.

In an interview a few years later, Platt expressed the opinion that the landscape architect should provide uncomplicated surroundings for a house on a hill, to avoid competing with the "larger setting."[23] He had followed his own precept at Faulkner Farm. Each garden "room" partakes of the view, but each has interior vistas as well. The several parts of the garden were all related by strong lines of sight.

After his work at Faulkner Farm, Charles Platt began

The pergola extends in a curve from either side of the casino, barely visible at the left. Neglect has brought a mossy antique quality to the garden that Charles Adams Platt designed for the Spragues at Faulkner Farm in Brookline, Massachusetts. (Photo by Peter Margonelli)

to design houses and gardens simultaneously. He is reported to have said later that the enormous problems he had experienced in working with architects caused him to become one.[24] Certainly, at Faulkner Farm he had walked into a complex disharmony between his clients, their architect, and his predecessor landscape architect. We can only guess at the extent of the rivalries and disagreements into which Platt was introduced. It is clear that the Spragues gave him sufficient authority to prevent a crippling entanglement.

Given the hindsight of eighty years, Faulkner Farm seems a period piece, a relic of that "golden afternoon" before income taxes, world wars, depression, and inflation made such creations unlikely. The garden may seem to be no more than one would expect to accompany a large formal house designed when garden labor was cheap and abundant. In fact, however, the Sprague garden attracted an enormous amount of attention when new, and it influenced countless garden owners and designers. As with any work of art, copies in plan or in detail devalue the originality of the prototype.

The fin-de-siècle shift to an older, more geometric style of garden, exemplified by Platt's work at Faulkner Farm, represented a turning away from the theoretically more natural style that had held sway for a half a century. This shift paralleled similar changes in architectural style. Even Charles Sprague Sargent, a staunch advocate of naturalistic landscaping, admitted that since all gardens are to some extent artificial, formal design was not without some merit. For *Garden and Forest*, the only American periodical of that decade to consider issues of landscape design, Sargent wrote two articles on formal gardening in 1893.[25] Historical precedents cited in the editorials included "your grandmother's garden in New England," the Mall in Central Park, and the "happy results" of the cooperation between architect and landscape gardener (Olmsted) at the 1893 World's Columbian Exposition in Chicago. If Olmsted, a leading proponent of the natural style, used a more architectural style on occasion, it could not be entirely without merit.

Bellefontaine in Lenox, Massachusetts, was devel-oped at about the same time as the Sprague garden, as was Indian Harbor at Greenwich, Connecticut, another grand and formal creation by the same Beaux-Arts–trained architects, Carrère & Hastings. During this period, Wilson Eyre, also an architect, designed comparable gardens, such as Ashford in Greenwich. Many architects were well equipped to design architectural gardens, but Charles Platt was not a product of the dominant Ecole des Beaux-Arts. He innovated his own style, adopting the Italian villa gardens as models and as inspiration.

Platt's initial interest in Italian gardens was that of an artist. His modest intention for his book on Italian gardens had been simply to illustrate them, even though he did comment on their merits or shortcomings. Platt was strongly impressed by the clarity of spatial organization in the nineteen villa gardens he depicted and described in his book. The component parts of each were treated as one entity. This became Platt's own desideratum in all his work. To achieve his ideal, he was compelled, finally, to become an architect. But even in his early projects around existing houses, as at Faulkner Farm, Platt attempted to create this harmony of structure and site.

"Pavilion, Villa Lante," a photograph from Platt's book. The casino Platt designed for Faulkner Farm may have been modeled on this pavilion. (Boston Athenaeum)

He intended his book to point the way toward the adoption in the United States of the Italian model. He noted similarities in the character of the landscape, at least in some parts of this country.[26] He became a strong advocate for the return to architectural form in garden design while favoring the restraint and individuality that to him were typical of the best Italian villa gardens.

Platt's reviews of specific Italian gardens reveal other features that appealed to him. Strong sight lines, satisfying perspectives, a view from a height, unity and balance: these he admired and strove to emulate. At Villa Medici, for example, he praised the elevated temple and the view of the city. At the Quirinal Palace garden he admired the perspective along the principal walk, a painting of which he used as a frontispiece. He missed this clarity of design at Villa Albani but found the straight lines of the Boboli Gardens "relentless" and wearisome. At Caprarola he noted how well integrated were the elements of its plan. The Villa Falconieri was unified, he felt, by a "system of stone-pines . . . planted at intervals."[27]

Italy had held American writers and artists in thrall for decades. Thomas Cole had painted a vast, glowing view of Florence in the 1830s, and Hawthorne completed *The Marble Faun*, a wildly romantic novel set in Rome, in 1859. Daniel Chester French was only one of the sculptors to study and improve his skill under the benign influence of Italy. More and more American travelers in search of culture, as well as collectors in search of artifacts, made pilgrimages to Italy after the Civil War. Out of their experiences there, returning artists produced an outpouring of Italian-based journals, novels, translations, paintings, and sculpture, with profound effect on American intellectual life. In Boston, interest in Italian culture was particularly intense, inspired by Harvard art historian Charles Eliot Norton's lectures and Longfellow's translations of Dante.

"This garden, I seem to have spent my whole life in it; and when we are settled in Providence, I'm going to have mother send back for some of these statues. I suppose Signor Cavaletti wouldn't mind our robbing this place of them if he were paid enough."[28] Thus spoke the heroine of William Dean Howells's *A Foregone Conclusion* (1874), referring to the garden of the Venetian palace where she and her mother were staying. The fictional Miss Vervain's proposal was acted upon by scores of actual Americans, who brought home the counterparts of the broken fountain and the marble naiad she admired. Certain art dealers were only too happy to furnish garden owners with "exact reproductions" of celebrated statues from the Vatican or some Florentine palazzo: "available in terra-cotta, bronze, or lead" if not the "best hard Carrara marble," as a 1910 catalog phrased it.

The importing or copying of mere incidents from Italian gardens was ridiculed by some American garden critics after the turn of the century. Edith Wharton, in her 1904 book on Italian gardens, stressed that these gardens could not be reproduced by simply importing old fragments.[29] An Englishman, Edward S. Prior, writing in *House and Garden*, was perhaps the only critic who faulted Faulkner Farm for being composed too much of fragments. The Spragues' "second-hand debris from European museums," "the nail-parings and hair-combings of European styles," created for Prior a "dreary stage scenery that it must be nausea to live with."[30] Even he, however, admitted that the overall design of the garden was not bad.

The design of Faulkner Farm met with almost universal acclaim. Horatio Hollis Hunnewell came from Wellesley to have a look in June 1898. He was astonished, impressed by the art but not uncritical. According to Hunnewell, "The sunken garden, when finished, will attract great attention and admiration, no doubt, but in passing judgement on the whole place, it must be said there are many serious blemishes and objections, to say nothing of the extravagance, for the cost must reach several hundred thousand dollars."[31]

Few American gardens have been so frequently analyzed in print. In a series on the Italian garden in a 1900 architectural journal, James Sturgis Pray concluded that the Sprague estate had all the characteristics of its Renaissance prototypes: the harmonious relationship between house and grounds, the use of water, and most important, sufficient elevation to provide a view.[32] Platt's Cornish, New Hampshire, friend, neighbor, and client, Herbert Croly, wrote an admiring article on Platt's work for *Architectural Record* in 1904. It was filled with praise and photographs of Faulkner Farm. To Croly, the Sprague garden marked a welcome return to the "original and classic" model typified by Italian villa gardens, where the house fits the landscape and architecture blends into nature.[33] The Italian style was made to seem a natural one for America.

Boston architect Guy Lowell's *American Gardens* (1902) included sixteen views and a plan of the Sprague

garden. Lowell admired the outdoor rooms as extensions of the house and considered Platt's adaptation of imported ideas entirely appropriate in the search for a national style.[34] Ralph Adams Cram, another architect, agreed with Lowell on the necessity of borrowing from European archetypes. In his 1901 series of articles on Faulkner Farm in *House and Garden*, "An architectural style of our own is denied us," he claimed, without saying why, "so we borrow of course."[35]

Platt himself expressed the belief that America was at last developing its own style, especially in the design of country places. The once fashionable picturesque gardens were to him but the "dime novel of architecture"—evidence of a period of transition. The newer, more spacious and restful style based on the "best historical models," especially those of Italy, was proof that America was "emerging from the formative period of alternate rebellion and imitation which has passed so

The Sprague garden when new, as seen from the house. The entrance drive at the left was soon hidden by trees. A ladder and scaffold inside the casino indicate that the frescos were not yet completed. (Courtesy of the Trustees of the Boston Public Library)

long for originality."[36] Platt was not, of course, the one to say it, but the new national style for country estates might have been termed the Platt style.

In his critique of the Sprague garden, Ralph Adams Cram particularly admired the use of sculptural elements. Roman vases and Olympian heads were not mere fragments to Cram but were evocative of "memories and fancies, dreams and visions, and all the phantasmagoria of an unhampered soul." What would have been merely "dumb and tongueless" relics if housed in a museum could, here at Faulkner Farm, "speak for all to hear."[37]

Guy Lowell, like other garden writers at the time, harked back to early American formal gardens as worthy antecedents. Only the ubiquitous carpet bedding of the late nineteenth century met with his scorn. Cram agreed with Lowell that the flower garden at Faulkner Farm avoided this "discredited mode." "Firm and noble restraint" had wisely curbed the "riotousness of nature." Sounding almost panic-stricken, Cram was convinced that flowers would "let loose riot and revolution" unless "held firmly in check by the kindly hands of their betters," as fortunately they were at Faulkner Farm.[38] Some of us may never before have appreciated the risks posed by flowers.

Paradoxically, carpet bedding—"foolish blots of curvilinear beds spattered over a green lawn" to Cram— undoubtedly required more restraining by gardeners than did the Faulkner Farm flower beds, where each

plant was allowed to develop more freely. The Spragues' flower garden was "a masterpiece of nobility and beauty," said Cram the elitist, noting that the absurd bedding style had "passed into the hands of the light-hearted suburbanite and the municipal gardener."[39] Snobbery played a part in changing popular taste, as it often does. Jessie M. Good, in her paean to the Sprague garden in *Country Life in America*, admired its harmonious relationship to the house. She, like Cram, could not resist a dig at the wretched, outmoded taste in flower beds at other places, "patterned after the heavenly bodies and placed as an excrescence wherever a bright grassy spot in the front lawn could be found."[40]

Good found more precedents for the Sprague garden than the Italian villa model alone. She concluded that the garden at Faulkner Farm conformed to the dictates of Sir William Temple and Lord Bacon, whose seventeenth-century essays on gardening had had wide influence in England. Another writer, Brooke Fish, in *New England Magazine*, agreed that Bacon would have approved the Spragues' "covert alleys" and the simplicity of their garden plan. Fish likened the curve of the garden at the casino to the apse of a great cathedral.[41] Writing for *Harpers'* in 1899, English art critic Charles Caffin admired Faulkner Farm's kinship with the six-

Sculptural relics were incorporated into the walls and balustrades at Faulkner Farm but with more restraint than in some other turn-of-the-century estate gardens. (Photo by Peter Margonelli)

teenth-century royal gardens of the Tudors at None-such and Hampton Court.[42] The list of possible antecedents seemed endless. The garden at Faulkner Farm had an instant pedigree.

While Platt was overseeing the building of their garden, the Spragues were spending part of the year in Washington, D.C., after Charles Sprague's election to the House of Representatives in 1896. He was reportedly the richest man ever to serve there, primarily because of his wife's inherited fortune. "It required a special train of nine cars to move his household possessions to Washington."[43] He fell ill in 1897, after being thrown from his horse, and became partially paralyzed. He consulted specialists and tried to conceal his illness from his constituents. Finally, he collapsed entirely and spent his last year in McLean Hospital, near Boston, where he died in 1902.[44]

Mrs. Sprague's tastes became more grandiose after the death of her husband. It seemed as though the new garden fostered her desire to "improve" her house. Brooke Fish, writing in *New England Magazine* in 1902, praised her garden at length but commented, "Barring the material of the house, which is wood, the whole is Italian from general scheme to smallest detail."[45] The wood soon disappeared under a veneer of brick. Herbert Browne added another story to the house, a ballroom, a conservatory, wall and ceiling murals, gilt carving, and marble floors. The house lost in coherence what it gained in grandeur. It also lost its affinity to New England without becoming more Italian. During the first two years of her widowhood, Mary Sprague spent more on alterations than the entire house had cost just a few years earlier. Figures on the cost of constructing the garden have unfortunately been lost.

Mrs. Sprague's enormous expenditures on her house and garden during the years of her husband's illness and her subsequent widowhood can be viewed as frivolous or callous. Another interpretation is that at thirty-one she was just coming into her own as a confident, strong-willed patron. Entrusted for the first time with power, she was willing to take risks, willing to place confidence in an artist who at Faulkner Farm was attempting something of greater scope than anything in his previous experience. An innovative creator needs this degree of support. Mary Sprague's backing enabled Platt to achieve all he did at her country place and, incidentally, to start a new style.

Charles Platt went on to a long and distinguished career as both an architect and a landscape architect. In

White wisteria at Faulkner Farm, 1932. (From *Horticulture;* Frances Loeb Library, Harvard University)

1901, soon after the Faulkner Farm garden was completed, Platt designed a garden for Mr. and Mrs. Larz Anderson at their adjoining estate, Weld. (Mrs. Anderson and Mrs. Sprague were first cousins.) At Weld, as at Faulkner Farm, Platt worked around an existing house. Thereafter he insisted on designing both house and garden at the same time. Although later in his life he designed urban buildings, his fame rests chiefly on his work on country estates. Platt died in 1933.

Two years after her husband's death, Mary Sprague married Edward D. Brandegee, a college friend of Charles Sprague and a pallbearer at his funeral.[46] Unlike many owners of country houses, the Brandegees spent most of each year at Faulkner Farm, where their four children grew up. A friend who often visited Faulkner Farm as a child recalls the dominating presence of Mrs. Brandegee. She was "the captain of her ship," a fitting metaphor for a granddaughter of shipowner William F. Weld, the strong and vibrant woman portrayed by John Singer Sargent.[47]

Mrs. Brandegee lived to be eighty-five, continuing to oversee the management of her farm and her garden. With an outdoor staff of up to forty during the growing season, Faulkner Farm was regularly opened to the public.[48] Estate owners were generous in the early years of this century; they had apparently little reason for paranoia.

In the 1920s, Mrs. Brandegee enlarged the lawn area in her flower garden to allow for social gatherings, including debutante parties and wedding receptions. She had an iron trellis for wisteria installed at the end of the house toward the flower garden.[49] The essence of the garden in the 1920s and 1930s was the mass of white wisteria one saw in the spring upon emerging from the marble ballroom with its Gobelin tapestries. Even if flowers played only a minor role in the villa gardens of Italy, as Edith Wharton so firmly maintained, America's first and best-known Italian garden was, in its prime, admired for its floral display.

Notes

1. New England Historical and Genealogical Society, *Index* (Boston, 1981) 45:115–17; Isabel Perkins Anderson, *Under the Black Horse Flag* (Boston: Houghton Mifflin, 1926).

2. On Charles F. Sprague, see the Harvard Class of 1879 Secretary's Reports for 1885, 1890, 1895, 1900, clipping files, Harvard University Archives

3. Charles F. Sprague obituary, 30 January 1902, clipping files, Harvard University Archives.

4. Boston Department of Parks, *Nineteenth and Twentieth Annual Reports of the Board of Park Commissioners*, 1894 and 1895.

5. Correspondence between Charles F. Sprague and Olmsted, Olmsted & Eliot, job file B-29:299 and letterbooks 28–40, 1893–95, Olmsted Archives, Manuscript Division, Library of Congress.

6. Sprague to Olmsted, Olmsted & Eliot, 7 July 1893 and 12 September 1893, Olmsted Archives.

7. Olmsted, Olmsted & Eliot to Sprague, 5 September 1894, Olmsted Archives, 36:62.

8. Sprague to Olmsted, Olmsted & Eliot, 14 April 1895, Olmsted Archives.

9. Olmsted, Olmsted & Eliot to Little, Browne & Moore, 14 June 1895, Olmsted Archives, 40:422.

10. Olmsted, Olmsted & Eliot to Sprague, 6 June 1895, Olmsted Archives, 40:363.

11. Sprague to Olmsted, Olmsted & Eliot, 13 October 1895, Olmsted Archives.

12. Herbert Browne Account Book, Browne Collection, Society for the Preservation of New England Antiquities (hereafter cited as SPNEA).

13. See *Monograph of the Work of Charles A. Platt* (New York: Architectural Book Publishing Co., 1913), introduction by Royal Cortissoz; Keith N. Morgan, *Charles A. Platt: The Artist as Architect* (New York: Architectural History Foundation, 1985); Keith N. Morgan, ed., *Shaping an American Landscape: The Art and Architecture of Charles A. Platt* (Hanover, N.H.: Dartmouth College and University Press of New England, 1995).

14. Morgan, *Charles A. Platt*, 36–37.

15. Catalog of Herbert Browne's Garden Library, Browne Collection, SPNEA; Charles Eliot, review of *Italian Gardens*, by Charles A. Platt, *Nation* 57 (28 December 1893): 491.

16. Charles H. Caffin, "Formal Gardens and a New England Example," *Harpers' Monthly Magazine* 99 (September 1899): 557–65.

17. Charles A. Platt. *Italian Gardens* (New York, 1894), 6.

18. "A Gold Medal Estate in Massachusetts," *Horticulture* 8 (15 December 1930): 571–72.

19. Lee Albright, interview by author, Brookline, Mass., 19 January 1983.

20. Platt, *Italian Gardens*, 52, 139.

21. Morgan, *Charles A. Platt*, 34–35, 80.

22. Edith Wharton, *Italian Villas and Their Gardens* (New York, 1904), 5.

23. "From an Interview with Charles A. Platt," *Outing* 44 (June 1904): 353.

24. Charles Downing Lay, "An Interview with Charles A. Platt," *Landscape Architecture* 26 (April 1912): 129.

25. "Formal Gardening: Does it Conflict with the Natural Style?" *Garden and Forest* 6 (15 March 1893): 119–20; "Formal Gardening: Where It Can Be Used to Advantage," *Garden and Forest* 6 (22 March 1893): 129–30; "The Columbian Exposition," *Garden and Forest* 6 (6 December 1893).

26. Platt, *Italian Gardens*, 154.

27. Ibid., 115.

28. William Dean Howells, *A Foregone Conclusion* (1874; reprint, New York: Library of America, 1982), 134.

29. Wharton, *Italian Villas*, 12.

30. Edward S. Prior, "American Garden-Craft from an English Point of View," *House and Garden* 4 (November 1903): 211–15.

31. Horatio Hollis Hunnewell, *Life, Letters, and Diary*, ed. Hollis Horatio Hunnewell, vol. 2 (Boston: privately printed, 1906), 6 June 1898.

32. James Sturgis Pray, "The Italian Garden," *American Architect and Building News* 67 (10 February 1900): 43–45. Pray's series of articles continued in the issues of 17 February, 17 March, and 24 March.

33. Herbert Croly, "The Works of Charles A. Platt," *Architectural Record* 15 (March 1904): 195–98.

34. Guy Lowell, *American Gardens* (Boston: Bates & Guild, 1902).

35. Ralph Adams Cram, "Faulkner Farm, Brookline, Massachusetts," *House and Garden* 1 (August 1901): 1.

36. "From an Interview with Charles A. Platt," 349–50.

37. Ralph Adams Cram, "The Sculptures of Faulkner Farm," *House and Garden* 1 (September 1901): 9–10.

38. Cram, "Faulkner Farm," 10–11.

39. Ibid.

40. Jessie M. Good, "The Art of Formal Gardening," *Country Life in America* 1 (April 1902): 209.

41. Brooke Fish, "Faulkner Farm," *New England Magazine*, n.s., 25 (January 1902): 585.

42. Caffin, "Formal Gardens," 565.

43. Charles F. Sprague obituary.

44. Ibid.

45. Fish, "Faulkner Farm," 585.

46. Harvard Class of 1881 Secretary's Reports, 1884, 1898, and 1906, Harvard University Archives; Edward D. Brandegee obituary, 11 September 1932, biography files, Brookline Public Library Archives.

47. Mrs. Richard C. Storey, interview by author, 9 February 1983.

48. *Boston Herald*, 13 June 1920, rotogravure section.

49. "Gold Medal Estate," *Horticulture* 8 (15 May 1932): 571–72.

Chapter 15

The Great Good Place

Edith Wharton at The Mount,

Lenox, Massachusetts

EDITH WHARTON, at thirty-eight, was tired of Newport, the spot where she had spent every summer of her life. The year was 1900. You would think she might have been satisfied. After all, she had gotten her way in everything.

Edith Jones had married Teddy Wharton, an amiable bon vivant thirteen years her senior, in 1885, when she was twenty-three. Together, they followed the pattern of Edith's life as a child: New York City winters, Newport summers, and frequent trips to Europe. After fifteen years they had no children but plenty of money, especially after Edith's fortunes were unexpectedly enhanced by the legacy of a remote Jones cousin. They lived in the style to which they were both accustomed.

The Whartons had bought a Newport cottage called Land's End in 1893, a house well away from her mother's. Edith promptly embarked on a radical remodeling of Land's End with help from Ogden Codman, then in his early twenties and just embarking on his ambitious career as a society architect. She and Codman discovered their shared admiration for a restrained classicism in architecture and interior design. They collaborated on a book that promulgated the classical style. *The Decoration of Houses* was barbed with blasts at the frowzy, overstuffed rooms and houses in which they and most people they knew had grown up and still lived. First published in 1897, the book was an immediate success. Two years later, Edith Wharton's second book came out, *The Greater Inclination*, a collection of her previously published stories.

Even though she had now achieved recognition and success as a writer, Edith Wharton wanted to change her life, starting with Newport. The setting of Land's End is bleak, as its name implies, and might on gray days depress one who was not entirely enamored of the sound of surf forever crashing against cliffs. Edith pined to get away from the gloom and dampness, but she was also determined to flee from the social constraints, the "watering place trivialities" of Newport.[1] She yearned for the deeper, richer life in the arts that her literary accomplishments seemed to offer. She longed to be with creative people who shared her interests. She knew well by then that her dull, benevolent husband did not.

During the summer of 1899, while Teddy and his mother were in Europe, Edith stayed in her mother-in-law's summer cottage in Lenox, in the Berkshire hills of Massachusetts. The following year the Whartons rented a house there and began looking for a property to buy. Edith Wharton confided her enthusiasm to Ogden

Edith Wharton early in her writing career. (The Beinecke Rare Book and Manuscript Library, Yale University)

Codman: "I am in love with the place—climate, scenery, life & all—& when I have built a villa . . . & have planted my gardens & laid out paths through my bosco, I doubt if I ever leave here."[2] In the summer of 1901 the Whartons purchased the Sargent farm in Lenox, 113 acres sloping down to Laurel Lake. Their reasons differed, but both Edith and Teddy embarked eagerly on the project of making a country place for themselves in the Berkshires.

For her escape to "real country," it is ironic that Edith Wharton chose Lenox, a community already known popularly as "the inland Newport."[3] Although in an earlier, simpler time, Lenox, like Stockbridge, had been a mecca for intellectual vacationers such as Nathaniel Hawthorne and the Reverend Henry Ward Beecher, by the 1890s both towns were enormously fashionable resorts. The glamour once attached in the public eye to writers and artists had faded when faced with the glitter of the purely rich.

August and September marked the height of the Berkshire social "season." House-party guests filled the giant cottages; others flocked to Curtis's Hotel in Lenox or the Red Lion at Stockbridge.[4] Hillsides were claimed as the most desirable house sites, providing the views that had originally attracted summer residents to the region. In the 1880s, Joseph H. Choate, a New York lawyer, began building the house and now famous garden at Naumkeag on a hill in Stockbridge. During the 1890s the industrialist Stokeses, Sloanes, Schermerhorns, and Westinghouses built mansions of unprecedented size over former hill farm pastures. The earliest of these "cottages," in shingle style, were soon outclassed by oversize Colonial Revival mansions that were in turn superseded by palaces of brick and marble. Shadowbrook (1893) had one hundred rooms; the builder of Blantyre (1901) had his wife's ancestral Scottish castle copied, antlers and all. The winner in terms of ostentation may have been Bellefontaine (1899), modeled on the Petit Trianon by architects Carrère & Hastings, who also laid out the grounds. To Edith Wharton, Bellefontaine's elaborately decorated architectural gardens were cold, impersonal, and the epitome of vulgar ostentation. She told Ogden Codman that he really ought to see the place "—as an awful warning!"[5]

This was the Lenox that Edith Wharton had chosen for what she hoped would be a home for her spirit and for a life of the mind. She was to thwart the conventions of her upbringing many times in her life, but her choice of Lenox was entirely conservative. She was, after all, merely moving from the summer resort her mother had chosen to that of her mother-in-law. Her attitude toward "society" was always ambivalent. She scorned the busy social "inanities" of both Newport and Lenox, which did not endear her to her new neighbors. She could not stand the pretentious flaunting of wealth. According to Ogden Codman, Mrs. Wharton was rude to Mrs. Sloane, the queen of Lenox society.[6] On the other hand, Edith did not intend to be an outcast; in fact, her efforts to belong and contribute to the Lenox summer community cut into her writing time and eventually exhausted her.[7] She was very sociable—as long as she could choose her companions. The Whartons' new house was planned from the outset as the setting for continual hospitality.

The deed to the Lenox property was in Edith Wharton's name. It was she who selected the site for the house, a knoll with a view southeast to Laurel Lake and the hills of Tyringham. The Whartons asked Ogden Codman to design their house, Edith knowing that Codman shared her penchant for rooms, facades, and landscapes of cool restraint. She and he adhered with religious zeal to the articles of faith that lay behind such designs. They chose as their model a seventeenth-century English manor house attributed to Christopher Wren.[8]

The Whartons liked his plans, Codman told his mother in February 1901, "but I don't know what they mean to spend."[9] That was the first hint of what soon grew into a full-blown quarrel over money. Codman vented his anger at the Whartons in letters to his mother, letters that reveal him as childish and arrogant. He complained peevishly that "[t]he Whartons' house instead of being my first is my sixth & the smallest of the four now building."[10] Codman, at last successful and busy, felt that the Whartons still treated him as their pet protégée and resented his new prosperity. When Teddy Wharton tried to beat down his commission, Codman waved the American Institute of Architects rule book at him; when Wharton shouted and slammed a door, Codman walked away from the job, expressing relief and telling his intimates that Wharton was an idiot. Teddy Wharton was probably showing signs of the instability and paranoia that blighted the

remainder of his life. Two years after the fight with Codman, he suffered his first "sort of nervous collapse" in the summer of 1903.

Edith Wharton was undoubtedly a difficult and demanding client in her own way. Even though she shared Codman's taste and wanted to keep him as a friend, she told him she too thought it best that they not collaborate on the house after all.[11] Codman, however, continued to feel vindictive toward them both; he delighted in recounting their problems over the house and enumerating the defects he was sure he would have avoided.

The Whartons turned to another architect, Francis Hoppin, whom they had known in Newport, to design the house they christened The Mount. According to Codman—a biased reporter, to be sure—Hoppin's life was made miserable by fussy Mrs. Wharton, who telegraphed him almost daily and made him revise the plans continually. By the spring of 1902, Codman's feud

Postcard view from the flower garden to the Wharton house, Lenox, Massachusetts. An awning shaded the long terrace. Edith Wharton penned the verse for Charles Eliot Norton in 1906. (bMS AM1193[336]; by permission of the Houghton Library, Harvard University)

with the Whartons was superficially over, and he was invited back to decorate the interior of their house. He told his mother gleefully that the Whartons rued the day they had quarreled with him and were hoping now that he could redeem Hoppin's failure.[12] Edith Wharton was pleased with Codman's designs for her rooms. Both Whartons were "very humble," gloated Codman; "[h]owever I will try to be kinder now."[13] The patched-up friendship nevertheless became permanently un-glued three years later, when Teddy, refusing once again to pay Codman's bills, called in a lawyer.[14] By that time, however, Codman had married a rich wife and no longer really cared.

The Whartons' house was named The Mount, "not because it was one," as Edith Wharton's friend Daniel Berkeley Updike put it, "but because some old family place had been so named."[15] The house was entered in the European style from a walled, statue-lined fore-court, which Codman considered "an utter failure," so small that "it looks like a clothes yard and is all out of proportion."[16] This enclosed introductory space an-nounced that privacy was valued here. Indeed, one pro-gressed only gradually and in stages to the main rooms of the house. "Privacy would seem to be one of the first requisites of civilized life," the authors of *The Decoration of Houses* had declared.[17]

Each of the principal rooms at The Mount opened onto a broad brick-floored terrace that ran the length of the house on the rear, or garden, side. Shaded by a fes-tive striped awning, the terrace overlooked the garden. Beyond the garden, D. B. Updike recounted, "a lawn sloped to a meadow stretching to the border of a little wooded lake. One day when a party for lunch had gath-ered on the terrace, Mr. Choate [of Naumkeag] arrived, accompanied by the Austrian Ambassador. 'Ah, Mrs. Wharton,' he said as he stepped from the house, 'When I look about me I don't know if I am in England or in Italy.'"[18] Mrs. Wharton may not have been entirely pleased by this remark, presumably intended as a com-pliment. The ambassador had missed the point, for The Mount was intended to be distinctly *American*, Mrs. Wharton's attempt to synthesize and adapt the histori-cal principles of harmony and proportion to the New England scene. Rugged outcrops of limestone, native white pines, and a giant American elm were featured in her landscape. The house was painted white, with green shutters, that quintessentially American combination. The Whartons' barns and livestock enhanced the typi-cal rural New England character of their view toward the lake. Edith Wharton developed her gardens within this regional context.

.   .   .

At the time she was involved in the building of The Mount, Edith Wharton was immersed in Italian his-tory and culture. Her first novel, *The Valley of Decision* (1902), was set in Renaissance Italy. Impressed by this book, her Berkshire neighbor Richard Watson Gilder, editor of *Century* magazine, commissioned Edith Whar-ton to write a series of articles on Italian villa gardens. Edith and her eccentric English friend, Vernon Lee, with Teddy in tow, traveled from villa to villa in 1903. With the addition of painted illustrations by Maxfield Parrish, the articles were published as a book, *Italian Villas and Their Gardens.* The book was a popular suc-cess, more ambitious than Charles Adams Platt's pio-neering book on the same subject, published a decade earlier. Edith Wharton wrote her book with the hope of encouraging in her American readers a return to form and structure in the planning of their gardens. Her opening sentence was guaranteed to shock: "The Ital-ian garden does not exist for its flowers; its flowers exist for it."[19] What really counted, the chief lesson to be learned from the great Italian country houses, was the intimate relation between the house and its garden. Mindful of some new American estate gardens, she cautioned, "a marble sarcophagus and a dozen twisted columns will not make an Italian garden." Instead of struggling to make a literal copy, one should strive for "a garden as well adapted to its surroundings as were the models which inspired it."

Edith Wharton had plunged right into a contro-versy that had torn the garden world in two when she plunked herself down on the side of formality and structure. She could not abide the "laboured natural-ism" of the English landscape style and its later off-spring. She had no use, either, for the flashy formless gardens favored by some of the very rich. Mr. Mindon, the harried protagonist of her 1900 story, "The Line of Least Resistance," looks out at the grounds of his Newport villa: "The lawn looked as expensive as a vel-vet carpet woven in one piece; the flower borders con-tained only exotics. . . . A marble nymph smiled at him from the terrace; but he knew how much nymphs cost."[20] Wharton's own garden at The Mount, indeed her entire place, could be characterized by the phrase she used to describe a Roman villa she admired: "the day-dream of an artist who has saturated his mind with the past."[21]

Having sited the house on a hillside, Mrs. Wharton was forced to deal with the slope. "We are going to ruin ourselves in terraces," she told Ogden Codman, "but the effect will be jolly."[22] Before construction of the house could begin, however, there must be an entrance drive. For assistance with this project she called upon her niece, Beatrix Jones (later Farrand). "Trix," ten years younger than Edith, was already well trained and established as a "landscape gardener," to use her term for her professional role. From the white-picket entrance gate and the lodge, the drive runs for half a mile through a double avenue of sugar maples, past the stable, then dipping and turning through a dense wood and emerging into a clearing, from which the house comes suddenly into view.

The next project, also designed by Beatrix Jones, was a kitchen garden, surviving now only in plans and a photograph or two. No mere vegetable plot, this was an elegant parterre 250 feet long, divided by paths into eight squares and enclosed by a clipped hedge with topiary archways. At one end was a grape arbor; along the other end ran a double row of pear trees. In the summer of 1902, when the house was nearing completion but before they moved in, Edith came nearly every morning to work in the kitchen garden. In the afternoons she took long rides on her horse, returning "stupid with fresh air." She wrote her friend Sara Norton that "Lenox has had its usual tonic effect on me, & I feel like a new edition. . . . It is great fun out at the place now too—Everything is pushing up new shoots—not only cabbages & strawberries, but electric lights & plumbing."[23]

Ogden Codman came to visit. In a typically snide comment he told his mother, "The place looks *forlorn* beyond my powers of description and it will take years and a small fortune in Landscape gardening to make it look even decent."[24] But to Edith Wharton, when they moved into The Mount in September 1902, "[t]he views are exquisite, & it is all so still & sylvan—I have never seen the Michaelmas daisies as beautiful as this year—the lanes are purple."[25]

After months in Italy, the Whartons returned to The Mount in June 1903 with happy anticipation. Edith Wharton was devastated by what she found:

Beatrix Jones (later Farrand), perspective drawing of the kitchen garden at The Mount, 1901. (College of Environmental Design Documents Collection, University of California, Berkeley)

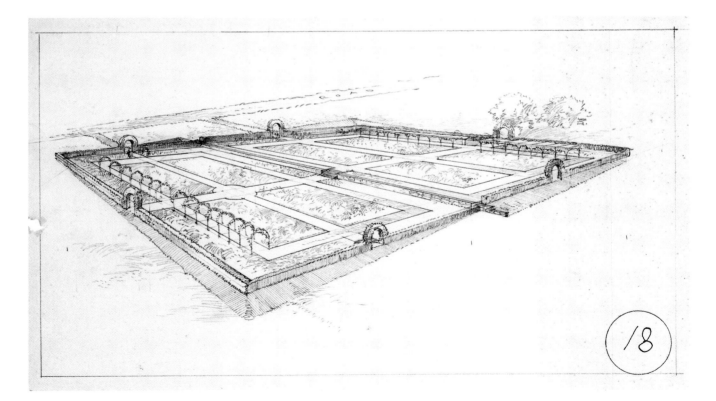

Dolphin fountain in the flower garden, surrounded with white petunias. (Beinecke Library)

Edith Wharton's friend Walter Berry posing as a statue with one of her dogs in the trellis niche designed by Ogden Codman, ca. 1904. The niche had been moved to The Mount from Mrs. Wharton's Newport garden. (Beinecke Library)

. . . out of doors the scene is depressing. There has been an appalling drought of nine weeks or more, & never has this fresh showery country looked so unlike itself. The dust is indescribable, the grass parched & brown, flowers & vegetables stunted, & still no promise of rain! You may fancy how our poor place looks, still in the rough, with all its bald patches emphasized. In addition, our good gardener has failed us, we know not why, whether from drink or some other demoralization, but after spending a great deal of money on the place all winter there are no results, & we have been obliged to get a new man. This has been a great blow, as we can't afford to do much more this year—I try to console myself by writing about Italian gardens instead of looking at my own.[26]

The new head gardener, Reynolds, was a great success; he and Mrs. Wharton got on well. Despite the drought, she and Reynolds and his crew planted the eighty-by-one-hundred-foot flower garden below the house. In the center of the garden was a pool with a spouting dolphin fountain. At the far end was an arched trelliswork niche that Codman had designed for the Whartons' garden in Newport. The garden was filled with rosy-colored flowers. The terrace and the room above, where Edith Wharton wrote each morning, overlooked the glowing flower garden far below.

The friend who best understood and shared Edith Wharton's passion for plants and gardening was Sara Norton. Miss Norton was a daughter of Charles Eliot Norton, an eminent professor of art history at Harvard and a translator of Dante's *Divine Comedy*. In summer the Nortons lived simply on an old farm in Ashfield, a small town in the Berkshires that was removed from Lenox by miles but even more by its utter lack of pretense. Edith described her flower garden to Sara Norton in 1905, urging her to come to see it:

[My garden] is really what I thought it never could be—a "mass of bloom." Ten varieties of phlox, some very gorgeous, are flowering together [by August, thirty-two varieties were in bloom], & then the snapdragons, lilac & crimson stocks, penstemons, annual pinks in every shade of rose, salmon, cherry & crimson—the Hunnemania [a yellow Mexican poppy], the lovely white physostegia, the white petunias, which now form a perfect hedge about the tank—The intense blue Delphinium Chinense, the purple & white platycodons, & c.—really with the background of hollyhocks of every

shade from pale rose to dark red, it looks, for a fleeting moment, like a garden in some civilized climate.[27]

The Whartons never reached The Mount before June, and the weeks in midsummer when the phlox was in bloom may have been the most brilliant season in the garden.

A highlight of the Lenox social season was the Midsummer Flower Show. Edith Wharton worked with the committee on arrangements and fretted over her own entries, tying and labeling little clusters of flowers, many of them raised in her small greenhouse. She was competitive, anxious to do well in this field as in every other aspect of her life. In 1906 she was delighted when, as usual, she won a bundle of first prizes for her phlox, snapdragons, lilies, poppies, and gladioli. In her diary, Edith noted the number of first prizes she had collected at the flower show and on the next page the number of weeks that her new novel, *The House of Mirth*, had been the best-selling book in New York.[28] One might assume that both accomplishments were equally gratifying to her.

Daniel Berkeley Updike, a frequent and charmed recipient of the hospitality of The Mount, had mixed feelings about his hostess's avid gardening:

Edith was very learned about gardens, and she and a neighbor, Miss Charlotte Barnes, used to hold interminable, and to me rather boring, conversations about the relative merits of various English seedsmen and the precise shades of blue or red or yellow flowers that they could guarantee their customers. . . . Edith was conscious of my half-hearted interest in horticulture, and on one particularly dull autumn afternoon when she was directing some planting, I asked her if there was not something I could do—hoping that there wasn't! With a malicious glint in her eye she replied, "Yes, you can pick off the withered petunias that border the fountain." If you have ever tried that particular task you will realize the punishment inflicted.[29]

From the terrace at The Mount a grand double staircase led down into the garden. The flower garden on the left was balanced visually by a sunken garden on the right. The two gardens were linked by a straight gravel walk, bordered by lindens. On a slope around the corner of the house was Edith's rock garden, where she grew sun-loving alpines between natural outcrops of limestone.

The flower garden at The
Mount, as seen from the
terrace at the house, 1905.
(Beinecke Library)

Still shuttling architects, Edith Wharton had Francis Hoppin return to The Mount in 1905 to design steps and walls for the sunken garden. She wrote Sara Norton, "Did I tell you that we are building a high wall around the sunk garden? It will be charming when it is quite 'tapisse' with creepers."[30] The shadowy walled garden echoed with the cooling plash of water falling from a single jet. Edith knew from her experience of Italian gardens how welcome were shade and the sight and sound of water in the heat of the day. And how refreshing was a view; tall arched openings in the wall revealed the countryside beyond.

In *The House of Mirth* (1905), the novel that was Edith Wharton's first large success, her doomed heroine, Lily Bart, wanders off during a house-party weekend to lean pensively against the balustrade of a broad terrace that overlooked "a landscape tutored to the last degree of rural elegance. In the foreground glowed the warm tints of the gardens. Beyond the lawn, with its pyramidal pale-gold maples and velvety firs, sloped pastures dotted with cattle; and through a long glade the river widened like a lake under the silver light of September."[31]

Edith Wharton's description fit the scene spread out before her as she wrote. It was the view *from* the house that held meaning for her; house and landscape were parts of one felicitous whole. She conveys this sense of the harmony she had evoked in a passage from *Sanctuary*, a novella she wrote in 1903: "The large coolness of the room, . . . its outlook over field and woodland toward the lake lying under the silver bloom of September; the very scent of late violets in a glass on the writing table; the rosy-mauve masses of hydrangea in tubs along the terrace; the fall, now and then, of a leaf through the still air—all, somehow, were mingled in the suffusion of well-being."[32]

A biographer of Beatrix Farrand, prejudiced perhaps in favor of her subject, castigated the garden Edith Wharton made without her niece as "a designed disaster" that appeared to be "stretched on a rack."[33] There is more than one angle of vision, but this one seems to ignore the view and the setting. With her keenly developed visual sense, her self-confident taste, and her years of studying gardens in Italy and elsewhere, Edith Wharton was quite capable of arranging the landscape about her house in such a way as to please herself and others. She no longer needed the help of the talented Beatrix, who seems never to have returned to The Mount after 1901, when she had planned the entrance drive and the kitchen garden. Edith urged Trix to visit in July 1903, to recuperate from an appendectomy, but there is no indication that she came. Even if she had, she would have been unable to work. "[T]his house has been a hospital all summer," Edith told Sara Norton in early August while Teddy was in a state of collapse.[34] Beatrix or her mother (Edith's sister-in-law, Minnie Jones) would occasionally propose over the next few summers to bring the other to The Mount to convalesce from nervous illness, but Mrs. Jones seems always to have come alone.[35]

Edith Wharton was intimately involved with her garden, from its overall design to "every tiniest little bulb and shoot." Each time she returned to Lenox in June after a winter's absence, she would walk through the garden with Reynolds, her head gardener, checking to see how each "tree, shrub, creeper, fern, 'flower in the crannied wall'" had come through the winter.[36] Sometimes she was dismayed. Her emotional attachment was such that *she* suffered when her garden suffered.[37] During recurrent "cruel" droughts, she agonized over "parched grass and starved skinny trees." She raged at the hill-country winters that interfered with her gardening plans and injured her plants. "Even the clematis paniculata I had established so carefully is dead," she wailed one spring. Another year she cried, "Don't talk to me about this climate! I don't think anything has grown an inch since last year."[38] She pined for a more "civilized climate" than that of the region she had chosen.

Morton Fullerton visited The Mount in October 1907, setting the stage for a passionate affair with Edith Wharton. After this the growth of plants was linked, for Edith, to sexual awakening. Her novel, *Summer,* published in 1916, is filled with erotic metaphors: "the crowding shoots of meadowsweet and yellow flags . . . this bubbling of sap and slipping of sheathes and calyxes." Flowers sometimes represented physical passion. "Under his touch, things deep down in her struggled to the light and sprang up like flowers in the sunshine."[39] To Fullerton she compared her efforts as a gardener to her writing: "[T]he place is really beautiful. . . . I was amazed at the success of my [efforts]. Decidedly, I'm a better landscape gardener than novelist, and this place, every line of which is my own work, far surpasses the House of Mirth."[40]

Not everyone understood Edith Wharton's direct and intimate connection with her garden. She was much amused by a review in the *Atlantic,* which stated that her book on Italian villa gardens made it clear that she had "never worked in a garden!!!"[41] The reviewer was convinced that "Mrs. Wharton has never spent an hour in a garden uprooting weeds, hunting rose-bugs, squashing caterpillars. . . . She betrays no acquaintance with the trowel and a broken back . . . the heat and sweat of noon."[42] This was so far from the truth that it made her laugh, but some who actually visited Edith Wharton's garden came away feeling that it lacked the owner's personal touch. Ironically, the very perfection she struggled so hard to achieve made it seem *less* than perfect to some observers. In her book on the gardens of well-known people, Hildegarde Hawthorne complained that Mrs. Wharton's garden lacked "intimate charm . . . the sense of personal and loving supervision," in contrast to the "special spiritual quality" emanating from Mrs. Jack Gardner's garden at Green Hill in Brookline, for example.[43] Sara Norton's sister Lily found The Mount quite chilling: "Her house, her garden, her appointments were all perfect—money, taste, and instinct saw to every detail; yet the sense of a *home* was not there."[44]

Daniel Chester French and his wife, Mary, who had made their own garden at Chesterwood, perceived more clearly Edith Wharton's artistry. Her place, with its view "like an old tapestry," was, according to Mrs. French, "one of the most exquisite to be found anywhere in the Berkshires."[45] Edith Wharton visited the Frenches' garden, and they came sometimes to The Mount. Mrs. French described how "when we went to her place, she and Mr. French would wander about the grounds, exchanging ideas, she courteous enough to ask his advice, but artistic enough to need little from any one." The Frenches considered The Mount a model of "what can be done in landscape gardening by developing every little natural beauty, instead of going in with preconceived ideas and trying to make it like some other beautiful place to which the lay of the land bears no resemblance whatever."

. . .

In a letter to a friend, Edith Wharton described the daily routine at The Mount: "Here I write every morning, & then devote myself to horticulture, while Teddy plays golf & cuts down trees."[46] This may have been how she thought she would like to spend her days, but her account bore little resemblance to reality. In fact, such a disciplined and solitary life would not have suited her, for by choice she led such an overwhelmingly social existence that her steady literary output seems miraculous. The writing was done early, in the privacy of her own room. Serious gardening followed, as she said. But always there were friends coming to stay, servants to manage, guests for lunch or dinner, meals to plan, and letters to write. Her little dogs—Miza, Jules, Nicette—clamored for attention. Then Mrs. Wharton would dash off to a committee meeting or a social call. The Whartons traveled continually: to Europe and to New York as a matter of course, but even when supposedly settled at Lenox, they would frequently depart for a few days visit here or a week there.

The more involved and successful Edith Wharton became as a writer, the more she was drawn to friendships with artists and intellectuals. Teddy Wharton, increasingly cantankerous, was left out. His wife's friends often found him as trying as he found her literary life. To Charles Eliot Norton he wrote, "I should like you to see 'The Mount,' to prove to you that Puss [Edith's nickname] is good at other things besides her to me rather clever writing."

The Whartons found one mutual interest when they acquired their first automobile in 1904, "a little sputtering shrieking American motor in which we hope to see something of the country."[47] How difficult it is to imagine the sense of liberation that the first motorcars brought to their privileged owners. Edith Wharton thrilled at "the escape from the railways, the charm of exploring new roads, of being able to flit from point to point as the fancy takes us."[48] With their chauffeur, Charles Cook, Teddy Wharton beside him, and accompanied at the best of times by her new friend Henry James, Edith Wharton whirled over the hills and valleys of New England, each year in a new and more powerful car.

The Whartons introduced Henry James to the motorcar. Both he and the motor figured largely in Edith Wharton's life at The Mount and in the meaning the place held for her. James, then in his sixties and at the peak of his literary powers, paid three visits to The Mount. At that beautiful place and on their motor

The Whartons' motorcar at The Mount, 1904. Edith Wharton and Henry James are seated in the back, with chauffeur Charles Cook at the wheel and Teddy Wharton beside him. (Lilly Library, Indiana University)

The view from the terrace at The Mount, toward Laurel Lake and the Tyringham hills, ca. 1905. (Beinecke Library)

"flights" over the countryside, he was in some measure consoled for the depressing changes he had found on his return to his homeland after twenty years abroad. "I have been won over to motoring, for which the region is, in spite of bad roads, delightful."[49] As they spun along through the glorious autumn afternoons, amid colors "like molten jewels," James was overwhelmed by "the sweetness of the country itself, this New England rural vastness."

For Edith Wharton, too, motoring provided "an immense enlargement of life."[50] By motor they drove often to visit the Nortons in Ashfield, trying different routes through the hill country. One day they drove to Litchfield, Connecticut, a town that charmed James. On a jaunt to Cornish, New Hampshire, the Whartons visited the Maxfield Parrishes and others in that colony of artists and gardeners. On longer motor trips, Edith Wharton visited more gardens. After lunching one day in 1905 with the Coolidges at the old Governor Benning Wentworth place near Portsmouth, New Hampshire, the Whartons drove on to tea with Mrs. Tyson at Hamilton House. Another time they called on Mrs.

Sprague at Faulkner Farm in Brookline and visited the Thayers' gardens in Lancaster.[51]

Riding through the back country, away from the resorts of the prosperous, both Henry James and Edith Wharton were struck by the bleak desolation of lonely farmsteads and villages. Even in summer the starved aspect of New England's hinterland was a reminder of the long months of wintry chill, against which Edith Wharton so fruitlessly railed as it affected her garden. Out of her sense that the weathered gray facades were prisons of a sort, she wrote of desperation and hopeless entrapment in *Ethan Frome* and of rural degeneracy in *Summer*. The barren lives of her characters were ostensibly the reverse of her cushioned existence, but as her husband's mental state deteriorated, her own life became so fraught with uncertainty and anguish that she may herself have felt imprisoned. The Mount itself became one of the complexities of her life as her husband and her marriage disintegrated.

. . .

One of Henry James's stories, "The Great Good Place" (1900), still strikes a responsive note in those who have felt the frantic despair of the protagonist, a man beset and bound by a web of worldly concerns, a web no less constricting for his having woven it himself. In a vivid dream he finds himself at a place of peace and beauty, where hours of solitude are spent in the serenity of a fine library, and companionable hours are passed in conversation of a high order. James may have thought of this as an ideal spiritual state or as a vision of what civilization at its best might be. While staying at a former monastery in France in 1910, Edith Wharton felt that she had found James's Great Good Place.[52] All her efforts at The Mount had been directed toward making such a place of her own. For a few years she succeeded, balancing creative work with social intimacy in a beautiful and harmoniously ordered setting of her own making.

Writing to Bernard Berenson in 1911, Edith Wharton summed up her delight in her "really beautiful" place: "the stillness, the greenness, the exuberance of my flowers, the perfume of my hemlock woods, & above all the moonlight nights on my big terrace, overlooking the lake." The terrace was the focus of The Mount, where, on precious fleeting occasions during her ten years there, her ideal was made real. From "that dear wide sunny terrace" she and those she loved could feast their eyes on the landscape she had composed with just this vantage point in mind. The view of the gardens, woods, lake, and hills soothed her mind and spirit. Evenings too brought serenity: "I went out on my terrace last night, and took up my interrupted communion with Vega, Arcturus, and Altair." One night "the terrace was saturated with real white moonlight, & it was hot enough to sit out late & listen to the Aristophanes chorus in the laghetto."[53]

On the terrace, Edith Wharton also found social communion of the highest order, justifying all her efforts at The Mount. The memory of one evening in particular stayed with her, "when we sat late on the terrace with the lake shining palely through dark trees." In response to an allusion to his Albany relatives, his "labyrinthine cousinship," someone asked Henry James to "tell us about the Emmets—tell us all about them."

Late into the moonlit night, James held as charmed captives the little "inner group" of friends while he spun tales and evoked visions of his lost youth.[54]

The Mount had to be sold. After too many scenes, too many arguments over money, too many unsuccessful attempts to mend Teddy Wharton's mind, Edith Wharton finally concluded that life with him was impossible. She could no longer afford to keep The Mount, with or without Teddy. In September 1911, she left Lenox for the last time and sailed for France. The Mount was sold in 1912. The Whartons were divorced in 1913. Edith Wharton lived in France for the rest of her life, making there two homes for herself and two memorable gardens.

The house and gardens at The Mount are being restored now, thanks to the timely intervention of Edith Wharton Restoration, Inc. The view has been recovered; garden walls and walks have been reclaimed. From her terrace, on an autumn afternoon, the ideals of harmony, proportion, and beauty that inspired Edith Wharton seem distinctly possible. She came quite close to achieving her goal at this great good place.

Notes

1. Edith Wharton, *A Backward Glance* (New York: Appleton-Century, 1934), 124. Biographies of Edith Wharton include R. W. B. Lewis, *Edith Wharton* (New York: Harper & Row, 1975), and Eleanor Dwight, *Edith Wharton: An Extraordinary Life* (New York: Abrams, 1994).

2. Edith Wharton (hereafter cited as EW) to Ogden Codman Jr. (hereafter cited as OC), 1 August 1900, Codman Family Manuscripts Collection, Society for the Preservation of New England Antiquities (hereafter cited as CFMC), box 84.

3. *Picturesque Berkshire* (Northampton, Mass.: Picturesque Publishing Co., 1893), 22.

4. George A. Hibbard, *Lenox* (New York: Charles Scribner's Sons, 1896), 35–38.

5. EW to OC, 27 September 1900, CFMC, box 84. See Edwin Hale Lincoln, *A Pride of Palaces*, ed. Donald T. Oakes (Lenox, Mass.: Lenox Library Association, 1981).

6. OC to Sarah Bradlee Codman, 25 February 1901 and 1 July 1901, CFMC, box 50.

7. Daniel Berkeley Updike, quoted in Percy Lubbock, *Portrait of Edith Wharton* (New York: Appleton-Century, 1947),

17–18; EW to Sara Norton, 23 August 1905, folder 6, Edith Wharton Papers, Beineke Library, Yale University.

8. Richard Guy Wilson, "Edith and Ogden: Writing, Decoration, and Architecture," in *Ogden Codman and the Decoration of Houses*, ed. Pauline C. Metcalf (Boston: Boston Athenaeum, 1988), 164.

9. OC to Sarah Bradlee Codman, 17 February 1901, CFMC, box 50.

10. OC to Sarah Bradlee Codman, 7 February 1901, CFMC, box 50.

11. EW to OC, 25 March 1901, CFMC, box 84.

12. OC to Sarah Bradlee Codman, 3 March 1902, CFMC, box 50.

13. OC to Sarah Bradlee Codman, 5 October 1902, CFMC, box 50.

14. OC to Sarah Bradlee Codman, 8 June 1905, CFMC, box 50.

15. Updike, in Lubbock, *Portrait of Edith Wharton*, 17.

16. OC to Sarah Bradlee Codman, 8 October 1902, CFMC, box 50.

17. Edith Wharton and Ogden Codman Jr., *The Decoration of Houses* (1897; reprint, New York: W. W. Norton, 1978), 22, 49.

18. Updike, in Lubbock, *Portrait of Edith Wharton*, 20.

19. Edith Wharton, *Italian Villas and Their Gardens* (1904; reprint, New York: Da Capo Press, 1988).

20. Edith Wharton, "The Line of Least Resistance," in *The Stories of Edith Wharton*, ed. Anita Brookner, (New York: Carroll & Graf, 1989), 2:35.

21. Wharton, *Italian Villas*, 101.

22. EW to OC, 29 July 1901, CFMC, box 84.

23. EW to Sara Norton, 7 June and 4 July 1902, folder 3, Wharton Papers.

24. OC to Sarah Bradlee Codman, 8 October 1902, CFMC, box 50.

25. EW to Sara Norton, 30 September 1902, folder 3, Wharton Papers.

26. EW to Sara Norton, 5 June 1903, folder 4, Wharton Papers.

27. EW to Sara Norton, 23 July 1905, folder 6, Wharton Papers.

28. EW diary, 15 August 1906, Wharton Papers.

29. Updike, in Lubbock, *Portrait of Edith Wharton*, 19–20.

30. EW to Sara Norton, 26 October 1907, folder 8, Wharton Papers.

31. Edith Wharton, *The House of Mirth* (1905; reprint, New York: New American Library, 1964), 52.

32. Edith Wharton, *Sanctuary* (New York: Charles Scribner's Sons, 1903), 86.

33. Jane Brown, *Beatrix: The Gardening Life of Beatrix Jones Farrand, 1872–1959* (New York: Viking, 1995), 79.

34. EW to Sara Norton, 9 August 1903, folder 4, Wharton Papers.

35. EW to Margaret Terry Chanler, 7 September 1902; EW to Sara Norton, 5 June 1903, 23 September 1906, 26 October 1906, folders 4 and 7; EW diary, 24 October to 5 November 1906, Wharton Papers.

36. EW to Morton Fullerton, 3 July 1911, in *The Letters of Edith Wharton*, ed. R. W. B. Lewis and Nancy Lewis (New York: Charles Scribner's Sons, 1988), 242.

37. Judith Fryer, *Felicitous Space: The Imaginative Structures of Edith Wharton and Willa Cather* (Chapel Hill: University of North Carolina Press, 1986), 175.

38. EW to Sara Norton, 17 June 1905 and 14 June 1906, folders 6 and 7, Wharton Papers; 3 July 1911, No. 1015, Norton Family Papers, Houghton Library, Harvard University.

39. Edith Wharton, *Summer* (New York: Signet Classic, Penguin, 1993), 33–34, 122.

40. EW to Morton Fullerton, 3 July 1911, *Letters of Edith Wharton*, 242.

41. EW to Sara Norton, 2 August 1906, folder 7, Wharton Papers.

42. Henry Dwight Sedgwick, *The New American Type and Other Essays* (Boston: Houghton Mifflin, 1908), 73.

43. Hildegarde Hawthorne, *The Lure of the Garden* (New York: Century, 1911), 135–36.

44. Elizabeth G. Norton, quoted in Lubbock, *Portrait of Edith Wharton*, 40.

45. Mrs. Daniel Chester French, *Memories of a Sculptor's Wife* (Boston: Houghton Mifflin, 1928), 205.

46. EW to Mrs. Alfred Austin, 14 August 1906, *Letters of Edith Wharton*, 107–8.

47. EW to Sara Norton, 12 July 1904, folder 5, Wharton Papers.

48. EW to Sara Norton, 24 January 1904, folder 5, Wharton Papers.

49. Henry James to Jessie Allen, 22 October 1904; Henry James to Edmund Gosse, 27 October 1904, in *Henry James's Letters*, ed. Leon Edel (Cambridge, Mass.: Harvard University Press, 1984), 4:329.

50. Wharton, *Backward Glance*, 176.

51. EW diary, 27 August and 29 October 1905, 29 June 1906, Wharton Papers.

52. Lewis, *Wharton*, 291.

53. EW to Margaret Terry Chanler, 18 July 1903, Wharton Papers.

54. Wharton, *Backward Glance*, 192–94.

Chapter 16

A New Palette

Eolia, the Harkness Estate,

Waterford, Connecticut

THE SEA is all around—the sky, the air, the space, the flowers, the quiet—and the sea. The air is always moving. Mr. and Mrs. Harkness called this place of theirs Eolia, after the island home of King Aeolus, keeper of the winds. According to Greek mythology, Aeolus could give mariners a favorable breeze or a wild tempest, as he chose. He gave Odysseus a month of hospitality and a fair wind toward home. A fitting name, Eolia, for the Harknesses' summer retreat, where guests were welcome and where the wind influenced the design of house and garden and set the pattern of daily life.

This twentieth-century Eolia is on a promontory, not an island. It sits on Goshen Point, just south of New London, Connecticut, where the Thames River enters Long Island Sound. The Harkness mansion, its outbuildings, and gardens had only half a century to grow when the widowed Mary Stillman Harkness died, leaving the property to the state of Connecticut. Since 1953 two-thirds of the 234-acre estate has been open to the public as a park.

. . .

Edward S. Harkness (1874–1940) was the youngest son of Stephen V. Harkness, a man who, by luck and keen business intuition, had amassed a great fortune in his lifetime from an Ohio whiskey distillery. In 1870 the elder Harkness had become a "silent partner" of John D. Rockefeller in the newly formed Standard Oil Company. The company grew rapidly, as did the fortunes of its stockholders.

Edward's father set an example for his children of integrity, modesty, and charitable generosity. No robber baron he. Edward was fourteen when his father died. After graduating from Yale in 1897, Edward surpassed his father by devoting his entire life to giving away the ever-growing Harkness fortune so that it would do the most good for the most people. Unlike many rich inheritors he was not concerned with collecting nor with expanding his wealth.

In 1904, Edward married Mary Stillman of New York, the daughter of a successful lawyer. The couple held in common the belief that material prosperity must be accompanied by a social conscience. They lived in comfort, even luxuriously, but still, in light of the possibilities, with relative simplicity. According to one account, Edward Harkness gave away more than $129

Courtyard of the Harkness house, Eolia, Waterford, Connecticut. This photo by Floyd S. Baker, New York, was published in the magazine *Architecture* in 1908. (Frances Loeb Library, Harvard University)

million in his lifetime.[1] To Yale alone he donated eight residential colleges, a theater, and an art gallery.

The Connecticut coast was part of Mary Harkness's family heritage. Among her later charities was the historical museum, Mystic Seaport, located in the Connecticut town where her mother's family had long been engaged in shipbuilding. Mary's sister, Jessie Stillman, and her husband, William Taylor, bought land along the shore at Goshen Point in 1902. They began building a house, but Jessie soon decided she did not like the windswept promontory after all.[2] In 1904 she and her husband sold the property to the newly wed Harknesses, who purchased contiguous pieces of farmland on the point that became Eolia until they owned almost a mile of shoreline.

A green tile roof, littered with chimneys and dormers, covers the forty rooms of the Harkness house, designed by architects Lord & Hewlett—a large house but no more flamboyant than the Harknesses themselves. Mr. Harkness's tiny bedroom, overlooking the garden but not the water, is almost spartan. *Architecture* magazine published exterior views of the house in 1908.[3] The house has little grace or charm. The vines that have covered it are an asset.

Within a few years the Harknesses had added a whole village of supporting outbuildings, including green-

houses, athletic facilities, a cow barn, stables, poultry houses, and silos.[4] As was typical of American country estates early in the twentieth century, Eolia incorporated genteel farming activities. Unlike Seward Webb's enterprise at Shelburne, this was not serious agriculture. But Eolia had showcase facilities, bearing little resemblance to those of the average subsistence farm of the period, that provided the Harknesses with a year-round supply of fresh milk, butter, poultry, eggs, vegetables, fruit, and flowers. They spent only summers at Eolia, but the head gardener delivered produce by car to the Harkness's New York City home all through the winter.[5] Right from the start, Eolia was an estate of the automobile age. Its several garages even included a turntable for washing cars.

A series of photographs taken in 1908 show the earliest garden landscape, immediately adjacent to the house. At the front door was a circular bed of flamboyant cannas. The driveway ellipse was bordered with young maples and hydrangeas in wooden tubs. West of the house, where the ground sloped away, was an ornamental garden with squared-off flower beds, each bed displaying either cannas or phlox with a border of marigolds. On the south-facing, ocean side of the house, the space enclosed by two arcaded, awninged porticos was treated as a cloister court, bisected by gravel walks that centered on a fountain. The courtyard was lined with tubbed bay trees, a common feature of American formal gardens in the early twentieth century.

Even as these photographs were taken, Mr. and Mrs. Harkness were making plans for more elaborate gardens with the Boston landscape architecture firm of Brett & Hall. In its layout, the garden they designed still survives.[6] The firm is little remembered today, but the two principals had impeccable credentials. Franklin Brett, an 1887 graduate of Massachusetts Institute of Technology, had worked for several years in the Olmsted office in Brookline, Massachusetts. In 1901 he spent a year in New York working for Charles Adams Platt on the design of country estates. In Platt's office Brett got to know fellow-employee George D. Hall, a 1902 alumnus of Harvard's first landscape architecture class, the first formal program in the United States. In 1903, Brett and Hall established their own firm in Boston.[7]

The commission that may have been Brett & Hall's most exciting took them to British Columbia in 1908. They had been hired by the president of the Grand Trunk Pacific Railway to plan a port city for ten thousand or more people at the rail terminus. The city of Prince Rupert, 550 miles north of Vancouver, was expected to equal Vancouver or Seattle in importance. The landscape architects spent several months in the rough settlement, planning idealistically for an uncertain future. They foresaw a great city on mountainous terrain, with a grid of streets for the business district, a Beaux-Arts–inspired section with radial avenues centered on an opera house, and a residential area of sinuous streets and large lots. Unfortunately, Prince Rupert's chief promoter, the railway president, went down with the *Titanic* in 1912, and the city never lived up to his dreams. Still, most of the Brett & Hall scheme was carried out, even to an opera house. Brett & Hall also landscaped the seven-hundred-acre grounds of Hatley Castle, the estate of a mining baron near Vancouver, British Columbia. The firm went on to design numerous gardens in eastern Canada. The partners closed their Boston office during World War I and served as military camp planners. After the war, Hall, always drawn to the Far West, moved to California, and Brett returned to practice in Massachusetts.

To Brett and Hall, fresh from their work in Prince Rupert in 1908, the Harkness project must have seemed rather small and tame. Although their drawings for Eolia

bear no date, three 1912 postcard views of the completed garden suggest that work was begun about 1910. The Brett & Hall plan is balanced, architectural, and strongly axial, but it includes curved, irregularly planted shrub borders where the formal gardens meet the wider landscape. The Harknesses had Brett & Hall lay out a golf course along the shore and two tennis courts, one clay and one grass. Around the courts was a border of spring-flowering shrubs: purple and double white lilacs, yellow forsythia and kerria, white *Viburnum opulus*, and dogwood.

The landscape architects devised a simple bedding-out scheme for the courtyard at the house: tulips and hyacinths succeeded by red geraniums. They opened the view of Long Island Sound by adding a broad grass terrace all along the house. At the center of the terrace, steps led down onto a lawn. Brett & Hall defined the extent of the lawn by a long curve planted with *Spiraea vanhouttei* and Japanese barberry and anchored at either end by *Hydrangea paniculata*. These shrubs would have seriously interrupted the view had they been allowed to grow up.

West of the house is a long rectangular garden with the end nearest the water bowed out into a semicircle. At the opposite end is a U-shaped pergola centered on a pavilion. "The teahouse of Mrs. Edward Harkness is particularly beautiful," according to one star-struck critic. "With its cosy steps, sphinx, and luxurious flowers and vines all bathed in sunshine, it is reminiscent of the Garden of Allah."[8] Eolia, a more earthly garden than Allah's, can at least be actually seen. Here twin flights of steps curve down from the pergola to the garden itself, where long grass panels, now hedged, flank a fountain basin. Flower beds run around the garden's perimeter, and a low stone wall encloses the whole.

The pergola was planted with Chinese wisteria, native grapes, and Dorothy Perkins roses. On its shady side were white and crimson rhododendrons interplanted with lilies, a combination recommended by a then-popular garden writer, Wilhelm Miller, who favored native or natural-looking plantings.[9] Enclosed by the arms of the pergola were two American elms, and other elms framed the view across the garden. The flower beds were planted in strict rows or blocks of single species, with the tallest in the center. At the corners of each bed were standard box or bay trees. A rainbow of brightly colored flowers bloomed all summer long, a bland and tidy garden, perhaps a bit dull.

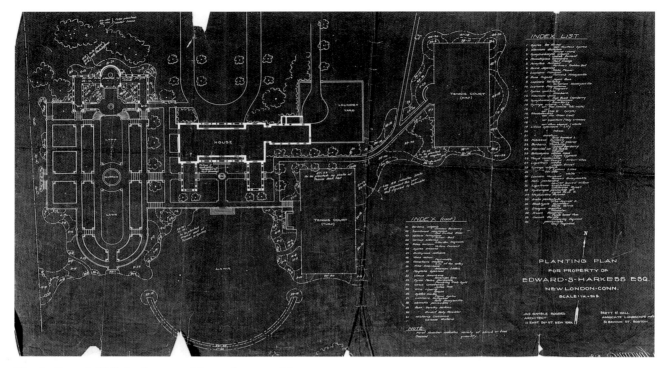

Plan by Brett & Hall, landscape architects, for part of the
Harkness property, ca. 1909. The turf tennis court later became the East Garden, designed by Beatrix Farrand. (College of Environmental Design Documents Collection, University of California, Berkeley)

Teahouse and pergola in the
West Garden at Eolia, with
later planting by Beatrix
Farrand; photo by Mattie
Edwards Hewitt, 1920s.
(Connecticut Department
of Environmental Protec-
tion)

A wrought-iron arch designed by Beatrix Farrand marked the entrance to the East Garden; photo by Edna Leighton Tyler, 1933. (LaMare collection, Connecticut Department of Environmental Protection)

In 1919 the Harknesses turned to another landscape designer, Beatrix Farrand. Typically, they never expressed overt dissatisfaction with Brett & Hall. Indeed, that firm's major contribution, the West Garden plan, was never changed. But the Harknesses wanted more beautiful gardens, more interesting gardens. These Mrs. Farrand gave them, imposing her personal and very different planting style.

. . .

Beatrix Jones Farrand (1872–1959) had learned to know and love flowers, gardens, and the seacoast as a child in Newport and at Bar Harbor.[10] Her parents' divorce may have shocked their families and friends, but Beatrix and her mother, Mary Cadwalader Jones, were by no means rejected by the polite social circle to which they belonged. Their unorthodox situation probably helped to propel Beatrix on her independent course—that and the example of her aunt, writer Edith Wharton. Mrs. Jones herself had written an article on the fields of activity open to women.[11]

As the result of a fortunate introduction, Beatrix Jones had lived for three years in the 1890s with the Charles Sprague Sargents at Holm Lea, in Brookline, Massachusetts. She studied under Professor Sargent at Harvard's Arnold Arboretum and in his own naturalistic garden. After this unique firsthand education on plants and planting, Beatrix spent several years in Europe, looking at gardens in Italy, Germany, and England. She visited Gertrude Jekyll at her garden, Munstead Wood, in Surrey and had a chance to absorb Jekyll's theories on color and planting. In 1899, Beatrix

Jones was one of the founding members of the American Society of Landscape Architects. She did not hesitate to speak her mind at the society's meetings during the years when she was beginning her long career of designing for private clients. In 1913 she married Max Farrand, a professor of history at Yale, who was probably instrumental in bringing Beatrix and the Harknesses together. Max Farrand and Edward Harkness were both members of the first board of directors of the Commonwealth Fund, a charitable foundation established by the Harkness family in 1918.[12] In the 1920s and 1930s, Beatrix Farrand herself worked at Yale, where one of her landscape design projects was for the Harkness Memorial Quadrangle.

Beatrix Farrand was actively involved with Eolia from 1919 until about 1935 and for much longer as an advisor to ensure proper maintenance.[13] She worked on many seaside gardens, including her own Reef Point at Bar Harbor, Maine, and she knew how to cope with winds off the water. Her first project at Eolia was the East Garden, which was built on what had been a tennis

Beatrix Farrand's planting plan for one section of the West Garden, with perennials in many shades of yellow as well as blue. (College of Environmental Design Documents Collection, University of California, Berkeley)

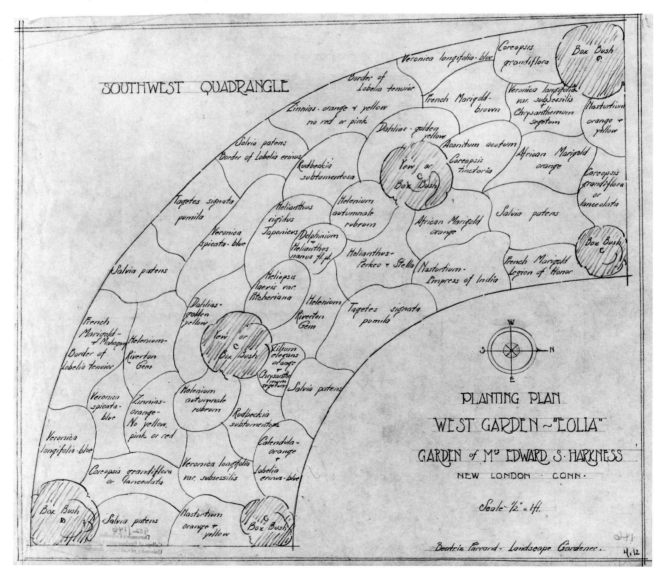

Planting and stone elephants at the foot of the steps that led from the West Garden into a rock garden; photo by Samuel Gottscho, 1935. (Connecticut Department of Environmental Protection)

court. The garden's name had a double meaning: not only was it east of the house but with its Chinese and Korean sculpture it explicitly evoked the Orient. Mrs. Farrand never traveled to the Far East, but she incorporated oriental ornament in several gardens, most notably the Rockefeller garden at Seal Harbor, Maine. The Rockefellers had brought back wall tiles and antique sculpture from China and Korea for their garden. Mr. and Mrs. Harkness also had traveled to the Orient and returned with statuary. Beatrix Farrand made no pretense of designing truly oriental-style gardens. Describing the Rockefeller place, the plan of which is closer to Chinese precedents than that of the Harknesses, she wrote, "As flower gardens in the occidental sense of the word are unknown in China and Korea, it was clearly necessary to disassociate the figures from the actual flowers and to keep them as guardians of the entrance walk and surrounded by naturalistic and inconspicuous planting."[14]

The Harknesses' East Garden is surrounded by a low wall of rough granite blocks laid dry. At its center is a sunken grass panel surrounded by a two-foot retaining wall. At the center of *that* is a tiny rectangular pool, which looked stark recently and like a mistake. Originally, however, the pool was a charming centerpiece, surrounded by feathery astilbe and decorated by the delicate figure of a bronze crane. The East Garden contained blue Chinese vases, Korean statues representing the "seven ages of woman," and a screen of green glazed tiles. As was her custom, Mrs. Farrand submitted alternative schemes to the Harknesses, showing them sketches for the screen and for garden gates. The gates they chose were delicate wrought-iron arches, soon embowered in roses.

The flower beds in the East Garden were devoted to pink and white lilies and pale, sweet-scented annuals in shades of lavender and blue. There were standards of heliotrope and lemon verbena, carpeted with dwarf heliotrope. Baby's breath, lavender, and dianthus added their own fragrances to this sunny, sheltered garden, but the dominant strain was the spicy scent of heliotrope.[15] A small walled sundial circle rounds off the East Garden as one looks toward Long Island Sound. Guarding this circle were two stone Chinese dogs, small but so heavy that it took two men and a dolly to move them in and out of their winter storage each spring. When they disappeared one year, no one could imagine how or where they had gone. Eventually, the dogs were found in a Yale student's room, the unharmed victims of a ponderous prank.

Beatrix Farrand never doubted that a garden was "an absolutely artificial thing," similar to a stage set and requiring definite spatial limits.[16] Even when she was just beginning her life work as a "landscape gardener"—the term she always adhered to—she believed strongly that the design of the garden should relate closely to the architecture of the house. In a discussion of Italian villa gardens at an early meeting of the American Society of Landscape Architects, Beatrix Jones, as she was then, remarked that if American garden designers were to follow Italian models, they should not simply copy or import details, a tendency she had begun to observe.

American designers would, she hoped, be inspired by the "grand idea," that unity of site, house, and garden plan that typified the best Italian examples.[17]

In her work at Eolia, Beatrix Farrand followed her own precepts in her strongly architectonic plan for the East Garden. In the much larger West Garden she accepted and incorporated the existing formal layout. Her contribution to the West Garden was a new and entirely different planting plan. Brett & Hall's original design had called for rigid rows of plants, whereas the Farrand plans illustrate her method of planting in "drifts," to use a word of Gertrude Jekyll's. Her 1895 visit to Miss Jekyll's garden and her subsequent study of Jekyll's books had helped inspire Beatrix Farrand.[18] The vitality of Farrand's admiration for Gertrude Jekyll is indicated by her later purchase of all Jekyll's garden photographs and drawings. The Farrand planting plans for Eolia contain no straight lines; a curving arc of one flowering plant simply flows into groups of others. Often two species are shown sharing the same space, either to prolong the period of bloom or to provide a low-growing cover for the ankles of a taller plant.

Another important difference between the two plant-

The East Garden, designed by Beatrix Farrand, at Eolia, the Harkness estate in Waterford, Connecticut. Edna Leighton Tyler took this photograph of the East Garden, looking toward Long Island Sound, in 1933. (LaMare collection, Connecticut Department of Environmental Protection)

Opposite: Samuel Gottscho photographed the garden at Eolia in 1935. Here a wrought-iron squirrel runs across a chair back, and roses cover a wall of the West Garden pergola. The planting among the paving stones was probably in accord with Beatrix Farrand's plans. (Connecticut Department of Environmental Protection)

ing schemes is in their use of color. For Brett & Hall, colors were expected simply to be varied and bright. Long rows of chrysanthemums, for example, included every shade available. Scarlet oriental poppies abutted yellow daylilies; brilliant red geraniums flanked the pergola steps. In matters of color, Beatrix Farrand was again

influenced by Gertrude Jekyll, who, having started out as a painter, was always keenly aware of pictorial effects. She handled garden color—lights and darks, flower and foliage—as a painter would. An American garden writer, Mabel Cabot Sedgwick, also heightened public awareness of garden color in *The Garden Month by Month* (1907). Sedgwick described the perennials that blossom each month, keying them to a chart of sixty-three colors. A useful tool for gardeners then and still more accurate than most color photographs.

Beatrix Farrand's plans specify varieties to provide the exact shade of color she wanted. The predominantly yellow southwest section of the border, for example, contained the sun-loving heleniums, heliopsis, and helianthus in shades from pale cream to deep gold. Some of the marigolds were almost brown and some of the nasturtiums a deep mahogany. This was not a one-color garden, however. She boldly introduced a few drifts of complementary color, spikes of violet salvia and veronica. Beatrix Farrand shared Gertrude Jekyll's belief that rigid adherence to a monochrome palette—a fad early in the century—was foolish. "Surely the business of the blue garden is to be beautiful as well as to be blue," Miss Jekyll wrote, noting that flower colors appear more intense when juxtaposed with others in a complementary hue.[19]

Another garden bed at Eolia was based on a cool color scheme of white flowers and gray-leaved artemesias, nepetas, and verbascum, with the silvery blues of globe thistles, *Eryngium*, lavender, and *Nigella "Miss Jekyll,"* as well as pale lemon lilies and creamy hollyhocks. At the center of this square bed was a dark evergreen *Chamae-cyparis* with a pale Silver Moon rose and a purple clematis trained over it. This draping of vines upon trees was frequently advocated by followers of William Robinson on both sides of the Atlantic. Robinson's books, *The Wild Garden* (1870) and *The English Flower Garden* (1883), had helped to inspire the use of more herbaceous perennials in gardens, arranged with vines, shrubs, and bulbs in what appeared to be a casual, unstudied way. Beatrix Farrand typically used informal planting within a formal setting, as she did at Eolia, thus synthesizing the styles of two feuding factions in garden design.

Mrs. Farrand designed a small parterre garden of clipped box below the West Garden wall. As usual, she offered the Harknesses several possibilities before she and they were satisfied with the plan or with details such as a wrought-iron garland to ornament a fence. With her usual flair but in a different vein, she began in 1927 to design a secluded rock garden where the ground below the West Garden sloped toward the waterfront. Here she used dwarf evergreens, alpine plants, and spring bulbs in a naturalistic setting. Mrs. Harkness was particularly fond of this garden, with its path winding among the rocks. A small rocky pool and the sound of running water evoked a landscape far from the coast of Connecticut.

Among Beatrix Farrand's papers at the University of California at Berkeley are almost two hundred drawings done in her office for the Harknesses at Eolia. Many are proposals for the small details so important to Mrs. Farrand: flower boxes, fountains, brick paving patterns, and more. Women did all the drafting in her New York office. Several memos bear the initials "A. B." for Anne Baker, her chief design assistant; other drawings bear Mrs. Farrand's own penciled notations.

Mattie Edwards Hewitt, a prominent garden photographer, took picures at Eolia in the 1920s. Another set of photographs was made in 1933 by Edna Leighton Tyler, who had known the property since childhood.[20] Her photographs include long views and also close-ups of fine details now gone: gates and arches of delicately wrought iron and little stone elephants and lions from the Orient. Many of the Tyler photographs are hand-colored, conveying what may be a false impression of the softest gradations of subdued color: pale yellow, gray, gray-green, gray-blue, lavender, and mauve. Mrs. LaMare, whose husband was the Harknesses' superintendent at Eolia, says that the subtle coloration in these photographs accurately reflects the pale tints that Mrs. Harkness preferred. She must have liked the light creamy yellow she chose for the window awnings; the wooden farm buildings and estate cottages were always painted that same shade, too. After 1950, when Mrs. Harkness died and the state took over Eolia, C. J. LaMare continued to stick to her favorite pastels when planting the gardens and the window boxes.

The Harknesses left little of themselves at Eolia. No revealing letters, no gossip, no scandals; no children who might have lived on there; and not even a word about the garden, only photographs and the place itself. I imagine Mr. Harkness as polite, always considerate of his guests and the servants, his voice never raised, deferring to others even on his own golf links. And at night, after dinner and perhaps a round of bridge, I see him shaking hands with his houseguests, giving his wife a dry kiss on one cheek, and slowly climbing the stairs to his monkish bedroom. Mrs. Harkness was apparently as restrained as her husband, as subdued as the colors she chose. Recently, in one corner of the garden the initials "M. S. H." were meticulously trimmed in boxwood, a topiary advertisement of which Mary Stillman Harkness in life would surely not have approved. She and her husband are shadowy figures now, but the peaceful seaside place they cherished is appreciated at all seasons, by many people, just as they intended. The gardens they commissioned, the work of one of the country's greatest designers, are slowly being restored just as Beatrix Farrand planned them.

Notes

1. George W. Pierson, *Yale: College and University, 1871–1937* (New Haven, Conn.: Yale University Press, 1952) 1:213. See also James W. Wooster, *Edward Stephen Harkness, 1874–1940* (New York: privately printed, 1949), and John Tebbel, *The Inheritors: A Study of America's Great Fortunes and What Happened to Them* (New York: G. P. Putnam's Sons, 1962).

2. Margaret M. LaMare, interview by author, 7 December 1982.

3. *Architecture* 17 (15 September 1908): 138–41.

4. Mrs. LaMare, interview; Fred Van Name, *Harkness Memorial State Park* (Deep River, Conn.: New Era Press, 1961).

5. Mr. and Mrs. Orlando Gengo, interview by author, 19 October 1982.

6. Layout and planting plans, James Gamble Rogers, architect, and Brett & Hall, associate landscape architects, drawings 902-164 and 902-166, Beatrix Farrand Collection, College of Environmental Design, University of California, Berkeley.

7. George D. Hall, "A Biographical Minute," *Landscape Architecture* 42 (April 1952): 129.

8. Amy L. Barrington, "Here's Flowers for You," *Arts and Decoration* 11 (May 1919): 42.

9. Wilhelm Miller, "Rhodendrons and Lilies: A Perfect Combination," *Country Life in America* 9 (1906), 429.

10. Biographical material about Beatrix Farrand includes Marlene Salon, "Beatrix Farrand, Landscape Gardener: Her Life and Work" (master's thesis, University of California, Berkeley, 1976); Robert W. Patterson, "An Appreciation of a Great Landscape Gardener," *Landscape Architecture* 49 (summer 1959): 216; *Beatrix J. Farrand (1872–1959): Fifty Years of American Landscape Architecture* (Washington: Dumbarton Oaks, 1982); Jane Brown, *Beatrix: The Gardening Life of Beatrix Jones Farrand, 1872–1959* (New York: Viking, 1995).

11. *Garden and Forest* 8 (January 1895): 29 includes a reference to *The Women's Book*.

12. Wooster, *Edward Stephen Harkness*, 44.

13. According to Mrs. LaMare, even after Mrs. Harkness's death in 1950, C. J. LaMare continued to receive advisory letters, now lost, from Beatrix Farrand.

14. Quoted by Diane K. McGuire, "Beatrix Farrand's Contribution to the Art of Landscape Architecture," *Beatrix J. Farrand*, 40.

15. Mrs. LaMare, interview. Planting plan, center panels, East Garden, drawing 902-137, Farrand Collection, University of California, Berkeley.

16. Quoted in Marlene Salon, "Beatrix Farrand, Landscape Gardener," 32.

17. Remarks by Beatrix Jones in a paper by F. Vitale, *ASLA Transactions (1898–1908)* (American Society of Landscape Architects, 1908). See also Beatrix Farrand, "The Garden in Relationship to the House," *Garden and Forest* 10 (7 April 1897): 132–33.

18. See David Hinge, "Gertrude Jekyll, 1843–1932: A Bibliography of Her Writings," *Journal of Garden History* 2 (July–September 1982): 285–92.

19. Gertrude Jekyll, *Colour Schemes for the Flower Garden* (1908; reprint, Woodbridge, Suffolk: Antique Collectors' Club, 1983), 221.

20. The garden photographs are held by the Connecticut Department of Environmental Protection.

Chapter 17

The Mind's Eye and
the Camera's Eye

The apple-tree, in New England,

plays the part of the olive in Italy,

charges itself with the effect of de-

tail, for the most part otherwise too

scantily produced, and, engaged in

this charming care, becomes in-

finitely decorative and delicate.

What it must do for the too under-

dressed land in May or June is eas-

ily supposable; but its office in the

early autumn is to scatter coral

and gold.

—Henry James, *The American Scene*

HE IS BENT OVER, trimming his horn-beam hedge skillfully, thoughtfully, one gray twig at a time. His back is to the main street of Williamstown, but he is unaware of the sounds of passing cars, a dog barking, a woman calling her child, people walking into the white church next door. The man is absorbed in his hedge, absorbed in perfecting what anyone else would say was already perfect. The leaf buds are just beginning to unfurl—thin shining silk, pale newborn green. The man has his work cut out for him, and he knows it. He has nearly eighty feet of hedge to finish before the leaves are fully opened.

The hedge encloses the garden on three sides, along the road and beside the obscure cul-de-sac that leads to the house. Almost twenty years ago the man planted tiny sprigs of hornbeam. The hedge is nearly seven feet high now; the man has prudently topped it off at exactly the height to which his extended arm and pruners can reach without a ladder. The hedge is beautiful even without leaves—a dense interlacing of smooth gray branches, thick as an arm near the ground and thin as a pencil higher up, with twigs that look as delicate as soda straws. In his mind the man sees the hedge in summer, a solid wall of leafy green on which only he will be able to spot the tiny imperfections: the two wayward leaves up here that must be cut out that very August minute, or the small peephole over there through which with fury he will spy the unwelcome flash of red from a passing truck. He would make a mental note: I must encourage every twig just there to close that horrid aperture.

But now it is early April, and his mind is focused on the corner of the hedge, where it makes a ninety-degree turn, where he is working now. Each snip of his sharp neat clippers represents a decision: this twig or that? Cut it here or back there? Even as his mind races along ahead of his hand, he is thinking of other possibilities. Should I or should I not let the hedge grow higher here at the corner and perhaps at the two ends? I could shape a finial here and there, which would be fun. Leafy green ornaments. Would that be an improvement, or would they spoil the straightforward simplicity that the hedge has now? And then I would need a ladder. . . . He weighs the pros and cons now while pruning, as he does sometimes if he wakes up during the night.

"Excuse me, sir." The man turns slowly on his heel and straightens up. He had not heard them approach, but three people stand there on the sidewalk, smiling and nodding, none of them as high as the man's shoulder.

"So sorry to bother you, sir. We are from Japan. We are tourists to your lovely town."

"Ah, yes," says our man, removing his tweed hat. "How may I help you?"

"This is my wife; this my daughter. We admire very much your hedge. We have not seen such a hedge. We would like please to take a picture. With your permission." The tourist was festooned with cameras, light meters, camera bags.

"But of course," said the man, his palms held wide in welcome.

The tourist fixed the eye of the camera on the man with his small sharp pruning shears and on the silvery twigs of his majestic hedge.

. . .

All the gardens in these pages started in the mind of the gardener: dreams, images, pictures that the gardener tried to bring to life. Looking at the gardens—those that survive or have been resuscitated, as well as the places that we can know only through old photographs and written records—we are the camera's eye. We are outside, looking in. We are spectators.

The garden makers pass before us, different people living in different times and different places, dreaming their own dreams. We see them, but what were they seeing? One thing they had in common, even perhaps the only thing, was a wish to make an elysium on earth for themselves, their families, and perhaps their heirs. Mark Girouard, describing certain English and French landowners of the eighteenth-century Enlightenment, could have been talking about these Americans who also strove toward their own imagined Edens: "Their hopes were boundless; their achievements tended to fall depressingly short of their hopes. But it is hard not to warm to their enthusiasm, even when it verged on the ridiculous."[1]

The image in a garden maker's mind, the picture that inspires the planning and the plantings, comes from something the gardener has seen and remembered. The sources could be long ago and far away: Kirk Boott trying to grow the English wildflowers of his childhood or Shepherd Tom Hazard in his eighties resorting to spiritualism to reenter the garden paradise of his early married life. Often people try to recapture the atmosphere of other gardens they have admired: Daniel Chester French remembering the sculptors' gardens he had wandered through during his earliest Italian sojourn; John Perkins Cushing, whose horticultural exploits under glass and in the open rivaled those of his uncle Perkins, on whose estate Cushing had grown up. For Mrs. Tyson only a "colonial" garden would suit the old house she had bought. Garden fashions were spread by books and magazines: Downing, for example, had a literary hand in what Joseph Potter and Henry Bowen did with their grounds.

Most of these garden makers were artists in their own gardens. Celia Thaxter focused on the color, the scents, the minute details. Ogden Codman Jr. laid out a garden for his mother, a modest but skillful rendition of the Italianate style then fashionable among estate owners. Edith Wharton started out with help from her niece Beatrix Farrand but took over the design of the most important parts of her garden herself. French, already a renowned sculptor, brought all his assurance and skill to bear on his grounds at Chesterwood, discovering then how much he loved horticulture.

The professional landscape designer did not make an appearance in New England until late in the nineteenth century. There were no academic programs of training. Horticulturists proffered precepts and advice, engineers laid out towns, and Frederick Law Olmsted, with his radical integration of social and environmental concerns, began designing parks, suburbs, and campuses. Not until late in his career did Olmsted branch into the designing of private estates, and even then—most notably at Shelburne Farms and Biltmore—he clung to the ideal that his work would eventually have a public benefit.

Before there were landscape architects, we had architects. With the 1890s revival of interest in classical design principles, Beaux-Arts–trained architects extended into the garden the architecture of the houses they were designing. Charles Adams Platt reversed this process in his career, first designing gardens like that at Faulkner Farm, radiating from the house with seeming inevitability. Only gradually did Platt come to realize that he must become the architect of the house as well. The architect-designer of the Hamilton House gardens was Herbert Browne, whose enthusiasm for colonial revival forms matched that of his client, Mrs. Tyson. For the Harknesses, landscape architect Beatrix Farrand took over and extended the gardens laid out by the designers who preceded her at Eolia, making of them a work of art.

The image of the gifted amateur designing his own

garden is more than a charming conceit. It can happen and, as we have seen, often does happen. It is still happening right now, for which we should be thankful. But those who employ professional designers play major parts, too. The patron's role is crucial in encouraging, supporting, and providing latitude for talent. It takes a patron as well as an artist to turn landscape into art.

Money clearly helped. A great deal of money made possible the most lavish display. Particularly during the so-called Gilded Age of the late nineteenth and early twentieth centuries, there were plenty of estate owners in the United States who wished chiefly to impress others with their wealth. More interesting, however, are the garden makers who were not simply making a statement but who *cared*. Particularly appealing to me are those whose dedication to their own landscapes verged on excess. Picture Sarah Parker Goodwin of Portsmouth working away till dark had fallen, then creeping in with an aching back for her tea, a hot bath, and bed.

In his book *Old Money*, Nelson W. Aldrich Jr. describes how "in this New World, the Old Rich (and the New Rich seeking to become Old) have had to grab on to every old work of art, . . . every old style and fashion, and set them up as props, in every sense of the word, of their historical legitimacy."[2] He was writing about the decades after the Civil War. But even when the nation was young, people like Colonel Boyd or Theodore Lyman, having acquired the means to improve and embellish their homes and grounds, still turned to the Old World for models. John Codman, touring English country seats in 1800, was plotting all the while how he might transform his own estate, at home in Massachusetts, to look more like those he was admiring.

The earliest fortunes in New England came from trade: merchants, shipowners, importers, exporters, buyers, sellers; these were the ones making money. Many, like Kirk Boott, rose from "humble beginnings." Some, including Boott, believed that they had risen higher or to more secure heights than turned out to be the case. Fortunes were quickly made and as quickly lost.

Like Thomas Handasyd Perkins, the uncle who set him on his way, John Perkins Cushing accumulated great wealth in China, primarily from trading in opium. Others, like Isaac Royall of Medford, profited from West Indies sugar, which meant chiefly rum. Another source of riches, the most unsavory of all, was the human trade that forced West Africans into slavery. The whole truth of an enterprise that made many New Englanders rich is still hidden in shame.

Technological advances opened new opportunities. The Hazards of Rhode Island profited from the woollen manufactories. The great Lowell cotton mills brought money to their Boston-based proprietors. Horatio Hollis Hunnewell, following success as a banker in Paris, gained even greater wealth from his investments in railroads. For a time there seemed to be no limit to the money to be made from railroading, as the network expanded to cover the country. Mrs. Tyson lived off the railroad money left her by her husband, George, never having to worry about all she spent restoring and ornamenting Hamilton House, both inside and out, while she lived with appropriate luxury there and in her Boston townhouse. William Seward Webb started out with the inheritance—chiefly from railroads—of his wife, Lila Vanderbilt, and it grew with Webb's help. The fortunes of the 1880s and 1890s were of a greater magnitude than ever before. People like the Vanderbilts, the Webbs, and the Harknesses hardly knew what to do with all their money. One thing they did, of course, was create great estates

Some fortunes, more limited in extent, were made by true Horatio Alger entrepreneurship. Henry Bowen, who shook off the dust of his small hometown in Connecticut at twenty-one to seek his fortune in the big city of New York, found what he was looking for by selling silk thread and founding an antislavery newspaper. Returning home, he became the biggest man in town, the companion of presidents and senators, with the flashiest house and the fanciest garden. Joseph Potter, too, rose from obscurity, learning the printing business, forging political connections, and then, taking swift advantage of an unmet need, supplying the entire Union army with socks from nine mills he built for the purpose. His garden, aways open to the public, was his goodwill offering.

Inheriting money sometimes made all things seem possible. Think of Mary Pratt Sprague, whose share of her ship-owning grandfather Weld's fortune built Faulkner Farm in all its neo-Renaissance magnificence, or the Harknesses, earnestly giving away their inherited Standard Oil money but saving enough to create and maintain Eolia.

But some of these people did not have quite enough to fulfill their dream or, in Celia Thaxter's case, to keep herself and her troubled son. She depended on her "pome money," as her brother referred to her literary earnings, and on the china she painted and sold. Her garden from seeds and cuttings supplied by friends required the outlay of more labor than cash. Edith Wharton, who moved among the affluent and whose classical tastes could not be satisfied on the cheap, depended on the money she made from her books. The Codmans had expensive tastes, too, so much so that they were forced to live for years in France, in a colony of fellow expatriates, just to save money. When they were finally able to reclaim The Grange, they made do, clinging like leeches to what they had.

The golden age of some of these gardens was very brief. For Potter it was a mere ten years before his small paradise was converted into house lots. Edith Wharton's tenure at The Mount was also only ten years, over half of them spent in the pleasurable process of creation. But all these gardens resulted from the impulse to create something beautiful and lasting. The reasons some survived and others did not are tangled. Sometimes the creator or the heirs made plans that they hoped would ensure the survival of a place they loved. The Codmans, sticking together in their sibling eccentricity, never quarreled with their brother Ogden's scheme of leaving their estate to the Society for the Preservation of New England Antiquities. Maybe that was why only one of them ever married. French's daughter Margaret struggled for the last two decades of her life to arrange permanent support for Chesterwood; the hardest part for her was relinquishing control. But she was a sole heir. More heirs usually mean more problems. Subdivision among members of succeeding generations, while admirably fair, democratic, and typically American, usually spells the end of what was once a whole.

There are so many questions and so few answers. Why did Cushing's four children sell off Bellmont, the sole focus of their father's life for thirty years, almost before he was cold in the ground? Why, on the other hand, has the Hunnewell place been handed down with apparent amiability from generation to generation, each concerned with maintaining and preserving it? Perhaps the charitable impulse plays a part. Horatio Hollis Hunnewell started out with a benevolent public concern for expanding horticultural knowledge. Dr. Webb tried to improve the lot of Vermont's farmers. And the Harknesses, who had no children, were determined that Eolia, as well as their entire fortune, should be devoted to the public good.

. . .

J. B. Jackson once described a cosmic historical drama: "First there is that golden age, the time of harmonious beginnings. Then ensues a period when the old days are forgotten and the golden age falls into neglect. Finally comes a time when we rediscover and seek to restore the world around us to something like its former beauty. . . . But there has to be that interval of neglect."[3] This Jackson called "the necessity for ruins." The original state takes on the sacred quality of myth. The half-ruined skeleton of an old garden can be wondrously appealing to the imagination, resonant with allusions to memory and hope. The crumbling casino, the ancient sculptural fragments, the mossy balustrades, and even the remaining view at Faulkner Farm have an antique quality that could not be bought at any price. As one Hunnewell once said of his towering evergreens, none of us, had we all the money in the world, could buy one. Time is what it takes.

As the Machine becomes ever more dominant in the Garden of America, attempts at regaining Eden become more precious and more elusive. Searching after old gardens, we are like Mary unlocking the Secret Garden. We are outside, looking in, awed and delighted. In discovering and recovering old gardens we may even find for ourselves those dreams in the mind's eye of their makers, dreams of an earthly paradise.

Notes

1. Mark Girouard, "The Chateau de Canon, Normandy," *Country Life* (15 December 1994): 34.

2. Nelson W. Aldrich Jr., *Old Money: The Mythology of America's Upper Class* (New York: Random House, 1988), 63.

3. John Brinckerhoff Jackson, *The Necessity for Ruins and Other Topics* (Amherst: University of Massachusetts, 1980), 101–2.

Contents